Erratum

The last two lines on p. 362 of *Environmental Policy in the 1980s* should read:

A review of the most significant environmental policy actions and public statements by administration officials leads us to conclude that little change in

(For your convenience, this correction has been typeset in a size and width that may be pasted or taped over the error.)

ENVIRONMENTAL POLICY
IN THE 1980s

ENVIRONMENTAL POLICY IN THE 1980s:
Reagan's New Agenda

Norman J. Vig
Carleton College

Michael E. Kraft
University of Wisconsin, Green Bay

a division of
Congressional Quarterly Inc.
1414 22nd Street, N.W., Washington, D.C. 20037

Library of Congress Cataloging in Publication Data

Main entry under title:

Environmental policies in the 1980s.

1. Environmental policy — United States. 2. United States — Economic policy — 1981-   . I. Vig, Norman J. II. Kraft, Michael E.
HC110.E5E49865   1984   363.7′056′0973   84-1868
ISBN 0-87187-305-2

For
Teddy and Jesse
Steve and David

TABLE OF CONTENTS

vii

PREFACE

The Reagan administration is rapidly gaining a reputation as one of the most effective presidencies in recent history. At least in domestic policy, Ronald Reagan has accomplished greater change in less time than any president since Franklin D. Roosevelt. He has used the video pulpit and the silent levers of government to reverse many previous policies and to define a new agenda for the future. "America is back," he proclaimed in his State of the Union address in early 1984. But, perhaps unwittingly, his campaign slogan invites the rejoinder: back to what?

Democratic candidates will no doubt focus on several "setbacks": back to the highest levels of unemployment since the Great Depression, back to the worst poverty levels in a decade, and back to fears of nuclear war not experienced since the Cuban missile crisis. This book treats another prominent reversal: the Reagan administration's attempt to undo many of the nation's commitments to environmental quality during the past 15 years. The National Environmental Policy Act of 1969 pledged the federal government "to create and maintain conditions under which man and nature can exist in productive harmony." President Reagan's agenda for the 1980s sharply tilts the balance back toward man's production at nature's expense.

There are many ways to measure policy change, and one common indicator frequently invoked by the administration is money. By this criterion, the environmental policy reversal under Ronald Reagan is unmistakable: his administration found less money to spend on environmental programs than its predecessors. Whereas expenditures for environmental protection and natural resources increased from 1.5 percent of the federal budget in 1970 to 2.4 percent in 1980, they had fallen back to 1.2 percent by 1984. The Environmental Protection Agency's projected 8.5 percent budget increase for 1985 over its 1984 budget will roughly restore its purchasing power to that of 10 years ago.

But fiscal commitment, such as that evident during the "environmental decade" of the 1970s, is not the only criterion for evaluating policy change. It is quite literally true that throwing money at a problem does not necessarily solve it. The contributors to this book make it abundantly clear that environmental problems have not been solved in this country, taking issue with what Reagan frequently implied during his 1980 presidential election campaign. Indeed, the administration has faced one crisis after another in responding to toxic waste emergencies: dioxin contamination at Times Beach, Missouri; leaking waste dumps from New Jersey to California; and unsafe levels of ethylene dibromide (EDB) in Florida's water supplies, citrus crops, and much of the nation's grain stockpile. These and other problems are not of this administration's making. Unsafe chemicals and other hazardous substances have accumulated in our soil, water, and air for many decades, and it is evident that the policies of the past were often ineffective in controlling them.

By the end of the first environmental decade there was certainly a case for reassessment and regulatory reform. The costs and benefits of many environmental programs needed to be reexamined in light of experience. But this required careful policy analysis sensitive to the long-term and often intangible benefits of sustained program commitments. It also demanded recognition of strong public and congressional support for the environmental goals of the 1970s, if reform efforts were to gain legitimacy and consensus. Instead, the Reagan administration has ignored public opinion, bypassed Congress, and imposed a massive deregulatory effort throughout the federal government. Presidential powers have been stretched to the limit in carrying out this "administrative strategy." In the process, environmental agencies and natural resource programs have been gravely weakened without compensating economic benefits. Ideological fervor rather than sound policy analysis has carried the day.

This book argues that many of Reagan's policy changes will not be successful because they lack both political legitimacy and a rational foundation in technical and economic analysis. These are critically important criteria for evaluating policy success, even though the substantive impacts may not be measurable for some years to come. Policy making that violates constitutional norms, democratic accountability, and empirical evidence is doomed to frustration and failure. From this perspective, Reagan's performance as president loses much of its alleged luster. The ability to exercise presidential power is not an adequate criterion for evaluating presidential leadership.

The contributors to the book represent different disciplines and fields of expertise. They have written extensively on environmental issues, and many have served in government, as consultants, or on the staffs of conservation organizations. The authors recognize the heavy costs entailed in environmental protection, the need for trade-offs to achieve other social values, and the necessity for greater efficiency or "cost-effectiveness" in much environmental regulation. Although they do not hide their concern that many of Reagan's policy changes hold perilous consequences for the future, they offer an informed professional critique that they hope will contribute to more constructive reform in the remainder of the 1980s.

The book thus provides a needed text for students of environmental policy and politics, of the presidency and other national governmental institutions, and of policy analysis and public administration. It should be of interest to all concerned with environmental quality and the use of natural re-sources. In presenting a detailed account of environmental policy changes through 1983, the book provides one of the most penetrating case studies of the Reagan presidency. Citizens as well as professional scholars will find much to reflect upon in gauging the broader requisites for effective presiden-tial leadership. But each of the authors also analyzes specific impacts of the Reagan administration on other governmental institutions, processes, or programs, allowing the reader to assess the consequences from many different perspectives.

The organization of the book reflects these objectives. The introductory chapter establishes a framework for evaluating policy change, reviews past environmental policy development in this light, and suggests how the evaluation criteria might be applied to President Reagan's policy departures. Part I focuses on the policy environment: Reagan's electoral campaign of 1980 and alleged mandate for policy change as well as public opinion on environmental policy and the response of citizens and the environmental movement to the administration's policy changes. Part II concentrates on changes in the methods and processes of environmental policy making. Administrative tactics used to achieve substantive policy change are stressed: political appointments, budget and personnel cuts, government reorganiza-tion, and oversight and control of the regulatory process. The roles of the presidency, the Congress, and the courts are discussed explicitly. Part III then presents detailed studies of policy change in six specific areas: energy, air pollution, water pollution, toxic and hazardous waste disposal, public land and water management, and international environmental policy. Part IV concludes with summary economic and political evaluations of the Reagan policy changes.

We gratefully acknowledge the exceptional cooperation of all of the participants in this project. A more conscientious and punctual group of contributors would be difficult to imagine. Support from the Science, Technology, and Public Policy Program at Carleton College (funded by the Alfred P. Sloan Foundation) and the Department of Public and Environmen-tal Administration at the University of Wisconsin, Green Bay, has been essential. Seemingly endless typing, duplicating, and mailing by Kathy Hayden, Nancy Gustafson, and Hendrika Umbanhowar have been much appreciated. Finally, special thanks are due to Joanne Daniels and Nancy Lammers at CQ Press for their encouragement and professional assistance throughout. The text is far better than it would have been without their careful editing. But any errors and omissions are, of course, our own responsibility.

Norman J. Vig
Michael E. Kraft
February 1, 1984

INTRODUCTION

1. ENVIRONMENTAL POLICY FROM THE SEVENTIES TO THE EIGHTIES

Norman J. Vig and Michael E. Kraft

"I do not think they will be happy until the White House looks like a bird's nest."

President Ronald Reagan
March 11, 1983

With these sarcastic words, President Reagan vented his frustration over one of the most embarrassing chapters of his presidency. Two days earlier he had announced the resignation of Anne McGill Burford (Gorsuch) as administrator of the Environmental Protection Agency (EPA) amidst an escalating political scandal that threatened to engulf the White House itself. On December 16, 1982, Gorsuch had become one of the highest executive officials ever cited for contempt of Congress by the U.S. House of Representatives. The citation was prompted by her refusal, on presidential orders, to deliver subpoenaed documents on alleged mismanagement of the "Superfund" program for cleaning up the nation's chemical waste dumps. More than 20 other top EPA officials were fired. On March 21, 1983, William D. Ruckelshaus, who had served as the first EPA administrator (1970-1973), was designated her successor.

Six months later Reagan's other chief environmental appointee, Interior Secretary James G. Watt, was in equally deep trouble. In a speech given on September 21, he jokingly referred to the membership of a commission set up to examine his controversial coal-leasing policies as comprised of "a black. . . . a woman, two Jews, and a cripple." Public outrage over this thoughtless remark was swift, and within a week it appeared that the Republican-led Senate was prepared to pass a resolution calling for Watt's removal. He resigned on October 9 rather than face "deconfirmation" by his own party. Four days later Reagan astounded everyone by appointing his national security adviser, William P. Clark, to succeed Watt at Interior.

Although Reagan praised both Watt and Gorsuch for their outstanding performance in office and defended his environmental record in other public statements, it was obvious that his environmental and natural resource policies had run into a wall of opposition by the third year of his presidency.[1] Rarely before had Congress so exercised its powers to check the executive as in driving these two agency heads from office. Nor did these remarkable events reflect only the competence and personal demeanor of the incumbents: behind the dismissals lay fundamental differences over the environmental policies of the Reagan administration.

To many the president's "bird's nest" charge and defense of Watt symbolized an attitude profoundly antagonistic to the environmental community and oblivious to his policies' consequences. Reagan had entered office with the most conservative political agenda in half a century and had used executive powers to the maximum in seeking to carry it out during the first two years of his presidency. His deregulation program called for major changes in energy, health, consumer, and environmental policies to reduce the government's scope and to promote economic recovery. The policies of Watt, Gorsuch, and other agency officials accurately reflected these priorities, resulting in massive changes at the administrative level.

This "administrative strategy," which largely bypassed Congress by changing regulations through the rule-making process carried out within the agencies, prompted serious questions about whether the president was violating his constitutional obligation to "take care that the laws be faithfully executed."

In fact, the Reagan administration had embarked on a new policy course that has altered radically the environmental agenda of the 1980s. The guiding principles, set out by the president's Council on Environmental Quality, are: (1) regulatory reform, including extensive use of cost-benefit analysis in determining the value of environmental regulations and programs; (2) reliance as much as possible on the free market to allocate resources; and (3) decentralization or environmental federalism, shifting responsibilities for environmental protection to state and local governments whenever feasible.[2] If carried out literally, these goals would reverse much of the policy development of the 1970s and return environmental administration to an earlier era in which private interests largely had their way. The federal government no longer would have a major role in controlling the social costs of pollution and economic development. Many public lands and facilities would be turned over to private ownership or management.

The environmental community, which found itself almost wholly excluded from policy making beginning in 1981, responded with furor to the Reagan administration. In March 1982, 10 leading environmental and conservation organizations issued a formal "indictment" of the president, charging that he had "broken faith with the American people on environmental protection" by taking or proposing "scores of actions that veered radically away from the broad bipartisan consensus in support of environmental protection that has existed for many years." The document listed 227 examples of the ways in which environmental policies allegedly were being subverted. "In the name of 'getting the government off our backs,'" the environmentalists asserted, "they are giving away our natural heritage."[3]

But the criticism was not limited to such groups. Many conservationists—including current and former Republican officials, senators, representatives, and even members of Reagan's own environmental policy transition team—bitterly questioned the administration's policies and the White House's insensitivity to environmental issues.[4] Membership in environmental organizations grew by leaps and bounds during 1981 and 1982 as public concern spread. A confrontation was inevitable as it became increasingly evident that the administration was out of touch with public sentiment on environmental matters.

The Reagan administration's radical policy departures must be judged in relation to the prior record of environmental policy development as well as to the administration's own policy agenda; moreover, such a review and evaluation must be based on specific criteria. In the following section we set out such a general framework for analyzing and evaluating policy change. Then, using that framework, we analyze the so-called environmental decade, beginning in 1969 and ending in 1980. Finally, we turn to evaluating Reagan's effort to redefine the environmental agenda for the 1980s.

Policy Change and Evaluation

A policy is a means to an end. It expresses an intent to achieve certain objectives, through a conscious choice of means, and usually within some specified time period. Public policy making is distinctive in several respects: it must be done through constitutional processes, it requires the sanction of law, and it is binding on all members of society. In a democracy, it normally is open to public scrutiny and debate, although secrecy often is permitted in matters involving national security and diplomatic relations.

Policy change pervades modern political life. Every election is in part a referendum on past policy performance, and most candidates promise to introduce new policies or to change old ones. Yet dramatic policy change is much easier to espouse than to achieve, especially in our system of divided authority and dispersed power. The Founding Fathers created a system of multiple checks and balances that has served its purpose by moderating policy change in the absence of widespread social and political consensus. Thus policy changes normally come slowly and incrementally, involving broad consultation and agreement among diverse interests. Still, our system has proved flexible enough to permit substantial innovations when the public supports them and when political leaders act cohesively.

The study of public policy, and especially policy change, has become increasingly important as objectives have become more complex and difficult to achieve.[5] Indeed, traditional government approaches to administration and regulation have come under widespread attack from a diverse community of policy analysts as well as from conservative interest groups that resent the growing burdens of government.[6] Political scientists have placed greatest emphasis on problems of policy design and implementation, while economists have attacked the logic of compulsory regulation without regard to positive market incentives.[7] Yet care must be exercised in policy analysis and evaluation lest simplistic generalizations be allowed to guide policy change.

The environmental policies of the last decade, for example, were based on a deep conviction that various types of industrial and business activity must be regulated by laws forcing companies to adopt new technologies and processes to clean up pollution emissions by specified dates. It was recognized that this would impose other economic and social costs, but that such a trade-off would have to be made in the long-term interest of preserving human health and environmental integrity. These fundamental goals must be kept firmly in mind when evaluating policy success.

It must also be recognized that all policies undergo change as they are put into practice. There is always some slippage between intention and outcome, in part because all of the problems cannot be foreseen when policies are designed, and in part because policy implementation is an interactive process in which new knowledge and experience inevitably lead adminis-trators to adjust policies to fit changing circumstances. In fields such as environmental regulation, changing scientific and technical knowledge re-quires continual reassessment and modification of specific objectives and methods for achieving them. Rational policy making necessitates such flexibility in the implementation process, provided always that policy adjust-ments do not violate statutory intent. Congress and the courts maintain oversight of administrative decision making to ensure that implementing agencies stay within the bounds of the law.

Policy Cycles

As already suggested, the policy-making process involves a series of stages, all important in evaluating the overall success of the outcome. Six stages often are distinguished as comprising a "policy cycle": *agenda setting* (identification and definition of problems and advocacy of action), *policy formulation* (specification of goals and choice of means for achieving them), *policy legitimation* (mobilization of support and formal enactment), *policy implementation* (mobilization of resources and application to goal achieve-ment), *policy evaluation* (measurement of results and redefinition of goals or agenda), and *policy revision* or *termination*. The terminology varies, but most students of public policy employ some model of this kind in analyzing ongoing processes of policy development.[8]

Real-life action does not always neatly fit abstract models. Likewise, policy evaluation does not simply follow the accumulation of experience or reflect systematic measurement of results. Nevertheless, the policy-cycle model provides essential benchmarks for analyzing policy change through time.

Agenda setting is an important preliminary stage in policy making because it determines when action is taken, how the basic issues are defined, and what general direction the policy response will take. Policy formulation and legitimation are closely intertwined, since they ordinarily involve extensive consultation among different actors who seek to build support for their proposals. Even if policies are formulated in the executive branch, for example, this usually is done with a keen eye toward congressional approval, since most policy changes require legislative enactment or other congressional support. Policy legitimation is critical to the success of any policy in our system of government. This requires not only constitutionality—adherence to constitutional processes and the rule of law—but also political legitimacy in the sense that policies represent a majoritarian agreement among representatives of the public who share authority in policy making. This in turn implies broad public support for major policy initiatives.

The desired results still may not be achieved unless effective methods are developed for implementing the policy. It is especially important in new policy areas that competent institutions be created to refine the decision-making criteria and find workable administrative solutions. Policies still must be reevaluated in light of changing circumstances and needs, and new techniques for monitoring and assessment may be required if such evaluation is to produce constructive policy revision. Cumulative experience, as well as new information or changing values and priorities, may lead to the policy agenda's revision. A new cycle will begin.

Policy Evaluation

In light of these diverse considerations, policy evaluation must encompass a number of criteria. There is no single "bottom line" for assessing policy success. Public policies usually involve much more than delivering a particular product or service to a policy "consumer" at an anticipated date and price. They often entail long-term commitments to broad social values or goals that are not easily quantified or measured. Their impact depends on the response of the private sector, which may or may not cooperate despite legal requirements. Such opposition, as well as unforeseen events and changing perceptions or values, may delay policy implementation and shift priorities over time.

However, criteria for policy evaluation tend to fall into two broad categories. The first involves *substantive* or *ends/means* assessment. At the simplest level, we can ask to what extent the substantive policy goals have, in fact, been achieved. In the case of air pollution, for example, we can ask how much cleaner the ambient air has become since passage of the Clean Air Act. Even at this level problems arise. For example, how do we know how clean (or dirty) the air would be in the absence of the Clean Air Act? Even if we attribute all emission reductions to this policy (a rather unrealistic assumption, given other developments such as the trend toward smaller automobile engines), how do we evaluate the impact on human health and the environment? Such cause-effect relationships are very difficult to establish.

And what if we determine that most rivers and lakes have not become noticeably less polluted in recent years? Does that mean that the Clean Water Act is a failure, or that effluent controls are thus far only sufficient to prevent further deterioration? Does limited success mean that the original goals were unrealistic, or that the means for attaining them need improvement? In short, both measurement problems and value judgments are likely to impinge at this level of analysis.

Another substantive or end/means assessment involves measuring achieved benefits and related costs, and then comparing the two measurements to determine a cost/benefit ratio. Economists almost invariably advocate this approach, usually on the assumption that all important elements in the equation can be expressed in dollar values.

The underlying logic—that we should attain maximum social value from the investment of scarce resources—is hard to refute. But this approach does not adequately address the complications in evaluating environmental policy.[9] Many of its goals have diffuse collective benefits, such as clean air, that cannot be assigned a surrogate market price. Scenic beauty and the ecosystem's stability, for example, have intrinsic values unrelated to what this generation may be willing to pay for them. Nor is there any adequate method for "discounting" future benefits since we do not know how much future generations will value them. Given such limitations, the economic approach may be most useful for comparing the cost-effectiveness of one administrative strategy against another for the purpose of achieving legislative goals at least cost.

Another approach, adhered to by many political scientists including most of this book's contributors, accepts the need to measure substantive progress (insofar as it can be done) but places greater emphasis on the processes used for achieving policy results.

From this perspective, two criteria emerge as especially important in evaluating ongoing policies or policy changes: (a) *legitimation*—is the process by which policies are made or changed constitutionally and politically legitimate? (b) *institutional implementation*—do administrative agencies have the institutional resources necessary to implement policies in light of statutory goals and changing technical knowledge?

The assumption is that if policies lack political or legal support, fail to achieve competent administration, and/or disregard empirical evidence, they are not likely to produce anticipated results. Conversely, policies meeting or progressing toward these criteria can be considered effective.

In the following section we discuss the broad environmental policy cycle that began in 1969 and continued through 1980. We evaluate policy development using the process criteria as well as available evidence on goal achievement and costs and benefits. Space does not permit a full evaluation of past policies, nor is that the purpose of this book. But even this brief summary will serve to highlight the changes that President Reagan has attempted.

Environmental Policy Development: 1969-1980

Until 1969 the federal government's role in environmental policy making was sharply limited. One major exception was in public land management, where for nearly a century Congress had set aside portions of the remaining public domain for preservation as national parks, forests, grazing lands, recreation areas, and wildlife refuges. The "multiple-use" and "sustained-yield" doctrines that grew out of the conservation movement at the turn of the century ensured that this national trust would contribute to economic growth under the stewardship of the Interior and Agriculture departments. Yet steady progress also was made both toward managing the lands in the public interest and protecting lands from development.[10] After five years of debate, Congress passed the Wilderness Act of 1964 to preserve some of the remaining forestlands in pristine condition, "untrammeled by man's presence."

Agenda Setting for the 1970s

Controlling human waste and industrial pollution was another matter. Air and water pollution long were considered local matters and kept off the political agenda. After World War II policies to control the most obvious forms of pollution were developed gradually at the local, state, and eventually federal levels. The federal government began assisting local authorities in building sewage treatment plants in 1948 and initiated a limited program for air pollution in 1955. But it was only in the 1960s that Washington began actively prodding the states to set pollution abatement standards and formulate implementation plans based on federal guidelines.

By the end of the 1960s it was widely recognized that this limited federal-state partnership was totally inadequate to address what by then was perceived as a national environmental crisis.[11] A new environmental movement was sweeping the country that catapulted environmental policy onto the national political agenda. This movement, drawing inspiration from the developing science of ecology, demanded far more vigorous and comprehensive federal action to prevent irreversible environmental degradation. In almost unprecedented fashion, a new environmental policy agenda was formulated that was implemented throughout the 1970s.

Congress set the stage for policy innovation at the end of 1969 when it passed the National Environmental Policy Act (NEPA), which declared

> it is the *continuing policy of the Federal Government,* in *cooperation with* State and local governments, and *other concerned public and private organizations,* to use *all* practicable means and measures, including financial and technical assistance, in a manner calculated to foster and promote the general welfare, to *create and maintain conditions under which man and nature can exist in productive harmony,* and fulfill the social, economic, *and other* requirements of present *and future* generations of Americans. [emphasis added] [12]

The law required detailed environmental impact statements (EISs) on all major federal actions, and established the Council on Environmental Quality to advise the president and Congress on environmental matters. President Richard Nixon then seized the initiative by signing NEPA as his first official act of 1970 and proclaiming the 1970s the "environmental decade." The race was on as the White House and congressional leaders vied for environmentalists' support.

Table 1-1 Major Federal Environmental Legislation, 1969-1980

Legislation	Implementing Agency	Major Provisions
President Nixon		
National Environmental Policy Act of 1969 (PL 91-190), 1970	All federal agencies	Declared a national policy to "encourage productive and enjoyable harmony between man and his environment," required environmental impact statements; created Council on Environmental Policy.
Clean Air Act Amendments (PL 91-604), 1970	Environmental Protection Agency (EPA)	Required administrator to set national primary and secondary air quality standards and certain emission limits; required states to develop implementation plans by specific dates; required reductions in automobile emissions.
Resources Recovery Act (PL 91-512), 1970	Dept. of Health, Education and Welfare (later EPA)	Set up a program of demonstration and construction grants for innovative solid waste management systems; provided technical and financial assistance to state and local agencies in developing resource recovery and waste disposal systems.
Federal Water Pollution Control Act Amendments (PL 92-500), 1972	EPA	Set national water quality goals; established pollutant discharge permit system; increased federal grants to states to construct waste treatment plants.

Federal Environmental Pesticide Control Act (PL 92-516), 1972	EPA	Required registration of all pesticides in U.S. commerce; allowed administrator to cancel or suspend registration under specified circumstances.
Noise Control Act (PL 92-574), 1972	EPA	Gave federal government authority to set standards limiting certain commercial sources of noise.
Marine Protection Act (PL 92-532), 1972	EPA	Regulated dumping of waste materials into the oceans and coastal waters.
Coastal Zone Management Act (PL 92-583), 1972	Commerce Dept.	Authorized federal grants to the states to develop coastal zone management plans under federal guidelines.
Endangered Species Act (PL 93-205), 1973	Fish & Wildlife Service, Dept. of Interior	Broadened federal authority to protect all "threatened" as well as "endangered" species; authorized grant program to assist state programs; required coordination among all federal agencies.
Energy Supply and Environmental Coordination Act (PL 93-319), 1974	EPA, Federal Energy Administration	Amended Clean Air Act to allow auto manufacturers more time to meet emission deadlines; eased requirements for certain industrial polluters.

President Ford

Safe Drinking Water Act (PL 93-523), 1974	EPA	Authorized federal government to set standards to safeguard the quality of public drinking water supplies and to regulate state programs for protecting underground water sources.
Federal Land Policy and Management Act (PL 94-579), 1976	Bureau of Land Management, Dept. of Interior	Gave Bureau of Land Management authority to manage public lands for long-term benefits; officially ended policy of conveying public lands into private ownership.
National Forest Management Act (PL 94-588), 1976	U.S. Forest Service, Dept. of Agriculture	Gave statutory permanence to national forest lands and set new standards for their management; restricted timber harvesting to protect soil and watersheds; limited clearcutting.
Toxic Substances Control Act (PL 94-469), 1976	EPA	Authorized premarket testing of chemical substances; allowed EPA to ban or regulate the manufacture, sale, or use of any chemical presenting an "unreasonable risk of injury to health or environment; prohibited most uses of PCBs.
Resource Conservation and Recovery Act (PL 94-580), 1976	EPA	Required EPA to set regulations for hazardous waste treatment, storage, transportation, and disposal; provided assistance for state hazardous waste programs under federal guidelines.

President Carter

Clean Air Act Amendments (PL 95-95), 1977	EPA	Amended and extended Clean Air Act; postponed deadlines for compliance with auto emission and air quality standards; set new standards for "prevention of significant deterioration" in clean air areas
Clean Water Act Amendments (PL 95-217), 1977	EPA	Extended deadlines for industry and cities to meet treatment standards; set national standards for industrial pretreatment of wastes; increased funding for sewage treatment construction grants and gave states flexibility in determining priorities.
Surface Mining Control and Reclamation Act (PL 95-87), 1977	Dept. of Interior	Establishes environmental controls over strip mining; limits mining on farmland, alluvial valleys, and slopes; requires restoration of land to original contours.
Alaska National Interest Lands Conservation Act (PL 96-487), 1980	Dept. of Interior, Agriculture	Protected 102 million acres of Alaskan land as national wilderness, wildlife refuges, and parks.
Comprehensive Environmental Response, Compensation, and Liability Act (PL 96-510), 1980	EPA	Authorizes federal government to respond to hazardous waste emergencies and to clean up chemical dump sites; creates $1.6 billion "Superfund"; establishes liability for clean up costs.

Policy Formulation and Legitimation

Although NEPA was enacted with little fanfare at the end of 1969, events in 1970—especially the massive Earth Day rallies of April 22—galvanized the 91st Congress to action. Sen. Edmund Muskie, then the leading Democratic hopeful for the presidential nomination, emerged as the dominant political figure in national policy formulation. He was chairman of the Senate Public Works Committee, and its staff developed proposals for amending the Clean Air Act that went well beyond the president's. The committee's recommendations carried both houses of Congress and were passed with little opposition. Thereafter Congress retained the initiative in formulating most environmental legislation in the 1970s.

The outpouring of new federal legislation in the next decade truly was remarkable. Table 1-1 lists 20 major environmental statutes passed during the administrations of Nixon, Gerald R. Ford, and Jimmy Carter. But many others could be cited. Although the Nixon administration's commitment waned as business counterpressures mounted, a bipartisan coalition in Congress continued to support environmental reform. During Nixon's tenure major breakthroughs were made in air and water pollution control (the latter over the president's veto), solid waste recovery, pesticide regulation, noise abatement, and ocean, coastline, and endangered species protection. Only the Energy Supply and Environmental Coordination Act of 1974 slowed progress as deadlines for auto emission controls were extended and some utilities were encouraged to convert to coal burning in the wake of the great oil price increases. President Ford signed five pieces of major legislation that tightened environmental planning over public lands and established a framework for controlling toxic chemicals. President Carter added his signature to another five major laws that revised and extended the clean air and water laws, required restoration of strip-mined lands, set aside more than 100 million acres of Alaskan wilderness for varying degrees of national protection, and created the $1.6 billion "Superfund" to clean up toxic waste sites in the 1980s.

Congress and the incumbent administrations cooperated on many other aspects of environmental policy. For example, area designated as national wilderness (excluding Alaska) more than doubled, to more than 23 million acres in 1980 from about 10 million in 1970. Seventy-five units, totalling some 2.5 million acres, were added to the National Park Service in the same period. The National Wildlife Refuge System grew similarly. Throughout the 1970s the Land and Water Conservation Fund, financed primarily through royalties from offshore oil and gas leasing, was used to purchase additional private land for park development, wildlife refuges, and national forests.

The most obvious threats to both antipollution programs and land preservation came from conflicting demands for increased energy production in the aftermath of the Arab oil embargo. The Nixon, Ford, and Carter administrations all attempted to formulate national policies for increasing energy supplies, although Carter also emphasized conservation and environmental safeguards.[13] These pressures largely were responsible for air pollution deadline extensions, but Congress was unable to enact any comprehensive energy program and unwilling to sacrifice its basic commitment to environmental quality. Indeed, the Clean Air Act was strengthened in many respects by the 1977 amendments.

This confirmed that the environmental policies of the 1970s were legitimated by strong congressional and public support. Although some of the initial legislation—especially the Clean Air Act of 1970—received rather hasty deliberation, most policy was formulated through extensive debate, consultation, and compromise. Both Republican and Democratic presidential administrations recognized the need for strong federal legislation, even though they may have differed with Congress over details.

Institutional Development and Policy Implementation

The most important institutional innovation in the field of national environmental management was undoubtedly the establishment of EPA by President Nixon in December 1970. The agency was the product of the President's Advisory Council on Executive Organization, headed by Roy Ash, which concluded that an independent agency reporting directly to the president was needed to coordinate and enforce all major pollution control programs. The reorganization presented formidable difficulties as dozens of scattered offices and programs and thousands of personnel were brought together under one umbrella. Many tensions and delays resulted as older transferred officials — often with their own traditional sense of mission — had to be melded into a new structure that included many young and energetic lawyers and others who saw the need for radical changes.[14] Nevertheless, William Ruckelshaus, as the first EPA chief, effectively implemented the new functional organization recommended by the Ash council. The legislative mandate of EPA grew rapidly, requiring additional programs, offices, and staffs. EPA's budget (excluding construction grants for sewage treatment plants) grew to $1.3 billion in 1980 from about $500 million in 1973; full-time employees increased from 8,200 to 10,600, two-thirds of them in the agency's 10 regional offices. Even then, the nation's leading environmental agency found it increasingly difficult to meet the new program obligations with available resources.

Virtually every federal agency was forced to develop some capabilities for environmental analysis under NEPA, which required that EISs be prepared on all "major federal actions significantly affecting the quality of the human environment." Although consulting firms prepared most EISs, the statements had to meet detailed requirements established by the Council on Environmental Quality and enforced in the courts. Provisions for public hearings and citizen participation allowed environmental and community groups to block some projects and delay many others, often by filing legal suits challenging the adequacy of impact statements. More important, many design changes were made in projects to anticipate or accommodate such objections. Although the EIS process was criticized from all sides and was revised in

1979 to focus more sharply on critical issues, most careful studies indicate that it forced greater environmental awareness and more careful forward planning in many agencies.[15] More than 12,000 EISs were prepared by 70 federal agencies during the 1970s, and by the decade's end the process had become routine.[16]

Established natural resource agencies, such as Agriculture's Forest Service and Interior's Bureau of Land Management, generally made the transition to better environmental planning more easily. Longstanding doctrines of multiple use and strong professional norms of land management were gradually adapted to serve new environmental goals and interests.[17] Wilderness preservation, never a dominant purpose of these agencies, came to be accepted as part of their mission. Even development-oriented agencies such as the Army Corps of Engineers made great strides in environmental planning and design.[18]

Competent and experienced administrators were appointed to environmental posts. Carter gave especially high priority to environmental issues and drew heavily on the established environmental organizations for appointments and advice. Carter's appointees brought professional expertise to their jobs and avoided overt partisanship (as had their predecessors). As the decade progressed the environmental groups increasingly were willing to accept compromises that these officials found necessary. The agencies themselves moved from single-minded advocacy of the environmentalist perspective toward greater emphasis on balance and compromise to achieve long-term goals. Most students of environmental administration observed growing proficiency and flexibility as implementation "matured."[19]

Nevertheless, policy implementation lagged considerably behind schedule. Much of the initial legislation overestimated the speed with which new technologies could be developed and applied. The laws also underestimated the compliance costs and the difficulties of writing standards for hundreds of major industries. As a result, most of the original compliance deadlines were missed or postponed, and some of the required regulations fell years behind schedule. Frequent legal challenges, as regulated industries sought to block implementation and environmental organizations tried to speed it up, compounded the backlog.[20] Other delays were caused by personnel and fund shortages, scientific and technical uncertainties, and the need for extensive consultation with other federal agencies, Congress, and state governments.

Many industrial complaints about environmental regulations were understandable. The volume of federal regulations increased enormously in the 1970s, including new requirements for occupational health and safety, consumer product safety, and energy conservation. These regulations placed multiple and oftentimes conflicting burdens on the same industries, as did the different environmental laws. The environmental legislation and regulations were extremely complicated and sometimes inconsistent; the priorities and compliance procedures were not always clear, often creating confusion and uncertainty over requirements. Still, more than 90 percent of industrial firms were on air and water pollution abatement schedules by the decade's end.

Successful agencies must be able to balance short-term political pressures against long-range missions and goals, while maintaining external constituent support. Evidence suggests that EPA was successful in the political aspect of administration. Indeed EPA, often caught in the middle of regulatory disputes, postponed actions when interest group pressures could not be reconciled. The agency also experimented with new techniques for mediating disputes and with flexible alternatives for achieving pollution reductions. The "bubble" concept, which allows individual plants to determine the optimal mix of emission controls to meet air pollution standards for the plant as a whole, provides an example of this. At the same time, more emphasis was placed on environmental research and monitoring to improve the informational bases for decision making. Scientists and engineers played an increasingly important role in EPA as more difficult technological issues were tackled in the latter half of the decade. In short, the adversarial style of early environmental regulation gave way to more flexible and practical problem-solving approaches, contributing to EPA's reputation as a competent regulatory agency.

Policy Evaluation

Our evaluation thus far has focused mainly on process criteria: the legitimation of new environmental policies and the development of institutional capabilities for administering them. We will now examine the existing evidence on substantive goal achievement and relative costs and benefits to complete the evaluation.

Environmental Quality. How much did environmental quality improve in the environmental decade? The Council on Environmental Quality's annual reports provide a running account of national trends in air quality, water quality, and other indices of pollution, and these have been supplemented by other studies by private organizations.[21] Environmental monitoring capabilities gradually have improved, but all data must be viewed with caution. According to 1981 CEQ estimates, total emissions of the five major air pollutants (particulates, sulfur oxides, nitrogen oxides, hydrocarbons, and carbon monoxide) declined by 21 percent (by weight) between 1970 and 1980. The result was a significant reduction in the ambient concentrations of some pollutants as measured between 1974 and 1980. Overall levels of sulfur dioxide and carbon monoxide declined by a quarter and a third, respectively, while others (particulates and ozone, or "smog") declined only slightly. The level of nitrogen dioxide actually increased. "Unhealthful," "very unhealthful," or "hazardous" days due to air pollution declined by about one-third in 40 large metropolitan areas beween 1974 and 1980; nevertheless, seven cities still averaged more than 100 such days a year from 1978 to 1980 (led by Los Angeles with 231).[22] The acid rain problem had been aggravated by the construction of tall smokestacks to meet ground-level ambient standards in the 1970s, and there were still few regulations to control emissions of more hazardous air pollutants such as mercury and vinyl chloride. Thus, while significant progress was made in some areas, air pollution remained a serious problem at the decade's end.

Even less tangible progress was made in other areas of pollution control. With some notable exceptions, national water quality does not appear to have improved measurably in the 1970s; yet considering that the economy grew by more than a third during the decade, even holding even could be considered an achievement.[23] Most U.S. cities still did not have adequate secondary sewage treatment plants by 1980, and almost nothing had been done to control pollution from "nonpoint" sources, which accounts for half of all surface water pollution. Many types of hazardous and toxic wastes remained uncontrolled and became increasingly worrisome. Almost no progress was made in halting ground-water contamination, despite the Safe Drinking Water Act of 1974 and the Resource Conservation and Recovery Act of 1976. Regulations for implementing the toxic waste disposal provisions of the latter still had not been issued by the EPA in 1980, and the mammoth task of cleaning up thousands of potentially dangerous chemical waste dumps had yet to begin. The Superfund act of 1980 provided only a small fraction of the total resources needed to complete this process. Finally, only a few chemicals had been regulated under the Toxic Substances Control Act of 1976, even though thousands of new chemicals are produced each year.

These results fell short of expectations; they reflect both the magnitude of the task being undertaken and the complexities encountered in implementing environmental policies. However, the seriousness of hazardous and toxic waste problems was not fully recognized until Love Canal and similar incidents brought them to public attention in the second half of the decade.[24] EPA budgets and staffs were not increased rapidly enough to cope with these "second generation" problems, and many scientific and technical issues remained to be resolved.

Costs and Benefits. As indicated earlier, many environmental benefits cannot be assigned a dollar value. Nevertheless, the costs of environmental programs were substantial and continuing to rise; by the decade's end the relative costs and benefits of environmental programs were being actively debated.[25] New methods were being applied to improve cost-effectiveness, and some environmental groups were more willing to consider alternative, less costly approaches. Many economists argued that regulatory strategies that placed more emphasis on market incentives would improve efficiency and compliance, and EPA experimented with this approach.[26]

It is always easier to measure the costs of programs than the benefits. Costs can be calculated in terms of budgetary outlays and expenditures made by the private sector to comply with regulations, although there is no way of knowing how much industry would have spent without these requirements. By this standard, the commitment to environmental and natural resource programs in the 1970s was quite impressive. Whereas total federal budget outlays (in current dollars) rose from $197 billion in fiscal 1970 to $577 billion in 1980, or by 193 percent, expenditures on "natural resources and environment" increased from $3 billion to $13.8 billion, or 360 percent. If one corrects for inflation, these environmental expenditures were still more than twice in 1980 what they had been a decade earlier. In real terms, spending increases averaged about 9 percent a year during 1971-1976 and 6 percent annually in the Carter years. Put another way, the federal government invested a total of $73 billion in the omnibus natural resources and environment category during the decade (1970-1979), which amounted to about 2 percent of all budget expenditures.[27]

This was not the total environmental bill, since state and local governments also increased their spending appreciably, and most costs for pollution control equipment were borne by the polluting industries (and ultimately by consumers). About 85 percent of all industrial pollution control investment was for new technology to meet air and water pollution control standards. By 1980 governments at all levels and the private sector together were spending about $55 billion annually on pollution abatement.[28] In constant dollar terms, this represented an increase of nearly 50 percent since 1972 or more than 5 percent a year. (The real growth rate for the economy as a whole averaged 3.2 percent during 1972-1980.) Taken together, these pollution control expenditures amounted to about 2 percent of the Gross National Product in 1980, compared with 1.5 percent in 1972. In sum, it appears that about one-half of 1 percent of national income was reallocated to pollution control during the environmental decade.

Quantitative estimation of the current and future benefits of environmental regulation is extremely difficult, if not impossible. The results depend largely on what assumptions are made about the impact of policies on things such as the incidence of disease, property damage, or recreational opportunities, and how one assigns monetary values to these "goods." Even so, the CEQ and EPA made increasing efforts to estimate benefits in relation to costs in the late 1970s, as did many individual economists and some business organizations. As one might expect, the results varied widely depending on who was doing the research.

In its Tenth Annual Report (1979), CEQ summarized the data from various government studies on environmental costs and benefits to the economy. The report estimated the total cost of complying with all existing federal pollution control and environmental quality programs to be $26.9 billion in 1978, but it also found annually accruing benefits to be substantially greater. The annual benefit from air quality improvements alone was calculated to be $21.4 billion. The benefits as of 1979 from other programs were not estimated, but the annual benefits to be enjoyed from water pollution programs and enhanced recreational opportunities were projected to total another $19 billion by the year 1985. CEQ found these programs' effects on the economy to be marginal. While environmental costs contributed slightly to the inflation rate, this was offset by reducing the unemployment rate a similar amount. Environmental investments increased the economic growth rate through 1977, but thereafter they could be expected to exert some "drag" on the economy (so that by 1986, GNP could be nearly 1 percent lower than it would be in the absence of *any* environmental controls).[29]

These estimates were challenged by some business economists and individual researchers. For example, a study conducted for the Business Roundtable estimated that cumulative environmental expenditures of $400 billion by 1985 would produce only half this level of benefits.[30] A well-respected economist, A. Myrick Freeman, found the CEQ estimates somewhat optimistic but concluded that "where state of the art analyses of environmental benefits have been undertaken ... they strongly suggest that environmental protection is good economics."[31] Other private studies have found substantial net benefits from some programs, such as controlling stationary air pollution sources, but negative benefits from others, such as auto emission controls.[32] Although the evidence was mixed, it scarcely supported the view that environmental investment was unproductive.

Summary

The environmental policy cycle that began in 1969-1970 was maturing by 1980. Programs initiated early in the decade were in the middle stages of implementation and beginning to undergo evaluation, while those enacted later were still in the early phases of implementation. Environmental protection appeared to be a well-established function of national government, strongly legitimated and increasingly well institutionalized. Improvements in environmental quality were more incremental in the 1970s than anticipated, and there was growing awareness of costs as well as benefits. But processes for environmental decision making had advanced greatly, and agencies such as EPA were making progress toward greater administrative efficiency. The 1980s would be more difficult as even larger pollution abatement expenditures were required, but few observers expected major changes in the environmental agenda.

Agenda Setting for the 1980s

In his last environmental message to Congress, President Carter offered this assessment of the past and future:

> During the 1970s, the government and people of this Nation showed an extraordinary grasp of the ties between human beings and their environment and demonstrated strong leadership in creating a sustainable relationship. The 1980s are presenting new challenges. Our Nation must continue to move forward and extend the progress we have made — progress for which we are being repaid many times over.[33]

In his final budget of January 1981, Carter called for renewed efforts to control pollution and conserve resources, and he proposed budget increases of 12 percent for environmental programs by 1984.[34] While this rate of increase was only half that of 1977-1980 and one-third that of 1970-1976 (in real terms), it reflected the prevailing view that progress could be maintained with existing programs and some cost savings in the 1980s.

The outgoing CEQ, whose staff had been cut from 60 to 6 by President Reagan shortly after he assumed office, issued a departing statement in which it summarized the most pressing environmental issues to be faced in the coming decades and suggested ways to reduce spending. The statement concluded with a reaffirmation of the past's environmental values:

> Beyond these strictly economic considerations are the intangible values associated with conservation and environmental protection—values arising from bedrock feelings about the relation between humans and nature. Many people—irrespective of their place on the political spectrum—feel that human beings are part of the natural world and should live in harmony with it, rather than seek to be masters of nature, attempting to dominate it entirely for their own purposes. . . .

> Clearly, our concern for the human environment must recognize economic realities. But it would be false economy indeed to limit our economic vision to the needs of the present. We recommend the long view— the view that looks toward the world of our children and our children's children, linking their destiny to the values of our past that have always depended on a healthy, rich and beautiful earth.[35]

The Reagan Agenda

President Reagan brought an entirely different perspective to office. He also spoke of enduring human values and obligations in his inaugural address, but it was economic issues that he stressed:

> These United States are confronted with an economic affliction of great proportions. . . . Idle industries have cast workers into unemployment, human misery, and personal indignity. . . . For decades we have piled deficit upon deficit, mortgaging our future and our children's future for the temporary convenience of the present.[36]

These economic difficulties indeed were uppermost in the minds of most Americans as the new decade began. But did that mean that people were willing to sacrifice prior commitments to environmental quality? Did they want to cut environmental programs in order to reduce future government deficits? Could Reagan legitimately translate his electoral mandate into a program of fiscal retrenchment that substantially reduced the federal role in environmental protection?

As noted at the outset of this chapter, Reagan's CEQ took a very different stance than its predecessors, reflecting his economic philosophy. It called for reevaluation of all environmental programs in terms of their economic costs and benefits. Without waiting for the results, the new CEQ suggested that environmental regulation had gone too far during the environmental decade without commensurate social benefits. But the reevaluation did not stop there. After summarizing the entire history of federal resource management since 1776, the council reached this sweeping conclusion:

> The most striking lesson to be learned from a review of the nation's environmental history is that resources held in common, that is, resources which have not been assigned as a property right, have almost inevitably deteriorated.[37]

This "tragedy of the commons," it is suggested, can be remedied only if much of the national trust is turned over to those with a private economic stake in its use. This utilitarian philosophy, rooted in the pages of Adam Smith and in the spirit of the pioneers who subdued nature for their own perpetual benefit, was to be the guiding principle of the Reagan administration.

It is difficult to imagine a more abrupt and dramatic policy shift than that illustrated by the statements of the old and the new CEQ. The ideology of the president clearly penetrated what had been considered a relatively independent and objective source of environmental advice, and that was evident in other environmental agencies as well. Reagan did not try simply to reform environmental management; he set out to reverse the policy cycle of the 1970s and redefine the entire environmental agenda.

Evaluating Reagan's Environmental Policies

The environmental impacts of the Reagan administration will be felt for years to come. Many will be impossible to measure for some time. But the process by which policy changes have been made as well as the impact on environmental institutions and decision-making processes already can be evaluated. Two major issues are raised throughout this book: policy legitimation and institutional implementation.

Policy Legitimation. The administration has attempted to reverse existing policy commitments without any apparent electoral or public opinion mandate to do so. Private environmental organizations, which always have provided the impetus for conservation in this country, have been denigrated and excluded from the policy-making process. Requirements for citizen participation, written into most of the laws of the 1970s, have been ignored or reduced. Most importantly, virtually all the changes in environmental policy have been implemented by executive means without the advice or approval of Congress (with the exception of congressional acquiescence to the administration's initial budgetary reductions). Although no legislative revision had been achieved by the end of 1983, environmental policy had been altered extensively by Reagan's political appointees. Executive agencies traditionally have considerable discretion in implementing specific provisions of federal law, but Reagan's use of administrative powers has gone much beyond precedent in reordering *policy* objectives. This eventually contributed to the congressional counterattack on abuses at EPA, but many of the other policy changes also raise fundamental questions of democratic accountability and constitutional propriety.

Institutional Implementation. Asserting that it could "do more with less," the Reagan administration has radically diminished the institutional resources and capabilities for administering environmental programs. Sheer reductions in budgets and staffs have curtailed many functions, particularly in areas such as research, information gathering and dissemination, monitoring, and enforcement. As many experienced officials have been displaced, talent and professional competence have been lost. The capacities for bringing environmental analysis and advice to bear on policy making throughout the government have atrophied. Finally, although many environmental responsibilities have been delegated to the states, these have not been accompanied by additional funding to support state environmental administration. Thus, despite much improved management at EPA under Ruckelshaus, it appears to most observers that the Reagan administration has permanently weakened the institutional and professional competence of environmental agencies.

Despite administration claims to the contrary, most of its environmental policy changes appear to be motivated by ideological preferences rather than sound economic and scientific analysis. Massive budget cuts and changes in regulatory priorities were made at the outset of the administration, before any new studies could be conducted. Cost-benefit analyses of existing and proposed regulations have had very little effect, nor have convincing economic data been produced to justify major program changes. The administration made it clear that it rejects many previous findings on national and global environmental hazards—including those in the *Global 2000 Report*—while new research continues to underscore past health and ecological warnings.[38] As of late 1983 the administration had begun to modify its position on some issues, such as acid rain, in the face of overwhelming scientific evidence. Yet it has undermined its credibility by seeking technical advice largely from the regulated industries and by massively cutting environmental research budgets (EPA's by over half). By politicizing much of environmental administration, it has downgraded the importance of technical specialists at all levels. Finally, there is worrisome evidence that the administration has screened scientific personnel for political loyalties and suppressed certain kinds of research. All this further undercuts the agencies' abilities to effectively manage an environmental protection program.

The following chapters contain extensive documentation and analysis which will allow the reader to judge whether these charges are justified, and what the longer-term consequences of the Reagan presidency are likely to be for environmental quality.

Notes

1. Steven R. Weisman, "Reagan, Assailing Critics, Defends His Environmental Policy as 'Sound,' " *New York Times,* June 12, 1983.
2. Council on Environmental Quality (CEQ), *Environmental Quality 1981* (Washington, D.C.: Government Printing Office, 1982), iii-iv and chapter 1; CEQ, *Environmental Quality 1982,* 3-4.
3. *Ronald Reagan and the American Environment* (San Franciso: Friends of the Earth, 1982).
4. Philip Shabecoff, "Memo: Meese and Environmentalists," *New York Times,* February 5, 1982; John B. Oakes, "Reagan Making a Bad Start on Nature," *New York Times,* August 31, 1981.
5. David Nachmias, *Public Policy Evaluation: Approaches and Methods* (New York: St. Martin's Press, 1979); Stuart S. Nagel, *Policy Evaluation: Making Optimum Decisions* (New York: Holt, Rinehart & Winston, 1982); Peter H.

Rossi, Howard F. Freeman, and Sonia R. Wright, Evaluation: *A Systematic Approach*, 2d ed. (Beverly Hills, Calif.: Sage Publications, 1982).

6. Alan Stone, *Regulation and Its Alternatives* (Washington, D.C.: CQ Press, 1982); Eugene Bardach and Robert A. Kagan, eds., *Social Regulation: Strategies for Reform* (San Francisco: Institute for Contemporary Studies, 1982); Robert E. Litan and William D. Nordhaus, *Reforming Federal Regulation* (New Haven: Yale University Press, 1983).

7. Daniel A. Mazmanian and Paul A. Sabatier, *Implementation and Public Policy* (Glenview, Ill.: Scott Foresman, 1983); Garry D. Brewer and Peter deLeon, *The Foundations of Policy Analysis* (Homewood, Ill.: Dorsey Press, 1983); Lester B. Lave, *The Strategy of Social Regulation: Decision Frameworks for Policy* (Washington, D.C.: Brookings Institution, 1981).

8. Charles O. Jones, *An Introduction to the Study of Public Policy*, 2d ed. (North Scituate, Mass.: Duxbury Press, 1977); Walter A. Rosenbaum, *Energy, Politics, and Public Policy* (Washington, D.C.: CQ Press, 1981).

9. Daniel Swartzman, Richard A. Liroff, and Kevin G. Croke, eds., *Cost-Benefit Analysis and Environmental Regulations: Politics, Ethics, and Methods* (Washington, D.C.: Conservation Foundation, 1982); Michael S. Baram, "Cost-Benefit Analysis: An Inadequate Basis for Health, Safety, and Environmental Regulatory Decision-Making," *Ecology Law Quarterly* 8 (1980): 473-531; Ian G. Barbour, *Technology, Environment, and Human Values* (New York: Praeger, 1980), chapter 8.

10. Paul J. Culhane, *Public Lands Politics: Interest Group Influence on the Forest Service and the Bureau of Land Management* (Baltimore: Johns Hopkins University Press, 1981), especially chapter 1.

11. One striking and influential study documenting this was John C. Esposito, *Vanishing Air* (New York: Grossman, 1970). See also Walter A. Rosenbaum, *The Politics of Environmental Concern*, 2d ed. (New York: Praeger, 1977), chapter 5; Helen Ingram, "The Political Rationality of Innovation: The Clean Air Act Amendments of 1970," in *Approaches to Controlling Air Pollution*, ed. Ann F. Friedlaender (Cambridge, Mass.: MIT Press, 1978), chapter 2.

12. Public Law 91-90 (42 USC 4321-4347), Sec. 101. NEPA was primarily the work of Sen. Henry Jackson, chairman of the Senate Interior and Insular Affairs Committee, Rep. John Dingell, chairman of the House Merchant Marine and Fisheries Committee, and Professor Lynton K. Caldwell, then a congressional adviser. See Caldwell, *Man and His Environment: Policy and Administration* (New York: Harper & Row, 1975), chapter 4; and Richard A. Liroff, *A National Policy for the Environment* (Bloomington: Indiana University Press, 1976).

13. On energy policy developments, see Rosenbaum, *Energy, Politics and Public Policy;* Congressional Quarterly, *Energy Policy*, 2d ed. (Washington, D.C.: Congressional Quarterly, 1981); and Regina S. Axelrod, ed., *Environment, Energy, Public Policy: Toward a Rational Future* (Lexington, Mass.: Lexington Books, 1981).

14. J. Clarence Davies III and Barbara A. Davies, *The Politics of Pollution*, 2d ed. (Indianapolis: Pegasus, 1975), chapter 5; John Quarles, *Cleaning Up America* (Boston: Houghton-Mifflin, 1976); John C. Whitaker, *Striking a Balance: Environment and Natural Resources Policy in the Nixon-Ford Years* (Washington, D.C.: American Enterprise Institute, 1976).

15. See Richard N. L. Andrews, *Environmental Policy and Administrative Change: Implementation of the National Environmental Policy Act* (Lexington, Mass.: Lexington Books, 1976); Liroff, *A National Policy for the Environment;* Lynton

K. Caldwell, *Science and the National Environmental Policy Act: Redirecting Policy Through Procedural Reform* (University, Ala.: University of Alabama Press, 1982).

16. The annual CEQ reports contain the full text of NEPA, the current guidelines, and updates on their application. New regulations were made mandatory in 1979; see CEQ, *Environmental Quality 1979*, 577ff.

17. Culhane, *Public Lands Politics.*

18. Daniel A. Mazmanian and Jeanne Nienaber, *Can Organizations Change: Environmental Protection, Citizen Participation, and the Corps of Engineers* (Washington, D.C.: Brookings Institution, 1979).

19. Helen M. Ingram and Dean E. Mann, "Environmental Policy: From Innovation to Implementation," in *Nationalizing Government: Public Policy in America*, ed. Theodore S. Lowi and Alan Stone (Beverly Hills, Calif.: Sage, 1979); Dean E. Mann, ed., *Environmental Policy Implementation: Planning and Management Options and Their Consequences* (Lexington, Mass.: Lexington Books, 1982); Alfred A. Marcus, *Promise and Performance: Choosing and Implementing Environmental Policy* (Westport, Conn.: Greenwood Press, 1980).

20. Lettie McSpadden Wenner, *The Environmental Decade in Court* (Bloomington: Indiana University Press, 1982). Congress was also unwilling to enforce strict deadlines; see R. Shep Melnick, "Deadlines, Common Sense, and Cynicism," *The Brookings Review* (Fall 1983): 21-24.

21. One parallel effort is *State of the Environment 1982* (Washington, D.C.: Conservation Foundation, 1982). A great deal of useful information is included in *Environment and Health* (Washington, D.C.: Congressional Quarterly, 1982).

22. CEQ, *Environmental Quality 1981*, 33, 243, 246.

23. *State of the Environment 1982*, chapter 3.

24. Adeline Gordon Levine, *Love Canal: Science, Politics, and People* (Lexington, Mass.: Lexington Books, 1982); Michael H. Brown, *Laying Waste: The Poisoning of America by Toxic Chemicals* (New York: Pantheon, 1979); and The Environmental Defense Fund and Robert H. Boyle, *Malignant Neglect* (New York: Vintage Books, 1980).

25. CEQ, *Environmental Quality 1979*, chapter 12; Paul R. Portney, ed., *Current Issues in U.S. Environmental Policy* (Baltimore: Johns Hopkins University Press, 1978).

26. There is a large literature on economic incentives; see, for example, Allen V. Kneese and Charles L. Schultze, *Pollution, Prices and Public Policy* (Washington, D.C.: Brookings Institution, 1975); Frederick R. Anderson et al., *Environmental Improvement Through Economic Incentives* (Baltimore: Johns Hopkins University Press, 1977); and Lave, *The Strategy of Social Regulation.* For a good current study, see Robert W. Crandall, *Controlling Industrial Pollution: The Economics and Politics of Clean Air* (Washington, D.C.: Brookings Institution, 1983).

27. *Economic Report of the President* (Washington, D.C.: Government Printing Office, 1982), 316-317.

28. CEQ, *Environmental Quality 1982*, 307.

29. CEQ, *Environmental Quality 1979*, 655-659, 665. Subsequent analyses using the same econometric model indicate that effects on economic growth would be even less; see chapter 16 in this volume.

30. Richard Liroff, "Cost-Benefit Analysis in Federal Environmental Programs," in *Cost-Benefit Analysis and Environmental Regulations*, 45.

31. Ibid.

32. See, for example, A. Myrick Freeman, *Air and Water Pollution Control: A Benefit-Cost Assessment* (New York: Wiley, 1982); Lester B. Lave and Gilbert S. Omenn, *Clearing the Air: Reforming the Clean Air Act* (Washington, D.C.: Brookings Institution, 1982); and Crandall, *Controlling Industrial Air Pollution.*

33. CEQ, *Environmental Quality 1980,* iv.

34. Executive Office of the President, *Budget of the United States Government, Fiscal Year 1982* (Washington, D.C.: Government Printing Office, 1981), 151.

35. Council on Environmental Quality, "Environment in the '80s—the Carter CEQ Says Farewell," *Sierra* (September/October 1981), 34-37.

36. "Inaugural Address of President Ronald Reagan," *Weekly Compilation of Presidential Documents* (Washington, D.C.: Government Printing Office, January 23, 1981), 5.

37. CEQ, *Environmental Quality 1981,* 12.

38. Council on Environmental Quality and Department of State, *The Global 2000 Report to the President: Entering the Twenty-First Century* (Washington, D.C.: Government Printing Office, 1980). See also Martin W. Holdgate et al., eds., *The World Environment 1972-1982: A Report by the United Nations Environment Programme* (Dublin, Ireland: Tycooly International Publishing, 1982). For comments on these and other international reports, see CEQ, *Environmental Quality 1981,* 205-207, and chapter 15 of this volume.

Part I

SETTING THE AGENDA:
OPPORTUNITIES AND CONSTRAINTS

2. A NEW ENVIRONMENTAL POLICY AGENDA: THE 1980 PRESIDENTIAL CAMPAIGN AND ITS AFTERMATH

Michael E. Kraft

The 1980 presidential election put Ronald Reagan in the White House and began an unprecedented period of upheaval in U.S. environmental and natural resource policy. The "environmental decade" of the 1970s was brought to an abrupt halt as Interior Secretary James G. Watt, Environmental Protection Agency (EPA) Administrator Anne Gorsuch, and other officials in the new administration fashioned an environmental policy agenda more in tune with their conservative ideology and probusiness sympathies. Policy officials from the president on down brought with them a strikingly different view of environmental quality issues and their relationship to economic revitalization and development. Virtually all environmental protection policies enacted during the 1970s were to be reevaluated as part of the president's larger agenda of reducing the scope of government regulation, cutting back on the role of the federal government, shifting responsibilities when possible to the states, and relying more on the private sector than on government intervention.[1]

How did the Reagan administration justify such a radical departure from the bipartisan consensus that had characterized environmental policies throughout the 1970s? The president and his aides cited the 1980 election results: the new agenda's legitimacy was based to a considerable extent on the presumed mandate that Reagan had received with his landslide victory over President Jimmy Carter on November 4, 1980. The results were impressive enough. Reagan won nearly 44 million votes (50.7 percent) to Carter's 35.5 million (41.0 percent), with John Anderson garnering 5.7 million (6.6 percent). The Electoral College vote margin was even greater; Reagan won in 44 states for a total electoral vote of 489 to Carter's 49. Carter received the lowest percentage of the popular vote of any incumbent Democratic president in U.S. history; he amassed fewer electoral votes than any incumbent president except William Howard Taft in 1912.[2] As president, Reagan interpreted that vote as a mandate for aggressive pursuit of conservative policy

29

goals and economic revitalization. Accordingly he launched a thoroughgoing attack on economic and regulatory policies and, as part of that effort, attempted a radical alteration in environmental policies.

Unfortunately for the president, he and his advisers seriously misjudged the public's commitment to environmental policy. In late July 1983 William D. Ruckelshaus finally acknowledged what should have been clear in 1981. He asserted that the administration had misread its mandate from the 1980 election. It had confused, he said, the public's wish to improve the way environmental and public health programs were administered with a desire to change the goals of the programs themselves. When it attempted to change some of those goals through deregulation, this caused the "perception" that the administration was hostile to environmental programs. While Ruckelshaus still believed there was a need to make environmental laws "more reasonable, rational, and less burdensome," he was convinced that this meant changing only the means used, not the goals: "We cannot deregulate in this area," he said.[3]

Regardless of the change of direction Ruckelshaus's statement may signal, his comment underscores the importance of understanding Reagan's rise to power and the way in which his environmental policy agenda developed. This chapter addresses critical questions focused on those concerns. What were the major elements of the Reagan agenda, and what political forces, organizations, and individuals were most influential in shaping it? How were the issues on that agenda presented during the 1980 presidential campaign and, in particular, how salient were environmental and natural resource issues in 1980? To what extent could the election's outcome be interpreted as public endorsement of Reagan's environmental or regulatory reform policies? What are the implications for the legitimacy of the aggressive strategy used by the administration to put that agenda into effect?

The Political Environment of 1980

No presidential election takes place in isolation from the larger political forces in the nation, and 1980 was no exception. Reagan's victory and his policy agenda must be explained in terms of underlying forces at work in the American political system during the previous decade and the immediate collection of issues, personalities, and events in 1980. Four particular changes in political institutions, practices, and issues in the late 1960s and in the 1970s are of special importance. These are (1) a decline of public trust and confidence in government and political institutions, (2) reforms in the presidential nominating process, (3) the rise of new political issues and narrowly focused interest groups that articulated those issues and mobilized the public, and (4) the growing influence of the mass media on electoral processes and on politics more generally.[4]

For various reasons during the late 1960s and 1970s the public became disenchanted with government, exhibited less confidence in political institutions from the presidency to political parties, and demanded greater openness and participation in political processes. To meet the new climate of expectations, a number of democratizing reforms were instituted. Those of particular relevance for the presidency focused on the party nominating process. Although scholars continue to debate the wisdom and effects of these reforms, they agree on one important consequence: the influence of party leaders and the nominating conventions themselves declined, and the moderating and coalition-building functions of political parties suffered.[5]

Most delegates to the conventions now are selected through a lengthy series of state-party primary elections, which are especially vulnerable to the well-organized single issue interest groups that had proliferated in the 1970s. To succeed in this string of exhausting primaries, candidates are forced to build expensive, media-oriented, and candidate-centered political organizations.[6] They also are forced to distinguish themselves sharply from the competition. Thus the new process puts a premium on narrow appeals to intensely motivated supporters whose political clout or financial resources might help ensure victory in the primary elections. It discourages the building of broader-based support that might dilute those appeals, and thereby hinders the effectiveness of governing after the election.

The new electoral process makes possible the nomination and election of individuals with only modest national reputations and little experience in the federal government. There is also a greater likelihood that having won the nomination and election through their own efforts, they will arrive in Washington owing little to those groups outside their narrow electoral coalition, convinced of their right to govern independently and unable to do so very effectively.[7] Jimmy Carter moved from relative obscurity as a former governor of Georgia to win the Democratic nomination in 1976 and to overcome a weak challenge by incumbent president Gerald R. Ford. His success owed much to the superior organizing skills of his supporters, particularly evident in the early presidential primary contests. But once in office Carter fared poorly and is widely considered one of the least effective presidents in U.S. history. In many respects, Reagan's rise to power was similar. He entered politics after a long career as a Hollywood actor, with strong support from wealthy personal friends, business interests, and right-wing organizations. Although governor of California for two terms, he had no experience in the federal government.

These changes in the U.S. political system not only made presidential leadership and effective government more difficult but also increased public frustration over the results. The haphazard presidential selection process, congressional incapacity to develop coherent public policy or to oversee effectively the federal government's vast operations, and the difficulty of building public consensus on any major issue combined to form what some political scientists called a "crisis of competence" in government.[8] As the 1980 election neared, certain related developments set the stage for Reagan's nomination and election. The U.S. economy was in deep trouble, with declining productivity, a loss of competitiveness in the world economy, and double-digit inflation; the Carter administration seemed to be making little headway in solving domestic economic problems or in reversing America's decreasing influence in the international arena. The rising costs of government and increasing taxation led to taxpayer revolts as the public voiced its frustration. In this climate, economic regulatory programs, including environmental regulation, became a vulnerable target.

Although environmental groups had become an established part of the Washington community and were well represented in policy-making positions in the Carter administration, many organizations saw their grass-roots support weaken.[9] The groups suffered some erosion in membership, financial resources, and public enthusiasm, and they were attacked by conservative critics for a variety of failings from elitism to continued support of inefficient and costly public policies.[10]

Business groups meanwhile were becoming highly adept at representing their interests in Washington and the states, and they increased their involvement in electoral politics through newly established political action committees (PACs). Conservative ideological groups also found in the new economic conditions and growing dissatisfaction with government an opportunity to expand their political activities. They developed an enormously successful direct-mail fund-raising strategy, particularly through New Right leader Richard Viguerie's operation, and the new electoral politics greatly increased their influence. In Ronald Reagan they found a candidate eager to lead a conservative counterrevolution in public policy.

Reagan's Nomination

Reagan won the Republican nomination for president in 1980 because he and his supporters understood the electoral game created by party rules changes in the 1970s, and because they devised a strategy tailored to the new political environment. The primary campaign was based on Reagan's considerable skills as a candidate: he was out of office and had the time and resources to devote to the campaign, he had experience from the 1976 Republican nomination contest, and he had staunchly loyal, well-organized supporters in each state in which he was to enter a primary. He also led the competition in the polls from the beginning and benefited from the attention the mass media showers on front runners. The result was that his Republican rivals dropped out fairly early in the primary season and allowed him to consolidate his position, gain broader support within the party, and devote more time to planning for the general election campaign. All these advantages were important to Reagan's defeat of Carter in November.[11]

The Primaries

From the start Reagan did very well. He won a state Republican convention straw vote in Florida in November 1979, even though he went to Florida only once. And although he lost to George Bush by a few points in the Iowa caucus straw polls, he went on to defeat Bush, John Connally, and John Anderson in the New Hampshire, South Carolina, and Illinois primaries. By March 19, 1980, the date of the Illinois primary, Reagan had won seven of the first nine primaries, and Ford had announced he would not be a candidate in 1980. Of the thirty-four Republican primaries, Reagan went on to win twenty-nine to Bush's six, and he captured 61 percent of the total votes cast.[12]

Perhaps more important, his early victories convinced journalists that he was certain to win the nomination, and he developed momentum; he retained his front-runner status, and the other candidates were winnowed out before managing to win a significant number of delegates. Bush continued the futile effort longer than Reagan's other rivals, finally conceding on May 26. By early July, before the opening of the Republican convention, Reagan had 1,540 delegates (or 77.2 percent of the total) to 267 for Bush, 58 for Anderson, and 129 shared among the other candidates.[13]

Although the outcome was in little doubt, the primary campaigns after Illinois nevertheless were important for Reagan. They helped to get his message across and mobilize supporters whose votes would be critical in the November election. The main message, according to Theodore White, was a simple one: "that government itself was choking the American people, wasting their money, forcing up prices, poking its nose into local affairs." [14] It was, White noted, the same speech Reagan had been giving for years to conservative audiences. The same people, including members of newer organizations in the New Right such as the Moral Majority and Right-to-Life committees, were out in force in the state primaries. But Reagan's early successes allowed him to pay more attention than might have been expected to broadening his base within the Republican party. That same strategy continued at the convention itself.

The Convention

Soon after accepting the nomination, Reagan began working to build a unified Republican party. It was an important decision for him and for his strategists. He selected Bush as his running mate, retained moderate Bill Brock as national party chairman, helped his defeated rivals for the nomination raise funds to pay off their campaign debts, and arranged a series of meetings with Republican members of Congress and governors.[15] The media helped Reagan deemphasize his right-wing views by reporting extensively on such overtures.

In addition to nominating the party candidate, conventions also approve platforms, which can be another device for building party unity. Such was the case in 1980. The platform was conservative without being right wing. It emerged from a long process of public hearings held nationwide (10 in all) and careful drafting by a moderate group of policy committees established by party chairman Brock. Reflecting the concerns of Washington-based issue activists, the overriding theme was how to restructure or reform government, not reject it. The final document's language apparently was cleared with the Reagan staff, although they had little direct involvement in its initial drafting. Congressional Quarterly concluded that Reagan's actions at the convention "demonstrated that he is more interested in winning in November than in ideological purity." [16] And Albert Hunt of the *Wall Street Journal* described the well-orchestrated convention as a "tour de force" for Reagan: he "touched all the right political bases" and had "no intention of emulating the right-wing strategy embraced by his original political mentor, Senator Barry Goldwater, in 1964." [17]

Reagan's Environmental Policy Agenda

Agenda setting is the first stage of the cycle of policy development and change. It includes how environmental problems are perceived and defined, the attention or priority given to them, and the kinds of solutions thought to be effective or appropriate. An environmental policy agenda will reflect not only particular positions on issues but also a president's general political beliefs about the role of government and the private sector, and priorities in the related areas of economic and regulatory policy. That was especially true of Reagan's agenda in 1980. One place to begin looking for a clear statement of a president's agenda is the party platform, but the search must extend beyond that. It must include statements made during the campaign itself, task force or transition team reports delivered to the president-elect, formal statements by the president or his leading policy officials, and, of course, legislative and budgetary proposals made to Congress.[18] Other chapters in this volume examine policy proposals, budgets, and the activities and statements of environmental policy officials after Reagan assumed office. This chapter focuses primarily on the pre-inaugural indicators of Reagan's broad stance on environmental and regulatory policy issues. Insofar as it is possible to determine the origin of the beliefs and issue positions on that agenda, some of the major sources will be suggested.

The 1980 Platforms

Table 2-1 provides excerpts from the Republican and Democratic platforms, the latter chiefly to allow comparison of Reagan's agenda with the Carter administration's and Democratic party's positions. Five broad topics are included: economy; government operation, reform, and decentralization; regulatory reform; energy; and environmental quality. The first four have important relationships to the direction of environmental policy, and the combination allows a fuller and more accurate comparison. Party platforms always are stronger on general rhetoric than specific policy proposals, and both parties tend to endorse certain widely shared beliefs and positions. Nonetheless, the major points of distinction emerge fairly well from Table 2-1.

The Republican party's commitment to economic policy change, deregulation, vigorous energy resource development, and greater reliance on the marketplace rather than government policies clearly indicated what one could expect with Reagan in the White House. If there were any doubts about that, Reagan's acceptance speech reinforced the positions stated in the platform:

America must get to work producing more energy. The Republican program for solving economic problems is based on growth and productivity.... [Energy development] must not be thwarted by a tiny minority opposed to economic growth which often finds friendly ears in regulatory agencies for its obstructionist campaigns.

Make no mistake. We will not permit the safety of our people or our environmental heritage to be jeopardized, but we are going to reaffirm that the economic prosperity of our people is a fundamental part of our environment.[19]

Environmental quality thus was defined to include "economic prosperity," and Reagan indicated that environmental policy would be judged in terms of economic costs and benefits and its contributions to economic revitalization. His statement assumed the goals were compatible.

Campaign Statements and Policy Advisers

Because environmental issues were of low salience and were not discussed much in the campaign itself, only a few statements reported by the press are worth noting. None points with any clarity to a well-defined environmental policy agenda. But, taken together, they suggest Reagan's general posture on the issues, and they are consistent with the Republican platform. At one point, Reagan asserted that air pollution in the United States had been "substantially controlled." On another occasion, he departed from his prepared statement to say that nature itself, not industry, was the chief air polluter (confusing nitrous oxide from decaying plants and trees with nitric oxide from industrial smokestacks), and he went on to call for major overhaul of the Clean Air Act to help the steel industry. A day later, he maintained he was an environmentalist and referred to his environmental record as governor of California; however, as a writer for the *National Journal* noted, "Reagan's environmental commitment as California's governor from 1967 to 1975 is not quite as sparkling as he claims." [20] On yet another occasion, Reagan was quoted as saying that if the EPA had its way, "you and I would have to live in rabbit holes." Such statements betrayed little understanding of environmental problems or familiarity with studies showing the modest impact of federal environmental policies on industrial development and unemployment.

Whether speaking of economic policy and regulatory reform (much more prominent in the campaign) or environmental policy, Reagan displayed a tendency to "shoot from the hip" and to propose simplistic solutions. Elizabeth Drew explained Reagan's tendencies more generally; his mind, she said,

appears to be a grab bag of clippings and "facts" and anecdotes and scraps of ideas. People who have worked with him describe him as an intelligent man with an open mind but strong political instincts of his own. He is inclined toward uncomplicated concepts: a balanced budget, a strong defense, patriotism.[21]

Such habits were reinforced by his close association with a group of supporters who shared his right-wing beliefs, including auto dealer Holmes Tuttle, steel magnate Earle Jorgensen, industrialists Henry Salvatori and Justin Dart, and the chairman of the board of Union Oil Co., A. C. (Cy)

Table 2-1 1980 Party Platforms

Republican Platform	*Democratic Platform*

Economy

Asserted that "nothing is more important to the nation's defense and social well-being than economic growth" and that "sweeping change in economic policy in America is needed." Promised a "bold program of tax rate reductions, spending restraints, and regulatory reforms that will inject new life into the economic bloodstream of this country."

Opposed any action "whose effect will be a significant increase in unemployment." Favored antirecession jobs programs, targeted tax reductions to stimulate production, and restraint on federal spending, but opposed "drastic cuts in social programs which impose unfair burdens on the poor and the aged, on women, on children, and on minorities."

Government Operation, Reform, Decentralization

Criticized the Democrats for having produced "a central government of vastly expanded size, scope, and rigidity," and announced "it is time for change." Asserted that "decentralization of the federal government" was a high priority and that the "best government is the one closest to the people." Pledged the party to a "comprehensive program of government reform."

"The Democratic Party has long stood for an active, responsive, vigorous government [but we have] a special obligation to ensure that government is also efficient and well managed." Pledged support for a variety of measures to ensure government openness and integrity, law enforcement, paperwork reduction, and election reform.

Regulatory Reform

The party "declares war on government overregulation." Stated that "where possible we favor deregulation" and that "we believe the marketplace, rather than the bureaucrats, should regulate management decisions." Supported agency "review of existing regulations" and the conduct of "cost-benefit analysis of major proposed regulations." Recommended legislation which would eliminate the "present presumption of validity in favor of federal regulations."

"Federal regulations are needed to protect consumers and providers in the areas of health, safety, and the environment." The Carter administration established a management system which includes "reviewing and eliminating outdated rules and analyzing the full impact of new rules before they are issued," "alternative regulatory approaches which can reduce compliance costs without sacrificing goals," and "increasing public participation in the regulatory process."

Energy

Stated that energy is "the lifeblood of our economy" and that "we are committed to aggressively boosting the nation's energy supplies" and "restoring maximum feasible choice and freedom in the marketplace for energy consumers and producers alike." The U.S. must "proceed on a steady and orderly path toward energy self-sufficiency," but that free markets will "allocate energy supplies to their most highly valued uses." Acknowledged that "conservation plays a vital role," but rejected "the position of the Democrats which is to conserve through government fiat." Asserted that "Republicans believe an effective balance between energy and environmental goals can be achieved," but that "we must maximize our domestic energy production capability" by moving "forward on all fronts simultaneously, including oil and gas, coal, and nuclear."

"For the past four years, the Democratic Party's highest legislative priority has been the development of our nation's first comprehensive energy policy." "America's energy future requires a continued strong national policy" based on "efficient use of energy" and "development of secure, environmentally safe and reasonably priced energy sources." The party "commits itself to a federal program for solar or other renewable resources that exceed the federal commitment to synthetic fuels" with a goal of "having solar energy account for 20% of our total energy by the year 2000." "We must make conservation and renewable energy our nation's energy priorities for the future."

Environment

Acknowledged that "virtually all major environmental legislation in the past decade reflected a bipartisan concern over the need to maintain a clear and healthful environment," and reaffirmed its standing commitment to conservation and wise management of America's renewable natural resources." But it noted "it is imperative that environmental laws and regulations be reviewed, and where necessary, reformed to ensure that the benefits achieved justify the costs imposed." "We strongly affirm that environmental protection must not become a cover for a 'no-growth' policy and a shrinking economy."

"Progress in environmental quality — a major achievement of the 1970s — must continue in the 1980s." During the next four years, "we must carry forward vigorously with these important policies, and move to address a series of new challenges. We must strive to ensure that environmental regulations cost no more than necessary and are streamlined to eliminate waste, duplication, and delay." The "benefits of these regulations far outweigh their costs," and "we must work to reform regulation without deforming it." The EPA and other environmental agencies must have "sufficient resources to carry out their mandates."

Source: The Republican platform is printed in its entirety in *Congressional Quarterly Weekly Report*, July 19, 1980, 2030-2056. The Democratic platform is in the August 16, 1980, issue, 2390-2420.

Rubel. Drew reported that for a time after the inauguration, some members of this "kitchen cabinet" actually moved into offices in the Old Executive Office Building next to the White House. The group is said to have played a large role in selection of cabinet members and other officials.[22] Similarly, Reagan relied heavily on Sen. Paul Laxalt of Nevada (chairman of the national campaign) and several other representatives of the western Sagebrush Rebellion, such as Joseph Coors of Coors Brewing Co., for his appointments to environmental agencies. Coors and Laxalt reportedly recommended both James Watt and Anne Gorsuch to the president. While all presidents depend on campaign aides and old friends for such suggestions, Reagan's decision to delegate authority for environmental programs to Watt provided yet another indicator of how the environmental agenda began moving away from more moderate Republican positions.

Task Force and Transition Reports

A similar shift was evident during the transition period between the November election and the inauguration. Two sets of reports and policy recommendations reached Reagan after his election in November. His choice of one and rejection of the other suggest the influence of a considerably more narrow set of ideas on the president-elect than indicated by the party platform. In effect Reagan was turning from a convention and campaign strategy of coalition building and moderation to a strategy for policy change that was far more aggressive, narrow, and ideological. That decision had major implications for the direction of his environmental policy initiatives and their legitimacy.

In fall 1980 Reagan appointed a transition task force on the environment to study proposals and make recommendations. Chaired by Dan Lufkin, a director of Columbia Picture Industries who previously had headed Connecticut's Department of Environmental Protection, the task force included two former EPA administrators (Russell Train and William Ruckelshaus) and several other environmental officers and scientists. It produced a voluminous report for the president, calling for moderate reforms in line with Reagan's agenda as expressed in the Republican platform and his other remarks during the campaign. The report recommended reexamination of environmental laws passed in the previous decade but did not advocate cutting programs on a wholesale basis. As Russell Peterson, head of the Council on Environmental Quality (CEQ) under presidents Richard Nixon and Gerald R. Ford, expressed it, the report "sought to maintain the momentum of environmental protection while allowing for some easing of regulation and for economic incentives for pollution control." [23] The Lufkin report was largely ignored: only three copies were ever made, according to one EPA official.

While the Lufkin committee was at work, a parallel and unofficial "task force" report was being assembled by the conservative Heritage Foundation (whose board of trustees includes founder Joseph Coors). Although the Lufkin committee was associated with the moderate Bush wing of the party, and included, according to Peterson, "some of the nation's most respected and influential Republican environmentalists," the Heritage Foundation group consisted of ideological critics of the environmental agencies and programs. They lacked both scientific expertise and experience with the administration of such programs.

The Heritage study's recommendations were contained in a massive 1,093-page tome, *Mandate for Leadership: Policy Management in a Conservative Administration*, covering virtually every major policy area. As its introduction noted, the study tried to answer the question, "What is the conservative agenda, particularly for the first 100 days?" A prepublication draft manuscript was given to the transition team and to the press in November 1980.[24] Unfortunately, the advice it contained reflected little experience with environmental programs and displayed little support for their legislatively mandated goals, thus inviting strong opposition from Congress and environmental groups.

The EPA chapter referred to the agency as a "morass of regulatory controls" and argued that it needed "proper administrative direction and not legislative remedy." Its general theme was that there was too much regulation at too much cost for risks that were not serious. The regulatory reform chapter advocated "the most comprehensive and far-reaching programs of regulatory reform ever undertaken by any administration in the nation's history." The Heritage Foundation's study expressed a true believer's confidence in public support for such actions:

> The conservative's dream of doing away with government controls and abolishing federal agencies is now more generally understood and accepted by large segments of the population, including skeptical business and consumer groups wielding political clout who had long favored such regulation.[25]

Louis Cordia, an environmental policy analyst at the Heritage Foundation and author of the EPA chapter, became a member of the agency's transition team and in November 1981 was appointed to a position there. His name surfaced later during the EPA Superfund scandal when he admitted he had prepared so-called hit lists, or pro and con assessments of hundreds of agency officials and prospective officials for the transition team.[26] Such screening of agency personnel later was described by Chester Newland as a prime example of "ideological political administration." [27]

There was little doubt that the Heritage Foundation and several similar groups had a major impact on the Reagan agenda. Various accounts in the press said the Heritage report was "widely used by Mr. Reagan's transition staff after his election." [28] But perhaps the best indication of their influence is simply that so much of their advice was identical to what James Watt and Anne Gorsuch set about doing once in office. Indeed, in a general review of the administration's record after one year, the Heritage Foundation said that almost two-thirds of its suggestions had been adopted.[29]

Why is any of this important other than to satisfy curiosity about the origins of the Reagan agenda? The issue is not so much who or what shaped Reagan's environmental agenda, but whether it was assembled from a sound base of policy experience, current scientific knowledge, and good administrative practice. If not, the administration was putting its environmental programs at great risk and engaging in an experiment that invited policy failure. Rejection of the Lufkin transition task force report and reliance on the Heritage Foundation study suggest that Reagan was indeed willing to run such a risk in pursuit of his larger objective of regulatory reform. His desire to satisfy the Sagebrush Rebels among his supporters was also a major factor in this choice.

The 1980 Election: What Kind of a Mandate?

The election results on November 4 were stunning, but counting votes is much easier than figuring out what voters meant to say. Fortunately, several studies on this subject give a reasonably accurate assessment of voter decision making. Some data on environmental issues are available, but it is also important to cast a wider net because Reagan's environmental agenda, as we have seen, is closely tied to the broader economic and regulatory reform goals.

Reagan's popular vote margin of 51 percent to Carter's 41 percent was not the only election result bearing on his future actions. The president picked up 33 seats in the House of Representatives, the largest Republican gain since 1966. Republicans also won 4 governorships out of 13 contested in 1980 and 189 state legislative seats nationwide. More important, however, was the gain of 12 Senate seats, giving the Republican party control of the Senate for the first time since 1955. Defeat of senior Democratic senators such as George McGovern, Birch Bayh, Frank Church, Gaylord Nelson, and Warren Magnuson symbolized the Republican successes in the Senate. Not only were some noted liberals retired early, but the election put 16 freshman senators in that body, 12 of whom were staunch conservatives. The 52 Republican freshmen in the House also were strongly conservative as a group.[30]

Reagan's surprising margin over Carter (the polls had indicated a closer election was likely) and the dramatic Republican and conservative gains led to a variety of assertions about party realignment, emerging Republican majorities, and a mandate for conservative policy change. The president-elect was quick to suggest as much. Asked if he felt wedded to the Republican platform, he replied:

> I am—I ran on the platform; the people voted for me on the platform. I do believe in that platform, and I think it would be very cynical and callous of me now to suggest that I'm going to turn away from it. Evidently, those people who voted for me ... must have agreed with the platform also.[31]

Speculation about the mandate and how politicians and parties might react extended to Congress. Two congressional scholars, Thomas E. Mann and Norman J. Ornstein, suggested that the 1980 election "provided as clear and distinct a message of general policy direction as any election since 1964." In Congress, they noted, the results of the 1980 election produced a clear and distinct change in the *political dialogue* and *the political agenda,* with both Democrats and Republicans talking about and focusing on the need to reduce public spending, balance the budget, and shore up our national defense. . . . [If] one can recall the items discussed on the political agenda in 1968, or 1972, or 1976, the change is . . . remarkable.[32] [Mann and Ornstein's emphasis]

The result was that few Democrats in Congress were prepared to challenge the president, or as Mann and Ornstein put it, they were "not anxious to step forward proudly as warriors carrying the spear of New Deal liberalism." [33] Reagan would be successful in getting Congress to accept his conservative revolution in the first year, including the massive cutbacks in environmental programs, in large part because of the widely shared belief that voters sent a message in 1980 saying it was "time for a change." To what extent was this a reasonable conclusion given the conduct of the campaign, the issues raised, and, most significantly, the basis for voters choosing Ronald Reagan over Jimmy Carter?

The Campaign

It would be difficult to characterize the 1980 campaign as sufficiently enlightening on the issues to allow the electorate to send a clear ideological message to Washington. It was not one of the more exciting contests in U.S. history, and the range of issues discussed was fairly narrow. Neither Reagan nor Carter distinguished himself with brilliant speeches or creative policy proposals. Public opinion polls and election studies tell us that the public was not especially impressed with either candidate; the Gallup poll favorability ratings Carter and Reagan received in October "were the lowest for any pair of major-party candidates for president, going back to 1952 when Gallup first employed this measure." [34]

The campaign reflected this lack of public enthusiasm. Carter's campaign aides failed to take Reagan very seriously, assuming he would self-destruct with right-wing rhetoric. The Reagan campaign indeed was afflicted with a series of gaffes, and the candidate tended to make extemporaneous remarks that later caused him political embarrassment. He was not well prepared, frequently got his facts wrong, and demonstrated an inability to think clearly about the consequences of his remarks. But Reagan did not directly attack popular programs such as Medicare, Social Security, or unemployment compensation, and he cultivated an image of moderation during the campaign.

Carter in turn found it difficult to run as an incumbent in the midst of a recession for which he bore some responsibility and with a major international crisis created by the Iranian seizure of the U.S. embassy and its personnel. At least initially he adopted the strategy of running as president—campaigning little and trying to appear presidential by staying in the White House. As part of that strategy, he refused to join Reagan and John Anderson in the September debate sponsored by the League of Women Voters. But he was severely criticized for that decision, and he discovered that the incumbent strategy was not very successful in 1980.

Explicit discussion of environmental issues was absent from the campaign, an important fact in any overall assessment of a particular mandate for environmental policy change. Albert Hunt reports that Reagan's main contribution on environmental issues was a tendency to make blunder after blunder. In an early October stop in Steubenville, Ohio, Reagan entered into a "rambling discourse":

> [He] claimed that the volcano on Mt. St. Helens produced more sulfur dioxide than all the automobiles had emitted over the previous ten years. He even suggested that the oil slicks off the coast of Santa Barbara, California, were once considered healthy in battling infectious diseases. In addition, he talked about some dangerous health hazards coming from trees. It was a silly performance, compounded a few days later when the candidate returned home to be greeted by one of the worst smogs in southern California history. (He also was welcomed by a sign on a tree reading: 'Chop me down before I kill again.')[35]

Perhaps the highlight of the campaign for most voters came during the second debate sponsored by the League of Women Voters, this one in Cleveland one week before the election. The sharp differences between the policy views of the two candidates were less noticeable than the distinctions between their personalities. Carter's tendency to attack Reagan made him appear mean and allowed his opponent to adopt the nice-guy role in response. Nor did he explain satisfactorily his dismal record in office. Most observers concluded that Reagan benefited more from the debate than Carter.

Later reports that the Reagan staff had used leaked or stolen material from a Carter briefing book to prepare their candidate perhaps help to explain why Reagan did so well.[36] His talent for public speaking, at least when well prepared, and his affable nature did not hurt.

Presidential campaigns are financed largely through public funding. Each major party candidate in 1980 received $29.4 million in federal funds, and the national parties were given another $4.6 million. State and local parties were allowed to spend unlimited funds for campaign literature, voter registration drives, telephone banks, and the like. Republicans were better at raising funds in 1980, and ultimately they spent another $15 million on those kinds of activities, about three times what the Democrats spent.[37]

Independent political action committees also contributed funds indirectly beneficial to the candidates. These committees are allowed to spend unlimited amounts of money supporting their candidates, as long as they have no direct contact with the candidate or his campaign. Reportedly, some $12 million was spent—mostly on television and print media advertising—by independent committees during Reagan's primary and general-election campaigns. This amount vastly exceeded the amount of independent funds spent to support Carter. Much of the money spent on Reagan came from the Fund for a Conservative Majority, Jesse Helms's Congressional Club, the National Conservative Political Action Committee (NCPAC), and two groups established specifically to support Reagan during the campaign: Americans for Change, headed by Sen. Harrison Schmitt of New Mexico, and Americans for an Effective Presidency, headed by Peter Flanigan, a former Nixon aide.[38] Elizabeth Drew's examination of the complex funding arrangements in 1980 suggested that the total amount of "extra private money" spent in support of Reagan was more than five times that spent on Carter ($26 million to Carter's $5 million).[39] One can only speculate on the degree to which such disparities in total spending affected the election's outcome. But it is a safe bet that money was another of Reagan's advantages in 1980, and thus another factor constraining claims of an issue mandate.

Voter Decisions

Scholars agree that it is difficult to conclude that any election grants a mandate on specific issues. The argument is simple: there are a great many issues in any campaign, and voters choose one candidate over another for many reasons. Thus election results do not necessarily imply that those voting for the winner favored his positions on the issues. To make a strong case for a mandate a number of conditions would have to be met, including the existence of significant issue differences between major party candidates, an electorate well informed about the candidates and their issue positions, and a large turnout of voters who decide largely on the basis of the issues. How well did the 1980 election meet these conditions, especially for environmental, economic, and regulatory reform issues?

Certainly Carter and Reagan held different opinions about the environment, but it is more difficult to establish that the other conditions mentioned above existed. Turnout was low (53.2 percent of the eligible electorate), voters were poorly informed on the issues, issue voting was not the predominant explanation for the outcome, and the particular policy preferences of the electorate were not in accord with Reagan's proposals, especially on government spending cutbacks. But the public was sufficiently inconsistent or ambivalent in its views to allow some competing explanations for the result. For example, the broad themes of overregulation and big government clearly struck a responsive chord in the public, even though that view did not extend to particular program changes.

The findings from several analyses of voting behavior are instructive on these points. One study concluded that "on average only two out of five [voters] could meet the criteria for issue voting on any given issue." The authors also noted that many failed to vote at all or voted for Carter or Anderson, that most voters were in between Carter and Reagan on the issues, and that "positional issues provided only one determinant of vote choice." [40]

A parallel study by Warren E. Miller and J. Merrill Shanks examined in exhaustive detail data collected through the National Election Studies for the Center for Political Studies (CPS). They found the public responded favorably to Reagan's "themes or symbols," such as attacks on government spending in general (or on welfare policies in particular), but that there was no such support for cuts in particular programs other than foreign aid and the space effort. On the contrary, they found pluralities favoring greater expenditure of funds in every other domain, including environmental protection. Thus they concluded that there was a "fragile base" for Reagan's subsequent across-the-board cuts.[41] The CPS surveys, like other polls in the last several years, found the public's policy preferences on environmental issues distinctly closer to Carter's positions than to Reagan's; for example, Miller and Shanks concluded that in 1980 "opposition to the relaxing of environmental protection regulations [to increase use of energy sources] remained firm throughout the year." A generous reading of such studies suggests that at best there was broad public approval of a change in the *direction* of public policy and a willingness to give Reagan's conservatism a chance; but there was no mandate for change, especially on environmental issues.

How salient were environmental issues in comparison to other issues in the campaign? Candidates raise many issues in appealing to diverse groups in the electorate, but clearly not all are of equal importance to voters. In 1980 economic issues (recession, unemployment, and inflation) consistently headed CPS's list of the most salient issues—the ones voters say are the most important problems "the government in Washington should take care of." In contrast, the so-called social issues used in appeals to conservative groups were far down the list. Except for "energy shortage," environmental and resource concerns did not make the list of the top ten; and the percentage of the public citing "energy shortage" as a major problem declined significantly by the end of the campaign in November.[42] These findings prompt the question of how Reagan could have received a mandate on such issues when voters were largely preoccupied with other matters during the campaign.

If support for particular policy positions does not entirely explain Reagan's success, what else was important? In many respects the 1980 election was a referendum on Jimmy Carter's performance in office, especially his handling of the economy. Carter entered the campaign with the lowest job approval rating of any president since Gallup began gathering that piece of data in the 1940s, and during the campaign he was judged harshly on his record. Voters were prepared to give Reagan a chance because they were less impressed with the alternative of Carter.

Kathleen Frankovic examined exit polls and found that "disapproval and dislike of the incumbent outweighed any other single explanation for supporting Ronald Reagan." She also found that nearly two-fifths of Reagan voters claimed their primary motivation was simply that "it was time for a change," as opposed to any positive quality or ideological views of their candidate.[43] Her findings are consistent with other data. There is evidence of voter dissatisfaction with both candidates in the low favorability ratings of the Gallup polls, the low turnout, and the volatility of the electorate in the campaign's last few weeks. Everett Carll Ladd reported that the proportion of the electorate undecided in the last several weeks of the campaign was the highest in the previous three decades; between 25 and 37 percent of voters made up their minds during the last week of the campaign, and 10 percent did so on election day.[44] Reagan increased his margin over Carter very substantially in the last week of the campaign, but these data suggest the reasons had little to do with ideology or well-considered policy preferences.

Both scholars and politicians will debate for some time the meaning of the 1980 election. Most scholars agree that no mandate for Reagan's conservative counterrevolution existed. Ladd found little evidence for "a pronounced, persisting conservative swing in the populace, likely to sustain a coherent Republican majority" and saw only a "brittle mandate" in the election results. Gerald Pomper asserted that "Jimmy Carter was not defeated in the marketplace of ideas; he was trounced in the marketplace of food and gasoline and mortgages." And Frankovic observed that the new president "does not have a mandate for conservative policies; he has a mandate to be different from Jimmy Carter." [45] Miller and Shanks were a little more generous toward Reagan, with a major qualification. They argue that public preferences for a policy change "appear to have played a significant role in his electoral victory":

> We believe that Ronald Reagan *did* become President with a base of support centered on a plurality of preferences for a conservative change in the *direction* of federal policy—changes consistent with the direction, if not the magnitude, of the new policies he has been implementing. The public may or may not like his performance in doing so, or the consequences of the new policies—and subsequent elections will surely hinge on the nature of those assessments.[46]

It is interesting that Richard Wirthlin, a key Reagan campaign official, put the mandate received in somewhat similar terms. The 1980 election should be viewed, he said, as initiating "a stewardship opportunity for the Reagan administration to reconsider and restructure the political agenda for the next decade." [47] If one views Reagan's postelection environmental policy actions as an attempt at such leadership in reconstructing the political agenda, there would be little basis for objection. Regardless of voter choice or the existence of a mandate, a new president has the authority to try to redefine the nation's agenda and to restructure policy priorities. The presumption is, however, that he will do so through constitutional processes and with appropriate regard for other elected officials, such as members of Congress, and for public opinion. As other chapters in the volume argue, there are important questions about the means the Reagan administration has chosen to pursue its goals. The apparent absence of a mandate from the election itself provides a basis for judging the legitimacy of both the goals and the means.

The 1982 Elections: A Mandate Challenged

The midterm elections following a particularly striking victory such as Reagan's in 1980 usually are watched carefully for signs of public reaction to the new administration. What did the electoral activities and the results in 1982 say about Reagan's new environmental agenda and public reaction to it? And what did they imply about the 1984 presidential election?

Thanks to the president and James Watt, environmental issues were far more salient in the 1982 elections than they were in 1980. As a movement under attack, with well-publicized battles with the administration, environmental groups found their membership rolls increasing sharply in 1981 and 1982 (the Sierra Club's membership increased by 44 percent in 12 months), and their financial resources much improved over the late 1970s.

They also were determined not to ignore electoral politics in 1982. Greatly expanded effort through the Sierra Club Committee on Political Education (SCCOPE) illustrated the new involvement. Key members of Congress and state officials were targeted for support, funds were raised for that purpose, and thousands of volunteers took up the battle through every means from voter registration drives to distribution of club literature. The group contributed more than $235,000 in cash and in-kind services to candidates. In their own words, they did "incredibly well. . . .In the Senate we were in 15 races and won 11. The Club had made 153 endorsements in House contests — and 121 won. In gubernatorial campaigns, 9 of 11 races went our way." [48] The club began planning for similar involvement in the 1984 elections.

Other groups were equally successful, if not endowed with quite as many members as the Sierra Club. The League of Conservation Voters, for example, had been active in electoral politics for more than a decade, endorsing and raising funds for congressional candidates, and distributing a widely read booklet on congressional voting records on environmental issues. In 1982 it selected 63 candidates to support, and 46 were elected. The environmental groups reported that they spent a combined total of nearly $2 million on the 1982 elections. They asserted that their primary objective, reelection of the environmental leadership in Congress, was achieved. That leadership included Republican senators Robert T. Stafford of Vermont, chairman of the Senate Environment and Public Works Committee, and John H. Chafee of Rhode Island, chairman of that committee's environmental pollution subcommittee.[49]

Despite some losses, environmentalists had made their point that the "green vote" was a force to be reckoned with in the 1980s. Before the election, the Democratic party was advised by pollster Peter Hart to make environmental protection a key campaign issue in 1982.[50] After the election, even the Republican National Congressional Committee acknowledged that virtually every candidate felt it necessary now to take a position on environmental issues. The impact of the election returns on the Reagan administration was less evident. An aide to James Watt was quoted as saying, "We see nothing that in any way would be interpreted as a renunciation of what we're doing. On the contrary, full speed ahead." [51]

Although most general assessments of the 1982 midterm elections acknowledged that the voter's verdict on the Reagan administration was far from clear, opinion polls during this period and throughout 1983 indicated that the administration's environmental policies were opposed by large majorities of the American public (*see Chapter 3*). Perhaps the most important change since the 1980 election was the degree to which the Reagan administration had propelled environmental issues to national prominence, thereby sparking a renewed environmental activism. The crisis in early 1983 that finally forced the ousting of the EPA's leadership temporarily increased the salience of environmental issues, but longer-term impacts were likely to follow.

At the end of 1983 environmental groups already were at work planning for the 1984 election. While they had not yet settled on a candidate for president, the League of Conservation Voters made an unusual announcement in early August 1983: *any* Democratic candidate would be preferable to Ronald Reagan in 1984. The announcement received extensive coverage, including a live interview with a league spokesperson on Cable News Network.

Conclusion

The 1980 election resulted in a major challenge to an environmental policy agenda that had matured during the 1970s. While Reagan's decisive victory over Carter may have implied a general willingness to give conservative policy officials a chance to make government more efficient and cost-effective, the evidence does not support a voter mandate for the radical environmental policy change that the administration attempted to implement. Whether one reviews the campaign itself, the issues raised, the election returns, or survey data on voter attitudes and behavior, there is little to suggest public enthusiasm for the Reagan agenda or the particular rhetoric and actions of the Watt-Gorsuch team.

What was the effect of the first two and one half years of the administration's effort to change the environmental policy agenda itself? Despite public opposition that was strong, persistent, and well reported in the nation's press, the administration did not alter its actions appreciably until early 1983. Like true believers in power, the White House seemed to disregard public criticism or to consider it of no political consequence. The administration gave free rein to its conservative ideology in every area of environmental and resource policy—from Watt's efforts to defend sharply increased energy and mineral development on public lands to a deemphasis of global resource issues and reversal of international environmental policy. Compared with the Carter administration, the Reagan administration's rhetoric, values, and policy commitments hardly could have differed more. While the administration did pay a steep political price eventually, it may well have succeeded in using the opportunity Richard Wirthlin described to restructure the political agenda for the next decade. The long-term impact of the Reagan administration's efforts to do so will depend on public reaction, the way the national media cover environmental and resource issues, the activities of the nation's environmental groups, and how other policy makers evaluate the new climate for environmental issues in the 1980s.

Notes

1. Council on Environmental Quality, *Environmental Quality 1981* (Washington, D.C.: Government Printing Office, 1982).
2. Gerald M. Pomper, "The Presidential Election," in *The Election of 1980*, ed. Gerald M. Pomper with colleagues (Chatham, N.J.: Chatham House, 1981). A discussion of election results also can be found in Paul R. Abramson, John H. Aldrich, and David W. Rohde, *Change and Continuity in the 1980 Elections*, rev. ed. (Washington, D.C.: CQ Press, 1983).
3. Philip Shabecoff, "Ruckelshaus Says Administration Misread Mandate on Environment," *New York Times*, July 27, 1983.
4. James L. Sundquist, "Congress, the President, and the Crisis of Competence in Government," in *Congress Reconsidered*, 2d ed., ed. Lawrence C. Dodd and Bruce I. Oppenheimer (Washington, D.C.: CQ Press, 1981); Nelson W. Polsby, *Consequences of Party Reform* (New York: Oxford University Press, 1983).
5. Polsby, *Consequences of Party Reform;* William Crotty, *Decision for the Democrats* (Baltimore: Johns Hopkins University Press, 1978).
6. Polsby, *Consequences of Party Reform;* Larry J. Sabato, *The Rise of Political Consultants: New Ways of Winning Elections* (New York: Basic Books, 1981).
7. Polsby, *Consequences of Party Reform* and "The Democratic Nomination," in *The American Elections of 1980*, ed. Austin Ranney (Washington, D.C.: American Enterprise Institute, 1981), 58-60; Charles O. Jones, "Congress and the Presidency," in *The New Congress*, ed. Thomas E. Mann and Norman J. Ornstein (Washington, D.C.: American Enterprise Institute, 1981).
8. Sundquist, "Congress, the President, and the Crisis of Competence"; Anthony King, "The American Polity in the Late 1970s: Building Coalitions in the Sand," in *The New American Political System*, ed. Anthony King (Washington, D.C.: American Enterprise Institute, 1978).
9. Bill Keller, "Environmental Movement Checks Its Pulse and Finds Obituaries Are Premature," *Congressional Quarterly Weekly Report*, January 31, 1981, 211-216.
10. William Tucker, *Progress and Privilege: America in the Age of Environmentalism* (New York: Anchor Press/Doubleday, 1982); Robert Cameron Mitchell, ed., "Symposium on 'Whither Environmentalism?'" *Natural Resources Journal* 20 (April 1980): 217-358.
11. Charles O. Jones, "Nominating 'Carter's Favorite Opponent': The Republicans in 1980," in *The American Elections of 1980*.
12. Gerald M. Pomper, "The Nominating Contests," in *The Election of 1980*. Pomper provides results of all primary elections.
13. Pomper, "Nominating Contests," 19.
14. Theodore H. White, *America in Search of Itself: The Making of the President 1956-1980* (New York: Harper & Row, 1982), 306.
15. Jones, "Nominating 'Carter's Favorite Opponent'," 88-90.
16. Charles Hucker and Christopher Buchanan, "Reagan: Pragmatism Over Ideological Purity," *Congressional Quarterly Weekly Report*, July 19, 1980, 1979. See also Michael J. Malbin, "The Conventions, Platforms, and Issue Activists," in *The American Elections of 1980*.
17. Albert R. Hunt, "The Campaign and the Issues," in *The American Elections of 1980*, 143.
18. For a detailed discussion of the concept of the president's policy agenda and various indicators of it, see Paul C. Light, *The President's Agenda: Domestic*

Policy Choice from Kennedy to Carter (Baltimore: Johns Hopkins University Press, 1982).

19. *Congressional Quarterly Weekly Report,* July 19, 1980, 2064.
20. Lawrence Mosher, "Talking Clean on the Hustings," *National Journal,* November 1, 1980, 1850.
21. Elizabeth Drew, *Portrait of an Election: The 1980 Presidential Campaign* (New York: Simon & Schuster, 1981), 115.
22. White, *America in Search of Itself*; Drew, *Portrait of an Election;* Drew, "A Report At Large: Politics and Money — II," *The New Yorker,* December 13, 1982, 72.
23. Russell W. Peterson, "Laissez-Faire Landscape," *New York Times Magazine,* October 31, 1982, 32.
24. Charles L. Heatherly, ed., *Mandate for Leadership: Policy Management in a Conservative Administration* (Washington, D.C.: Heritage Foundation, 1981).
25. Louis J. Cordia, "Environmental Protection Agency," and James E. Hinish, Jr., "Regulatory Reform: An Overview," in *Mandate for Leadership.*
26. Stuart Taylor, Jr., "Ex-E.P.A. Aide Says He Drew Up 'Pro and Con' Lists on Personnel," *New York Times,* March 17, 1983.
27. Chester A. Newland, "The Reagan Presidency: Limited Government and Political Administration," *Public Administration Review* 43 (January/February 1983): 1-21. A discussion of the influence of other conservative organizations in personnel selection can be found in William E. Schmidt, "Denver Lawyer's Role in E.P.A. Decisions Is Focus of Inquiries by Congress," *New York Times,* February 26, 1983, 7.
28. Schmidt, "Denver Lawyer's Role." See also Peterson, "Laissez-Faire Landscape."
29. B. Drummond Ayres, Jr., "Conservatives Bid Reagan Cut More," *New York Times,* January 22, 1983, 7.
30. Abramson, Aldrich, and Rohde, *Change and Continuity;* Pomper with colleagues, *The Election of 1980;* William Schneider, "The November 4 Vote for President: What Did It Mean," in *The American Elections of 1980.*
31. Drew, *Portrait of an Election,* 347.
32. Thomas E. Mann and Norman J. Ornstein, "The Republican Surge in Congress," in *The American Elections of 1980,* 300-301.
33. Ibid., 300.
34. Everett Carll Ladd, "The Brittle Mandate," *Political Science Quarterly* 96 (Spring 1981): 1-25, 5.
35. Hunt, "The Campaign and the Issues," 165.
36. *Newsweek,* July 11, 1983, 20-24.
37. Hunt, "The Campaign and the Issues," 163; Drew, "A Reporter at Large." See also Herbert E. Alexander, *Financing the 1980 Election* (Lexington, Mass.: Lexington Books, 1983).
38. Michael J. Robinson, "The Media in 1980: Was the Message the Message? " in *The Elections of 1980;* Drew, "A Reporter at Large," 86.
39. Drew, "A Reporter at Large," 96.
40. Abramson, Aldrich, and Rohde, *Change and Continuity,* 131.
41. Warren E. Miller and J. Merrill Shanks, "Policy Directions and Presidential Leadership: Alternative Interpretations of the 1980 Presidential Election," *British Journal of Political Science* 12 (July 1982): 299-356.
42. Miller and Shanks, "Policy Directions," 318.
43. Kathleen A. Frankovic, "Public Opinion Trends," in *The Election of 1980,* 103.

For a parallel argument, see Schneider, "The November 4 Vote for President," 240.

44. Ladd, "The Brittle Mandate," 9.
45. Ladd, "The Brittle Mandate," 24; Pomper, "The Presidential Election," 89; and Frankovic, "Public Opinion Trends," 117.
46. Miller and Shanks, "Policy Directions and Presidential Leadership," 354.
47. Richard B. Wirthlin, "The Republican Strategy and Its Consequences," in *Party Coalitions in the 1980s,* ed. Seymour Martin Lipset (San Francisco: Institute for Contemporary Studies, 1981), 264.
48. Denny Shaffer, "The 1982 Elections: An Environmental Impact Statement," *Sierra* (January/February 1983), 35. See also Robert Kutler, "SCCOPE: Getting Ready for the Elections," *Sierra* (September/October 1982), 31-36.
49. Philip Shabecoff, " 'Green Vote' Cited as Factor in Races," *New York Times,* November 7, 1982; Dale Russakoff, " 'Green Vote' Contingent Gains in Elections," *Washington Post,* November 6, 1982; League of Conservation Voters, *Election Report 1982* (Washington, D.C.: League of Conservation Voters, 1982).
50. Adam Clymer, "Democrats Seek to Balance Energy and Environmental Needs," *New York Times,* April 26, 1982.
51. Russakoff, "Green Vote."

3. PUBLIC OPINION AND ENVIRONMENTAL POLITICS IN THE 1970s AND 1980s

Robert Cameron Mitchell

Contemporary environmentalism was born in the 1960s. Its midwife was Rachel Carson, whose 1962 best-selling exposé of the unexpectedly destructive side effects of the miracle pesticide DDT, *Silent Spring,* articulated the subtle cumulative perils of modern technology. Its parents were the old line conservation groups—the Izaak Walton League, National Audubon Society, National Wildlife Federation, and Sierra Club. Throughout the 1960s these groups made a concerted effort to place the environment on the nation's policy agenda. During the decade their membership increased sharply, several new environmental groups were formed (such as Friends of the Earth, Environmental Defense Fund, and Natural Resources Defense Council), and the news media increased its coverage of environmental issues.

By 1969 signs abounded that significant grass-roots public concern about "ecology" was mounting; by the end of the year politicians—including President Richard Nixon, Rep. Gerald R. Ford, and Gov. Ronald Reagan—were responding to the shift in public mood by backing environmental initiatives.[1] The mammoth public response to Earth Day in 1970 marked the culmination of this effort to place the environment on the nation's policy agenda for strong remedial action.

A decade later the Reagan administration, responding to what it believed to be a shift in public priorities prompted by the nation's economic problems and by the high costs of pollution, attempted to reverse course on the federal government's commitment to strong environmental regulation. This chapter analyzes the Reagan administration's failure to win public support for its environmental program and the consequences of this failure for environmental politics in the 1980s.

Public Opinion in the 1970s

Hazel Erskine, an editor of *The Public Opinion Quarterly* and longtime observer of polling trends, described the "unprecedented" speed and urgency with which ecological issues burst into the American consciousness in the late

1960s as "a miracle of public opinion." [2] In 1965 few Americans recognized environmental quality as an important social problem. By 1970 a clear consensus had emerged that the side effects of growth and prosperity were causing unacceptable damage to the environment and that the problems were so serious that they should be the subject of strong, albeit costly, federal regulation. This consensus provided a mandate for environmental lobbyists and set the stage for the wave of environmental legislation that Congress passed during the first years of the 1970s, the so-called environmental decade. It is this consensus and its implied mandate that were strongly tested by the Reagan administration during its first two and a half years in office.

Public support of environmental groups provides them with a key lobbying resource because it lends credibility to the claim that they represent the "public interest." Although polls are only one measure of this support—referendum results, group membership trends, and spontaneous grass-roots activity are others—they are particularly influential in affecting decision makers' perceptions of the environmental mandate because they are up-to-date and representative of the entire U.S. population.[3] Those who live by the polls, however, can also die by the polls. Given the resistance by industry to environmental regulation and the high cost of environmental protection, any sign that public support for the stands taken by environmental lobbyists has weakened or that the public is unwilling to pay the costs could damage seriously the movement's political leverage.[4] Thus, whenever public opinion polls (Gallup, CBS News/*New York Times,* Harris, and others) include questions on environmenal issues, both environmentalists and their opponents closely scrutinize their findings and seek to promote their own interpretation of the data. Both groups also occasionally commission special polls when they think the findings may serve their purposes.

Throughout the 1970s support for environmental protection, reflected by impressive majorities in national polls, consistently confounded those who regarded environmentalism as a temporary fad. Twice during this period, however, the environmentalists' political clout was placed in jeopardy when policy makers misread the public's mood and assumed that support for strong environmental regulation had fallen off. The first doubts occurred in 1973-1974 when the Earth Day enthusiasm was dying down and the Arab oil embargo threatened the nation's energy security. The 1978 tax revolt, epitomized by the passage of California's antitax Proposition 13, and the economy's weakness at that time also gave rise to serious doubts. Each time poll results restored the movement's credibility and confirmed the continued existence of the environmental consensus.

Polls in 1973-1974, for example, showed that the public blamed oil companies rather than environmental protection laws for the oil shortage. Likewise, after California's Proposition 13 passed in June 1978, majorities—faced with trade-offs between protecting the environment and its possible costs, such as closing factories—consistently chose the environmental side. Also when asked whether we are spending too much, too little, or about the right amount to address various social problems, the public strongly supported environmental spending. Not once in the decade did the percentage of those saying that we are spending "too little" on environmental protection dip below 46 percent.[5] These expressions of environmental preferences were confirmed by California voters who passed a water pollution control bond issue that appeared on the same 1978 ballot as Proposition 13. Similarly, in the 1980 election when California went for Reagan, 64 percent of the state's voters favored another water pollution control bond issue and 52 percent voted for the Parklands Bond Issue.[6] California's Lake Tahoe Acquisition Bond Issue was the only environmental bond issue that failed to pass that year, and it was resubmitted and passed in 1982. Despite the rising resentment about taxes in the late 1970s, there was no backlash against the environmental movement. The national polls showed no increase in the small percent (around 10) who said they were "unsympathetic" to the movement.

President Ronald Reagan's three immediate predecessors gave every indication in their pronouncements and appointments that they believed environmental protection had strong popular support. Presidents Nixon, Ford, and Jimmy Carter expressed concern about pollution and took pains to associate their policies with the environmentalism symbolized by Earth Day. Their appointees to the two key environmental positions, interior secretary and administrator of the Environmental Protection Agency (EPA), for the most part were acceptable to environmental groups. Only Nixon's pre-Earth Day appointment of Walter Hickel as interior secretary was an exception, and even he, in most observers' estimations, turned out to be a friend of the environment. In these three administrations, the Council on Environmental Quality (CEQ) was allowed to serve as an advocate within the administration and as an active liaison with the environmental community. In particular, these administrations did not question the environmental groups' assertion that they speak for the broader public interest, nor did presidents Nixon, Ford, or Carter attempt to use the bully pulpit of the presidency to discredit their views. Whether they promoted proenvironmentalist policies or not, these administrations chose not to challenge environmentalism as such.[7]

Reagan Attempts to Reverse Course

The advent of the Reagan administration in 1981 marks the third and by far the most serious test of public support for environmentalist goals. For the first time since Earth Day, an administration actively sought to redefine the nation's environmental priorities and explicitly challenged the environmental consensus. It also sought to discredit the legitimacy of the environmental groups as representatives of the public interest. This occurred at a time of national stress, when concern about environmental goals was overshadowed by the need for economic recovery. Yet by spring 1983 it was apparent that the administration's environmental policies had failed to win public support. Reagan had failed to exhibit that important presidential skill, "the capacity to discern the direction, potential, and limits on policy action that the electorate is offering at any point...."[8] As a result, his environmental policies threatened to become a political liability. The administration was forced to limit the damage by appointing a respected, environmentally sensitive public figure as EPA administrator when the position suddenly became vacant, by accepting the combative interior secretary's resignation, and by moderating some of its more controversial administrative and legislative initiatives in the environmental policy area. The environmental consensus had held firm in the face of its third and greatest challenge.

The Reagan administration's attempt to reverse the course of the nation's environmental policies failed because it was based on three mistaken premises: that public support for strong environmental regulations was weak, that the environmental movement was out of touch with its constituency, and that the political consequences of a major change of course in environmental policy were negligible.

Strength of Environmental Support

The first mistaken premise was to assume that in the face of other urgent, apparently competing goals, the public would be willing to back off from the stringent environmental protection course charted by Congress in the early 1970s. Certain poll results supported this view. At the time of President Reagan's election, polls showed widespread public concern about the size of the federal government and about the harmful effects of government's regulation of business.[9] These two themes were emphasized in his campaign and subsequently were used to justify his administration's environmental and natural resource policies. Moreover, there was no evidence that environmental protection was a salient issue to more than a very small percentage of the general public. In poll after poll, economic issues received by far the greatest number of spontaneous mentions as "the most important problem facing the nation today," whereas no more than 1 percent ever mentioned the environment in this regard.

But poll findings such as these were not new. Since the early 1970s similar patterns had been found, leading public officials at the time to worry about the future strength of public support for environmental goals. As early as August 1973, Sen. Edmund Muskie, a Maine Democrat, lamented:

> Up to now those of us who are concerned with the environment have enjoyed a honeymoon period. It has been easy, relatively easy, to generate public support and congressional support for the goals that we have written into the law. Now we are getting into a crunch period and it is going to be difficult to avoid the pressures of those who would throw away much of what has been accomplished. . . .[10]

By 1974, according to John Quarles, deputy administrator of the EPA at the time, "every Congressman could feel" the drop in the intensity of grass-roots public concern about the environment.[11]

Strength and Salience. A decline in an issue's salience, such as that felt by Muskie and his colleagues, does not necessarily mean that public support for the issue is shallow or weak. There are two key dimensions that must be considered in assessing public opinion: the strength with which an opinion is held and the issue's salience for the person polled. The two dimensions are related but independent of one another.

Strength in public opinion about a social problem refers to the degree to which people regard the issue as a matter of national concern and are committed to improving the situation or solving the problem. Polls measure it by asking people to say how serious or how important they think a problem is, or how concerned they are about the problem. Pollsters also may ask people to make choices between improving the problem or not when the possible costs of doing so include higher prices, closed factories, and reduced energy production. Salience, in contrast, has to do with how much immediate, personal interest people have in the issue. One poll measure of an issue's salience is whether people spontaneously mention it when asked to name the one or two problems that they believe to be the most important facing the nation. Other ways polls can measure salience are to ask people whether they regard themselves as activists on the issue, or to ask them what actions they have taken or would take to promote their position on the issue.

Activists, by definition, have a great deal of interest in their issue. Occasionally, however, as in the case of Earth Day, a social problem suddenly becomes salient to the mass public and receives considerable coverage in the news media. During these periods when there is a great deal of active concern about the problem, the pressures on politicians to do something about it are particularly strong and can be exploited by legislators such as Muskie to aid their efforts to enact remedial legislation.[12]

Mass salience is transitory for all but the most momentous issues such as war or depression. The legislators Quarles referred to in his statement quoted earlier were feeling the inevitable decline in the mass salience of the environmental issue. (Nevertheless, the duration of the environmental issue's mass salience was impressive—three years or more.) Riley E. Dunlap, Kent D. Van Liere, and Don A. Dillman equate this decline with diminished public concern for environmental goals.[13] For Anthony Downs, the decline is an inevitable part of the "issue attention cycle" whose operation dictates a drop in support for environmental protection as its costs become apparent.[14]

Yet there are different reasons why people might not take an intense personal interest in an issue they nevertheless continue to feel strongly about. It may be that other issues are more important to them at the time, or that they believe there is nothing they can do about the problem despite the strength of their feelings. Still another possibility—one that seems plausible for the environment given the government's strong pollution control programs—is that they may believe the problem is being addressed satisfactorily.

In its belief that it had a mandate to de-emphasize environmental priorities in the name of economic recovery and less government, the Reagan administration disregarded the burden of evidence from polls taken in the late 1970s; it fell into the "salience trap" of believing that the absence of widespread, spontaneously expressed concern about environmental issues signified a weakening in the environmental consensus. The following excerpts from reports of polls taken in the 24 months after the Reagan election show this decidedly was not the case.

- *Gallup Poll for Newsweek,* June 1981: "... a large majority of the public believes that government regulation and requirements are worth the extra costs they add to products and services. A majority disapproves of slowing down the rate at which we are working to improve the environment in order to develop energy sources. Three-quarters believe that it is possible to maintain strong economic growth and still maintain high environmental standards."[15]

- *Opinion Research Corporation for the United States Chamber of Congress,* November 1981: "A significant minority—three people in ten—say there should be no air pollution of any kind and another four in ten say not only should there be no air pollution that would endanger health, but also none that interferes with recreation and natural resources. Only 23 percent of the public opts for the more limited goal of judging air quality just in terms of health. Also, only 22 percent support the proposition that environmental standards must be relaxed in order to achieve business and new job growth. . . ." [16]

- *Research and Forecasts for The Continental Group,* February-March 1982: (Seventy percent of the people interviewed for this poll said they had been hurt by the recession.) "There can be no doubt that there is sharp public concern for the environment. Six out of ten Americans think that pollution is one of the most serious problems facing the nation today. Even more significantly, the study uncovers signs that new ideas about man's relationship to his environment have entered the public consciousness. . . . We find the public does not wish to seek the attainment of a strong economy through indiscriminate growth. Rather, moderate, environmentally sound growth appears the order of the day." [17]

- *ABC News/Washington Post Poll,* April 1983: "Most Americans don't think air pollution, unsafe drinking water, or toxic wastes are serious problems in the area where they live, but most don't want the government to relax antipollution laws, either. On the contrary, even though the large majority of Americans believe compliance with antipollution laws costs business firms at least a fair amount of money, more than three out of four say those laws are worth the cost. . . . And two-thirds of Americans do not think antipollution laws should be relaxed in the troubled U.S. auto industry, one of the most hard hit by the recession." [18]

It also must be pointed out that polls during this period continued to show that the public did not regard the environment as a crisis issue. Moreover, they provided evidence that many people were relatively uninformed about environmental issues.[19] For example, an April 1983 ABC NEWS/*Washington Post* poll showed that 57 percent of those interviewed did not know enough about Interior Secretary James G. Watt, despite his high profile, to venture an opinion about him.[20] Polls undertaken during this period also show that people were willing to modify the major antipollution laws as long as the standards were maintained, and that majorities would support some trade-offs on specific environmental restrictions, particularly for the sake of developing needed energy sources.

Yet when we look beyond these findings, all of which relate to the salience of environmentalism, the public's basic commitment to environmental goals is unmistakable. Far from declining, support for these goals appears to have increased because of the Reagan attacks. William Schneider wrote in March 1983 that ". . . the public in recent months has shifted away from its preference for a balanced [between economic growth and environmental protection] policy and asserted a clear priority for environmental needs. . . ." [21] According to news reports, private Republican polling for the White House also has confirmed the conclusion that the public remains committed to environmentalism, even if the issue is less important personally than other more immediate and pressing concerns.[22]

Stimulated by the storm of controversy over EPA's toxic waste program, public opinion polls in 1983 sought people's views specifically about the administration's environmental policies. The president was not held personally responsible for the problems at EPA; but pluralities disapproved of his environmental programs and appointees, and majorities expressed the belief that he shared his appointees' probusiness views. In a spring 1983 *Newsweek* poll, 47 percent disapproved of his environmental policies (up from 40 percent the year before).[23] Several ABC News/*Washington Post* polls during this period found that 50 percent or more of their respondents believed the president "cares more about protecting the firms that are violating antipollution laws" than about enforcing those laws. This percentage was only slightly below the 60 percent who ascribed this view to EPA Administrator Anne Gorsuch at the height of her agency's controversy.[24] No more than one out of four of those polled believed the president cares more about enforcing the antipollution laws. Those who did have an opinion about Watt disapproved of Watt by a three to one margin.[25]

Causes of Environmental Concern. Why has the environment become such an enduring social concern that the environmental consensus persisted in the face of the Reagan attack? First, environmental issues have an inherently broad appeal. In contrast to many social problems that affect a particular group such as blacks or the handicapped, environmental problems potentially affect all citizens. Environmental quality improvements are true public goods in the sense that they are available to everyone. Moreover, and this is the so-called motherhood component, environmental improvements involve non-controversial goals, such as health, cleanliness, natural beauty's preservation, future generations' needs, and wildlife protection. Because numerous issues fall into the environmental category, diverse constituencies have an interest in supporting environmental regulation. Hunters as well as animal protection advocates favor wildlife habitat protection. Urban residents are affected particularly by air pollution, rural dwellers by strip mines and well contamination caused by toxic wastes. Citizens with little interest in nature and wildlife may be sensitive to the public health threat posed by toxic wastes or drinking water contamination.

A second reason for the public's persistent support lies in the fundamental shift in awareness experienced by many Americans in the late 1960s and early 1970s. This quiet revolution has profound implications for environmental politics because it has changed the public's value system.

Prior to the Earth Day period, the "human exemptionalism paradigm," according to Riley Dunlap, was dominant.[26] Those sharing this view—whose contemporary proponents include James Watt, Julian Simon, and the late Herman Kahn—tend to see life's possibilities and nature's bounty as infinite and humans as essentially omnipotent. They assume that human technological ingenuity can continue infinitely to improve the human situation as long as it is unfettered by unnecessary restrictions and self-imposed limitations. In this view it is imperative to use natural resources to promote human welfare through economic growth.

The "ecological paradigm" promoted by the Earth Day organizers offered a contrasting viewpoint. According to this theory, environmental limits are real, and natural ecosystems are subject to serious, sometimes irreversible, harm by human activities. Economic growth should be pursued in a way consistent with the need to maintain the quality of life. According to the Continental Group Report, which probed the public's environmental values in considerable detail, aspects of the ecological paradigm now are accepted widely by the general public. Moreover, it determined that fewer than one in ten of the general public and one in four of a business leadership sample hold strong human exemptionalist views.[27]

The other aspect of this new environmental awareness is an increased demand for cleaner air and water on the part of many who previously were willing to tolerate relatively high levels of environmental degradation as the necessary price of progress. In an important sense many Americans now view safety from harm caused by toxic substances, the provision of fishable and swimmable rivers, and cleaner air as entitlements. According to Everett Carll Ladd: "The meaning of 'more' has changed throughout American history with economic development—and today it includes a clean and healthy environment just as securely as it does good housing, motor cars, vacations, and television sets." [28]

Third, there is a widespread belief that environmental problems have not been solved despite the government's efforts over the past decade. One striking and little-noticed poll finding revealed that, on the average, people believe we have made only modest progress in improving the environment during the preceding five or ten years. In a Resources for the Future poll, undertaken in 1980, people were asked to rate the quality of the lakes and streams in their area—then and five years earlier—on a ten-point scale, where a score of one represented the cleanest water possible. The mean rating for present and past water quality was virtually identical (5.6 and 5.7 respectively). In a 1981 poll only 13 percent said they thought air quality in their area was better than five years earlier, whereas 24 percent thought it was worse.[29] A 1982 survey questioned people about the nation's environmental quality "compared to ten years ago" and found that more people felt it has "grown worse" (48 percent) than "improved" (34 percent).[30]

Unfortunately, no poll to date has asked people how much government

Table 3-1 Evaluation of the Effectiveness of
Selected Federal Government Programs

Federal government efforts have improved things

	Great deal	Some- what	Not at all	Made things worse	Don't know	
Protecting parks and wilderness areas	13%	43%	24%	8%	12%	100%
Reducing water pollution	8	41	29	13	9	100
Reducing air pollution	9	39	30	15	7	100
The quality of health care	9	37	26	21	7	100
Protecting the consumer	9	35	29	20	7	100
The availability of public transportation	5	26	30	27	12	100
The quality of education	6	24	27	36	7	100

Question: I am going to read a number of problem areas. For each, tell me if you feel that if in recent years, the federal government's efforts in this area have improved things a great deal, only somewhat, not changed things or made the problems worse. First, what effect has government activity had on: . . . .

Source: The Gallup Organization, Inc., "Public Opinion About Environmental Protection and Defense Spending: The Newsweek Poll," June 1981. Telephone poll of 745 adults was taken on June 17-18, 1981.

pollution control programs have kept environmental quality from declining further. Data from a June 1981 *Newsweek* poll, shown in Table 3-1, suggest that a majority or strong plurality believed the federal government's environmental programs had had a positive effect, especially in protecting parks and wilderness areas. Fewer than one in seven people believed air and water pollution had been made worse because of federal efforts. It is likely that people believe the government has not finished its worthwhile job of ensuring an acceptably safe and clean environment.

A final reason for the continued support for environmental protection is its high visibility in the news media. This stems from the persistence, multiplicity, and local character of environmental threats. Nearly each time Congress passes legislation that addresses a current environmental problem, new ones command the attention of the press and the public, ultimately requiring congressional action. In 1983, for example, toxic wastes and acid rain were two issues prominent in Congress, yet, as recently as 1975, few people had heard of either. By 1980, however, 64 percent of the public expressed "a great deal" of concern about hazardous chemical waste disposal, a level of concern even higher than had been expressed about air and water pollution in earlier surveys.[31] Site-specific toxic waste problems also contributed to this issue's visibility, as the Love Canal and Times Beach stories made for dramatic television and print media news coverage. It is not surprising, therefore, that of all the controversies surrounding Gorsuch's tenure at EPA, her administration of the $1.6 billion toxic-waste cleanup program would be the one to ultimately cause her downfall.

Environmentalists and the Constituency

A second fundamental mistaken assessment made by the Reagan administration was that the national environmental groups had lost touch with their constituency. Some ten national organizations, such as the National Audubon Society, Izaac Walton League, and Natural Resources Defense Council, lobby on environmental issues in Washington, D.C. These groups endeavor to be nonpartisan. They enjoy close ties with sympathetic legislators in both parties, and they have a long history of working with Republican and Democratic administrations. Many of their leaders publicly supported President Carter's reelection bid, revealing their fears of the antiregulation, probusiness bias they supposed would characterize a Reagan administration. Once in office, the administration made little effort to reach out to the environmentalists who, in turn, felt the administration's interior department and EPA appointments and policies had realized their worst fears. Environmental leaders quickly became outspoken opponents of Watt and Gorsuch but refrained initially from denouncing the president. Then in March 1982, not much more than a year after the president's inauguration, 10 groups shifted from blaming Reagan appointees to blaming their appointer, asserting the president had "broken faith with the American people on environmental protection." [32]

Support for groups that seek to speak for a public interest they believe otherwise would be underrepresented, such as the environmentalists, comes from several constituencies. The most visible are the groups' volunteer activists and professional staff. A larger body of members, although less active, contributes small amounts in membership dues and donations to support the cause. Approximately 2 million Americans belong to the major national groups.[33] Another important constituency is composed of those who are sympathetic toward the cause but are otherwise inactive. Polls consistently show this group numbers 100 million or more Americans.[34] Although passive, these sympathizers provide the majorities in the polls and referendums and the base from which the groups recruit new members.

Right from the beginning, the chief administration spokesperson on the environment, Watt, claimed these constituencies for his own. He eschewed the older, still respected, and more plausible label of "conservationist" for his "wise use" approach and chose to debate who was the truest environmentalist, a much more risky, and, as it turned out, disastrous course.[35] During the administration's first year in office, he vigorously portrayed its policies as representative of mainstream environmentalism in contrast to the "extremism" he ascribed to the national groups. Likewise, in defending their policies, both he and Gorsuch often employed the environmentalists' rhetorical symbols such as "environmental quality."

When interest groups characterized his policies as antienvironmental, Watt questioned their legitimacy as guardians of the environmental mandate, calling their leaders "hired guns," concerned about "membership, dollars and headlines."[36] Watt described other critics as members of "a left wing cult." He also declared the national environmental leaders out of touch with their rank and file and cited considerable national support for his policies. The Republican Study Committee, a conservative caucus made up of about three-quarters of the 192 Republican members of the House, issued a similar characterization. It endorsed journalist William Tucker's assertion that environmentalism served the selfish interests of the leisure class, further stating that *"environmental groups represent only a minority fringe of the American public."* [Tucker's emphasis] [37]

If the leaders were indeed out of touch, Watt's attacks should have stimulated membership drops as individuals became aware of the gap between their views and those of their organizations' Washington staffs. Just the opposite occurred. Watt provided the groups with an unwelcome but highly effective recruiting aid as thousands of sympathizers were moved by Watt's policies and rhetoric to join the national groups and to back their leaders. He also mobilized many of the environmental groups' existing members to become more active.

No group exploited Watt's attacks more skillfully than the Sierra Club. Soon after Reagan entered office, the club became an outspoken opponent of Watt. Sensing that many environmental sympathizers would feel threatened by the secretary's policies, it created direct-mail membership appeal letters featuring attacks on Watt. The club also led a highly publicized petition drive to replace Watt. Local activists collected more than one million signatures. On October 19, 1981, the petitions were delivered, with great fanfare, to Democratic members of Congress. The club also used the names and addresses as a prime source of new members, a fact little noted at the time but significant in the long run. By the beginning of 1983 the Sierra Club's membership had climbed to more than 335,000 from 180,000 in 1980. This represented a phenomenal membership growth, especially considering that in the three years prior to Reagan's election the club had experienced virtually no growth. The growth between 1980 and 1983 equaled the group's growth between 1965 and 1980, the Earth Day boom years.[38]

An even more significant rejection of Watt's claim as standard-bearer for the environmental mainstream was the break between the National Wildlife Federation (NWF) and the secretary in July 1981. By far the largest environmental organization, NWF long has had the reputation of being the most conservative. It has 800,000 associate members, who were recruited by direct mail and receive its magazine, and approximately 1.5 million affiliate members, most of whom are members of local sporting groups that belong to the state NWF affiliate organization. Neither set of members fits the environmental elitist stereotype. The sportsmen-affiliate members are drawn from Middle America for the most part. The associate members include many more people with less than a college education than the other environmental groups, and they are more conservative politically. Indeed, they voted for Reagan over Carter by 50 to 25 percent.[39] NWF resisted the temptation to condemn Watt flatly during the administration's first year in office, preferring instead to try to influence his policies without a direct confrontation. Disappointed with the results of this approach, its board finally took the unprecedented step for NWF of requesting a president to fire his secretary of the interior.

The group was sensitive to Watt's assertions that professional environmentalists were out of touch with their constituents' real views. NWF previously had conducted a random-sample mail survey of its associate members to see if they shared NWF's position on 11 specific issues on which NWF and the administration differed.[40] The answers to the questions, which had been carefully written to avoid influencing the members, revealed strong support of the NWF positions. NWF also surveyed the top affiliate leaders in each state with the same result. In each survey, those members who voted for Reagan were as supportive of NWF positions as those who voted for incumbent president Carter or John Anderson.

There is no doubt that the vast majority of the environmental groups' members rejected Watt's brand of environmentalism and strongly supported their leaderships' attacks. Far from splitting the national leadership from their members, Watt's attacks had the opposite effect. Did the administration's attacks on elitist environmentalists precipitate a falling off in those members of the general public who regard themselves as sympathetic with the movement? Again the answer is no. As shown in Figure 3-1, polls taken before and after the 1980 election revealed no significant shift in the large percentage who said they were sympathetic to the environmental movement. Nor was there any increase in the small percentage of those who professed to be unsympathetic, as one would expect if an administration-inspired antienvironmentalist backlash were to occur.

Other polls, conducted since Reagan's 1980 election, show that with environmental groups enjoy a relatively high level of public confidence, particularly compared to business, their chief lobbying rival. A poll undertaken for the Chamber of Commerce of the United States in 1981, for example, found 74 percent of the respondents would trust environmental groups—second only to the EPA—if they recommended changes in the Clean Air Act. The president was trusted by 59 percent, Congress by 55, and "business and industry" by only 39. [41] Likewise, a poll done for the Democratic National Committee found environmentalists in second place—after "farmers, agriculture groups" this time—in the percentage who believed

Figure 3-1 Views About the Environmental Movement
Before and After the 1980 Presidential Election

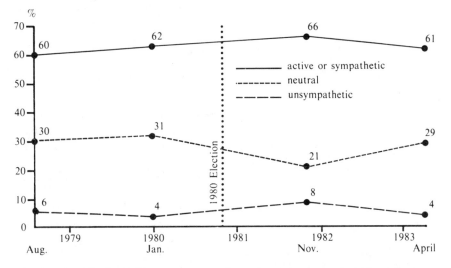

The question asked was: "In recent years, the environmental movement has been very active. Do you think of yourself as: an active participant in the environmental movement, sympathetic towards the movement but not active, neutral, or unsympathetic towards the environmental movement?"

Note: Surveys taken in August 1978, January 1980, November 1981, and April 1983. Percentages do not add up to 100 percent due to "Unsure" responses.

Sources: 1978, 1980, Resources for the Future; 1981, Opinion Research Corporation; 1983, ABC News/*Washington Post* poll.

they were "helping to make America a better place or have a positive influence." Twenty nine percent chose environmentalists. In third place with 24 percent was the Reagan administration, and "major business corporations" appeared in 15th place—with 7 percent—among the 21 groups listed.[42]

Contrary to those who brand environmentalists as elitists or as members of the "new class" because the national groups' members are disproportionately well educated, prosperous, and politically liberal, strong support for environmental protection has continued to be broad based. Everett Carll Ladd, who earlier had contended that environmental preferences did show a class basis, reviewed the polls taken after Reagan's 1980 election victory on environmental issues and concluded: "One of the most striking features of public opinion on environmental questions is the evenness of support across various groups in the population."[43]

For example, in a Roper poll that asked whether people felt environmental protection laws and regulations had gone too far, not far enough, or had struck about the right balance, the percentage who responded "too far" was relatively evenly distributed across the four income categories. Those with the lowest incomes were the least likely (18 percent) to choose the antienvironmental position, whereas those with the highest incomes were most likely to take this point of view (28 percent).[44] In short, while environmentalists certainly constitute a socioeconomic elite, the elitist label misses the mark because their policies receive wide support from all socioeconomic categories.

Political Consequences

The administration's third misperception about public opinion was to assume that the environmental issue and environmentalists were a negligible political threat to the president's supporters in Congress and to the president himself. If the administration had abided by the implicit rules followed by previous administrations instead of challenging the environmental consensus, this assumption would have been valid. But by making so little effort to placate environmental sentiment in appointments, in legislative initiatives, and in rhetoric during its first two years, the Reagan administration created the potential for the issue to have some political potency in the 1984 elections. In the longer run, the administration appears to have handed a previously nonpartisan issue to the Democrats.

The Harris-Ladd Debate. This political potency was the subject of a lively debate between two prominent public opinion analysts, Louis Harris and Everett Carll Ladd. Their debate reveals the unusual degree to which polling on environmental issues has become politicized during the Reagan years, as the combatants took extreme positions that were immediately used by members of Congress in the battle over the Clean Air Act.

Harris raised the issue first in his air-pollution poll testimony before the House Subcommittee on Health and the Environment on October 15, 1981, one year before the congressional midterm elections. He described the strength of public support for the Clean Air Act. Responding to questions from committee members, Harris gave his outspoken views on his poll-data's political implications. Public support for the act was so strong, he said, that any members of Congress who favored weakening the act ran a very strong risk of being voted out of office. This message delighted environmentalists, who circulated quotes from the colloquy all over Capitol Hill.[45]

Five months later, Harris restated his view before the Environmental Industry Council. He offered "startling" data to back up his earlier views. Harris's interviewers had asked a national sample of people in March 1982 first to reveal whether they favored or opposed nine single issues such as busing, abortion, and school prayer. Then they were asked if they would vote for a candidate who disagreed with their view on each of the issues even though they agreed with most of the candidate's other views.

The poll results are summarized in Table 3-2. Of all the issues, the most lopsided margin of approval was given to "strict enforcement of air and water pollution controls as now required by the Clean Air and Water Acts" with 83

Table 3-2 Harris Data on Potential Single Issue Voting in the 1982 Congressional Election

Do you favor or oppose. . . .	Percent Favor/Oppose (Percent who would certainly not vote for candidate who takes the opposite position.)[1]		Percent of potential lost votes[2] for candidates who take stands with which voters disagree		
			Favor/Oppose		Difference
(a) No cut in Social Security benefits, even if higher taxes.	71% (25%)	26% (15%)	18%	4%	+14%
(b) The federal government giving tax exemptions to schools that segregate whites and blacks.	24 (18)	71 (24)	4	17	−13
(c) Strict enforcement of air and water pollution controls as now required by Clean Air and Water Acts.	83 (15)	14 (15)	13	2	+11
(d) A constitutional amendment to allow daily prayers to be recited in classrooms.	69 (21)	28 (20)	14	6	+8
(e) A constitutional amendment to ban legalized abortion.	33 (32)	61 (30)	11	18	− 7
(f) Require affirmative action programs by federal law, provided no quotas.	68 (14)	24 (19)	10	5	+5
(g) Federal law to prohibit Justice Dept. and federal courts from ordering school busing to achieve social balance.	41 (27)	55 (28)	11	15	−4
(h) Federal law requiring registration of all handguns by federal authorities.	64 (20)	34 (28)	13	10	+3
(i) Federal law prohibiting birth control assistance to teenagers without parental permission.	45 (19)	52 (21)	8	11	−3

[1] For example, with reference to item (a), 25 percent of those in favor of no Social Security cuts would certainly not vote for a candidate who favored them; 15 percent of those who oppose no Social Security cuts would certainly not vote for a candidate who favored them.

[2] Potential lost votes are the percent of the total population who favor or oppose each issue and who declare they would "certainly" not vote for a candidate who took the opposite view.

Question: Now, suppose in the congressional elections this year, you found a candidate for Congress in your district whose views you mostly agreed with. Then suppose that same candidate took a position on (READ EACH ITEM) that you disagree with completely. Would you certainly not vote for that candidate, probably not vote for him, or could you still vote for him?

Source: The Harris Survey release #20, March 11, 1982. Poll was taken February 12-17, 1982. Sample of 1,253 adults nationwide. Telephone survey.

percent approving and 14 percent disapproving. Once again, however, the public showed that while they strongly supported environmentalism, the issue was less salient for them than many other concerns. Only 15 percent of those approving said they felt so strongly about pollution control that they "certainly" would not vote for a candidate who opposed strict enforcement. The same low salience level held for those who opposed strict air and water pollution enforcement.

What interested Harris was the balance of votes a candidate might win or lose because of his or her issue stand. This is calculated first by multiplying the support percent for each stand (pro or con) on an issue by the salience percent for that stand. This gives the percent of the total electorate for whom that stand is politically salient and is shown for each issue on the right hand of the table. Because of the exceptionally strong support for strict environmental regulation (83 percent), the low level of salience (15 percent) still translates into a sizable 13 percent (83% $\times$ 15% = 13%) of the total electorate who say that they would certainly not vote for a candidate who opposes strict enforcement. In contrast, those for whom opposition to strict enforcement is politically salient comprise only two percent (15% $\times$ 14% = 2%) of the electorate. The *difference* between these two figures represents the percent of potential lost votes for that issue stand. This calculation led Harris to tell his audience: "This means that the environmental vote alone, if fully mobilized, could make a swing of 11 points in this year's elections for the House and Senate. In real political terms, that is a balance of power." [46]

Politicians working to modify the Clean Air Act felt constrained to challenge this potentially damaging finding. Rep. James T. Broyhill, a Republican of North Carolina, solicited the views of Ladd, a well-known political scientist and polling expert at the University of Connecticut. Ladd just had published an article in which he criticized Harris's earlier statements about the political consequences of voting to weaken the Clean Air Act. [47] Ladd sent Broyhill a six-page critique of Harris's speech, which Broyhill then sent to the press accompanied by a release entitled "Leading Pollster Questions Objectivity of Louis Harris in Interpreting Polls on Environment." [48] This was hyperbole; Ladd had questioned Harris's interpretation, not his objectivity.

But in the press release Ladd minced no words:

> . . . One would conclude [from Harris's own data] that the striking feature of the environmental issue is that huge numbers of people want strict controls—but relatively few would vote against a candidate whom they saw against such controls. The point made by the Harris data is precisely the opposite Mr. Harris expressed in his speech of March 12. [49]

Ladd went on to point out that people's views about how they might vote eight months in the future are likely to be unreliable, especially given that their voting choices are determined by widely varying considerations. [50]

The dispute between Harris and Ladd centers on the relative meaning of the high level of support and low level of salience revealed in Harris's data. Harris chose to emphasize the former and Ladd the latter. In this exchange

Harris falls into what might be called a "reverse salience trap," wherein strength and breadth of support for an issue are equated with mass salience. He suggests there exists an angry environmental—or green—vote but downplays the difficulty of mobilizing this vote. Despite the environmentalists' exceptionally active political role in the 1982 election, for example, there was no sign of the mass uprising against antienvironmental candidates that Harris's more extreme statements implied would occur. Ladd, on the other hand, dismisses too cavalierly the marginal political *potential* of the net 11 percent potential lost votes. In particular, he ignores two factors: the organizational and the symbolic resources available to the environmentalists.

Green Political Resources. Environmentalists are organized. National and local environmental groups give the movement an exceptionally strong institutional base. Campaign contributions for favored candidates can be solicited efficiently by direct mail based on their fund-raising lists of several million people. Several national groups—National Audubon Society, Sierra Club, Izaac Walton League, National Wildlife Federation, and, to a lesser extent, Friends of the Earth—have existing networks of local chapters and groups that can be used to recruit volunteer campaign workers for targeted campaigns. Others, such as the League of Conservation Voters and Environmental Action, are able to hire field coordinators who use local environmental contacts to conduct political organizing. This infrastructure increasingly is being used for political purposes.

In the 1982 congressional elections, several groups for the first time publicly endorsed candidates for congressional and senatorial seats. Some candidates were challenging vulnerable incumbents viewed as unacceptably antienvironmental. Other favored candidates were proenvironmental incumbents facing close races, such as Democratic representatives Bob Edgar of Pennsylvania and the late Phillip Burton of California, and Republican Sen. Robert T. Stafford of Vermont. Environmental endorsements brought these candidates small amounts of money from one or more of the several environmental PACs, whose combined contributions in 1982 were about $2 million. Of greater significance, however, were the sometimes-impressive numbers of volunteer campaign workers the environmentalists were able to muster, such as the 400 who campaigned door to door for Burton during his campaign.[51]

The large number of very potent condensational symbols available to environmentalists is the second factor that contributes to the issue's political potential. In contrast to referential symbols, which refer to things using terms with narrow, neutral connotations such as "protection reaction strikes," condensational symbols involve concepts with diffuse yet powerful and emotionally charged meanings, such as "bombing runs."[52]

Powerful leaders, when pursuing unpopular policies, generally prefer to defuse the issue by using referential symbols, whereas weaker opponents use condensational symbols to arouse public concern.

The Earth Day paradigm shift changed environmentalist rhetoric by popularizing a large number of powerful condensational symbols, such as

"environmental quality," "scarcity," "spaceship earth," "endangered species," "toxic substance," "clean air," "acid rain," and "clean water." These
symbols arouse protective feelings and have come to overshadow symbols such
as "conservation" and "wise use," previously used to describe similar goals.
At the same time, the condensational symbols used by those opposed to the
environmentalists, such as "growth," "development," "wise use," and
"progress," have lost some of their favorable connotations. The rhetorical
disadvantage of appearing to oppose "clean air" in favor of "growth," or even
"economic recovery," is considerable. Watt's tactic of trying to wrest control of
these symbols from the environmentalists was risky and ultimately backfired.
The fight over who represented the mainstream heightened public awareness
of the environmentalists' complaints, and Watt's failure to win the fight gave
the environmentalists monopoly control of the symbols.

The electoral implications of Harris's consensus support-low salience
data thus lie somewhere between the Harris and Ladd interpretations. For
members of Congress, it appears that a proenvironmental voting record can
only help, not hurt, at reelection time. This holds true for Republicans as well
as for Democrats. Despite the propensity for Democratic voters to support
proenvironmental positions somewhat more than Republicans, the differences
between the two groups is typically small.

The electoral consequences for a member of Congress with an
antienvironmental voting record, the specific subject of the Harris-Ladd
debate, are more uncertain. Even among Republican voters, only a minority
support Reagan administration initiatives such as reducing the costs for
having clean air and relaxing environmental regulations for air and water
pollution; thus it is clear that few votes are to be won by backing these
programs.[53] Presuming the member is vulnerable on other grounds, being
perceived as antienvironmental could cause problems, especially if the
challenger is able to attract environmentalist volunteers. Recognizing that
they could not outspend their rival lobbies, environmental political strategists
experimented with techniques to mobilize their grass-roots activists to work
on the 1982 election campaigns of favored candidates. To this end they
hired full-time political organizers and ran numerous campaign workshops.
The various environmentalist postelection post-mortems agreed that their
ability to mobilize green workers was their important comparative advantage.
In the election in which Sen. Harrison Schmitt of New Mexico, a vulnerable
senator with a very low League of Conservation Voters score, lost his seat, the
claim is made that "more than 700 environmentalists walked precincts and
worked his [opponent's] telephone banks."[54]

Environmentalists aroused to political action by the administration's
environmental policies thus may influence the outcome in a few congressional
races. What about the threat to the president from environmentalists in 1984?
With one exception, all signs suggest that the impact of either green workers
or green votes in the 1984 presidential election will be overshadowed by the
economy and international affairs. The president's appointment of the
popular William Ruckelshaus to head the EPA is likely to ensure that his

environmental record will not cost him many votes if he seeks reelection. Only scandals are likely to command public attention sufficiently to interject the environment into presidential politics, and Ruckelshaus should be able to avoid those. Significant political damage to the president could occur only if Ruckleshaus were to resign as a matter of conscience for lack of White House support.

The exception, a very interesting one, concerns acid rain. The vagaries of the American presidential election process elevate the New Hampshire primary to a highly symbolic event. Acid rain in 1983 was of great concern in New England, as its impact differentially affects this region's waters. Local environmentalists seized on the issue—and also, to a lesser extent, the toxic waste issue that affects many places in the state—as a way to interject environmental concerns into presidential politics. They have enjoyed considerable success, according to an extensive July 1983 *Washington Post* analysis of New Hampshire politics: "Concern about the environment has become a potent political issue here, cutting across all elements in the state and seemingly destined to affect the outcome of next winter's highly publicized . . . primary." [55]

The environmental issue is especially salient in this conservative state because acid rain threatens the tourist industry and waste dumps the water supply. But the *Post* report also cites a renewed pride in the state's beauty and a feeling that the environmental improvements of the 1970s, such as the cleanup of many local rivers, are threatened. Feeling that things are getting worse is an even more powerful motivation for political action than a desire to improve the present situation.[56] The possibility therefore exists that the acid rain issue in New England, coupled with the Reagan administration's perceived environmental indifference, may have the potential to rekindle the mass salience of the environmental issue. This potential is summed up in the *Post*'s July 1983 poll of a sample of Manchester, New Hampshire, residents, which found Reagan outpolling both Mondale and Glenn by more than two to one. Yet it also found a high degree of concern about acid rain and toxic-waste dumps and, significantly, that nearly 60 percent of this sample described themselves as active environmentalists or sympathetic to the movement.[57]

The president's strategists were aware of the potential political damage posed by the environmental issue and apparently communicated this to the president. After meeting with Republican Gov. John H. Sununu of New Hampshire in June 1983, Reagan was described as seriously concerned about acid rain's growing importance in the primary.

Looking beyond the 1984 election, it will take more than the appointment of a credible EPA administrator to restore the Republican party's credibility on environmental issues. Until 1980 environmental protection was not viewed as a partisan issue despite the fact that Republicans on the average consistently score lower on the League of Conservation Voters' ratings than congressional Democrats. The Reagan administration's attack on environmental regulation has changed this. In November-December 1981, the

Democratic National Committee conducted a poll that led the committee's pollsters to conclude that environmental concerns are a "sleeper issue" for the Democrats. A memo to the chairman of the committee declared: "Voters perceive the Republican Party to be far from their views about environmental regulation and pick the Democrats as the party which would do the best job on environmental issues by a 51 to 11 percent margin." [58] This finding was publicized widely within the party, where it stimulated some candidates to campaign on the issue in the 1982 election. It also was shared with environmentalists to encourage them to work for Democratic candidates.

Pat Caddell, one of the pollsters, believes the demographics of the proenvironmental Republicans that this poll identified are potentially "devastating" for the Republicans because they involve sizable numbers of white, upper-income suburbanites, who traditionally have voted Republican. "These aren't marginal votes," he declared. "They are base votes." [59] Base votes are those a party takes for granted. It may be harder for Democrats to capitalize on this issue than they realize if John Anderson is on the ballot, however, because these demographics are a perfect description of his constituency.[60]

Conclusion: The Mistaken Mandate

The Reagan administration has tested the hypothesis that environmental quality is an enduring American concern. Here we had a popular president—blessed with a reassuring manner, an ability to make convincing speeches, and a coherent and appealing view of the world—supporting what environmentalists regarded as a significant cutback in the nation's efforts to improve environmental quality. He sought to legitimate this policy change by citing the nation's other, unmistakably important economic and foreign policy priorities and by branding his opponents as "environmental extremists." [61] Yet despite the president's best efforts, public support for the environmental consensus intensified rather than diminished.

The president was acting to fulfill a mandate to cut back on environmental regulation, which he sincerely believed he had been granted by the electorate in his landslide 1980 election. In pursuing this mandate, he ignored the advice of his transition team that the hallmark of his effort to protect and enhance the environment be "balance and consensus." [62] Instead he chose as his principal environmental adviser James Watt, a man committed to a view sharply at odds with the environmental consensus as it was revealed in numerous poll findings during the previous decade. The environmentalists' early opposition to Watt only stiffened the president's resolve. According to one White House adviser in an interview six months after the inauguration, Reagan's support for Watt ". . . reflects [the president's] belief that an election occurred in November, and the President was elected with a clear promise that he would appoint people in the regulatory and environmental areas that favor less regulation. He believes he had a mandate to appoint people like that." [63]

Even after the EPA controversy came to a head in spring 1983, and many of his advisers were convinced that the president's environmental policy differed from the voters' preferences, the president remained personally convinced that his program was sound. Perhaps in an effort to prove his sincerity on this point, in April 1983 Reagan instigated an extraordinary meeting with Ansel Adams, the famous photographer and naturalist who earlier had criticized Reagan's environmental policies as disastrous. According to Adams, the president began the 50-minute meeting by declaring: "We are not so far apart as you think we are. I've always been an environmentalist." The meeting only convinced Adams that he and the president had a "totally different concept of the world and it is very hard to break through." [64]

That the president finally accepted the resignation of Burford (formerly Gorsuch) and called upon William Ruckelshaus to head the EPA shows the degree to which his mistaken mandate cost him political leverage. Ruckelshaus had been a member of the original environmental transition team whose moderate recommendations were almost totally ignored. At the news conference announcing Ruckelshaus's nomination, the president noted his staunch commitment to protecting the nation's air, water, and land. He declared: "And I have given him the broad, flexible mandate that he deserves." [65]

Even if the White House allows Ruckelshaus to pursue the nation's ambitious environmental protection goals, he will have less latitude from the public to reform the laws than he would have enjoyed if he, not Gorsuch, had been the president's original EPA appointee. Changing some of EPA's environmental regulations and rewriting the Clean Air and Water acts in order to make them more workable at less cost is easiest to accomplish when the public has confidence in the decision makers' commitment to the laws' basic goals. The previous two years' experiences have eroded this confidence and enhanced the credibility of the environmentalists, who tend to believe strongly that regulatory reform of environmental laws inevitably results in weakened protection. A mandate for needed reform, which did exist in 1980, may have been squandered by the administration's pursuit of its mistaken mandate.

Notes

The author wishes to thank Susan Pharr for her helpful comments on earlier drafts of this chapter.

1. John C. Whitaker, *Striking A Balance: Environment and Natural Resources Policy in the Nixon-Ford Years* (Washington, D.C.: American Enterprise Institute, 1976); James E. Bylin, "Conservation Gains Political Weight," *The Wall Street Journal*, November 26, 1969.
2. Hazel Erskine, "The Polls: Pollution and Its Costs," *Public Opinion Quarterly* 35 (1971): 120-135.
3. This presumes that the poll is based on interviews with at least 750 people who represent a scientifically chosen national sample of people. If questions and interviewing are in accord with professional standards for survey research, polls should represent the entire nation's views with an error range of about 7 percent. Interviews are conducted in person or over the telephone. Unless noted otherwise, all the polls mentioned in this chapter meet these criteria. The meaning of the responses to a

particular question depend on the question's wording and its context in the questionnaire. Generally, polls are most useful when the same or similar questions are repeated in a number of different surveys because this allows the analyst to understand the underlying pattern of public opinion and to comprehend its complexity.

4. The Council on Environmental Quality's estimate of the cost to comply with federal environmental protection requirements can be found in *Environmental Quality - 1980, The Eleventh Annual Report of the Council on Environmental Quality* (Washington, D.C.: Government Printing Office, 1980), 387.

5. Robert Cameron Mitchell, *Public Opinion on Environmental Issues: Results of a National Opinion Survey* (Washington, D.C.: Council on Environmental Quality, 1980).

6. Laura M. Lake, "The Environmental Mandate: Activists and the Electorate," *Political Science Quarterly* 98 (Summer 1983): 215-233.

7. Joe Browder, "Decision-Making in the White House," in *Nixon and the Environment: The Politics of Devastation,* ed. James Rathlesberger (New York: Village Voice/Taurus Communications, 1972).

8. Erwin C. Hargrove and Michael Nelson, "Presidents, Ideas, and the Search for a Stable Majority," in *A Tide of Discontent: The 1980 Elections and Their Meaning,* ed. Ellis Sandoz and Cecil V. Crabb, Jr. (Washington, D.C.: CQ Press, 1981), 52.

9. *The Continental Group Report: Toward Responsible Growth. Economic and Environmental Concern in the Balance* (Stamford, Conn.: Continental Group: 1982).

10. John Quarles, *Cleaning Up America: An Insider's View of the Environmental Protection Agency* (Boston: Houghton Mifflin, 1976), 214.

11. Ibid.

12. Anthony Downs, "Up and Down With Ecology—the 'Issue-Attention' Cycle," *The Public Interest* 28 (Summer 1972): 38-50.

13. Riley E. Dunlap, Kent D. Van Liere, and Don A. Dillman, "Evidence of Decline in Public Concern with Environmental Quality: A Reply," *Rural Sociology* 44 (1979): 204-212.

14. Downs, "Up and Down With Ecology."

15. The Gallup Poll, "Public Opinion About Environmental Protection & Defense Spending: The Newsweek Poll," June 1981, 1.

16. Opinion Research Corporation, "Public Attitudes Toward the Clean Air Act" (Princeton, N.J.: Opinion Research, December 1981), 7.

17. *The Continental Group Report,* 19.

18. Paul Cramer, "Reagan Gets Bad Marks on the Environment: Public Does Not Want Pollution Laws Relaxed," ABC News/*Washington Post* Poll, April 1983, 4.

19. Mitchell, *Public Opinion on Environmental Issues;* Opinion Research Corporation, "Public Attitudes Toward the Clean Air Act."

20. Cramer, "Reagan Gets Bad Marks on the Environment."

21. William Schneider, "The Environment: The Public Wants More Protection, Not Less," *National Journal,* March 26, 1983, 676-677.

22. Dale Russakoff, "Gorsuch: A Loyal Soldier in the Center of a Constitutional Storm," *Washington Post,* December 19, 1982. Richard Wirthlin is President Reagan's pollster who conducts regular polls for the White House that assess public reaction to administration policies.

23. "Storm Over the Environment," *Newsweek,* March 7, 1983, 16.

24. Barry Sussman, "Poll Says Most Think Reagan Prefers to Protect Polluters," *Washington Post,* March 5, 1983; Cramer, "Reagan Gets Bad Marks on the Environment."

25. Cramer, "Reagan Gets Bad Marks on the Environment."

26. Riley E. Dunlap, "Paradigmatic Change in Social Science: From Human Exemptionalism to an Ecological Paradigm," *American Behavioral Scientist,* 24

(1980): 5-14.

27. *The Continental Group Report,* 63-65.
28. Everett Carll Ladd, "Clearing the Air: Public Opinion and Public Policy on the Environment," *Public Opinion* 5 (February/March 1982): 19.
29. Opinion Research Corporation, "Public Attitudes Toward the Clean Air Act."
30. *The Continental Group Report,* 25.
31. Mitchell, *Public Opinion on Environmental Issues,* 26-27.
32. Friends of the Earth et al., *Ronald Reagan and the American Environment* (San Francisco: Friends of the Earth, 1982).
33. This figure includes people who pay dues to at least one environmental group and takes into account that many individuals belong to more than one group.
34. See Figure 3-1. The 100-million figure is for adults and includes those who say they are active but who are not included in the two million members described above.
35. In his public statements Watt drew heavily on the "conservation" symbolism. His biographer emphasizes this paradigm in contrasting Watt's views with those of his environmentalist opponents. James Watt, "Prepared Remarks ... to the 46th North American Wildlife and Natural Resources Conference," release, March 23, 1981; Ron Arnold, *At the Eye of the Storm: James Watt and the Environmentalists* (Chicago: Regnery Gateway, 1982).
36. Joanne Omang, "Watt Finds Time to Hear Audubon Society," *Washington Post,* May 15, 1981.
37. William Tucker, "The Environmental Era," *Public Opinion* 5 (February/March 1982): 41-47; *Progress and Privilege: America in the Age of Environmentalism* (Garden City, N.Y.: Anchor Press/Doubleday, 1982); Tim Peckinpaugh, "The Specter of Environmentalism: The Threat of Environmental Groups," Republican Study Committee, Special Study, February 12, 1982.
38. Frances Gendlin, "Mike McCloskey: Taking Stock, Looking Forward," *Sierra* (January/February, 1983), 45, 125-127.
39. Robert Cameron Mitchell, "How 'Soft,' 'Deep,' or 'Left?' Present Constituencies in the Environmental Movement for Certain World Views," *Natural Resources Journal* 20 (April 1980): 345-358; Jay D. Hair and Patrick A. Parenteau, "Special Report: The Results of the National Wildlife Federation's Associate Membership Survey and Affiliate Leadership Poll on Major Conservation Policies" (Washington, D.C.: The National Wildlife Federation, July 1981), 20.
40. Hair and Parenteau, "Special Report."
41. Opinion Research Corporation, "Public Attitudes Toward the Clean Air Act."
42. Democratic National Committee, "A Survey of the Political Climate in America and Voter Attitudes Toward the 1982 Elections" (Washington, D.C.: Democratic National Committee, 1982).
43. Ladd, "Clearing the Air," 18; Robert Cameron Mitchell, "Silent Spring/Solid Majorities," *Public Opinion* 2 (August-September, 1979): 16-20, 55.
44. Ladd, "Clearing the Air."
45. Sierra Club, Washington Office, "Testimony of Louis Harris Before the Subcommittee on Health and the Environment, Energy and Commerce Committee, and Excerpts from Colloquy with Committee," release, October 16, 1981.
46. Louis Harris, "Address to the Environmental Industry Council," Washington, D.C., March 12, 1982.
47. Ladd, "Clearing the Air."
48. Office of Rep. James T. Broyhill, R-N.C., release, March 25, 1982.
49. Everett Carll Ladd, "Letter to Congressman Broyhill," March 19, 1982.
50. The debate continued as one of Broyhill's opponents in Congress on this issue, Rep. Henry A. Waxman, D-Calif., then solicited Harris's rebuttal to Ladd's critique. Although Harris did not back down from his version of a political apocalypse brought

on by environmental sentiment, he did acknowledge more clearly than before that a proenvironmental swing vote would not occur spontaneously but would have to be mobilized by the environmental groups.

51. Bob Chlopak, "PAC Wins 34 of 48," *Not Man Apart* (December 1982), 6.
52. W. Lance Bennett, *Public Opinion in American Politics* (New York: Harcourt Brace Jovanovich, 1980), 256.
53. Opinion Research Corporation, "Public Attitudes Toward the Clean Air Act"; Democratic National Committee, "A Survey of the Political Climate in America."
54. Chlopak, "PAC Wins 34 of 48."
55. "Environment Is Potent Political Issue Despite State's Economic Hardships," *Washington Post,* July 17, 1983.
56. Robert Cameron Mitchell, "National Environmental Lobbies and the Apparent Illogic of Collective Action," in *Collective Decision Making: Applications from Rational Choice Theory,* ed. Cifford S. Russell (Baltimore: Johns Hopkins University Press, 1979), 87-123.
57. "Environment Is Potent Political Issue," *Washington Post.*
58. Memo to Chairman Charles Manatt from Dotty Lynch, Democratic National Committee, February 24, 1982.
59. *Washington Post,* April 20, 1982.
60. Kevin Phillips, *Post-Conservative America: People, Politics, and Ideology in a Time of Crisis* (New York: Random House, 1982).
61. "Transcript of Reagan News Parley on Nomination of Ruckelshaus to E.P.A.," *New York Times,* March 22, 1983.
62. The President-Elect's Task Force on the Environment, "Protecting the Environment: A Statement of Philosophy," January 1981.
63. Howell Raines, "Reagan Reversing Many U.S. Policies," *New York Times,* July 3, 1981.
64. Dale Russakoff, "The Critique: Ansel Adams Takes Environmental Challenge to Reagan," *Washington Post,* July 3, 1983.
65. "Transcript of Reagan News Parley," *New York Times.*

Part II

POLICY MAKING:
INSTITUTIONS AND PROCESSES

4. THE PRESIDENT AND THE ENVIRONMENT: REVOLUTION OR RETREAT?

Norman J. Vig

Visiting an old friend, who had turned a bit cynical after 20-odd years in a remote part of the Third World, I asked him for a capsule description of the political process in the country where he lived.

"It's really quite simple," he said. "They have two parties, which you can most easily remember as the blues and the greens. Every now and again, tanks appear over there, and power changes hands. When the greens are in, their people get the jobs and the graft, and the blues get no civil liberties. After the next power shift, the blues get all the jobs and the graft, and it's the greens who have no civil liberties. The curious thing about it is that everyone seems to accept the system. No one but a professor would suggest that jobs or power could be shared or that everybody could have civil liberties all the time. They just think how nice it is to be in power now—or how nice it will be when they get back in power later. I sometimes suspect that even the press likes the system. Coups make more interesting reading than committee meetings."

What's now at issue in the United States is how much our system for resolving environmental and natural resources disputes resembles that of the greens and the blues. Were the 1970s the decade of environmental domination, making it now the turn of the aggressively pro-development forces to ride roughshod over the conservation community? Or did the 1970s begin lasting changes in our system, so that divergent points of view will continue to be heard and considered before decisions are made?

So wrote William K. Reilly, president of the Conservation Foundation, in the early winter of 1982.[1] Along with millions of other Americans, he wondered whether the Reagan administration, with its Sagebrush Rebellion supporters, was engineering a coup against the nation's system for environmental protection. In posing the issue in this way, Reilly raised a number of fundamental questions that this book seeks to answer. Does our political system allow radical change of this kind? Can a new presidential administration alter the rules of the game to exclude previous participants? Can it reverse the momentum of policy development over the previous decade or more? In short, what is the capacity of the presidency to achieve systemic, nonincremental change? Has Ronald Reagan achieved this in the field of environmental policy? If so, by what means?

The literature on the American presidency suggests caution in jumping to conclusions. Most scholars in recent years have argued that the days of the "heroic" and "imperial" presidency are past. They suggest that the "institutionalized presidency" is so constrained by its own internal bureaucracy and external constituencies that it rarely can impose its own goals. Hugh Heclo has written that "presidential government is an illusion—an illusion that misleads presidents no less than the media and the American public, an illusion that often brings about the destruction of the very men who hold the office." [2]

In domestic politics, especially, presidents rarely succeed in getting what they want.[3] The Congress, the courts, the bureaucracy, the interest groups, the multiple and varied state and local constituencies all tend to coalesce against radical policy departures. By 1980 even the most sanguine advocates of presidential leadership suggested that a new chief executive could only hope to achieve his objectives in a few priority areas.[4]

The controversy over current environmental policy provides an important test case for such theories of presidential leadership and policy making. Have the usual constraints operated in the case of Reagan's environmental policies or not? The new administration amazed most experts by passing the largest tax cut in history during its first year in office, marking the most radical break in fiscal policy since the New Deal. It demonstrated remarkable resourcefulness in devising new strategies for getting its economic program through Congress *(see Chapter 6)*. By forcing massive budget cuts as part of this program, it deeply affected the policies and programs of numerous government agencies, including those charged with environmental protection. It has shaped the discretionary policies of the bureaucracy through personnel appointments and new methods of regulatory oversight. The implementation of environmental laws and programs has changed substantially during the administration. Thus it is by no means certain that the limits of policy change stressed in most of the presidency literature will prove to be applicable in this case.

This chapter focuses on Reagan's use of the presidency as an instrument for policy change. I discuss the president's early success and scholarly reactions to it, and then summarize the literature on presidential opportunities and constraints in greater detail. I then consider Reagan's past record on environmental policy and the particular constraints and opportunities he faced in seeking to alter the environmental agenda when he entered the presidency. This sets the stage for analyzing the strategy he adopted for circumventing these constraints, and the policy dilemma in which the administration consequently found itself in the second half of his term. Finally, I conclude with an evaluation both of Reagan's performance as president in this important area of environmental policy and of the more fundamental issues raised by his radical departures from past methods of policy making.

A Different Presidency

As noted above, most recent studies of presidential policy making tell us why the chief executive must fail. One scholar speaks of "the no-win presidency,"[5] while another states flatly that "the 1970s marks the end of the presidential era in American politics."[6] The downfall of presidents Lyndon B. Johnson and Richard Nixon, the subsequent resurgence of Congress, and the manifest ineffectiveness of Jimmy Carter's leadership appeared to have reversed the trend toward growing presidential dominance during the past half century.[7] In reflecting on the Carter administration the dean of presidency scholars, Richard Neustadt, asked: "Is the Presidency possible? Even in the humble sense of keeping the game going, handing on the office reasonably intact?"[8]

But was this only a temporary phenomenon? Was it only part of the post-Watergate syndrome? Could a new and popular president such as Ronald Reagan reassert his powers? Despite his criticism of Carter's hyperactivity, he obviously sought an active presidency. He was undaunted by the Washington establishment and determined to move decisively whatever the obstacles. He would redefine the congressional agenda and mobilize popular support for his program. Where Congress refused to cooperate, he would find other ways of doing things. He would use the budget process as a weapon for policy change, and exert Executive Office control over the bureaucratic interests that survived. He would slow down administrative programs he disliked and accelerate others. He would, in short, defy the odds and prove that the president could lead the nation on a new course.

Reagan's early success caught most observers by surprise. As Hedrick Smith reported:

> Reagan the convinced conservative crusader, Reagan the strategist, Reagan the battler, Reagan the cheerleader, Reagan the political charmer, has staked the fate of his presidency on his single-minded campaign to enact a radical turn in the nation's economic policy. Using his capacity to persuade Congress to enact the largest budget and tax cuts in American history, he was able to move Congress on this one central issue, and establish his national leadership. In slightly more than six months, he achieved far more than political Washington had dreamed possible on the day of his Inauguration.[9]

Presidency scholars were impressed. James Sundquist of the Brookings Institution ranked Reagan's influence over Congress with that of only three other presidents this century: Woodrow Wilson, Franklin D. Roosevelt, and Lyndon B. Johnson.[10] Richard P. Nathan, one of the most astute critics of the Nixon administration, argued that Reagan was far more successful than his predecessors in achieving domestic policy change because he followed a dual legislative and administrative strategy from the outset.[11] The latter part of the strategy, involving White House control over the bureaucracy at the subcabinet level, so impressed Nathan that he called it "the Administrative Presidency."[12] He quotes with favor a *Wall Street Journal* article that noted that the new administration "has found a way to reshape federal government without necessarily changing laws. It is called Reaganizing." Nathan lauded this administrative approach as a way of *"making government work better. Doing so requires that politics penetrate operations, that the values politicians are elected to advance are reflected in the execution of laws, as well as in their enactment."* [Nathan's emphasis][13]

Other scholars took a very different view. Chester A. Newland, writing in the *Public Administration Review* in early 1983, noted that the president's agenda was being pursued largely as ideology.[14] He decried the fact that Reagan had filled the government with political appointees who had no governmental experience and who set out to politicize the bureaucracy with the president's ideological doctrines. Second-level appointees were screened carefully for ideological loyalty rather than professional competence; they had little interest in working with career professionals and often sought to exclude them from policy making. The senior civil service was weakened badly by forced retirements and agency transfers. Newland concluded that *"public administration under President Reagan is, to a significant extent, ideological political administration."* [Newland's emphasis][15] But, in contrast to Nathan, he questioned "whether government is being administered in ways that are consistent with long-term excellence or even adequacy of the constitutional foundations." [16] An administration that treated government as the enemy, Newland implied, was hardly likely to make it "work better."

These assessments, different as they are, indicate that Reagan's is no ordinary presidency. This chapter seeks to cast light on the debate over Reagan's use of presidential powers as well as on his success in changing environmental policies. As Nathan points out, nowhere did Reagan apply the "administrative presidency" more than in the field of environmental protection. "The end result was that environmental policies of the prior fifteen years were substantially diluted." [17] How was the president able to accomplish this?

Presidents and Policy Change

Presidents usually come into office with some kind of mandate to enact policy change rather than to maintain the status quo. But in seeking policy change, the president must operate within an intricate system of checks and balances in which he is only one of the leading actors. Whether he can move the system in the desired direction depends heavily on his ability to seize the opportunities of the moment and to devise workable strategies for persuading others to go along. In this sense presidential power is inherently political, the "power to persuade," as Neustadt put it long ago.[18] But without skillful management of the policy agenda and careful attention to the legitimate bounds of his authority, the president may lose the opportunity for reform and succumb to the countervailing pressures of the system (as Carter largely did).

Opportunities

The opportunities a president has depend on many situational variables as well as on how he uses the powers of his office. The size and perceived strength of the president's electoral mandate will influence the willingness of

Congress and other participants in the policy-making process to follow the president's lead, as in the adoption of Reagan's economic recovery program in 1981. A new president traditionally is accorded a honeymoon, but this may be very short unless the president demonstrates that he can work with others to achieve results. The country's mood is also an important situational variable: in some periods people look to the president for strong and decisive leadership more than in others. In 1981 people apparently were tired of weak leadership in the White House and ready to give Reagan a chance to carry out his economic program.

The president has a formidable array of instruments at his disposal in the Executive Office to shape policy formulation and implementation. He has the power to appoint several hundred top officials to head the departments and agencies. He can restructure the entire White House staff and reorganize administrative functions throughout the bureaucracy. Through the Office of Management and Budget (OMB), he controls the budget requests for all agencies and can exert oversight over all units of the federal government. Through the White House machinery he can intervene in the implementation of policy and shape discretionary decision making at lower levels. In short, the president has many avenues for reorienting policy from within the executive branch as well as through Congress. How he uses these management tools will have a strong bearing on how successful the president is in capitalizing on broader political opportunities.

Constraints

Numerous constraints usually limit the president's ability to achieve substantial policy change. Many are constitutional or legal: the need for congressional assent to legislation, the obligation to "faithfully execute" existing laws and treaties, standard requirements of administrative procedure, and the power of the courts to review administrative actions and define constitutional limits. But many are informal and political. The president must have a "governing coalition" in Congress, but he may need to build a different base of support on each major issue. Despite the formal separation of powers, policy-making authority is shared between the branches of government, and in many cases other actors such as congressional committees have established expertise and authority over particular fields of policy that is not easily challenged by the president.

More broadly, the president has a limited amount of "political capital" to spend in influencing others. Every obligation he incurs entails future political costs that reduce his bargaining power; thus he must spend his political capital wisely if he is to achieve his primary objectives.[19]

Furthermore, the president is severely constrained by lack of time, information, and staff resources. The president himself has little time for details and must delegate responsibility for all but the most important and pressing matters to his aides and staff. The latter control the flow of information to the president and usually define the policy options when a top-level decision is required. Given the large executive establishment, the president can become isolated from many sectors of administration and policy making.

Congressional time and attention are also very limited, and unless the president's initiatives are geared carefully to the legislative timetable, they are not likely to be effective. These limitations usually mean that the president must concentrate on a few issues of overriding importance at any given time. Other matters often are delayed or allowed to drift until some crisis develops.

Finally, the president is constrained in less tangible but very real ways by the media and public opinion. He must continually guard his reputation against the appearance of failure, scandal, or loss of credibility.[20] He can try to shape his image through major television speeches, press conferences, and other media events, but the press and opposition leaders will be quick to challenge these and other public relations tactics. Media surveillance of the president of the United States is perhaps the most intense in the world, and he cannot afford to disregard negative coverage for very long. The president always must keep one eye on public opinion polls and the electoral calendar.

Political Cycles Within Administrations

Several scholars have posited a cyclical dynamic within presidential administrations. Opportunities for dramatic change are usually greatest in the first year. It is then that the president's prestige and political capital are at their peak, and the public and Congress expect him to take the initiative in defining the agenda. But the president must act quickly if he is to succeed. Unless he can demonstrate early success his reputation will begin to fade, and other interests will soon assert themselves. By the second year Congress is likely to slow up legislation as electoral considerations influence decisions and opposition to specific proposals develops. The third year may be propitious for renewed initiatives, but the president's party typically loses support in the midterm elections and may have to compromise more to consolidate its position. The fourth year is least likely to produce substantive policy change since all attention is usually focused on the president's reelection.

However, some students of the presidency suggest that even this model overstates the real opportunities for presidential impact. Paul Light, for example, notes two contradictory trends. The policy-making capabilities of the president and his staff usually are weakest at the beginning of an administration and increase in effectiveness over time; but this "cycle of increasing effectiveness" is offset by a "cycle of decreasing influence" as the president spends his political capital.[21] Others argue that the president's influence is much greater in the early phases of policy making (such as policy formulation) than in the later stages (such as implementation); thus the president may have little influence over the outcome of his initiatives.[22] Finally, ongoing policy cycles have a logic of their own whose timing does not coincide with that of the electoral calendar, and it may be very difficult to reverse their momentum without a strong consensus in support of radical change.

The Reagan Administration

Ronald Reagan and his advisers apparently had learned much from observing the failures of previous presidential administrations. They were fully aware of the limitations stressed by the presidency scholars and entered office with a great deal of strategic planning on how to overcome them. As Robert Bartlett argues in Chapter 6, the Reagan administration "hit the ground running" by imposing a new set of budget priorities that had been developed in advance by the new OMB director, David A. Stockman. The president's agenda was set by 20 years of campaigning for conservative causes. There was an overwhelming feeling that the moment to implement this agenda at last had arrived and that the opportunity to reshape permanently the scope and functions of government must not be lost. Stockman's "Economic Dunkirk" memorandum clearly expressed this sense of urgency, as did Reagan's inaugural address.[23]

The president gambled on asserting control across the entire domestic policy agenda by proposing one massive package of tax and budget cuts—and won. As Smith and others noted, Reagan accomplished more in his first year than had any president since Franklin Roosevelt.[24] Moreover, he was not content to depend on this legislative strategy to assert his agenda. As Nathan and Newland have explained, Reagan moved aggressively from the beginning to gain control over policy implementation in the bureaucracy. By centralizing policy making in the White House and OMB and delegating implementation to ideologically loyal subordinates in the various agencies, Reagan imposed his philosophy at all levels of government. The operating arms of the administration were put on automatic pilot, so to speak, in tune with the president's central agenda.[25]

But could this strategy succeed for very long? Would the cyclical, institutional, and political constraints discussed above reassert themselves after the first year? Could diverse policy changes, such as those in the field of environmental regulation, really be legitimized as essentially derivatives of the president's economic program? Could the president maintain control if he delegated such extensive powers to his subordinates? We can now turn to these questions by examining Reagan's environmental policies.

Environmental Policy: Reagan's Options

Reagan entered office with certain opportunities and constraints regarding environmental policy change. The climate for regulatory reform to improve the cost-effectiveness of environmental programs was relatively good; but, on the other hand, there was no public or congressional consensus favoring significant departures from established policy goals *(see chapters 1-3)*. Whether the administration clearly understood this is open to conjecture, but other factors intervened to give Reagan's environmental strategy a far more radical twist. In this section I discuss some factors that seem to have shaped the initial strategy.

Opportunities and Constraints

As indicated in Chapter 1, and by most of the other chapters in this volume, there were good reasons to think that environmental policy was ripe for some reforms in the early 1980s. Costs had risen throughout the previous decade and would escalate much more in coming years, while the results were somewhat disappointing. The Carter administration and Congress had shown growing interest in moderating the regulatory burden and already had begun deregulating certain sectors of the economy (such as airlines and oil). Most major environmental statutes, including the clean air and water acts, were up for renewal and revision during 1981-1984. Some key members of Congress, including Democrats such as John D. Dingell of Michigan, who would chair the House Energy and Commerce Committee, favored lowering existing environmental standards.

Moreover, Reagan had a mandate from the Republican platform of 1980 to review environmental laws and regulations to ensure that the benefits justified the costs. He also had many experienced advisers and former officials of the Nixon and Ford administrations to draw upon for advice.

As indicated in Chapter 2, Reagan set up a transition task force on environmental policy in the fall of 1980 under Dan Lufkin, who had headed Connecticut's innovative Department of Environmental Protection.[26] This group included William D. Ruckelshaus and others who were well attuned to the professional debate over environmental policy, and it represented some diverse viewpoints. However, even "moderates" such as Ruckelshaus—then a vice president at the Weyerhaeuser Corp., which had a large economic stake in the outcome—recommended far-reaching changes in the regulatory functions of the Environmental Protection Agency (EPA) and in basic legislation such as the Clean Air Act.[27] The president also received extensive advice from conservative groups such as the Heritage Foundation, which advocated wholesale deregulation. The extent to which regulatory reform was to mean deregulation was thus still an open question.

But any attempt to achieve extensive policy change was likely to encounter severe constraints. First of all, environmental policy making had been dominated overwhelmingly by Congress in the previous decade. Most major statutes had been drafted or negotiated by congressional committee staffs and members, with minimal influence from the White House. Congress also had exercised periodic oversight of environmental programs and agencies to maintain its control. Furthermore, as noted in Chapter 1, bipartisanship had characterized most congressional decision making in the 1970s. The coalition supporting strong environmental policies in the early 1980s cut across both parties in the Republican-dominated Senate as well as in the House of Representatives. Thus, despite some potential allies such as Dingell, it would be very difficult to obtain major legislative changes.

Second, although environmentalism was not the paramount issue it had been a decade earlier, public opinion polls indicated that exceptionally broad support for the earlier environmental goals still existed *(see Chapter 3)*. Furthermore, environmental organizations drew their memberships from all social classes and groups, in some cases more from Republican voters than from Democrats. Reagan thus would risk alienating large numbers of his own supporters if he embarked on radical changes in environmental policy.[28] Whatever electoral mandate he had for his economic program, there was no evidence that it extended to environmental issues *(see Chapter 2)*.

Third, while some environmental programs were up for review and revision, others, including all those dealing with hazardous and toxic substances, were still in the early stages of implementation. To seek to alter these programs without congressional approval surely would invite criticism. Finally, environmental administration involved intricate forms of cooperation between federal, state, and local authorities. All levels of government had vested interests in the existing system, even though none may have been satisfied with it. To alter this system would require major changes in federal-state relations ramifying far beyond environmental programs, and the new federalism would be very difficult to achieve.

Reagan thus faced some critical choices in defining his environmental agenda and in devising a political strategy to carry it out. Before considering these further, however, the president's own views should be taken into account. What can be said about Reagan's own predilections on environmental matters?

Reagan's Environmental Record

Interpretations of Ronald Reagan's stand on environmental issues prior to 1980 vary, in part because his record as governor of California (1967-1975) was mixed, and in part because he appears to have changed his views at different points in his career. Pollution was a vital issue in smog-ridden California long before it became a leading issue in the rest of the country. Shortly after becoming governor, Reagan called for an ambitious and comprehensive program to end air and water pollution. He proposed the most stringent air pollution standards in the nation and the creation of a centralized Air Resources Board with jurisdiction over both mobile and stationary sources of air pollution throughout the state.[29] Yet, once the board was operating, Reagan was frequently at odds with it and attempted to veto many of its recommendations. In assessing his two terms as governor, the League of Conservation Voters, a proenvironment group, concluded that Reagan "was responsible for undermining what could have been the most far-reaching air pollution program in the nation. . . ." For his overall record on air pollution, the league regarded him as a "total failure." [30]

Reagan's biographer, Lou Cannon, paints a somewhat different picture. He describes Reagan's attitudes, like those of many westerners, as a bundle of contradictions. Although Reagan always was prodevelopment, he also "considers himself a conservationist, an outdoorsman and a lover of nature." [31] Cannon argues that Reagan successfully handled conservation issues as governor, in large part by delegating them to his resources administrator, Ike Livermore, who enjoyed wide support in the environmental community. He notes, however, that Reagan's environmental convictions never were very strong, and that he became almost totally isolated from environmental decision making after he left the governorship. Indeed, by the late 1970s he had identified himself publicly with the Sagebrush Rebellion of the West *(see Chapter 14)*.

Still, Reagan's fundamental beliefs do not seem to have been so antithetical to environmental protection that he could not have chosen a more moderate course in 1980. What did become obvious during the presidential campaign was that Reagan had little personal grasp of basic environmental science—especially regarding air pollution—and that by this time he had come to see the issues in a very different framework.

Economics and Politics

Two crucial developments intervened to shape Reagan's environmental agenda during the campaign's closing stages. First, Reagan threw his support fully behind the group of economists advocating a radical experiment in supply-side economics.[32] This elevated the tax and budget cuts to overwhelming priority and made Stockman's OMB the central agency for refining the president's program. To Stockman and his associates, environmental programs were a prime target for budget cuts and regulatory relief *(see Chapter 6)*. Drastic reductions in environmental funding thus were scheduled on fiscal grounds before Reagan's environmental officials could even take office, let alone conduct cost-benefit analyses of the affected programs. In short, Reagan locked environmental policy into the economic policy framework to such an extent that it received no independent attention.

Second, politics intervened to determine the choice of appointees to head the environmental agencies. Reagan had a very diverse electoral constituency, but it was most strongly anchored in the West. All presidents distribute spoils to different geographic and interest group constituents, and the Interior Department usually goes to a westerner since its policies mainly affect that region. Reagan delegated this appointment to Sen. Paul Laxalt, his campaign chairman from Nevada, who in turn selected James G. Watt as secretary.[33] But Reagan went beyond precedent and awarded the EPA to the western conservatives as well, reportedly at the urging of Watt and wealthy campaign contributors from Colorado *(see Chapter 7)*. These were fateful choices, as both leading environmental agencies were in the hands of militant opponents of existing policies.[34] Of equal importance, the more moderate and experienced members of the Lufkin transition team were largely excluded from decision making. Some of them, including Lufkin himself, were to become bitter opponents of the Watt-Gorsuch team.

Given Stockman's role and these appointments—as well as Reagan's penchant for delegating extensive authority to agency heads—the die was cast for radical policy change. But these choices also reflected a broader assessment of the opportunities and constraints noted above. Recognizing the potential opposition, the Reagan leadership opted for an executive-administrative strategy that would largely bypass the legislative process. If Congress would not cooperate—as Ruckelshaus warned it would not[35]—then policy revision would be pursued by depriving the agencies of resources and putting loyal ideologues in charge of them who would implement the rules and regulations in a very different way. Like civil rights groups, women's groups, and consumer groups, the liberal environmentalists and their allies simply would be excluded from the process. Whatever his personal views on nature and the environment, the president bears full responsibility for this strategic choice.

The Administrative Strategy

Since most of the following chapters discuss the new administrative strategy in detail, I will briefly summarize its main features here. The strategy had four major components: (1) personnel policies designed to change the ideological orientation of the agencies; (2) governmental reorganization intended to facilitate centralized White House control over policy and to institute changes within departments and agencies that would help to further the president's policy agenda; (3) budgetary cutbacks to force the agencies to operate more "efficiently" and to reduce their regulatory activity; and (4) imposition of more detailed regulatory oversight to ensure implementation of the president's economic and regulatory relief goals. None of these tactics was illegitimate in itself; indeed, all but the third had some precedent in the Carter administration (and even Carter projected smaller budget increases for the 1980s). But, taken together, they had a devastating impact on environmental programs that exceeded the bounds of congressional and public toleration.

Personnel Policies

Personnel policies were used with a vengeance to clean house. The Reagan administration was convinced that government was filled with environmental zealots and developmental obstructionists who refused to consider the economic needs of the nation. Virtually all high-level positions thus were turned over to political appointees who came from the private sector and from the regulated industries. In EPA, for example, Rita Lavelle, a public relations officer for Aerojet-General, became assistant administrator for hazardous and toxic wastes; Kathleen Bennett, a lobbyist for the American Paper Institute, became assistant administrator for air, noise, and radiation; and Robert Perry, a lawyer for the Exxon Corp., became EPA general counsel. The same was true of bureau chiefs and office heads within the Interior Department.[36] Most had little or no prior experience in government, and certainly none in environmental administration.

But there were also major personnel reductions in nonpolitical staffs. Total employment at EPA, for example, dropped from 14,269 in January 1981 to 11,474 by November 1982. The agency headquarters' staff was reduced from 4,700 when Reagan took office to perhaps as low as 2,500 by September 1982.[37] These reductions in force (RIFs) crippled EPA.

Agency Reorganizations

Often reorganizations had similar effects. At EPA Gorsuch abolished the Enforcement Division, then reestablished it, and then reorganized it again. At

Interior, Watt streamlined the Office of Surface Mining and merged several environmental bureaus into other units, moves clearly designed to enhance the agency's resource development orientation. The Department of Energy, although not abolished as Reagan had threatened while campaigning, was reduced to a shadow of its former self (except for activities related to nuclear power and nuclear weapons supply).

But perhaps the single most important reorganization came at the White House level. Reagan fired almost the entire professional staff of the Council on Environmental Quality and then reconstituted it with a much smaller staff in the lower echelons of the Executive Office. He apparently did not feel the need for independent environmental advice at the top. Shortly after taking office, Reagan also established several "cabinet councils," including one on Natural Resources and Environment chaired by Watt. This council coordinated policy making at related agencies, including Interior, EPA (which was not represented), and the Department of Energy. It acted as liaison with the new Office of Policy Development, which had replaced Carter's Domestic Policy Staff, through its secretary, but otherwise there was no evidence of environmental expertise in the White House.[38] Instead, the president's economic program was the guide to all decision making.

Budgetary Decisions

The Reagan administration used the budget as a weapon for policy change to an unprecedented degree. By rolling massive budget cuts affecting nearly every domestic social program into the 1981 fiscal reform package, Reagan was able to get congressional assent to reduction in environmental staffs and activities. This was interpreted as a mandate for policy change in the agencies even though no specific authorization for such changes had been granted.

OMB sought further deep cuts in environmental budgets in 1982 and 1983. Although Congress appropriated somewhat more than the president requested after 1981, the cumulative impact of budget restrictions was enormous, especially at EPA. Adjusted for inflation, EPA's operating budget declined by about one-third between 1981 and 1983, and its research and development funding was cut by more than half *(see Chapter 6)*. The overall shift from the Carter to the Reagan administrations is perhaps best captured in the spending total for all federal programs that deal with natural resources and environmental protection. In January 1981 Carter proposed a $16.2 billion budget for fiscal 1984, whereas Reagan, for the same year, later proposed $8.9 billion. In contrast to all past experience, these cuts were welcomed by Gorsuch and other administrators as proof that their agencies could "do more with less." [39]

Congressional approval of the budget reductions provided limited legitimation for policy changes designed to promote federal deregulation and transfer of responsibilities to the states. But observers in and out of Congress concluded that the funding withdrawals were undermining severely the environmental agencies' capabilities to carry out their statutory obligations.

These had not been altered and in fact were growing rapidly as the implementation of toxic waste programs began. Environmentalists charged the administration with "back-door repeal" of environmental laws by depriving the agencies of the resources necessary to implement them.

Regulatory Oversight

Regulatory oversight was intensified greatly during the Reagan administration. One of Reagan's first actions was to appoint a new Task Force on Regulatory Relief headed by Vice President George Bush to examine all new and existing regulations to determine their economic impact. Then in February 1981 the president issued Executive Order 12291, requiring all agencies to conduct cost-benefit studies of new rules and regulations *before* proposing them. The order required that

> ... to the extent permitted by law, all agencies must adhere to the order's substantive criteria in their regulations. These include: (1) refraining from regulatory action unless potential benefits outweigh potential costs to society; (2) choosing regulatory objectives that maximize net benefits to society; (3) selecting the alternatives that will impose the least net cost to society while achieving regulatory objectives; and (4) setting regulatory priorities to maximize aggregate net benefits to society, taking into account factors such as the condition of the national economy and of particular industries.[40]

Economic criteria thus were to be considered in all agency decision making. The regulatory impact review process was to be supervised by the director of OMB through a new Office of Information and Regulatory Affairs (OIRA), which was empowered to delay publication of any new regulation in the *Federal Register.*

This process was designed to slow agency rule making and enhance the influence of the president and OMB in regulatory policy. Although few environmental regulations actually were rescinded or repealed, the application and enforcement of them reflected the president's economic priorities *(see Chapter 8)*. Unable to move regulatory reform legislation through the Democratic House, the administration depended on OIRA to carry out deregulation by executive means, believing that Congress would accept the fait accompli.[41] In the words of Christopher DeMuth, OMB administrator for regulatory affairs and executive director of the Task Force on Regulatory Relief:

> The history of deregulation is that major administrative reform is a necessary prerequisite to statutory reform. Before Congress itself will act, external changes are required to dislodge accumulated interests in the status quo and to assure the doubtful of the economy's ability to continue functioning in the absence of federal controls. ... If we are to achieve major statutory reform in the last two years of President Reagan's first term, we must first build a solid foundation of *administrative deregulation* in 1982. [emphasis added][42]

This "administrative deregulation" did not fully succeed, since it aroused opposition in Congress and frequently was challenged in the courts *(see chapters 5 and 9)*. But along with the budget and personnel reductions, organizational changes, and policy direction by Reagan appointees and the Watt cabinet council, it brought an entirely new set of political forces to bear on the implementation of environmental policy. Chapters 10 through 15 spell out the effects in six specific fields.

The Policy Dilemma

The actions discussed thus far were primarily administrative, but they had the effect of thoroughly disrupting previous institutional development and methods of decision making. Reagan himself made few public statements about environmental policy, but he expressed support on numerous occasions for the activities of Watt, Gorsuch, and other appointees. These officials were given a relatively free hand by the president, especially during the critical first year when new priorities were being established. Watt also became one of the most popular speakers on the Republican fund-raising circuit, perhaps increasing his influence and independence. Other White House advisers apparently did not pay much attention to environmental policy until problems began to develop. As one Reagan aide put it early in the administration, "We have two basic programs that we want for the first two years: the budget cuts and the tax plan. Everything else is secondary." [43] Later, when the crisis at EPA was at its height, another senior aide admitted that "a lot of us frankly have not been paying much attention to it in the last two years." [44] Thus, despite the formal mechanisms for policy coordination and review, a combination of excessive delegation and neglect accounts for some of the embarrassments that the president later had to face. But the White House also seemed content to let Watt and others take the heat for unpopular measures.

The fundamental dilemma was that the policy changes could not be legitimized by normal constitutional processes or by appeals to public opinion. Agenda changes and policy innovations that break with the established consensus require such legitimation The Reagan administration in effect reversed the usual process by implementing new policies *before* they gained congressional and public support.

The administration did make some attempts to gain legislative support. During the first two years, it proposed amendments or guiding principles for revision of such major statutes as the Clean Air and Clean Water acts *(see Chapters 11 and 12)*. It also threw its support behind certain congressional initiatives, such as the Luken-Dingell bill in the House that would have weakened or postponed many air pollution deadlines, as well as other bills putting general regulatory reforms on a more secure constitutional basis. But the administration was so preoccupied with its tax and budget legislation during 1981 and 1982 that these efforts received comparatively little attention in the White House. The initiative was left to Watt and Gorsuch, whose uncompromising positions and personal abrasiveness only succeeded in polarizing positions and infuriating those senators and representatives seeking compromise. As a result, no significant legislative revision was attained through 1983 despite the radical reorientation of environmental policies within the executive branch.

It is quite possible that this was the administration's intent: it would change policies to such an extent that Congress eventually would have to recognize the fait accompli and amend legislation accordingly. But if this was the strategy—or at least the preferred alternative to compromise with environmental interests in the amendment process—it ultimately backfired in Congress. Congress reasserted its prerogatives with a vengeance in launching the Watergate-type investigation that drove the Gorsuch team from office and revealed the broader illegitimacy of the administration's approach to environmental affairs. It is ironic that Rep. John D. Dingell, one of the strongest proponents of Clean Air Act revisions, led the attack on the administration's abuse of power.

The events leading up to Gorsuch's contempt citation in the House themselves reflected the administration's exceedingly poor judgment. The Justice Department reportedly was seeking a test case for establishing the president's broader claims to executive privilege.[45] If so, it could not have chosen a more doubtful opportunity than in the highly charged atmosphere of environmental policy, nor one in which the administration's claims to preserve secrecy in legal proceedings were more suspect. The administrative style at EPA had emphasized informal negotiation with the regulated industries to achieve voluntary compliance without the need for legal enforcement, especially in the Superfund program *(see Chapter 13)*.

By late 1982 the press was full of allegations of "sweetheart" deals, agency personnel with ties to former employers they were supposedly regulating, and political manipulation of EPA funding in California and elsewhere. Attempts to exclude Congress and the public from such informal dealings could only arouse suspicion and backfire.

The president, therefore, could not escape fully the systemic constraints that have humbled other administrations. After the first year Congress reasserted its constitutional powers, and public opinion moved clearly against the president. Environmental organizations launched a massive public campaign, which was widely reported in the press, against the administration. Several candidates supported by environmentalists unseated their opponents in the 1982 congressional elections, further reducing the administration's chances for any legislative reform. Many state governors attacked the administration for devolving environmental responsibilities on them without the requisite funding. James Watt, like Anne Gorsuch, had become a political liability to the administration long before he resigned in October 1983.[46] The president's credibility was shaken by their forced resignations, even though he did not admit that *his* policies were at fault.

In light of the four-year cyclical dynamics of presidential administrations, these developments are especially interesting. The administration surely had its greatest impact on environmental policy making in the first half of the term before sound professional and analytical capabilities for policy manage-

ment had developed. The sweeping budgetary and organizational retrenchment, the bungled legislative relations, and even the OMB regulatory review
process were carried out in accordance with ideological preferences rather
than careful evaluation and assessment.[47] The return of Ruckelshaus to
EPA—if not William Clark's replacement of Watt at Interior—suggested a
delayed cycle of increasing effectiveness in policy management. But by this
time the cycle of decreasing influence was in full swing as the president's political capital was badly depleted in Congress and elsewhere (at least on
environmental issues).

Conclusion

Ronald Reagan came into office pledged to "reverse forty years of
government mismanagement" and to restore the rights of private business and
local government. It is fair to say that he was determined to cut back the federal government (except for defense) by whatever means he could muster in
the Oval Office. But the most distinctive features of his presidency in domestic
affairs were (1) the reliance on essentially ideological criteria for policy
formulation and coordination, (2) the effort to justify changes in the entire domestic policy agenda in terms of his economic recovery program, and (3) the
pursuit of deregulation and policy change through administrative mechanisms
without congressional participation (with the exception of budgeting).

To some extent these tactics were congruent with the recommendations
of many students of the presidency who had come to deplore the inability of
recent chief executives to play an effective leadership role. But few, if any,
could have contemplated the radical approach that Reagan was to take. The
administrative presidency may be an attractive concept to those who see a
compelling need for clear priority setting and strong policy coordination
throughout the executive bureaucracy. However, when pushed to extremes, as
in the case of Reagan's environmental policy, politicized administration can
permanently damage the professional capabilities of government agencies and
undermine the legitimacy of their actions.

This is not to suggest that the Reagan administration has not had any
success in implementing its environmental goals. Some temporary regulatory
relief—if not genuine reform—has been achieved; numerous obligations have
been delegated to the states, and some cost savings have been realized (though
these are insignificant when compared to the growth of the federal deficit
under Reagan). EPA, for example, had fewer resources (in real purchasing
power) when Ruckelshaus returned to it in 1983 than it had when he left it
more than a decade earlier. Given the serious budget deficits of the federal
and many state governments, support for environmental programs is not
likely to be restored for many years to come.

What then can we conclude about Reagan's environmental "coup?"
First, at the end of 1983 it had not been fully carried out because political and
constitutional limitations do not allow a president to change policies arbitrarily by executive means. Many of the administration's initiatives had been
blunted by congressional opposition, public outcry, and legal challenges. The

environmental legislation of the previous decade remained intact. The president's chief environmental appointees had been driven from office, and their successors had begun a retreat to more defensible positions. Although the president did not admit to any change of direction, he recognized the need to cut political losses by appointing more respected figures to head the beleaguered environmental agencies.

Second, the Reagan experience nevertheless demonstrated that an aggressive president can more successfully implement a *negative* than a *positive* policy agenda. While he did not achieve any positive legislation, Reagan succeeded in reducing the scale and effectiveness of national environmental regulations. The constraints emphasized in the presidency literature are evidently less applicable to this type of cutback administration than to those that seek to enact new governmental programs.

Finally, the president's ability to offset policy failures by avoiding personal responsibility should not be underestimated. Although he was obviously shaken by the EPA scandal and the Watt controversy, Reagan managed to deflect much of the criticism away from the White House. As one observer put it, "The departure of former EPA Administrator Anne Burford and most of the agency's top officials have silenced the wolves howling at the White House's door. A few forced resignations and firings . . . was a very cheap price to pay for such political relief." [48] Thus it was not clear that he would be held accountable for his subordinates' actions, nor that he would not be able to pursue his environmental agenda in a second term.

The "blues" may yet rout the "greens" in the second half of the 1980s.

Notes

1. William K. Reilly, "President's Letter," The Conservation Foundation, *Resolve* (Winter 1982), 2.
2. Hugh Heclo, "Introduction: The Presidential Illusion," in *The Illusion of Presidential Government,* ed. Hugh Heclo and Lester M. Salamon (Boulder, Colo.: Westview Press, 1981), 1.
3. Aaron Wildavsky, "Two Presidencies," *Transaction* 4 (December 1966). For further discussion, see Steven A. Shull and Lance T. LeLoup, "Presidential Impact: Foreign Versus Domestic Policy," in *The Presidency: Studies in Policy Making,* ed. Shull and LeLoup (Brunswick, Ohio: King's Court Communications, 1979); and Thomas E. Cronin, *The State of the Presidency,* 2d ed. (Boston: Little, Brown, 1980), chapters 3-5.
4. Arnold J. Meltsner, ed., *Politics and the Oval Office: Towards Presidential Governance* (San Francisco: Institute for Contemporary Studies, 1981).
5. Paul C. Light, "Presidents as Domestic Policymakers," in *Rethinking the Presidency,* ed. Thomas E. Cronin (Boston: Little, Brown, 1982), 368.
6. Lester M. Salamon, "Conclusion: Beyond Presidential Illusion—Toward a Constitutional Presidency," in *The Illusion of Presidential Government,* ed. Heclo and Salamon, 287.
7. See, for example, Charles O. Jones, "Congress and the Presidency," in *The New Congress,* ed. Thomas E. Mann and Norman J. Ornstein (Washington, D.C.:

American Enterprise Institute, 1981); and James L. Sundquist, "Congress, the President, and the Crisis of Competence in Government," in *Congress Reconsidered,* ed. Lawrence C. Dodd and Bruce I. Oppenheimer (Washington, D.C.: CQ Press, 1981).

8. Richard E. Neustadt, *Presidential Power: The Politics of Leadership from FDR to Carter* (New York: Wiley, 1980), 241.

9. Hedrick Smith, "The President as Coalition Builder: Reagan's First Year," in *Rethinking the Presidency,* ed. Cronin, 274.

10. Ibid., 275.

11. Richard P. Nathan, *The Plot That Failed: Nixon and the Administrative Presidency* (New York: Wiley, 1975).

12. Richard P. Nathan, *The Administrative Presidency* (New York: Wiley, 1983).

13. Ibid., 13.

14. Chester A. Newland, "The Reagan Presidency: Limited Government and Political Administration," *Public Administration Review* 43 (January/February 1983): 1-21.

15. Ibid., 2.

16. Ibid.

17. Nathan, *Administrative Presidency,* 78.

18. Neustadt, *Presidential Power: The Politics of Leadership,* chapter 3.

19. Light, "Presidents as Domestic Policymakers"; Neustadt, *Presidential Power.*

20. Neustadt, *Presidential Power,* chapters 4-5.

21. Light, "Presidents as Domestic Policymakers," 355-56.

22. Steven A. Shull, *Presidential Policy Making: An Analysis* (Brunswick, Ohio: King's Court Communications, 1979), 299-305.

23. Stockman wrote that "if bold policies are not swiftly, deftly, and courageously implemented in the first six months, Washington will quickly become engulfed in political disorder commensurate with the surrounding economic disarray. A golden opportunity for permanent conservative policy revision and political realignment could be thoroughly dissipated before the Reagan administration is even up to speed." *Washington Post,* December 14, 1980.

24. Smith, "The President as Coalition Builder"; John L. Palmer and Isabel V. Sawhill, eds., *The Reagan Experiment* (Washington, D.C.: Urban Institute, 1982).

25. Aaron Wildavsky, "Putting the Presidency on Automatic Pilot," in *The American Presidency: Principles and Problems,* vol. 1, ed. Kenneth W. Thompson (Washington, D.C.: University Press of America, 1982).

26. *New York Times,* November 14, 1980, 10.

27. Philip Shabecoff, "Ruckelshaus Said to Have Wanted Air Rules Eased," *New York Times,* April 28, 1983, 11.

28. Council on Environmental Quality et al., *Public Opinion on Environmental Issues: Results of a National Public Opinion Survey* (Washington, D.C.: Government Printing Office, 1980). Ruckelshaus has stated that the administration misread public opinion on the environment: *New York Times,* July 27, 1983.

29. Ronald Reagan, *The Creative Society* (New York: Devon-Adair, 1968).

30. *The Presidential Candidates* (Washington, D.C.: League of Conservation Voters, 1976), 57. See also Lawrence Mosher, "Talking Clean on the Hustings," *National Journal,* November 1, 1980, 1850.

31. Lou Cannon, *Reagan* (New York: G. P. Putnam's, 1982), 349. Chapter 21 contains the most insightful portrait of Reagan's environmental attitudes.

32. A. James Reichley, "A Change in Direction," in *Setting National Priorities: The*

1982 Budget, ed. Joseph Pechman (Washington, D.C.: Brookings Institution, 1981); and Leonard Silk, "On the Supply Side," in *Reagan: The Man, the President,* ed. Hedrick Smith et al. (New York: Macmillan, 1980).

33. Cannon, *Reagan,* 369. Cannon states that Watt was Laxalt's second choice for Interior, after former senator Clifford Hansen turned the position down.
34. For an excellent portrait of Watt, see Cannon, *Reagan,* chapter 21.
35. Shabecoff, "Ruckelshaus Said to Have Wanted Air Rules Eased."
36. For background on the Reagan appointees, see Ronald Brownstein and Nina Easton, *Reagan's Ruling Class* (Washington, D.C.: Presidential Accountability Group, 1982).
37. Philip Shabecoff, "Budget Office Is Said to Be Asking 17% Cutback in Funds for the E.P.A.," *New York Times,* December 13, 1982. See also Dick Kirschten, "Administration Using Carter-Era Reform to Manipulate the Levers of Government," *National Journal,* April 9, 1983, 732-736.
38. On the cabinet councils, see Newland, "The Reagan Presidency," 6-10; and Dick Kirschten, "Reagan's Cabinet Councils May Have Less Influence than Meets the Eye," *National Journal,* July 11, 1981, 1242-1245. It should be added that Reagan's White House staff was uniformly conservative on environmental and natural resource issues. This is confirmed in a study by John H. Kessel based on personal interviews with nearly 40 top aides. They are found to be more conservative on natural resource issues than on any other issues studied (including international involvement, economic management, social benefits, civil liberties, and agriculture). Danny Boggs, secretary to the cabinet council, is classified as an "unalloyed conservative." See Kessel, "The Structure of the Reagan White House" (Paper presented at the annual meeting of the American Political Science Association, Chicago, September 1983).
39. Philip Shabecoff. "E.P.A. Chief Claims Victory on Budget," *New York Times,* October 13, 1982.
40. Richard A. Liroff, "Cost-Benefit Analysis in Federal Environmental Programs," in *Cost-Benefit Analysis and Environmental Regulations: Politics, Ethics, and Methods,* ed. Daniel Swartzman et al. (Washington, D.C.: Conservation Foundation, 1982), 39.
41. Diane Granat, "Business Groups Press Regulatory Reform Bill," *Congressional Quarterly Weekly Report,* November 20, 1982, 2891-92.
42. Christopher C. DeMuth, "A Strong Beginning on Reform," *Regulation* (January/February 1982), 18.
43. Light, "Presidents as Domestic Policymakers," 353.
44. Steven R. Weisman, "Reagan and E.P.A.: Week's Changes Reflect Seriousness of Issue's Threat to the Administration," *New York Times,* February 26, 1983, 8.
45. Philip Shabecoff, "EPA Chief Urges Opening All Files to Quash Dispute," *New York Times,* March 4, 1983.
46. "Battle Over the Wilderness," *Newsweek,* July 25, 1983, 22-30.
47. George C. Eads, "White House Oversight of Executive Branch Regulation," in *Social Regulation: Strategies for Reform,* ed. Eugene Bardach and Robert A. Kagan (San Francisco: Institute for Contemporary Studies, 1982); Susan J. Tolchin and Martin Tolchin, *Dismantling America: The Rush to Deregulate* (Boston: Houghton Mifflin, 1983).
48. Al Gordon, "Crisis Blows Over, But EPA Questions Remain Unanswered," *Minneapolis Star and Tribune,* December 8, 1983.

5. CONGRESS AGAINST THE PRESIDENT: THE STRUGGLE OVER THE ENVIRONMENT

Henry C. Kenski and Margaret Corgan Kenski

Environmental policy making under the Reagan administration has been marked by a protracted struggle between the president and Congress over the appropriateness and direction of change in the current system of environmental protection. The seeds of this conflict were sown during the 1980 campaign, when Ronald Reagan as a candidate supported easing environmental protection laws, attacked the Clean Air Act repeatedly, blamed environmental regulations for slowdowns in industrial growth, and declared that "air pollution has been substantially controlled." [1] Once inaugurated and faced with a Congress that historically had supported environmental protection, President Reagan opted for a political strategy that sought to achieve major change in environmental policy through budgetary cutbacks and the use of regulatory and administrative powers rather than attempting to push for substantive environmental legislation.

Congress thus was forced to move from the *proactive* posture in environmental affairs it had assumed during the 1970s into a *reactive* stance of defending environmental protection laws against the radical policy changes proposed by the Reagan administration. This chapter explores the ensuing environmental policy struggle between Reagan and Congress, with emphasis on the roles Congress has played in the policy-making process.

Our analysis of Congress as a check on presidential policy making in the environmental arena begins with an overview of the congressional response to Reagan's policy strategy. We then move to a more specific discussion of how Congress responded and identify its policy-making roles. This discussion is followed by an analysis of why Congress responded the way it did, an analysis focusing on the parameters around Congress as policy maker. Next we examine the floor votes on environmental issues in the 97th Congress (1981-1983), followed by a look at the beginnings of change in the 98th Congress. Finally, we summarize our findings and speculate about the future role of Congress vis-à-vis the executive in environmental policy making.

The Congressional Response

Reagan employed a "dual approach" in developing his environmental policy strategy, as he had in other policy areas; he combined legislative and administrative strategies to achieve his domestic policy goals. His legislative environmental strategy was indirect: he avoided initiating substantive environmental proposals for Congress to consider and instead opted for an agenda-setting strategy that placed major emphasis on the budget and tax battles. Thus he waged his legislative fight on the political turf where he was strongest and avoided a frontal assault and debate on the substance and content of environmental programs in which he was politically weakest.

His administrative strategy emphasized dramatic, nonincremental change in regulations and administration. This course avoids the difficult task of applying one's political skills to gain support from organized groups and the general public, circumvents the legislative arena, and ignores the need to build bipartisan support in Congress. Not surprisingly, this facet of the dual strategy ran into substantial opposition as the conditions necessary to its success—a passive Congress, weak organized group opposition, and an uninterested public—did not exist. Our concern here is to assess how Congress responded generally to this dual strategy.

Legislative Response

Unlike his predecessor Jimmy Carter, Reagan opted for a political strategy that would enable him to control the political agenda. He focused public and congressional attention on the one broad issue of economic recovery, thus avoiding Carter's mistake of inundating Congress and confusing the public with too many proposals. Reagan's priority was clear, and he persuaded Congress to accept his economic premise (domestic budget cuts, tax cuts, and defense increases) and a simplified legislative agenda. All other substantive issues were pushed into the background.[2] According to Norman Ornstein, the president reduced his economic recovery issues to "three beautifully timed blockbuster key votes, all well defined and highly publicized, and all smashing victories for the president."[3]

Considerable conflict and stalemate between the president and Congress after August 1981[4] did not result in the repeal of the 1981 cut of $35.2 billion from the fiscal 1982 budget. This budget cut significantly altered the scope and shape of many governmental programs, including those dealing with the environment. The House Budget Committee chairman, Oklahoma Democrat James R. Jones, called passage of the 1981 budget reconciliation measure "clearly the most monumental and historic turnabout in fiscal policy that has ever occurred."[5]

Reagan had stunned the opposition with an initial proposal of $50 billion in budget cuts and then captured political momentum before the House Democrats fully understood what was happening. Because the president's party controlled the Senate, his primary opposition came from the House Democrats, who scrambled in disarray to formulate their own budget package. The Democrats also proposed substantial budget cuts, but these differed from Reagan's plan in the kind and degree of specific program reductions. The House Budget Committee, for example, formulated an unsuccessful budget-cut package for fiscal 1982 that included more funding for environmental programs than the administration's bill.[6] Overall, however, as *New York Times* analyst Hedrick Smith observed, the Democratic "budget and tax proposals ultimately became variations on basic Reagan themes, an indicator of how thoroughly he dominated the political arena." [7]

In the legislative arena, the president's dramatic budget victory in 1981 resulted in deep cuts for environmental protection programs in fiscal year 1982.[8] The 97th Congress held the fiscal 1983 appropriations for these programs close to the 1982 levels; thus it "preserved deep cuts the administration proposed and Congress enacted in fiscal 1982." [9] Through his agenda-setting strategy, which placed major emphasis on the budget and tax battles, the president thus achieved significant policy change without a frontal assault on the substance of environmental programs.

In the 1981 budget battle, environmental programs were not exempt from attack. The operating budget for the Environmental Protection Agency (EPA) was slashed from $1.3 billion in fiscal 1981 to $1.09 billion in 1982. The administration requested further cuts for 1983 and a budget of $961 million. Congress resisted but ended up appropriating only $1.04 billion.[10] A major target for reductions at EPA was research and development. Congress appropriated $227.2 million for this purpose for fiscal 1983, a figure slightly above the administration's $219 million request but significantly below the 1982 level of $270.5 million and the 1981 appropriation of $358 million.[11]

Sizable cuts also were made in the Interior Department's budget. Congress appropriated about $7.5 billion for Interior and related agencies in fiscal 1983, $923 million above Reagan's $6.6 billion request, and $2.07 billion in "off-budget" appropriations to buy oil for the Strategic Petroleum Reserve (SPR). (The latter appropriations are transactions of federally owned or controlled agencies that are excluded from budget totals under provisions of the law, even though these outlays are part of total government spending.) "While the final amount was up slightly from the $7.36 billion enacted for 1982 (not including the SPR), it was still down from fiscal 1981 spending of $12.06 billion, which included the SPR." [12] Overall Congress, in the fiscal 1983 Interior appropriations bill, acted to restore funds Reagan wanted cut "from energy conservation, fossil fuels research, park land acquisition, historic preservation, and the arts and humanities endowments." [13]

One budget area in which Congress had some success regarding environmental programs was in financial aid to the states. Having granted Reagan the cuts he sought in this area for fiscal 1982, Congress blocked further administration efforts to phase out federal grants to the states for administering environmental programs. These grants, some $233.1 million in fiscal 1983, pay about half the cost of state programs. Persuaded by the National Governors' Association of the environmental damage that could result, Congress acted in an appropriations bill on September 29, 1982, to block Reagan's proposed 20 percent reduction.[14] It thus sided with the states in the debate over the meaning of environmental federalism, holding that federal money was necessary for the states to help protect the environment.

Although Congress acted as a brake on the president's budget strategy, the deep cuts enacted in fiscal 1982 remain. By winning a decisive budget victory in 1981 President Reagan has affected the content of environmental policies, as the cuts have dramatically altered the federal government's capability to implement environmental protection programs.

Administrative/Regulatory Response

Critical to the fate of any administration's policy endeavors are the executive appointments of personnel selected to implement policy goals. For certain key executive positions, the president appoints individuals with the consent of the Senate. If there are no serious questions about the nominees' competence or integrity, the Senate will confirm the president's choices with little opposition, reflecting the tradition and feeling that the incoming president deserves to choose the people who will make up his executive team. In many cases members will put aside partisanship in executive appointment voting. The president can be even more certain of his appointees' confirmations if his party controls the Senate, as was the situation with the Republican-controlled Senate in the 97th Congress.

Thus tradition and Republican control of the Senate contributed to the approval of prodevelopment and proindustry conservatives to the top environmental policy positions. James G. Watt became secretary of the interior; Anne Gorsuch (later Burford) took over as head of the EPA; and John B. Crowell, Jr., was selected as assistant secretary of agriculture for natural resources and the environment.[15]

Having given Reagan his nominees, Congress proceeded to watch them and their administrative and regulatory behavior. The general response of Congress was one of vigorous oversight, although traditionally oversight is not a strong congressional role. "During the 97th Congress, for example, Interior Department officials appeared at 383 hearings. EPA officials appeared at 97 hearings between October 1, 1981, and the end of 1982." [16]

Watt lived up to his prodevelopment reputation; his tough, abrasive style resulted in negative reactions from environmental groups, Congress, western governors, and even segments of the business community.[17] His tactics resulted in bitter disputes over wilderness leases, coal leases, and offshore drilling as he neglected to consult members of Congress, ignored procedural requirements for environmental assessments, and alienated many state officials.[18] Watt clashed frequently with House Democrats and embarrassed several Republican House members "when he moved to open up wilderness and off-shore areas in their states to oil and gas leasing." [19] Despite Watt's tendency to provoke controversy, President Reagan defended his overall environmental policy in a June 11, 1983, radio address and declared the attacks on Watt unfair.[20]

Led by its chairman, Arizona Democrat Morris K. Udall, the House Interior and Insular Affairs Committee twice acted in 1981 to block Watt's plans to accelerate oil and gas leasing; the House Appropriations Committee took similar action.[21] This pattern continued in 1982 with a major clash over the issue of oil and gas leasing in areas either designated as federally protected wilderness or as land under consideration for such designation. Although Congress in 1981 blocked Watt's efforts to open up some of these areas for energy development, there existed a one-year "window" before a permanent ban was to take effect. Distrusting Watt, Congress in 1982 closed the window "with a rider to the fiscal 1983 Interior appropriation bill that banned oil and gas leasing in wilderness and wilderness study areas." [22]

Congress was also vigilant in its oversight of Anne Gorsuch and the EPA. Congressional Quarterly's Joseph Davis notes, for instance, that after noisy congressional protests in 1982, "EPA backed off from a decision to suspend an existing ban on dumping toxic liquid wastes into unlined landfills, and from plans to consider relaxing or repealing restrictions on lead in gasoline." [23] Gorsuch, described by *National Journal*'s Richard Cohen as "an official who quickly gained a reputation of wanting to ease tough enforcement of environmental laws," eventually became a pawn in the battle between the White House and the House of Representatives over the claim of "executive privilege." [24] Having refused to furnish two House committees with documents on EPA's enforcement of hazardous waste cleanups required by the 1980 "Superfund" law, Gorsuch was held in contempt of Congress on December 16, 1982, by a 259-105 vote in the House that included "yea" votes from 55 Republicans.[25] In this matter members of Congress pursued investigations of charges of lax EPA enforcement of environmental laws, including allegations and denials of mismanagement, conflict of interest, missing funds, delays in hazardous waste cleanups due to political considerations, improprieties, political influence, personal financial gain, unethical conduct, and shredded documents.[26] Burford (formerly Gorsuch) resigned on March 9, 1983.[27]

Although Congress recorded some striking oversight victories in its battle with the president, it is clear that with its many other duties it cannot oversee all administrative behavior. Thus many important environmental decisions have been made at Interior and EPA, and not in Congress. Major and minor rule changes have been made to relieve industry's regulatory burden and to promote energy development. Despite Watt's defeat by Congress on a number of wilderness leasing initiatives, Joseph Davis observes that "the Interior Department's annual report suggested that he gained more ground in the regulation arena than he lost in the legislative one." Moreover, "federal oil and gas leasing for onshore public lands climbed dramatically. The tonnage of coal leased grew even more rapidly, with the total including the largest federal coal lease sale in history, for the Powder River region in Montana and Wyoming." [28] Although members of Congress played a key role in forcing the resignation of EPA chief Burford, considerable damage to environmental protection programs already had been done.[29]

In short, the general congressional response to Reagan's dual approach of combining legislative and administrative strategies was vigorous but reactive. Congress, particularly House Democrats, acted to temper the president's budget cuts. Although quite unsuccessful in 1981 with the fiscal 1982 budget at stake, Congress was more influential in 1982 with the fiscal 1983 budget. Overall, the president maintained a stronger hand in the legislative strategy of the budget battle. Reagan's administrative strategy encountered strong opposition, especially among House Democrats, and Congress recorded important victories, including its role in forcing the resignation of Burford as the head of EPA. This protracted struggle underscores that Congress with its many other responsibilities cannot oversee all the behavior of an administration seeking dramatic change through an administrative/regulatory route. An understanding of the role Congress plays in policy making, however, requires more than an awareness of its general responses. It involves knowledge about Congress's specific roles in the policy process.

The Policy-Making Roles of Congress

Congress plays various roles in policy making. We introduce a typology of congressional policy roles, drawn from research done by Charles O. Jones, in Table 5-1. [30] This typology modifies and expands the categories used by Jones, specifically applying them to the 97th Congress. [31] In our application of the concept, a role can be played by the Congress as a whole, as one chamber, or as one committee.

Our organization of these roles is adapted to the political realities of the Washington environment since the election of 1980. The Republicans control the White House and the Senate, and the Democrats, the House of Representatives. Given this division and widespread public support for environmental protection, little opportunity for dramatic or innovative policy initiation and formulation exists. Congress therefore is inclined to a reactive posture in the environmental arena.

The first role of Congress then is *defender of the status quo* and is characterized by the making of modest revisions in existing law or by the blocking of major policy initiatives. The battle over Clean Air Act revisions provides examples of both. This battle, over what was without doubt the single most important substantive environmental policy on the legislative agenda in the 97th Congress, ended in a stalemate. Despite the strong 1980 campaign pronouncements, the administration vacillated on whether and how to revise the Clean Air Act in 1981. It first promised to send Congress a proposal, next delayed submission, and finally rendered a broadly worded statement of 11 principles rather than specific recommendations. In the absence of specifics from the White House, Senate Environment and Public Works Chairman Robert T. Stafford, R-Vt., departed from normal procedure and opted to review the existing law section by section and amend it rather than work from a draft bill. His committee labored throughout 1981 and 1982 and produced a bill making modest revisions in the existing law and

Table 5-1 Policy Roles of 97th Congress

Role	Activities	Examples
Defender of Status Quo	Makes modest revisions in existing law	Senate Environment and Public Works Committee's revision of Clean Air Act
	Blocks major policy initiative	Stalemate in House Energy and Commerce Committee over Clean Air Act revisions
Overseer	Ensures proper implementation of existing laws	Various committee and subcommittee investigations of EPA's implementation of hazardous waste
Initiator	Formulates policy in absence of executive action	Congressional passage of Coastal Barrier Island legislation
	Offers a competitive policy to an executive proposal	House Budget Committee's 1981 budget resolution
Partner	Endorses presidential action with minimal change	Senate approval of nomination of Watt
	Accepts executive proposals with major revisions	Congressional reauthorization of federal sewage treatment grant program
Facilitator of Interests	Responds to special and public interests	House Energy and Commerce Committee and the retention of Federal Noise Control Act

adding new provisions for control of acid rain. Although the committee's bill never went to the Senate floor, it provides a good example of defending the status quo by fine-tuning existing law.

On the House side, the Energy and Commerce Committee fought for two years over the law. At the end of 1981, two Democrats, Chairman John D. Dingell of Michigan and Rep. Thomas A. Luken of Ohio, submitted a revised bill that was endorsed by the Reagan administration and industry groups, and which was intended to defuse charges that the existing law would be gutted. Environmental groups backed California Democrat Henry A. Waxman, an Energy and Commerce subcommittee chairman, who led the faction intensely opposed to the Dingell-Luken measure. The Energy and Commerce Committee was so divided that a deadlock resulting over a more sweeping rewrite that would have loosened auto emission standards led to a situation in which no proposal left the committee. Thus House action preserved the status quo by blocking proposed changes. The defender-of-the-status-quo role proved to be a potent one for Congress.

The second role for Congress is that of *overseer,* which we covered under the general response of Congress to Reagan's strategy and which focuses on the proper implementation of existing laws. As Morris Ogul observes, given the range of activity open to members of Congress, they do what they consider most important at the time and "oversight is frequently neglected." [32] During the 97th Congress, members perceived certain environmental issues such as hazardous waste to be sufficiently important, and presumably electorally useful due to publicity opportunities, that oversight was not neglected. The House felt strongly enough about its oversight role that it held the EPA administrator in contempt of Congress for refusing to turn over documents sought by two House panels. It registered protests through hearings to force the EPA to rescind some current regulations and to prevent new ones from coming into effect. Through riders on appropriations bills, the House forced Watt to reverse some of his decisions on wilderness leasing.

The third role is the textbook notion of Congress as an *initiator* of policies, either in the absence of presidential action or as an alternative to what the president offers. In most policy areas, Congress does not play a strong initiator role, although historically it has done so in the environmental arena. As previously noted, it was exceedingly difficult for the 97th Congress to play such a role with divided party control in Congress and a Republican president. Congressional Quarterly concludes that "the only significant new environmental legislation to clear the 97th Congress" was the 1982 Coastal Barrier Islands bill, which banned federal subsidies for the development of coastal barrier islands. [33] In the end the measure had the support of both the administration and environmental groups, but it had been formulated by Congress, specifically the House Banking Committee, in the absence of executive action. [34] The House Budget Committee also initiated policy in the formulation of its own 1981 budget resolution. Ultimately preempted on the floor of the House by the presidentially backed Gramm-Latta resolution, the House Budget Committee's resolution was the previously mentioned competing budget package that included more funding for environmental proposals than the administration's bill.

The fourth role for Congress is that of *partner,* in which it endorses presidential action with minimal change or accepts executive proposals after major revisions. The Senate's approval of presidential nominations, such as James Watt's, provides an example of the first type of partnership. Congressional reauthorization of the federal sewage treatment grant program in 1981 illustrates the more extensive partnership. The president initiated a proposal that cut spending on the program from $5 billion to $2.4 billion, and he insisted on a number of reforms. Congress reluctantly accepted the cut and many of his reforms, but the House and Senate differed from the president and from each other on how and where the remaining money would be spent. Reagan sought a halt of federal funds for future population growth, with less federal money for dozens of expanding Sun Belt sewer systems and more money for plants in urban Frost Belt cities. The House wanted to "grandfather in" Sun Belt projects already under way, while the Senate wanted to accept more administration cutbacks. A joint conference committee produced a compromise bill, accepted by Reagan, which gave him much that he wanted but phased the changes in more slowly and with less dramatic impact on Sun Belt construction.

Perhaps the most important example of the extensive partnership role was in the 1981 budget victory, which resulted in substantial cuts for environmental programs. In this battle the Senate endorsed the president's proposal with minimal revisions while the House voted for it after a divisive fight in which the Democratic budget alternative was rejected. Although the Democratic proposal lost, bipartisan cooperation in the House still resulted in the removal of a number of Watt's proposals in the administration's budget package. These included Watt's plans "to put a moratorium on land acquisitions for parks while using the money to upgrade existing parks, to eliminate funds for the independent Water Resources Council, and to reorganize the Office of Surface Mining." [35] Such bipartisan cooperation reflects congressional input into the partnership role.

The final role of Congress is *facilitator of interests.* Here neither Congress nor the president seizes the initiative, but Congress acts primarily as a representative body, reflecting the demands of special and public interests in a complex issue area. The endeavors of industrial lobbyists in petitioning the House Energy and Commerce Committee to retain federal noise standards exemplifies this role. President Reagan wanted the federal noise control program phased out by 1982 and held to this position despite objections from industry groups. The groups found a receptive audience in Congress, however, especially among House Energy and Commerce Committee Republicans. They argued that a uniform federal standard was necessary to avoid the probable chaos and confusion for the transportation carriers that would ensue from separate state regulations. The House played a facilitator role in voting to maintain the program, but the provision reauthorizing it was dropped in a conference committee due to lack of support from Senate conferees.

The Parameters Around Congress as a Policy Maker

We have focused thus far on general and specific congressional responses to Reagan's environmental strategy. To understand better why Congress focused more on defending the status quo and oversight than on initiation, partnership, or facilitation of interests, we need to examine the parameters or boundaries wherein Congress operates. These parameters present both constraints and opportunities to Congress as a policy maker. Among the parameters we examine are (1) the Constitution; (2) political culture and tradition; (3) political support; and (4) legislative structure.

The Constitution

The Constitution sketches the general framework for the operation of our system, with the details filled in by the Supreme Court and political experiences over time. Some of the general principles put forth in the document written nearly 200 years ago still have a strong impact on policy change today. One important principle is *separation of powers,* which Richard Neustadt correctly observes does not mean separate institutions with separate powers but really separate institutions with shared powers.[36] The lack of a clear demarcation of powers often results in conflict and protracted struggle. The exercise of prerogatives by Congress and the president often puts the two branches on a collision course. Louis Fisher notes that one such example is access to information.[37] This was the case in the 97th Congress when various committees seeking information from the executive branch on EPA's activities were rebuffed with the invocation of the doctrine of executive privilege. The battle culminated in a contempt of Congress citation for EPA head Anne Gorsuch.

Bicameralism, which divides legislative power between two chambers, is a constraint on policy initiation that makes it difficult for Congress to match the more unified power base of the executive, particularly when the two legislative chambers are controlled by different political parties. For policy to be enacted into law, an identical bill must pass both houses. On a number of occasions in 1982, the House passed legislation supported by environmental groups, only to see it die in the Senate. These bills ranged from a measure "to strengthen a major hazardous waste law to legislation protecting national parks from overuse and encroaching development." [38] The bicameral principle dispersing legislative power in two bodies hinders congressional policy making, except perhaps in those situations in which the same party controls both chambers by substantial margins. Even then, the more unified executive branch has the advantage. Although bicameralism is a constraint for a policy initiation role for Congress, it also provides an opportunity for Congress to defend the status quo or to conduct oversight. Each body can act separately to block the administration's budget or administrative actions and thereby play a major role in the policy process.

The *presidential veto* acts as a constraint on the policy-making capacity of Congress. The Constitution requires that bills passed by Congress and then vetoed by the president become law only if both Houses override the veto by a two-thirds vote. In the 97th Congress, President Reagan showed that he could block new environmental legislation he opposed. Three of his fifteen vetoes involved environmental and natural resource bills that designated Florida wilderness lands, settled a water rights claim by Arizona's Papago Indians, and set specific EPA research and development priorities. Given the extraordinary two-thirds majority vote needed to override Reagan, Congress did not even attempt to do so. Only the Papago bill survived, scaled down and repackaged with a reclamation water reform bill the administration wanted.[39]

Congress does have constitutional leverage in the *power of the purse,* its power and responsibility to appropriate money. This constitutional prerogative proved extremely important to the fate of environmental statutes in the 97th Congress. Reauthorization of five major environmental laws, including the Clean Air Act, came due in a sharply divided Congress, which ended up using its power of appropriations to keep all five laws on the books without revising any of them. Saved from termination by the power of the purse, the five laws were thus carried over as "unfinished business" onto the agenda of the 98th Congress.[40]

Political Culture and Tradition

Another parameter affecting the role Congress plays in policy making is the expectation that people have about its political leadership role compared with that of the president, who is expected to play *the* major role in the making of policy.[41] Media coverage, especially the scope of television coverage, tends to reinforce the importance of the presidency compared with Congress. The prominent media scholar Michael Robinson contends that "both the quality and quantity of national press coverage of Congress has hurt the Congress in its competitive relations with the Presidency."[42] Congress's policy-making attributes heighten this disadvantage. Roger Davidson and Walter Oleszek describe these attributes and note that congressional policies emphasize constituents' needs, particularly if they can be mapped geographically, rather than more comprehensive policy issues. Congress is reactive, and members tend to mirror prevailing public or elite opinion in their districts or states. Congress is oriented to the present and immediate past because of electoral pressures. Finally, these scholars observe that policy leadership of Congress also is restricted by policy making often more oriented toward appearance than substance.[43] In sum, neither public expectations nor congressional behavior underscores a strong role for Congress as an initiator of policy. Hence the president has a decisive edge as a policy innovator.

Political Support

Still another parameter affecting the policy-making role of Congress is the critical factor of political support. Successful policy making requires the support of the general public, elected officials, and prominent organized groups operating in the particular policy arena. These support factors are essential to both Congress and the president.

As the separate chapters in this volume by Robert Mitchell and Michael Kraft point out, the Reagan administration consistently has misread or minimized the strength of public opinion supporting tough environmental protection despite worries over unemployment and economic development. This support is continuous and widespread, and it cuts across all ages, regions, demographic and political groups.[44] More importantly, this support has been noticed by members of Congress and has provided backing for those members seeking to preserve or even improve the existing system of environmental protection. Polls in 1981 on the Clean Air Act by Louis Harris, for example, who presented his findings to House and Senate subcommittees, definitely influenced key members of Congress on the matter of revisions. Vermont Republican Stafford, influential chairman of the Senate Committee on Environment and Public Works, called one Harris survey "the most extraordinary poll I've ever read," as it found deep, widespread support for the Clean Air Act across all age and political groups.[45]

Public opinion support is not the only factor to consider, however, as those who seek change also must achieve accord among elected officials on the direction of change. Such cooperation is imperative in a system of separate institutions with shared powers but is difficult to attain in a Congress as divided as was the 97th. The Republicans controlled the Senate with a 53-47 margin in 1981 and a 54-46 one in 1982, while the Democrats controlled the House with a 243-192 edge. In this context the possibilities for congressional initiative were few and far between; the politically realistic scenario was one of advantage for the president in building congressional support for his environmental proposals. Crucial in this situation for the president was the retention of support for members of his own party in Congress.

Maintaining this partisan support for substantive environmental legislation is what President Reagan failed to do even in the Republican-controlled Senate. While winning spectacular victories on tax and budget issues based on a coalition of Republicans and conservative Democrats, he was unable to do the same on environmental issues. As noted previously, bipartisan congressional support prompted the removal of some of James Watt's proposals from the Gramm-Latta budget resolution; other of his proposals were defeated by substantial margins on the House floor. Some Republican House and Senate members were disturbed by Anne Gorsuch's record as EPA head and favored her resignation. Members also were critical of Reagan's strategy to accomplish as much change as possible by regulation rather than legislation. Republican Senator Stafford warned that two more years of "confrontation, shortcuts, and end runs" around Congress would not produce the policy results sought by the White House or business: "It will only mean more delays." [46] Congressional support would be even more difficult for the administration to obtain because the Democratic majority rose from 243 to 269 in the House after the 1982 elections. While the Republicans maintained their 54 to 46 edge in the Senate, several of the Republicans who were reelected in 1982 had close races and probably could prove to be more independent of the president than they were the previous session. This was particularly true of Republican senators Stafford and John H. Chafee of Rhode Island, two of the most influential senators·in the environmental area, who were reelected in part due to solid support from environmental groups in the form of campaign volunteers, media, and money.[47]

A final factor crucial to political support is the need to build support among those organized groups involved in the environmental policy arena. The administration had support from many business and industry groups to ease the laws and regulations on environmental protection. Many of these groups, however, have become disenchanted both with the administration's failure to achieve many of the changes they sought, and with the adverse publicity about the administration's mismanagement of environmental policy and the rise of new environmental problems. Now fearful "that Congress and the courts will swing the pendulum in exactly the opposite direction—toward new and more stringent controls to deal with the latest generation of environmental hazards," many of these groups were divided, as were administration strategists, on whether the president should adopt a more conciliatory approach to Congress and proenvironmental groups. Compromise was being urged by many.[48]

Legislative Structure

A final parameter affecting congressional policy making is legislative structure, including the bicameralism noted earlier. The legislative workload was apportioned among 22 standing or permanent committees with 139 subcommittees in the House and 16 committees with 102 subcommittees in the Senate for the 97th Congress.[49] This division leads to a piecemeal consideration of policies, a process reflecting a patchwork of committee and subcommittee jurisdictions that frequently lacks clarity. Congressional scholars often emphasize that this structure limits Congress's policy-making endeavors. Davidson and Oleszek remark that Congress "is decentralized, having few mechanisms for integrating or coordinating its policy decisions," [50] while Charles O. Jones observes that congressional committee reforms "appear to have dispersed policy influence and leadership without a clearly defined purpose in doing so." [51]

This decentralization, fragmentation, and dispersal of power within both the House and Senate also is reflected in the environmental policy arena. Table 5-2 presents information on the committee jurisdiction of major environmental statutes during the 97th Congress. Decentralization and fragmentation are evident, more so in the House than the Senate. Senate reforms in the 1970s reduced the number of standing committees and helped codify jurisdictional boundaries. Consequently, one Senate committee, Environment and Public Works, deals with most environmental legislation, although several other committees such as Energy and Natural Resources still play important roles depending on the issue. By contrast, environmental jurisdiction in the House is quite dispersed, with the Energy and Commerce Committee having more jurisdiction than most other committees. Our table is based on 15 major environmental statutes. If it included other legislation, even more committees would be involved in the formulation and legitimation of environmental policy. Davidson and Oleszek found that 12 of the 22 standing committees in the House have some environmental responsibilities.[52] An effort to consolidate House jurisdiction was made in the Bolling committee reform proposals in 1973-1974, but "environmental and consumer groups, fearing capture of the new committee by producer interests, rallied to defeat it." [53] Hence environmental jurisdiction remained dispersed and fragmented in 1983.

This fragmentation constrains Congress in its policy initiation and partnership roles. Yet it also could be viewed as an opportunity in its defender-of-the-status-quo and overseer roles. By creating a larger number of access points in the policy process, fragmentation makes dramatic change difficult to achieve while providing multiple opportunities for a forum to challenge those favoring change. Depending on one's perspective, then, the legislative structure can be viewed either as a constraint or an opportunity.

If one favors a more assertive Congress in its policy initiation or partnership role, the fragmentation and power dispersion must be overcome. One method Congress sometimes uses to overcome its structural limitations is to create an *ad hoc* (temporary) committee to deal with a particular problem. House Speaker Thomas P. O'Neill, Jr., D-Mass., used this technique successfully in 1977 when he set up an Ad Hoc Committee on Energy that sat in a review capacity over bills reported by regular standing committees. To avoid bitter jurisdictional controversies, the committee was composed of 40 members, including 5 committee and 15 subcommittee chairmen, and was balanced carefully with regard to party affiliation and geography.[54] Although the Speaker's experiment worked in 1977, it should not be viewed as a permanent solution to structural weakness, for members are not always receptive to the idea. In February 1983, for example, five House subcommittees were conducting their own investigations of allegations of mismanagement and wrongdoing at the EPA, with special attention to toxic waste dump cleanups under the 1980 Superfund law. Speaker O'Neill called in the chairmen of the five House panels to explore ways of avoiding duplication and coordinating their investigations. The chairmen declined to merge their efforts on grounds that, in Georgia Democrat Elliott H. Levitas's words, "there are enough problems at EPA and superfund to go around." [55] Although such a posture enhances the overseer role by increasing the capacity of members to criticize and get media attention, such behavior underscores the decentralization and fragmentation that constrain Congress's effectiveness as a policy initiator.

Floor Votes in the 97th Congress

No analysis of the role of Congress in environmental policy would be complete without some understanding of those factors critical to the policy success and failure on the floor of both chambers. Thus political scientists continually are interested in analyzing floor voting or roll calls. Such an analysis can clarify, for example, the degree of consensus or bipartisanship on

Table 5-2 Committee Jurisdiction over Environmental Statutes

Statute	*House Committee*	*Senate Committee*
Appropriations for EPA	Appropriations	Appropriations
Clean Air	Energy and Commerce	Environment and Public Works
Clean Water	Public Works and Transportation	Environment and Public Works
Coastal Zone Management	Merchant Marine and Fisheries	Commerce, Science, and Transportation
Endangered Species	Merchant Marine and Fisheries	Environment and Public Works
Environmental Research, Development, and Demonstration Authorization	Science and Technology	Environment and Public Works
Federal Insecticide, Fungicide, and Rodenticide	Agriculture	Agriculture, Nutrition, and Forestry
National Environmental Policy	Merchant Marine and Fisheries	Environment and Public Works
Noise Control	Energy and Commerce; Public Works and Transportation	Environment and Public Works
Ocean Dumping	Merchant Marine and Fisheries	Environment and Public Works
Safe Drinking Water	Energy and Commerce	Environment and Public Works
Solid Waste Disposal	Energy and Commerce	Environment and Public Works
Superfund (1980)	Energy and Commerce	Environment and Public Works
Surface Mining Control	Interior and Insular Affairs	Energy and Natural Resources
Toxic Substances Control	Energy and Commerce	Environment and Public Works; Commerce, Science, and Transportation

issues in a given policy arena such as the environment. The clarification takes place through the systematic analysis of the bases of congressional support for, and opposition to, legislation. If one is interested in the current success or failure and future implications for environmental legislation, some knowledge of floor voting is essential. We therefore examine patterns of environmental support in the House and Senate during the 97th Congress.

Although important environmental issues such as revisions in the Clean Air and Clean Water acts never reached the House or Senate floor during the 97th Congress, other environmental matters did. To identify these issues, we draw upon the publications of the League of Conservation Voters (LCV), an environmental organization noted for its careful and comprehensive assessment of congressional voting records on environmental issues.[56] From these sources, we find that there were 38 House and 29 Senate votes on environmental issues out of total votes in the respective houses of 924 and 836 in the 1981-1982 session.[57] These votes encompass a wide range of environmentally related matters from budget cuts and water projects to hazardous waste and nuclear power. A vote on the basing mode of the MX missile, for example, is viewed as an environmental as well as a defense issue because it involves massive withdrawals of land, growth of boom towns, drains on an area's water resources, and adverse effects on traditional rural life styles.

Also, the issues voted on in the House and the Senate are never entirely comparable. Some matters make it to the floor of one chamber and not the other. Even if the two chambers vote on the same issue, the form and content of the respective bills can vary significantly.

Our intent is to assess the pattern of support in House and Senate voting on environmentally related bills by focusing on factors found to be important in previous research. These are partisanship, ideology, region, and constituency. Our emphasis here is on the substantive findings, as we have discussed the methodology employed in greater detail elsewhere in our earlier studies.[58]

What we seek to explain is the level of environmental support, measured by the proenvironment scores on those bills judged by the League of Conservation Voters as the best indicators of environmental commitment among lawmakers. An overall 97th Congress score was computed for each member in each chamber by averaging his or her 1981 and 1982 LCV ratings. Based on this score, the environmental commitment of each House and Senate member also was classified into high (71-100), medium (31-70), and low categories (0-30).

Overall, the results are consistent and replicate patterns of environmental support found in previous research. The single most important variable in explaining environmental support is ideology, and it is equally important for both the House and Senate. A member's philosophical orientation on a range of policy issues (measured by the conservative coalition support ratio) best explains his or her floor vote, with liberals most supportive of environmental legislation, conservatives least supportive, and moderates in between. Although ideology is strongly related to party affiliation, as most liberals are disproportionately Democrats and most conservatives Republican, it is not a perfect relation because the Democratic party includes many southern Democrats who are conservative. Also, the Republican party includes a number of moderates and a few liberals.

Partisanship or party affiliation also is an important variable. The parties frequently oppose one another on environmental issues in floor voting. In the 97th Congress, for example, a majority of Republicans opposed a majority of Democrats on two-thirds of the House environmental votes (26 of 38) and on nearly seven-tenths of the Senate environmental votes (20 of 29). In the House partisan votes, Democrats favored the position of environmental groups on 24 of the 26 votes, and in the Senate the Democrats supported the environmental view on 18 of 20 partisan environmental votes.

Examining the average roll-call support percentage by party categories on environmental issues also is revealing. The average environmental roll-call support percentage for all members of the House is 54 percent, for Republicans 34 percent, and for Democrats 69 percent. If one subdivides the Democrats into northern Democrats and southern Democrats, the support percentages are 80 percent and 46 percent respectively. Thus northern Democrats are strongest in their environmental support and are followed by southern Democrats and finally Republicans. The same pattern exists for the Senate. The average environmental roll-call support percentage is 44 percent for all members, 30 percent for Republicans, and 61 percent for Democrats. Subdividing the Democrats, the northern Democratic average is 71 percent and the southern Democratic is 40 percent. Partisanship clearly plays a role in floor voting.

Findings on partisanship on floor voting should be put in a broader perspective, as bipartisanship on environmental issues exists in many areas. Most of the major and most significant environmental statutes such as the Clean Air Act or Clean Water Act were passed with decisive majorities of both Democrats and Republicans voting for them.[59] Membership and financial support for environmental organizations also are bipartisan. A 1983 Harris poll, for example, showed that a slightly larger proportion of Republicans (13 percent) than Democrats (10 percent) claim membership in one or another environmental group and that the pattern holds for financial support.[60] Finally, the legislative success of environmental legislation depends on the support of key committee members from both parties, even though a partisan division may later appear on the floor. Thus Republican senators such as Stafford and Chafee, and Republican House members such as James Jeffords of Vermont, Cooper Evans of Iowa, David Emery of Maine, and others played critical committee roles in supporting environmental legislation during the 97th Congress.[61] Although much bipartisanship on environmental issues exists, our analysis of floor votes reaffirms that considerable partisanship spanning a range of environmental issues also exists.

Table 5-3 provides data on levels of environmental support, and it is based on the voting records of individual members across issues and not on average roll-call support percentages. Although the findings of these two methods of calculation are similar in substance, the actual percentage results sometimes differ by a percentage point or two. As can be seen, the national scores suggest medium levels of environmental support, with the Senate lower than the House. In both the House and Senate the East is the region most supportive of environmental issues, while the South is the least supportive. Using party/region combinations, House Democrats in the East, Midwest, and West virtually tie for high environmental support, while the South scores the lowest. Republican members in the East record the highest level of environmental support while those in the West and South are least support-ive. For the Senate, Democrats and Republicans in the East score highest among their party groupings while Democrats and Republicans in the South have the lowest party-based environmental support scores.

Finally, we looked at constituency characteristics in the House, but found a less significant pattern that was strongly influenced by the fact that urban districts tend to be both more Democratic and more liberal. Our analysis shows that high levels of environmental support are accorded to 54 percent of urban, 33 percent of suburban, 16 percent of rural, and 23 percent of mixed districts. Low levels of support are registered by 13 percent of urban, 24 percent of suburban, 40 percent of rural, and 31 percent of mixed districts. Urban districts are clearly the most supportive and rural districts the least supportive of environmental issues.

In short, ideology, party affiliation, region, and constituency all are important factors affecting environmental support on floor votes in both the House and Senate. Because the 1982 election results produced a 98th Congress that was more Democratic in the House and somewhat less conservative in both chambers, it appears that floor votes in the newer Congress should reflect more support for environmental issues.

The 98th Congress and the Beginning of Change

Because of Republican losses in the 1982 elections, the 98th Congress began in January 1983 with 269 House Democrats, an increase of 26 over the 97th, while the Senate division remained 54 to 46 with the majority Republican. Despite the electoral setbacks, the administration showed few initial signs of policy retreat either in its administrative or legislative strategy. Congress was more aggressive, however, particularly the Democratic House.

The Reagan administrative strategy received a serious setback as the furor over EPA mismanagement was pursued aggressively by House Demo-crats and culminated in the March 1983 resignation of EPA Administrator Burford (formerly Gorsuch). Among White House officials, "the Burford affair was seen as harmful to Reagan's reelection chances and weakening his leadership posture," and "the selection of Ruckelshaus was a major effort at damage control." [62] It is clear that William D. Ruckelshaus, the new EPA chief, favors compromise and conciliation over the confrontational tactics of Gorsuch and Watt. It is even more remarkable that Ruckelshaus publicly stated in July 1983 that the Reagan administration had misread initially its mandate from the public on environmental laws.[63] How effective Ruckelshaus will be in repairing the distrust between Congress and the

Table 5-3   League of Conservation Voters Environmental Support Scores in the House and Senate for the 97th Congress (1981-1983): Mean Percentages by Nation, Region, and Party

Category	House LCV %	House N	Senate LCV %	Senate N
National	52	434	43	100
East	67	116	65	24
South	36	121	28	26
Midwest	56	121	47	24
West	48	76	35	26
Democrats	67	242	60	46
Republicans	33	192	29	54
Democrats East	79	66	82	12
Democrats South	43	79	39	15
Democrats Midwest	79	58	65	10
Democrats West	76	39	60	9
Republicans East	50	50	48	12
Republicans South	21	42	14	11
Republicans Midwest	35	63	33	14
Republicans West	20	37	22	17

executive branch in the end will depend on how much support he has from President Reagan. Although the environmental outlook appears more positive at EPA, an assessment of how far the Reagan administration has changed also will depend on the administrative behavior of William P. Clark, Watt's successor as secretary of interior.

Reagan's legislative strategy still remains an indirect one, with heavy emphasis on budget cuts. The 98th Congress began with a Reagan budget proposal that called for a further 9 percent cut in the EPA's operating budget. The administration also requested another 25 percent cut in financial and technical support for state environmental programs, with the largest cuts in grants to the states to protect water quality.[64] This strategy too received a setback, as both the House and Senate resisted further environmental cuts. As of summer 1983, the administration began to make concessions and retreated from its earlier budget position. This was most evident in the budget battle, when on June 13 President Reagan had a letter sent to Republican senator Jake Garn of Utah confirming that he approved Ruckelshaus's recommendation to add $165.5 million to EPA's 1984 operating budget and $100 million to the Superfund to clean up hazardous waste sites. On June 21 the Senate adopted the revised administration budget and thus avoided slashing the EPA budget for the third consecutive year.[65]

The House was more aggressive in the summer of 1983. Earlier, on June 2, in a highly unusual move, it chose to overrule its own Appropriations

Committee "and voted to give EPA $353 million more than the administration had requested and $222 million more than the committee sought." The vote was 200-167, with 36 Republicans voting affirmative, to boost EPA to $1.3 billion, just $49 million less than its 1981 level.[66] Three years had passed, however, during which the agency had acquired increased responsibilities in the areas of toxic substances and hazardous waste management while its purchasing power had been reduced. Thus the House action, a challenge to Reagan, may not turn out to be enough to make up lost ground in the area of environmental protection.

Generally, the 98th Congress, bolstered by the addition of 26 House Democrats, has been more assertive in its battle with President Reagan over the environment. Vigorous administrative oversight, a stronger partnership role on budget allocations for environmental programs, and a strong commitment to defending the status quo with respect to environmental protection are thus far the predominant characteristics of congressional behavior during the 98th Congress. More effective opposition to Reagan's administrative and legislative strategies has slowed if not halted the administration's environmental policy momentum and has marked what appears to be the beginnings of change.

Congress and the Future

The Reagan administration has pursued a dual administrative and legislative strategy in seeking environmental policy change. Congress, particularly the Democratic House, has opposed the former by oversight and the latter by seeking a more extensive partnership role in budget decisions. While achieving many oversight victories, including the forced resignation of the head of EPA, Congress simply could not oversee all administrative and regulatory behavior given its other duties. Although Congress did mitigate environmental budget cuts in 1982 for fiscal 1983 and more recently restored some of the earlier budget cuts for fiscal 1984, it could not prevent the deep cuts enacted in Reagan's first year. A Republican-controlled Senate and the support of both Republicans and southern Democrats in the House provided the necessary margin for the president's budget victory, and the subsequent cuts in environmental protection programs.

Congress plays various policy roles in environmental politics, including defender of the status quo, overseer, initiator, partner, and facilitator of interests. Of these roles, Congress seems best at defending the status quo and conducting oversight and weakest at initiating policy change. Certain parameters affect why Congress plays the roles it does, and these include the Constitution, political culture and tradition, political support, and legislative structure. Although these parameters seem to make it difficult for Congress to initiate policy change, the very same parameters appear to enhance Congress's opportunity to defend the status quo and conduct oversight, particularly in a setting of divided partisan control. Congress was a strong initiator in previous years when the same party, the Democrats, controlled both chambers by decisive majorities. Given the current political setting, it appears unavoidable that Congress has turned toward its roles of defender of the status quo and overseer.

Floor voting is important and it is characterized by clear partisan differences in both chambers with the Democrats consistently more proenvironment than Republicans. The most significant factor in environmental support is ideology, but partisanship, region, and constituency factors also are important.

Reagan's environmental strategy has thus far received serious setbacks in the 98th Congress, with respect both to administrative policy (removal of Burford) and to the budget. Policy changes in the future (for example, the 99th Congress in 1985-1987) will be influenced strongly by the 1984 election outcomes. Prominent Republican senators such as Howard H. Baker, Jr., of Tennessee and John Tower of Texas are retiring, and more Republican incumbents face election than do Democratic incumbents. The possibility exists that the Democrats again will control the Senate and pick up a few more seats in the House. Should this occur, our research suggests that some reversal of Reagan's policies would occur and that the change would be in the direction of stronger environmental protection policies. Serious problems would remain, however, concerning what policy initiation to pursue and how to change the status quo.

The duration of the 98th Congress likely will continue to be characterized by a struggle between the Congress and the president over the environment. There is little doubt that the Ruckelshaus appointment and the replacement of Watt by Clark at Interior have minimized political damage at the symbolic and stylistic level and that Reagan's budgeting concession was welcome on Capitol Hill. How all these factors finally are weighed will make environmental policy making in the 98th Congress interesting to watch. One thing is certain—style alone will not be enough for the president to triumph over the Congress in the struggle over environmental policy.

Notes

1. Lawrence Mosher, "Talking Clean on the Hustings," *National Journal*, November 1, 1980, 1850.
2. Hedrick Smith, "The President as Coalition Builder: Reagan's First Year," in *Rethinking the Presidency*, ed. Thomas E. Cronin (Boston: Little, Brown, 1982), 277.
3. Norman J. Ornstein, "Assessing Reagan's First Year," in *President and Congress: Assessing Reagan's First Year*, ed. Norman J. Ornstein (Washington, D.C.: American Enterprise Institute, 1982), 89.
4. *Congressional Quarterly Weekly Report,* December 19, 1981, 2505-2524; Ibid., December 31, 1982, 3143-3157.
5. Congressional Quarterly, *Budgeting for America* (Washington, D.C.: Congressional Quarterly, 1982), 131.
6. "First FY 1982 Budget Resolution," Democratic Study Group *Fact Sheet*, April 24, 1981, 22.
7. Smith, "The President," 277.

8. "Congress Works a Minor Revolution — Making Cuts to Meet its Budget Goals," *National Journal,* June 20, 1981, 1123-1124.

9. Joseph A. Davis, "Environment," *Congressional Quarterly Almanac 1982,* vol. 38 (Washington, D.C.: Congressional Quarterly, 1983), 423.

10. Ibid.

11. Ibid.

12. Ibid.

13. Ibid.

14. Joseph A. Davis, "EPA, States Differ in Views of Environmental Federalism," *Congressional Quarterly Weekly Report,* November 27, 1982, 2915.

15. Kathy Koch, "Environment," *Congressional Quarterly Almanac 1981,* vol. 37 (Washington, D.C.: Congressional Quarterly, 1982), 503.

16. Davis, "Environment," 424.

17. Lawrence Mosher, "Tough Issues, Tough Style Could Lead to a Backlash Against Watt," *National Journal,* December 5, 1981, 2144-2148; and "Environmentalists More of a Political Force," *Business Week,* January 24, 1983, 85-86.

18. Henry C. Kenski and Michael Bowers, "The View From Capitol Hill," in *Energy and the Western States: Politics and Development,* ed. James L. Regens, Robert W. Rycroft, and Gregory A. Daneke (New York: Praeger, 1982), 175-179.

19. Koch, "Environment," 504.

20. Steven R. Weisman, "Reagan, Assailing Critics, Defends His Environment Policy as 'Sound,'" *New York Times,* June 12, 1983.

21. Koch, "Environment," 503.

22. Davis, "Environment," 424.

23. Ibid.

24. Richard E. Cohen, "The Gorsuch Affair," *National Journal,* January 8, 1983, 80.

25. *Congressional Quarterly Weekly Report,* December 18, 1982, 3077.

26. S. Huntley, with R. A. Taylor, J. P. Shapiro, and S. Fritz, "After Burford — What Next for EPA?" *U.S. News & World Report,* March 21, 1983, 25-26.

27. Hedrick Smith, "Reagan's EPA Retreat," *New York Times,* March 10, 1983, 1 and 11.

28. Davis, "Environment," 424.

29. Joseph A. Davis, "EPA and Congress at Odds over Budget Policy Issues," *Congressional Quarterly Weekly Report,* July 31, 1983, 1828 and 1830.

30. Charles O. Jones, "Congress and the Making of Energy Policy," in *New Dimensions to Energy Policy,* ed. Robert Lawrence (Lexington, Mass.: Lexington Books, 1979), 161-178.

31. The environmental policy examples cited in this section come from the *Congressional Quarterly Almanac* for 1981 and 1982 and from various issues of *Congressional Quarterly Weekly Report,* but particularly the summaries in December 19, 1981, 2513-2514, and December 31, 1982, 3151-3152.

32. Morris S. Ogul, "Congressional Oversight: Structures and Incentives," in *Congress Reconsidered,* 2d ed., ed. Lawrence C. Dodd and Bruce I. Oppenheimer (Washington, D.C.: CQ Press, 1981), 327.

33. *Congressional Quarterly Weekly Report,* December 31, 1982, 3151.

34. Joanne Omang, "Environmental Clashes Loom in Budget Bill," *Washington Post,* June 16, 1981.

35. Koch, "Environment," 503.

36. Richard E. Neustadt, *Presidential Power: The Politics of Leadership from FDR*

to *Carter* (New York: John Wiley, 1980), 26-27.

37. Louis Fisher, *The Politics of Shared Power: Congress and the Executive* (Washington, D.C.: CQ Press, 1981), 14-15.
38. Davis, "Environment," 423.
39. Ibid.
40. Ibid.; and Koch, "Environment," 503.
41. William J. Keefe, *Congress and the American People* (Englewood Cliffs, N.J.: Prentice-Hall, 1980), 108; Charles O. Jones, "Congress and the Presidency," in *The New Congress*, ed. Thomas E. Mann and Norman J. Ornstein (Washington, D.C.: American Enterprise Institute, 1981), 224-225; and Stephen J. Wayne, "Great Expectations: What People Want from Presidents," in *Rethinking the Presidency*, 185-199.
42. Michael J. Robinson, "Three Faces of Congressional Media," in *The New Congress*, 92.
43. Roger H. Davidson and Walter J. Oleszek, *Congress and Its Members* (Washington, D.C.: CQ Press, 1981), 427-428.
44. See, for example, Lou Cannon, *Reagan* (New York: G. P. Putnam's Sons, 1982), 363-364; "Environment," *Congressional Quarterly Almanac 1981,* 512; and "Business Week/Harris Poll," *Business Week,* January 24, 1983, 87.
45. *Congressional Quarterly Almanac 1981,* "Environment," 512.
46. Andy Pasztor, "Reagan Goal of Easing Environmental Laws Is Largely Unattained," *Wall Street Journal,* February 18, 1983, 15.
47. Dale Russakoff, "Getting Out the Green Vote," *Today,* October 29, 1982, 5.
48. Pasztor, "Reagan Goal," 15.
49. Davidson and Oleszek, *Congress and Its Members,* 206-207.
50. Ibid., 427.
51. Jones, "Congress and the Presidency," 241.
52. Davidson and Oleszek, *Congress and Its Members,* 217-218.
53. James L. Sundquist, *The Decline and Resurgence of Congress* (Washington, D.C.: Brookings, 1981), 431.
54. David J. Vogler, "Ad Hoc Committees in the House of Representatives and Purposive Models of Legislative Behavior," *Polity* 14 (Fall 1981): 89-109.
55. Joseph A. Davis, "House Subcommittees Begin Reviewing EPA Documents; Two More Officials Are Fired," *Congressional Quarterly Weekly Report,* February 26, 1983, 412.
56. League of Conservation Voters, *How Congress Voted on Energy and the Environment: 1981 Voting Chart* (Washington, D.C.: League of Conservation Voters, 1982); *How Congress Voted on Energy and the Environment: 1982 Voting Chart* (Washington, D.C.: League of Conservation Voters, 1983).
57. For total floor votes see the *Congressional Almanac* for 1981 and 1982.
58. For a more detailed explanation of the methodology, see Henry C. Kenski and Margaret C. Kenski, "Partisanship, Ideology, and Constituency Differences on Environmental Issues in the U.S. House of Representatives," *Policy Studies Journal* 9 (Winter 1980): 325-335; "Partisanship, Ideology and Constituency Differences on Environmental Issues in the U.S. House of Representatives and Senate: 1973-78," in *Environmental Policy Formation*, ed. Dean E. Mann (Lexington, Mass.: D. C. Heath, 1981), 87-102.
59. Douglas M. Costle, "Environmental Regulation and Regulatory Reform," *Washington Law Review* 57 (July 1982): 410.
60. "Business Week/Harris Poll," 87.
61. League of Conservation Voters, *Election Report 1982* (Washington, D.C.:

League of Conservation Voters, 1983), 6-7.

62. Dick Kirschten, "Ruckelshaus May Find EPA's Problems Are Budgetary As Much As Political," *National Journal*, March 26, 1983, 660.

63. Philip Shabecoff, "Ruckelshaus Says Administration Misread Mandate on Environment," *New York Times,* July 27, 1983.

64. "Reagan's Major Budget Proposals for Fiscal 1984," *Wall Street Journal,* January 31, 1983, 5.

65. Lawrence Mosher, "Ruckelshaus's First Mark on EPA — Another $165.5 Million for Its Budget," *National Journal,* June 25, 1983, 1344.

66. Ibid.

6. THE BUDGETARY PROCESS AND ENVIRONMENTAL POLICY

Robert V. Bartlett

Budget is policy.

No American president before Ronald Reagan ever began his term of office evincing greater appreciation for the strategic significance of this aphorism. No previous administration ever came into power more determined or better prepared to achieve substantial domestic policy change through the budgetary process. And after 30 months in office, few previous administrations could point to more success in the accomplishment of their domestic policy objectives. In the case of the Reagan presidency, unlike those of, say, Franklin D. Roosevelt or Lyndon B. Johnson, policy objectives were accomplished *without* persuading Congress to adopt major new substantive legislation. Rather, the Reagan approach was to exploit fully the range of executive and administrative powers available to the president, including those of personnel management, administrative rule making and enforcement, and reorganization. Occupying a prominent place in the Reagan strategy was the budgetary process, both executive and legislative. By drastically reducing the funds available for many domestic programs, the Reagan administration sought not only to control overall spending but also to achieve sweeping policy changes.

The initial budget agenda of the Reagan administration was extraordinarily broad and cut across nearly all policy areas—including education, labor, social services, transportation, intergovernmental aid, housing, health, and income support. But Reagan's departures from previous budgetary patterns and trends were nowhere more dramatic than for the group of programs typically labeled "environmental policy." Few environmental programs, whether for conservation of resources, construction of pollution control facilities, demonstration of technologies, acquisition and management of land, or regulation of environmentally harmful activities, escaped the Reagan budgetary scalpel (or meat axe). Although a few concessions were made in 1983 in the aftermath of an Environmental Protection Agency (EPA) scandal, many changes in environmental policy obtained by the Reagan administration through the budgetary process were profound and could not be reversed easily. Some changes in funding for research and development, for example, likely would have lasting consequences, leaving environmental programs and regulations in future decades still vulnerable to a criticism frequently leveled by Reagan partisans—that such programs and regulations lack an adequate scientific foundation and justification.

Budgets are simultaneously, among other things, tools of macroeconomic policy, means for establishing the priorities of government, and instruments for influencing the execution of particular laws and programs. All three of these dimensions of budgetary impact were stressed by the incoming Reagan administration, and all three must be kept in mind in any fair assessment of Reagan administration budgets for environmental quality and natural resources.

Inflation was a major issue in the 1980 election campaign, and without question it was a serious problem with widely ramifying negative consequences. President Reagan promised to bring inflation under control, in part by balancing the federal budget and thus dampening the stimulative effect of greater government spending. At the same time Reagan sought to spur economic activity through enactment of massive tax cuts, cuts that would have future spending implications.

But neither the proposed spending reductions nor the tax cuts were strictly macroeconomic policies in intent or in effect. President Reagan and his advisers also were strongly committed to reducing the level (or at least the rate of growth) of federal expenditures as a matter of political principle, if not of economic necessity. Beyond the emphasis on spending restraint, the Reagan administration was dedicated to achieving a substantial reordering of federal priorities as reflected in the budget. Most notably, Reagan sought to dramatically increase military expenditures, both in terms of real (inflation-adjusted) dollars and as a proportion of the total budget. Much of the nondefense budget—which included programs that ran against the grain of Reagan's conservative-libertarian ideology, programs Reagan thought more appropriately administered at other levels of government, and programs toward which he was relatively indifferent—naturally would have a low priority in Reagan administration budgets.

Unquestionably, both the defense and nondefense portions of the budget included funding for some programs of dubious or marginal merit. The budgetary process provides an opportunity to improve administration through improved efficiencies, anticipation and prevention, decreased waste, innovation, and the shifting of resources toward more critical problems and more successful approaches. Improved management is promised routinely by all presidential candidates, Ronald Reagan no less than others. And whether admitted or recognized, administration always offers opportunity for pursuit of political objectives. For the Reagan administration, improved management did not mean merely or even primarily greater efficiency and effectiveness in administering existing laws, agencies, and programs; rather, improved management meant above all else achieving the objectives of regulatory relief and smaller government.

Indeed, from whatever perspective one views the budgetary process, environmental agencies and programs were unlikely to be awash in budgetary resources in the 1980s, regardless of who was president. In a decade of budgets perennially in deficit, so-called uncontrollable spending (outlays for entitlement programs, interest on debt, and other obligations that are not controlled by the annual appropriations process) had risen by 1981 to account for three-fourths of the total budget. Under policies initiated by President Jimmy Carter, growth of defense spending in real dollars was scheduled to continue into the 1980s. Sluggish performance of the economy for several years had contributed to slow revenue growth and budgetary stringency. Moreover, as political scientists John L. Palmer and Isabel V. Sawhill note, any president taking office in 1981 would have had to respond to the public's concerns about the economy, national security, the growth of spending and taxes, and the ability of government to solve problems.[1]

This, then, was the context in which the Reagan administration began its budget-making efforts; these are the perspectives that ought to be kept in mind while assessing the impact of Reagan budgets on environmental policy and while seeking an answer to the question, is government "being administered in ways that are consistent with long-term excellence?"[2]

The Reagan Administration Program and Strategy

The foremost characteristic of the Reagan administration, contributing greatly to its success in making policy through the budgetary process, was its reliance on strategic planning and coordinated tactics to implement a predetermined agenda.[3] Unlike most previous administrations, the Reagan administration began its first day in office with a set of detailed and ideologically guided policy objectives and a relatively well developed and sophisticated strategy for accomplishing many of its objectives *(see chapters 2 and 4)*.

Ronald Reagan and his advisers adopted a strategy for domestic affairs that emphasized the administrative presidency (an approach that had been planned for Richard Nixon's second term but had been aborted because of the Watergate scandal) complemented by a selective, focused, well-coordinated legislative strategy.[4] Key to *both* the legislative strategy and the administrative strategy was the budgetary process.[5] A bold legislative program would be pursued through the congressional budget process, while the administrative powers inherent in the executive budgeting process would be used simultaneously to reduce the size and reach of government, to control the bureaucracy, and to achieve further substantive policy change. Early in the Reagan presidency, Secretary of the Interior James G. Watt declared, "We will use the budget system to be the excuse to make major policy decisions."[6] Large budget cuts in the nondefense budget were crucial to several broad goals. "The intended impact on public policy was to be greater than the sum of the parts: to reduce the scope of government, to reduce the governmental interference on the economy, to reduce reliance of individuals on the government."[7]

In this regard, perhaps no single action of Ronald Reagan before inauguration was more propitious for the early success of his administration than the appointment of David A. Stockman as director of the Office of Management and Budget (OMB). Stockman proved to be a master of bureaucratic detail. Moreover, his ideological commitment to retrenchment in the ends, size, and range of government activity matched that of Reagan himself. In a memorandum drafted before his appointment as OMB director, Stockman stressed the importance of early and resolute action by the new administration.[8] Because he and his staff and associates were able quickly to compile a detailed budget-cut package with justifications, the new administration was able to "hit the ground running." Stockman played a dominant role in forging the domestic program that would be enacted through the congressional budgetary process in 1981; in reality it was Stockman's program, developed in the context of broad goals and constraints established by the president.

Reagan had set as a goal of his administration substantial change in the direction of several long-term budgetary trends, notably rapid growth of total federal spending and slow or no growth of defense outlays. Total federal outlays adjusted for inflation had increased dramatically in recent decades, with entitlement programs accounting for much of that growth. Similarly, total federal outlays had expanded as a percentage of the gross national product. But in the quest to reduce by billions of dollars a proposed Carter administration budget of $740 billion, Stockman and his staff were limited to proposing cuts in only a fraction of the overall budget. In the 1981 fiscal year, which had begun on October 1, 1980, most federal outlays were for programs that could not be cut for various reasons. Twenty-four percent was budgeted for national defense, a proportion Reagan was committed to increase, ten percent for interest on the national debt, and thirty-three percent for "social contract entitlements"—Social Security, Medicaid, Medicare, and unemployment insurance. Thirteen percent of outlays supported other entitlements such as revenue sharing, veterans' benefits, guaranteed student loans, federal employee pensions, subsidized housing, food and nutrition assistance, Supplemental Security Income, and Aid to Families with Dependent Children. Only twenty percent of outlays consisted of spending on "other nondefense" programs—a category that included most of the regulatory and traditional service delivery activities of the federal government. For political reasons, many "other nondefense" programs were much more vulnerable to an aggressive budget-cutting effort than were most entitlement programs.[9]

With interest payments off limits, the defense budget slated for large increases, and many entitlement programs too entrenched politically to be touched, the huge spending cuts sought by Reagan and Stockman would have to be borne disproportionately by the other nondefense category. "Stockman's tactic, as he privately described it, was not to shear flocks of sheep, as would be inevitable with broad Social Security cuts, but to cull goats from the herd—

goats whose shearing would be more politically acceptable." [10] Large and well-publicized cuts would be made in some entitlement programs, such as housing assistance, food stamps, student loans, and Aid to Families with Dependent Children, but many more of the Stockman-Reagan "goats" would come from the other nondefense category. Reagan conservatives had objected strenuously to many of these programs before coming to power. The severe cuts proposed and subsequently enacted for many agencies thus had significance transcending the relatively modest impact on the size of the total budget.

Particularly hard hit were regulatory and environmental programs. Many environmental, health, and safety regulatory programs had been excoriated by Reagan partisans as being economically unreasonable and based on a weak scientific foundation, thereby imposing unjustifiable costs on business and consumers and unnecessarily discouraging desirable economic activity *(see Chapter 8)*. Murray Weidenbaum, Reagan's first chairman of the Council of Economic Advisers, had frequently criticized governmental regulation as a cause of inflation and reduced productivity. Weidenbaum had estimated the total annual cost of federal regulation to exceed $100 billion in 1979, a figure Reagan referred to in his first economic speech as president.[11] Before his appointment as OMB director, David Stockman had estimated that compliance costs for *new* environmental, safety, and energy regulations scheduled for the 1980s would exceed $100 billion.[12] A few weeks after Reagan's inauguration, the new OMB Office of Information and Regulatory Affairs estimated that federal environmental regulations would cost the economy a total of $500 billion in the decade of the 1980s.[13] One way to reduce the "regulatory burden" generated by environmental programs was to incapacitate them through drastic budget cuts.

Congress and the Budget, 1981-1983

The first-year legislative budget strategy decided upon by Stockman, Reagan, and Republican congressional leaders involved packaging the administration's requested budget cuts in an omnibus reconciliation bill and forcing Congress to vote on a single measure. Because impoundment as had been practiced by Richard Nixon was prohibited explicitly by the 1974 Congressional Budget and Impoundment Control Act, the Reagan administration needed congressional acquiescence to obtain budget reductions of any size. It is ironic that, in his efforts to obtain congressional approval of his budget proposals, Reagan was able to use to his distinct advantage provisions of the 1974 act, a law intended to enhance congressional control over the budget and to restrict presidential budgetary policy making.

Provisions of the 1974 law had established House and Senate budget committees and had superimposed a congressional budget review process on top of the annual congressional appropriations process. Both houses of Congress were directed to adopt each year budget resolutions setting spending, taxing, and borrowing goals, broken down by functional categories such as defense, transportation, and education. In conjunction with these resolutions, Congress could pass reconciliation instructions directing both appropriations and authorization committees to recommend changes to reduce spending or increase revenues by specific amounts. Then a single reconciliation bill could be adopted to implement measures necessary for conformity with binding totals in a second budget resolution.[14] Rather than voting on each individual cut, a situation in which committee politics and interest group pressures would favor spending, under the reconciliation procedure a package of cuts would be considered together in one bill. Opponents of particular cuts could cast only an up-or-down vote for the entire package. Political pressures for reduced spending would not be dissipated but would be focused on a single vote in each chamber, a vote to support the president or oppose him. Moreover, and perhaps more significant, reconciliation also could serve as a means for forcing action to revise authorizing laws having budgetary consequences. Thus, the reconciliation procedure provided an opportunity to deal with an extraordinary amount of substantive legislation in a single process, under severe deadlines.

The reconciliation procedure never had been used before 1980. But building on precedents established the previous year, the Reagan administration in 1981 skillfully used reconciliation to enact a sweeping legislative program through the budgetary process.[15] In his revision of the 1982 budget, submitted in March, President Reagan proposed cuts in the Carter budget of $44 billion in outlays and $37.5 billion in budget authority. In April the Republican-controlled Senate passed reconciliation instructions ordering 14 Senate committees to cut outlays by $36.4 billion. In the House, a similar Reagan-backed substitute resolution was approved in May. After authorization and appropriations committees reported measures making the required cuts and policy changes, Congress approved a reconciliation bill in July that cut $35.1 billion in outlays from the fiscal 1982 budget. The Reagan administration received nearly all of what it had asked for, including changes in the basic authorizing legislation for many programs. Indeed, Congress went beyond the original Reagan proposals in several respects, cutting budget authority by $57.9 billion. Far-reaching substantial policy changes in more than 200 programs were accomplished in a single vote on a single bill.

However notable its initial budget achievements, both administrative and legislative, the administration did not relent. In September 1981, even before the previous budget cuts had taken effect, President Reagan asked for further reductions of 12 percent in nonentitlement, nondefense programs, for a projected savings of $8.4 billion. Eventually Congress approved additional domestic spending cuts totaling $4 billion.

The first executive budget produced from the ground up by the Reagan administration was poorly received when sent to Congress in February 1982. A deep recession, combined with the budgetary effects of the enacted tax cuts and the accelerated defense buildup, left an estimated deficit of $91.5 billion in the fiscal 1983 budget proposed by Reagan—even with further drastic and probably unrealistic cuts proposed for many domestic programs. Without these additional cuts, OMB projections (based on highly optimistic assumptions) showed growing deficits in future years. Following widespread criticism by senators and representatives of both parties, Congress took the lead in drafting its own budget resolution, which Reagan later endorsed. While changing many priorities, Congress through its budget reconciliation process nevertheless made additional cuts in discretionary nondefense programs and some entitlements, going beyond cuts made the year before.

In February 1983, the third budget cycle of the Reagan presidency began with the administration proposing a budget totaling $900 billion in budget authority. Once again, the Reagan budget was characterized by a substantial defense increase, reductions in many domestic spending categories, and a long-term "structural" deficit (that is, a deficit caused by reasons other than poor performance of the economy). Congress again indicated its unwillingness to go along with Reagan proposals, but laborious negotiations and several votes were needed before Congress was able to pass a budget resolution incorporating different priorities and budget targets—namely, a tax increase, less military spending, and more domestic spending than called for by Reagan. The president continued to lobby hard for large increases in military expenditures and promised to veto bills increasing taxes or nondefense spending. The final shape of the overall budget for the 1984 fiscal year was highly uncertain as of midsummer 1983.

Reagan Budgets and Environmental Programs

Although Congress softened the budgetary blows directed by the Reagan administration at the whole range of environment and natural resources programs, the effect nevertheless was substantial. Sweeping, substantial changes—some attributable to nonbudgetary administrative actions—occurred between January 1981 and the end of 1983. Table 6-1 presents the budget projections submitted by the Carter and Reagan administrations, reflecting the policies of each. In the budget submitted shortly before leaving office in 1981, the Carter administration estimated that $16.2 billion in budget authority would be needed in fiscal 1984 for all natural resources and environment programs. For the same year the Reagan administration proposed $8.9 billion—32 percent less than actually obligated in 1980, without accounting for inflation—and projected a decline in that amount to $8.7 billion by 1986. (The 1983 Reagan budget had projected even more severe cuts for 1984 and 1985.) Regardless of who would be president after 1984, environmental policy would be influenced markedly by the actions of the Reagan administration for years to come.

Several federal agencies have significant responsibilities for natural resources and environmental quality, and each was affected differently by Reagan's budgets. The proposed 1984 Reagan operating budget for the Environmental Protection Agency (EPA) was $948.6 million, down from the $1,039 million approved by Congress for fiscal 1983 and roughly 70 percent of the $1,346.8 million obligated in fiscal 1981, without accounting for inflation. As Congress had assigned additional responsibilities to EPA in the

1970s under several pieces of major legislation, the agency's spending (excluding sewage treatment construction grants) had grown, in both Republican and Democratic administrations, from $447.6 million in 1972 to $771.5 million in 1976 to $1,346.8 million in 1981 *(see Table 6-2)*. Under Reagan, there was no reduction in the tasks EPA was mandated by law to carry out; indeed, its responsibilities for hazardous wastes and toxic substances were increasing. Critics charged that the Reagan administration was not pushing hard for specific legislative changes in environmental laws because it could achieve its objectives through the budgetary process. Republican Robert T. Stafford of Vermont, chairman of the Senate Environment and Public Works Committee, warned that the cuts proposed "amount to a de facto repeal of some of our environmental laws." [16] Reagan officials, including EPA Administrator Anne Gorsuch, described EPA budgets as "lean," "trim," and "sufficient," claiming that increased efficiency, completed tasks, and delegation to the states allowed such large cuts.

Although Reagan got nearly all that he had asked for by way of EPA budget cuts in 1981, Congress was less willing in 1982 to go along with administration proposals for further cuts. As can be seen in Table 6-3, Congress reduced budget authority for EPA in fiscal year 1982 below the level originally requested by the Reagan administration—largely in response to subsequent administration requests for cuts. But during deliberations on the 1983 budget, at a time when the way EPA was being managed was causing considerable controversy, Congress did not go along with the full extent of proposed Reagan administration cuts. Nevertheless, the agency was provided fewer resources than it had had the previous year. Budget cuts were spread across nearly every EPA operating program, with only two—management and support and interdisciplinary—receiving a net increase over the 1980-1984 period.

By January 1983 consideration of the EPA budget was overshadowed by the controversies and scandals that had developed concerning the activities of several agency political appointees, including the administrator and deputy administrator. In addition to conducting hearings and investigations into the management of EPA, Congress indicated a determination to allocate more resources for the agency. In February, prior to the resignation of Anne Burford (formerly Gorsuch), the Senate Environment and Public Works Committee recommended a 9.6 percent increase in the EPA operating budget over fiscal 1983 appropriations, instead of the 9.0 percent decrease sought by Reagan for fiscal 1984. The House Appropriations Committee also recommended a slight increase in EPA operating funds. Later, during hearings on the appointment of William D. Ruckelshaus to head the agency, the administrator-designate indicated that a review of budgetary needs would be a high priority for him following confirmation. White House chief of staff James A. Baker III, concerned about limiting the administration's political losses from its environmental policies and the EPA scandal, reportedly ordered EPA staff to prepare a supplemental budget request as an option for consideration by Ruckelshaus.[17] In both the Senate and the House, proposals

Table 6-1 Natural Resources and Environment, 1980-1988

	1980	1981	1982	1983	1984	1985	1986	1987	1988
				Budget Authority (in millions of dollars)					
Carter 1982 Budget	actual	estimate	estimate	estimate	estimate				
	13,051	12,705	13,572	15,310	16,170				
Reagan 1984 Budget	actual	actual	actual	estimate	estimate	estimate	estimate	estimate	estimate
	13,051	11,128	11,199	11,234	8,906	8,950	8,703	8,200	8,000

Source: Office of Management and Budget, *Budget of the United States Government*, fiscal years 1982 and 1984.

were made to restore EPA's operating budget to the fiscal 1981 level, and in June the House approved such an amended appropriations bill. Subsequently, EPA Administrator Ruckelshaus requested an additional $165.5 million in operating funds and $100 million in hazardous waste cleanup funds—a request that OMB Director Stockman approved. The Senate incorporated Ruckelshaus's request into its appropriations bill, which the House-Senate conference committee accepted. In July President Reagan signed the bill providing the increased support for fiscal year 1984. Still, excluding funding for hazardous waste cleanup and sewage treatment construction grants, the agency's operating budget was less in constant dollars than it had been when Ruckelshaus had headed the agency 10 years earlier. Given the diminished capacity and the managerial turmoil of the previous two years, the ability of EPA to quickly absorb more than a modest resource increment was doubtful.

Of course, the EPA is not the only federal agency with significant responsibilities for environmental quality, nor is it even the largest. Several vitally important bureaus, offices, and funds are organized under the Department of the Interior, including the Bureau of Land Management, the National Park Service, the Office of Surface Mining, the Bureau of Reclamation, and the Fish and Wildlife Service. The Carter administration's fiscal 1982 budget proposal for Interior's various bureaus and offices totaled $6.6 billion in budget authority; two years later Reagan was proposing only $6.4 billion for the 1984 fiscal year. Table 6-4 summarizes the overall budgets for five Interior Department agencies in the first two years of the Reagan presidency. Showing substantial growth were the Office of Surface Mining Reclamation and Enforcement, reflecting increasing obligations from the abandoned mine reclamation fund, and the Bureau of Reclamation, involved in funding of ongoing western water projects (several of which have been severely criticized by environmentalists). Hardest hit by cuts was the National Park Service—especially since most of the responsibilities of the former Heritage Conservation and Recreation Service (which had a budget of $719.2 million in 1980) were assigned to the National Park Service under a Reagan administration reorganization of the Interior Department. The decline of the Park Service's budget reflects drastic reductions in appropriations for land acquisition, which declined from $538.8 million in 1980 to $142.5 million in 1983. The Reagan administration had requested only $59.8 million for 1983, and its request for 1984 was even smaller, $54.7 million. The administration also sought to "zero-out" two related grant programs, the urban park and recreation fund and the historic preservation fund, which were provided $164.8 million in 1980 and, at the insistence of Congress, $26.0 million in 1983. ("Zero-out," a favorite phrase of David Stockman, meant elimination or abolishment of a program.)[18]

Several other agencies with major environmental or natural resource management responsibilities also fared poorly under the Reagan administration *(see Table 6-4)*. In each of its annual budgets the administration requested large budget cuts for the National Oceanic and Atmospheric

Table 6-2 EPA Operating Budget, 1972-1984

Budget Authority
(in millions of dollars)

	Excluding Superfund			With Superfund		
	Nominal	Deflated (constant 1972 dollars)	Percent change from prior year (constant 1972 dollars)	Nominal	Deflated (constant 1972 dollars)	Percent change from prior year (constant 1972 dollars)
1972	447.6	447.6				
1973	527.2	499.2	+11.5			
1974	618.9	541.9	+ 8.6			
1975	850.4	663.3	+22.4			
1976	771.5	568.5	−14.3			
1977	783.7	542.0	− 4.7			
1978	998.6	649.3	+19.8			
1979	1,202.6	740.1	+14.0			
1980	1,269.4	701.3	− 5.2	1,269.4	701.3	
1981	1,346.8	659.6	− 5.9	1,421.6	696.2	− 5.1
1982	1,086.0	516.2	−21.7	1,276.0	606.5	−12.9
1983 estimate	1,039.0	470.7	− 8.8	1,249.7	565.7	− 6.7
1984 Reagan budget	948.6	409.1	−13.1	1,258.6	542.7.	− 4.1
1984 initial appropriation	1,114.1	480.4	+ 2.1	1,524.1	657.2	+16.2

Note: Funding for sewage treatment construction grants is not included. Amounts are deflated to 1972 dollars using implicit price deflators for federal government purchases of nondefense goods and services, as calculated by the Bureau of Economic Analysis, Department of Commerce. The inflation rate for 1983 and 1984 is assumed to be 5.0 percent.

Source: Office of Management and Budget, *Budget of the United States Government*, fiscal years 1974-1984, and Council of Economic Advisers, *Annual Report of the Council of Economic Advisers*, 1982.

Administration (NOAA), but Congress refused to go along fully with these proposals. The Army Corps of Engineers had its budget reduced—unlike the Bureau of Reclamation, the other large water project construction agency of the federal government. The Reagan administration continued the Carter policy of recommending few or no new construction starts, contributing to a substantial cut in funding for the general construction program of the Corps. The Soil Conservation Service (SCS), the third and smallest water project construction agency, also suffered large cuts in its watershed planning and construction activities. Moreover, the Reagan administration sought to eliminate the SCS resource conservation and development program. Likewise, the budget of the Forest Service was cut, even as the Reagan administration was proposing increased timber sales from national forests. Large cuts were included in funds for forest research, for state and private forestry, for land acquisition, and for management, protection, improvement, and utilization of the national forest system. Along with presentation of the 1984 budget, the administration announced that it would propose legislation to provide for sale of about 10 percent of the national forest system.

But no environment or natural resources agency fared as badly as the Council on Environmental Quality (CEQ), a tiny but significant agency with appropriations that had grown to only $3.1 million in the last full fiscal year of the Carter presidency. CEQ was very nearly zeroed-out in the first weeks of the new administration, but President Reagan ultimately settled for firing the entire professional staff and reducing the budget by nearly three-fourths. Ironically, this action was officially taken less than two weeks before issuance of an evaluative report by the General Accounting Office that described CEQ as "effective," "successful," "unique," "important," and fulfilling "a continuing need" in the Executive Office of the President.[19] CEQ fared particularly poorly at the hands of Congress, which approved devastating rescission requests in 1981. Congress appropriated substantially less for 1984 ($.7 million) than the administration had requested ($.9 million) because of dissatisfaction with CEQ's function and performance under the Reagan administration.[20]

Budgeting for Environmental Research and Development

One of the recurring themes of conservatives and other critics of environmental regulations over the last decade has been the weakness of the scientific basis for many regulations. The general inadequacy of scientific understanding of existing and potential environmental problems has worried many scientists, environmentalists, and policy analysts as well. The EPA in particular has a strong need for good science to support its many regulatory programs. It conducts an extensive research program under several legislative mandates but has been criticized repeatedly and challenged in court for basing standards and regulations on inconclusive scientific evidence. The agency's research program has been studied and criticized by, among others, congressional committees, the National Research Council of the National Academy of

Table 6-3   EPA Operating Budget and Appropriations Under Reagan

*Budget Authority
(in millions of dollars)*

Carter 1982 budget	Reagan 1982 budget	1982 actual	Percent change, Reagan request to actual
1,376.3	1,191.4	1,086.0	− 8.8
	Reagan 1983 budget	1983 estimate	
	961.4	1,039.7	+ 8.1
	Reagan 1984 budget	1984 appropriated	
	948.6	1,114.0	+17.4

Note: Figures exclude funding for sewage treatment construction grants and for Superfund.

Source: Office of Management and Budget, *Budget of the United States Government*, fiscal years 1982-1984, and *Fiscal Year 1982 Budget Revisions;* Bureau of National Affairs, *Environment Reporter*, July 8 and July 15, 1983.

Sciences, and the General Accounting Office.[21]

The opportunity existed for the new Reagan administration to make improvements. One of the administration's highly touted regulatory reforms was a presidential executive order requiring cost-benefit analyses in decision making. Good science obviously would be necessary for sound cost-benefit analysis of environmental and other regulations. And at July 1982 House hearings, EPA Administrator Gorsuch reiterated that "one of the objectives of this administration is to improve the quality of the scientific basis underlying the regulatory decision-making process."[22]

Nevertheless, beginning in 1981, an administration committed to improve cost-benefit analysis of regulatory initiatives cut back severely on the scientific research needed to design innovative, effective, efficient regulations. The $205.5 million requested for EPA research and development in the 1984 Reagan budget represented a 46.7 percent decline from the $385.4 million spent in 1981, without accounting for inflation *(see Table 6-5)*. In constant dollars, the three-year reduction totaled 53.9 percent, compared with a budget reduction for the agency as a whole of 39.1 percent. The policy impact was greater than the numbers alone suggest, since the cuts were made in the context of chaotic internal politics, temporary leadership, reorganizational uncertainty, and changing objectives. Suffering disproportionate cuts were "independent" extramural research—the target of less severe criticisms than EPA's in-house research—and long-term basic research. A 1983 EPA budget document declared, "Research not directly linked to regulatory needs has been eliminated." [23]

The research and development budget of EPA was a focus of controversy over the first two years of the Reagan administration, but as Table 6-6 indicates, Congress appropriated little more than Reagan requested.

In 1982 Congress passed a bill authorizing substantially more research spending than Reagan had requested and more than Congress had already appropriated for fiscal year 1983, although less than the actual 1981 research appropriation. The bill also would have mandated that 20 percent of EPA's research budget be spent on long-term research, and it would have required substantial expenditures on matters such as energy-related pollution research, indoor air pollution research, and monitoring of environmental quality and the impact of federal programs. But President Reagan vetoed the bill (only the 10th bill he had vetoed as president).[24] In his veto message, Reagan emphasized his opposition to a provision requiring representation of states, industry, labor, academia, consumers, and the general public on EPA's Science Advisory Board—a provision similar to requirements that apply to science panels of other agencies such as the Food and Drug Administration. The Reagan administration had not objected to the science board provision before the bill was passed. Some critical members of Congress and skeptical environmentalists charged that the stated reason was a cover for the administration's opposition to the rest of the bill, but leaders of some scientific organizations defended Reagan's objection as consistent with the premise that scientific advice should be above politics.[25] (In early 1983 it was disclosed that political and ideological considerations had in fact played a role in Reagan administration appointments to EPA's Science Advisory Board as well as to a supposedly nonpartisan offshore oil advisory panel for the Interior Department.)[26]

Reduction in funds for environmental research was not limited to the EPA, which is only one of several agencies with environmental research and data collection as part of its mission. A major activity of the CEQ, before its impoverishment under the Reagan administration, was the collection, analysis, and distribution of information. Overall, federal funding for research and development fared well in Reagan budgets, with the administration proposing a 17 percent increase in the 1984 budget over the fiscal 1983 level. Within those totals, however, substantial cutbacks were proposed for several environmental research programs. Various NOAA research programs have been the targets of Reagan budget-cutting proposals for fiscal years 1982, 1983, and 1984, although Congress refused to go along with many of the reductions proposed for 1982 and 1983. For 1984, the Reagan administration proposed cutting NOAA's 1983 research and development budget from $191.1 million to $133.9 million. Impacts would include:

> . . . reduction in data buoy research, reduction in instrumentation R&D, termination of all weather modification research, reduction of the Global

Table 6-4 Budgets of Selected Agencies

| | Budget Authority (in millions of dollars) | | | | | | |
	1981 actual	1982 Reagan budget	1982 actual	1983 Reagan budget	1983 estimate	1984 Reagan budget	Percent change 1981-1984
Environmental Protection Agency (excluding funding for sewage treatment construction grants)	1,421.7	1,391.5	1,276.0	1,147.4	1,249.7	1,258.6	−11.5
Bureau of Land Management	1,035.4	1,166.0	1,240.7	1,256.3	1,163.1	584.2*	−43.6*
Bureau of Reclamation	795.1	849.5	778.6	950.3	824.7	1,002.6	+26.1
Fish and Wildlife Service	427.6	397.8	441.4	416.1	468.9	476.0	+11.3
National Park Service	857.8	720.5	802.4	736.3	887.3	739.2	−13.8
Office of Surface Mining	178.0	180.0	173.8	159.8	222.2	282.3	+58.6
Forest Service	2,295.3	2,236.0	1,993.0	2,132.2	2,191.8	1,866.4	−18.7
Soil Conservation Service	589.0	552.2	575.9	516.5	519.0	475.0	−19.4
Council on Environmental Quality	2.5	1.0	.9	.9	.9	.9	−64.0
Corps of Engineers	3,181.0	3,135.0	3,064.9	2,816.0	3,063.2	2,665.1	−16.2
National Oceanic and Atmospheric Administration	857.2	800.0	909.9	781.0	964.3	835.1	− 2.6

* The primary reason for the 1984 reduction for the Bureau of Land Management was transfer to the Minerals Management Service of the responsibility for payment of mineral receipts to the states.

Source: Office of Management and Budget, *Budget of the United States Government*, fiscal years 1982-1984, and *Fiscal Year 1982 Budget Revisions*.

Atmospheric Research Program, ... termination of solar-terrestrial research ..., elimination of ocean energy research, reduction of environmental impact studies, elimination of ocean minerals resource evaluation, termination of the undersea research program, closing of the Great Lakes Research Laboratory, termination of the Chesapeake Bay study, reduction of the ocean technology engineering research, termination of the Sea Grant program, reduction of significant fisheries research, [and] the lay-up of the two research vessels (SURVEYOR and FERREL) and eight fishery research vessels....[27]

Funding for research and development by the Interior Department declined from $424 million in 1981 to $373 million in 1983, with the Reagan administration recommending a further decrease of $44 million for 1984. Forest Service research funding was reduced from $127 million in 1981 to $105 million in 1983; the Reagan administration requested $101 million for 1984. In fiscal years 1981 and 1982, the Reagan administration attempted virtually to eliminate funding for nonnuclear research from the budget for the Department of Energy. For 1984 the administration again proposed substantial cuts in conservation, fossil fuel, and solar and other renewable energy research programs *(see Chapter 10)*.

Some program cuts do not show up under "research and development" but nevertheless have consequences for future research and future environmental policy. Most notably, many federal statistics-gathering activities of all kinds were cut back severely under the Reagan administration, which generally placed a low priority on information gathering and dissemination. A comprehensive, coordinated, and reliable environmental information system never had existed before 1981, despite repeated recommendations by prestigious panels and committees. But Reagan budget cuts led to the elimination of many existing monitoring, compiling, and analyzing programs, reduction in the frequency of reporting for others, and a decrease in sample size, periodicity, and geographic detail for numerous surveys.[28] *Science* magazine reported that "virtually all the 70 or so programs in the government involved in collection and analysis of statistics have suffered from federal budget cuts."[29] Data about environmental quality, already glaringly inadequate, became more so—even in the face of "the high priority the public attaches to environmental quality, the extent of environmental regulation, and the high costs of both environmental damage and compliance with regulations."[30]

Conclusion

The consequences of Reagan's budgets for environmental programs, particularly for research, development, and data collection, will provide a long-term legacy of this administration. To be sure, the environmental policy impact of the Reagan presidency has not been entirely malignant. In many of its activities the federal government is a significant degrader of environmental quality, and many budgetary cutbacks have beneficial environmental ramifications.[31] For example, environmentalists in 1981 supported efforts to end the federal practice of subsidizing flood insurance for construction on

Table 6-5   EPA Research and Development Budget

	Nominal	Deflated	Percent change from prior year, constant dollars	Percent change from 1981, constant dollars
	Budget Authority (in millions of dollars)			
1981	385.4	385.4		
1982	311.1	301.7	−21.7	−21.7
1983 estimate	228.6	209.9	−30.4	−45.5
1984 Reagan budget	205.5	177.6	−15.4	−53.9

Note: Amounts are deflated to 1981 dollars using implicit price deflators for federal government purchases of nondefense goods and services, as calculated by the Bureau of Economic Analysis, Department of Commerce. The inflation rate for 1983 and 1984 is assumed to be 5.0 percent.

Source: Intersociety Working Group, *R&D in the FY 1984 Budget: A Preliminary Analysis,* American Association for the Advancement of Science, March 1983.

undeveloped coastal barrier islands. And, as environmentalists long have pointed out, many federal water resources projects are economically as well as environmentally unsound; Reagan administration cuts in the water-development budgets of the Corps of Engineers and the Soil Conservation Service probably had a net beneficial impact on environmental quality. Moreover, Reagan policies of increasing user fees for many federally funded facilities and resources will have the effect of reducing demand for subsidization of additional environmentally damaging projects. Likewise, the reforms in the sewage treatment construction grant program advocated by the Reagan administration may over time lead to improvements in water quality, even with lowered expenditure of federal funds—by giving state and local governments a greater financial stake in the design of plants, by ending the practice of funding plants large enough to encourage future growth, and by better focusing funds on priority problems.

But while the administration sought to make some overdue reforms and curtail some programs of dubious value, it also sought to cut to the bone a great many programs for environmental protection. At the same time, it continued to support large, economically questionable, and environmentally damaging projects such as the Clinch River breeder reactor, the Tennessee-Tombigbee waterway, and the Garrison Diversion project—projects that were inconsistent with the rhetoric and the stated budget principles of the administration.

The Reagan administration always was sensitive, however, to the political realities of budgeting, and it repeatedly demonstrated a remarkable ability to learn from experience whenever it was rebuffed by Congress. This can be seen by the tempering in subsequent years of initially radical proposals for cutting EPA, NOAA, and various energy programs. The administration's environmental policies likely will be moderated in its 1985 fiscal year budget proposals as posturing begins for the 1984 elections. In any event, OMB's ability to dictate policy to EPA through the budgetary process has been restricted by the political consequences of the controversies and scandals that enveloped EPA in the first two years of the Reagan presidency.

As macroeconomic policy, environmental budgeting under Reagan had little impact on the rate of growth of federal expenditures or on the performance of the economy, and it contributed little toward balancing the budget as Reagan had promised *(see Chapter 16)*. In some instances, the Reagan administration truly has taken a "nickel and dime" approach to environmental budgeting, gutting highly effective agencies such as CEQ and engendering international ill will by trying to cut United Nations environmental programs, only to achieve minuscule budgetary savings *(see Chapter 15)*.

Reagan's success in influencing the priorities of national government is undeniable. But, given the nature and extent of environmental problems faced by modern society and given the values and attitudes of the American public *(see Chapter 3)*, it is another question whether the budgetary priorities established by the Reagan administration are appropriate. *Not* spending money on some environmental problems can be a shortsighted and counterproductive policy, penny-wise but pound-foolish. "Many short term budgetary gains could result in more acute problems with larger remedial costs shifted to later years." [32]

It is at the level of management and execution, however, that Reagan's environmental budgeting is vulnerable to the most severe criticism, especially with regard to the EPA. Donald Lambro, author of *Fat City: How Washington Wastes Your Taxes* — a book Reagan sent to all his cabinet members — rated EPA, as inherited by the Reagan administration, as one of only three agencies "given high marks for maintaining scandal-free administrations as well as conducting themselves with a high degree of professionalism and competence." [33]

Opportunities for reforming EPA existed. But reform is no simple task, as noted by Peter B. Hutt, an attorney who represented the Chemical Manufacturers Association:

> You can slim down a regulatory agency and make it more efficient, if you do it the right way. That requires a good deal of insight and people who really know how to regulate. And that's difficult to pick up quickly. But if you go too far, you can cut the heart out of an agency, and then you have a moribund institution. [34]

The Carter administration had taken great strides in making environmental regulation more flexible and cost-effective. The Reagan administration's approach was blunt: it sought primarily to enfeeble EPA by depriving it

Table 6-6 EPA "Research and Development"
Appropriation Category

			Budget Authority			
			(in millions of dollars)			
1981	1982			1983	1984	
actual	Reagan budget	actual	Reagan budget	esti- mated	Reagan budget	appro- priated
198.6	190.6	154.3	108.7	119.0	111.7	142.7

Note: Additional funds for research and development are budgeted under the "Salary and Expenses" appropriation category.

Source: Office of Management and Budget, *Budget of the United States Government,* fiscal years 1982-1984, and Bureau of National Affairs, *Environment Reporter,* March 13, 1981, and July 15, 1983.

of resources. Whereas such a strategy has a certain degree of guaranteed effectiveness, it may also discredit the principles and ideology behind it. The Reagan record is just as discouraging for many of President Reagan's original supporters as it is for environmental activists: opportunities for lasting conservative revisions of regulatory policy may be lost for years as a consequence.

The lack of knowledge sufficient to justify action is still a pervasive weakness of many environmental policies. The failure to establish, competently manage, and generously fund a long-term research operation to fill the large gaps in our knowledge constitutes "a disgraceful failure to respond to the true interests of the next generation." [35] This shortcoming of environmental policy was not ameliorated by the budget policies of the Reagan administration:

> Because of the budget cuts, the information base for environmental policy, always weak, is likely to be even weaker in the future. We will be less able to sort out important problems from unimportant ones, less able to tell which environmental programs are working effectively and which are not. Perhaps most important, the perennial dilemma of whether available information is sufficient to justify action will become more pervasive and difficult.[36]

Of course, some of the blame (or credit) for the impacts of the environmental budget cuts also must be apportioned to Congress, which before 1983 went along with most of the administration's budget proposals. The task and responsibility of rebuilding government institutions for protecting and enhancing environmental quality fall on both the president and Congress. But institutions are not easily rebuilt once decimated. The long-term legacy of the first two years of the Reagan administration may turn out to be the institutional and research capabilities lost because of short-term budget reductions.

Notes

1. John L. Palmer and Isabel V. Sawhill, "Perspectives on the Reagan Experiment," in *The Reagan Experiment: An Examination of Economic and Social Policies under the Reagan Administration*, ed. John L. Palmer and Isabel V. Sawhill (Washington, D.C.: Urban Institute, 1982), 2.
2. Chester A. Newland, "A Mid-Term Appraisal—The Reagan Presidency: Limited Government and Political Administration," *Public Administration Review* 43 (January-February 1983): 2.
3. Ibid.
4. Richard P. Nathan, *The Administrative Presidency* (New York: Wiley, 1983).
5. Ibid., 92.
6. *New York Times*, March 29, 1981, 1.
7. Rowland Evans, Jr., and Robert Novak, *The Reagan Revolution* (New York: E. P. Dutton, 1981), 135.
8. David A. Stockman, "The Stockman Manifesto," *Washington Post*, December 14, 1980.
9. Henry J. Aaron, "The Choices Ahead," in *Setting National Priorities: The 1984 Budget*, ed. Joseph A. Pechman (Washington, D.C.: Brookings Institution, 1983), 202-204.
10. Evans and Novak, *The Reagan Revolution*, 126.
11. Murray L. Weidenbaum, *The Future of Business Regulation: Private Action and Public Demand* (New York: AMACOM, 1979), 23.
12. Stockman, "The Stockman Manifesto."
13. Lawrence Mosher, "Reaganites, with OMB's List in Hand, Take Dead Aim at EPA's Regulations," *National Journal*, February 14, 1981, 256.
14. Allen Schick, *Reconciliation and the Congressional Budget Process* (Washington, D.C.: American Enterprise Institute, 1981).
15. Hedrick Smith, "The President as Coalition Builder: Reagan's First Year," in *Rethinking the Presidency*, ed. Thomas E. Cronin (Boston: Little, Brown, 1982), 271-286; Congressional Quarterly, *Budgeting for America: The Politics and Process of Federal Spending* (Washington, D.C.: Congressional Quarterly, 1982).
16. Lawrence Mosher, "Making Them Hire," *National Journal*, March 20, 1982, 514.
17. *National Journal*, April 2, 1983, 687.
18. William Greider, "The Education of David Stockman," *Atlantic Monthly*, December 1981, 34.
19. General Accounting Office, *The Council on Environmental Quality: A Tool in Shaping National Policy* (Washington, D.C.: Government Printing Office, 1981).
20. Constance Holden, "CEQ Staggering Under Latest Budget Cut," *Science* 221 (August 5, 1983): 529.
21. General Accounting Office, *Improving the Scientific and Technical Information Available to the Environmental Protection Agency in its Decision-making Process* (Washington, D.C.: Government Printing Office, 1979); General Accounting Office, *Promising Changes Improve EPA's Extramural Research; More Changes*

Needed (Washington, D.C.: Government Printing Office, 1980); U.S. Congress, House Committee on Science and Technology, Subcommittee on the Environment and the Atmosphere, *Organization and Management of EPA's Office of Research and Development*, 94th Cong., 2d sess., June 1976; National Research Council, *Perspectives on Technical Information for Environmental Protection* (Washington, D.C.: National Academy of Sciences, 1977); and National Research Council, *Research and Development in the Environmental Protection Agency* (Washington, D.C.: National Academy of Sciences, 1977).

22. *Congressional Quarterly Weekly Report,* July 31, 1982, 1829.

23. Eliot Marshall, "EPA's Troubles Reach a Crescendo," *Science* 219 (March 25, 1983): 1403.

24. *Congressional Quarterly Weekly Report,* October 30, 1982, 2774.

25. R. Jeffrey Smith, "President Vetoes EPA R&D Bill," *Science* 218 (November 12, 1982): 663; Joseph A. Davis, "Reagan Vetoes Legislation Authorizing EPA Research," *Congressional Quarterly Weekly Report,* October 30, 1982, 2769.

26. Eliot Marshall, "EPA's Troubles Reach a Crescendo," 1404; Marshall, "Hit List at EPA?" *Science* 219 (March 18, 1983): 1303; Marshall, "Hit Lists Claim a Victim at EPA," *Science* 220 (April 1, 1983): 38; and Joseph A. Davis, "Environmentalists Shift Focus to Interior, Reagan Policies," *Congressional Quarterly Weekly Report,* April 2, 1983, 670.

27. Fred D. White, "FY 1984 R&D in the Atmospheric and Ocean Sciences," in *R&D in the FY 1984 Budget: A Preliminary Analysis,* Intersociety Working Group (Washington, D.C.: American Association for the Advancement of Science, 1983), 179-180.

28. U.S. Congress, Hearing, House Committee on Post Office and Civil Service, Subcommittee on Census and Population, *Impact of Budget Cuts on Federal Statistical Programs,* 97th Cong., 2d sess., March 16, 1982; also, M. Margaret Conway, "Reaganomics and the Federal Statistical Programs," *PS* 15 (Spring 1982): 194-198.

29. Constance Holden, "Statistics Suffering Under Reagan," *Science* 216 (May 21, 1982): 833.

30. Herbert C. Morton, "The Environmental Data Dilemma," *Resources* (Spring 1981): 22.

31. Christopher K. Leman, "An Era of Limits?" *Resources* (March 1982): 1-2; Michael E. Lowry, "Understanding the Budget," *Sierra,* March-April 1983, 62-63; Paul R. Portney, "Natural Resources and the Environment," in *Setting National Priorities: The 1982 Budget,* ed. Joseph A. Pechman (Washington, D.C.: Brookings Institution, 1981), 103-107; *Ronald Reagan and the American Environment* (San Francisco: Friends of the Earth, 1982), 85-136.

32. *Conservation Foundation Letter,* May 1981, 4.

33. Donald Lambro, "The Best and the Worst Government Agencies," *Washingtonian,* May 1981, 144-150.

34. Lawrence Mosher, "Move Over, Jim Watt, Anne Gorsuch is the Latest Target of Environmentalists," *National Journal,* October 24, 1981, 1902.

35. Bruce A. Ackerman and William T. Hassler, *Clean Coal/Dirty Air* (New Haven: Yale University Press, 1981), 72.

36. Conservation Foundation, *State of the Environment 1982* (Washington, D.C.: Conservation Foundation, 1982), 7-8.

7. ENVIRONMENTAL INSTITUTIONS AND THE REAGAN ADMINISTRATION

J. Clarence Davies

By the time the Reagan administration took office in January 1981 the effort to improve environmental quality already had been institutionalized. Strong and stable environmental agencies existed at the state and federal government levels; both political parties were committed to environmental improvement; environmental interest groups were a potent and respected political force; and opinion polls showed repeatedly that environmental protection had become a basic value for the American public.

The changes made in the first two years of the Reagan administration were designed largely to reverse the institutionalization process. During those two years, the resources of the environmental regulatory agencies, notably the Environmental Protection Agency (EPA), were sharply reduced, and their competence and authority weakened. The offices and individuals responsible for environmental awareness in the nonregulatory agencies were mostly eliminated. State pollution-control agencies, many already financially hard-pressed, found that their federal grants were not immune to the Reagan budget cuts. Environmental interest groups were excluded from policy debates in the executive branch, and partisan strife over environmental issues increased markedly.

In some respects those changes demonstrated a remarkable flexibility in the federal government. In a very short period of time, the president was able to reverse a process that had been ongoing for more than 10 years. It may be exceedingly difficult for a modern president to initiate new programs, but Reagan showed dramatically the power of a president to stop programs he dislikes and to weaken institutions of which he disapproves.

The inherent fragility of institutions makes it easier for a president to successfully implement negative initiatives. Much has been made of the intractability and stability of government agencies, and indeed the difficulty of completely abolishing an agency cannot be exaggerated. But mere existence is a very minimal criterion. To perform its mission an agency requires skilled personnel, leadership, and cooperation from institutions both inside and outside the government. As we shall see, the Reagan administration succeeded in depriving the environmental agencies of these requirements.

In EPA the Reagan changes were abruptly halted by a series of dramatic events culminating in the resignation of all of the top political leadership of the agency. This controversy and the approach of the 1984 election also slowed the weakening of environmental functions in other agencies. But the legacy of the first two and a half years of the Reagan administration will stay with us for some years to come. Although the effort to improve environmental quality in the United States still is strongly supported by the public and also is firmly rooted in a network of private organizations, the government's environmental institutions will have to undergo a long and difficult process to rebuild their former strength.

The Reagan Administration's Approach

As discussed in Chapter 2, Ronald Reagan's presidential campaign gave clear indications that he would try to reverse many of the changes in environmental institutions that had taken place in the 1970s. Several characteristics of his administration as it assumed power are particularly important in considering the institutional changes that were to occur.

The Reagan philosophy was characterized by a hostility toward all nonmilitary functions of government, especially of the federal government, and regulation of business was the most abhorrent. Thus, in the eyes of Reagan and most of his appointees, reducing the scope of federal activity and weakening federal civilian agencies were positive goods in themselves. This was particularly true for regulatory agencies such as the Occupational Safety and Health Administration, the Consumer Product Safety Commission, and the EPA.

A corollary of the antigovernment philosophy was a complete mistrust of, if not outright disdain for, career civil servants. There had been a tendency in the Carter administration to believe that all policy wisdom resided in former residents of the state of Georgia and that the career civil service was an obstacle to implementing the new administration's policies. Richard Nixon as president was paranoid about the civil service and formulated elaborate plans to gain political control over it.[1] However, the antagonism and lack of communication between Reagan's political appointees and the civil service reached a new high, and the result in many cases was a political lobotomy to the institutional memory and expertise of federal agencies. The administration was convinced that the regulatory agencies were staffed largely by consumer and environmental "extremists" who were hostile to Reagan.

The Reagan administration's antagonism to the federal regulatory agencies also was fueled by the fact that the business community was a mainstay of the administration's political constituency. The administration shared the view of the Chamber of Commerce of the United States, the National Association of Manufacturers, and other business interests that federal regulation to protect the environment, workers, and consumers had been carried to excess during the 1970s and that such regulation was a major cause of the slowdown in the national economy.

A large portion of the American public shared Reagan's views on high taxes, excess regulation, and the incompetence of the civil service. The two views diverged, however, on the importance of environmental protection, and the administration's actions to change environmental institutions indicated that it sided with the business community.

Personnel Changes

Most Reagan administration appointments to the top posts in the Interior Department and EPA were drawn from a narrow circle of right-wing, Republican, business-oriented westerners. James G. Watt, secretary of the interior, was the first and most visible of such appointees. Watt had served six years at Interior during the Nixon administration and then two years on the Federal Power Commission. Prior to his appointment as secretary, he headed the Mountain States Legal Foundation, an organization that devotes most of its efforts to legal action to curb or repeal federal actions in Colorado and other western states.

Watt made no secret of his views that most resource problems could be solved by letting the free market have its way and that organized environmental groups represent a threat to the capitalist system and the American way of life.

The top EPA posts were left vacant for a long time. Finally, on May 5, 1981, a Watt protégé, Anne Gorsuch (later Burford), was confirmed as administrator. Gorsuch had been an attorney for the Colorado telephone company and a member of the Colorado legislature. In the legislature she was identified with a group of conservatives devoted to the unfettered free market and opposed to environmental and other regulation, especially federal regulation. She had no management experience, no experience in Washington, D.C., and no in-depth knowledge of environmental policy.

The people most responsible for the appointments of Watt and Gorsuch were Joseph Coors, a Colorado brewer, and Sen. Paul Laxalt, a Republican of Nevada. Coors was a major contributor to the Reagan campaign and an important figure in right-wing Republican politics. Laxalt chaired the president's national campaign organization in 1980; later Reagan named him national chairman of the Republican party. Rumors circulated in 1981 that Coors and Laxalt had been given control over appointments in Interior and EPA, Coors in exchange for his campaign support, Laxalt in exchange for a pledge not to object to the president's appointments to the State Department. Those rumors cannot be confirmed, but little doubt exists that both men did exercise considerable influence over Interior and EPA appointments. Gorsuch appears to have had almost no control over the appointment of her subordinates. Partly because of this, partly because of her management style of relying almost exclusively on a few personal assistants, and partly because of the myriad problems in the agency, other top EPA posts were plagued by difficulties. Gorsuch created two new key associate administrator positions, but her appointees to these positions lasted only three months before resigning. Of the six existing assistant administrator positions, two stayed vacant for seven months after the administration took office, one for ten months, two for fifteen months; one office (research and development) did not have a permanent head during Gorsuch's entire tenure.

The political appointees at both EPA and Interior were mostly associated with the business community, in sharp contrast with the Carter appointees, many of whom had come from environmental organizations. However, especially at EPA, the appointees were not themselves business executives, but rather lobbyists, lawyers, or scientists who had represented business interests. Few had any management experience, and most had some ties with the industries they were responsible for regulating.

The EPA appointees were perhaps only slightly less well prepared for their new jobs than Reagan's appointees to other agencies. A study of nearly 150 middle-level appointments made by the administration in the first half of 1981 showed that nearly 60 percent of the subcabinet offices, nearly 80 percent of the independent agencies, and virtually 100 percent of the independent regulatory commissions were staffed by people with no prior experience in the executive branch.[2] Chester Newland, appraising the first two years of the Reagan administration, observed that "under Reagan, most key administrative positions have been staffed on the basis of partisan and personal loyalties."[3] A study comparing Reagan's appointments to regulatory agencies with appointments made by the four presidents who preceded him confirmed that the Reagan appointees were less likely to have had previous government experience. However, they were not any more likely to have been politically active prior to their appointment. Sixty percent of the Reagan appointees had ties to regulated companies, but this was slightly lower than the comparable percentage for appointees of Dwight D. Eisenhower and Richard Nixon. Forty percent of the Kennedy and Carter appointees had been associated with regulated firms.[4]

The career civil service suffered in various ways under the new regime. The most obvious impact was the sheer reduction in personnel. As Table 7-1 shows, almost all of the environmental agencies suffered cuts in personnel, and EPA was particularly hard hit, losing almost a quarter of its total work force. Even in those agencies that did not lose in overall employment, such as the Agriculture Department's U.S. Forest Service and Interior's Bureau of Land Management, environmentally related offices suffered staff cuts at the same time that offices devoted to timber production and other resource-utilization functions received additional employees.

The most sweeping personnel change made by the administration was at the Council on Environmental Quality, part of the Executive Office of the President. The White House considered abolishing the council but decided the political costs of doing so would be too high. Instead, the administration fired the entire council staff, some of whom had been appointed originally during the Nixon and Ford administrations. The overall size of the staff was reduced by more than half, and new appointments were drawn largely from

Table 7-1 Federal Agency Employment, 1981 and 1983
(number of positions)

Agency	Fiscal 1981 actual	Fiscal 1983 estimated	Percent change 1981-1983
Office of Surface Mining, DOI	1,036	638	−38.4%
Consumer Product Safety Commission	789	556	−29.5
EPA (excluding Superfund)	10,498	8,129	−22.6
Federal Trade Commission	1,587	1,235	−22.2
Occupational Safety and Health Administration, DOL	3,009	2,354	−21.8
Mine Safety and Health Administration, DOL	3,808	2,996	−21.3
National Highway Traffic Safety Administration, DOT	755	645	−14.6
Bureau of Indian Affairs, DOI	13,152	11,410	−13.2
National Oceanic and Atmospheric Administration, DOC	13,563	11,794	−13.0
Federal Highway Administration, DOT	4,020	3,500	−12.9
Urban Mass Transportation Administration, DOT	575	509	−11.5
Corps of Engineers — Civil Works, DOD	27,445	24,689	−10.0
Coast Guard, DOT	6,321	5,773	−8.7
National Park Service, DOI	9,945	9,291	−6.6
Fish and Wildlife Service, DOI	4,914	4,600	−6.4
Bureau of Mines, DOI	2,699	2,559	−5.2
Geological Survey, DOI	9,517	9,070	−4.7
Bureau of Reclamation, DOI	7,351	7,371	+0.3
Forest Service, USDA	29,818	29,975	+0.5
Nuclear Regulatory Commission	3,277	3,303	+0.8
Bureau of Land Management, DOI	6,041	6,096	+0.9
EPA — Superfund	270	516	+91.1

Note: Employment figures include permanent positions only.

Source: The Conservation Foundation, *State of the Environment 1982* (Washington, D.C.: The Conservation Foundation, 1982), 388.

the ranks of the Reagan presidential campaign.[5]

In a number of cases the civil-service rules governing the Carter-instituted Senior Executive Service (SES) were used to force senior civil servants from their jobs.[6] The SES rules gave members of the service a choice between accepting reassignment to a different location or resigning. Many faced with an order to move on short notice from Washington to some remote location chose to resign.

The most important changes in the civil service, in agencies such as EPA and the Department of Energy, resulted not from formal actions but from the policy and political orientation of the Reagan political appointees. The civil servants were not consulted about policy and saw key positions go to people who were not sympathetic to the goals of the programs for which they were responsible. The jobs of many of the more senior civil servants became so unrewarding that those with an option (that is, the most competent) left the government. Because there are no objective measures of the competence of individual civil servants, there are no good measures of the extent of this phenomenon. However, at least at EPA, there is little question that the average experience and qualifications of those in senior civil service positions have declined markedly since 1981.

Organizational Changes

Two kinds of organizational changes were made to reflect the policy views of the Reagan administration. Small but often important changes were made within agencies, and the governmentwide mechanisms for policy review and approval also were changed.

Within the environmental agencies some programs that were considered particularly undesirable were merged with other programs, thus losing their organizational identity. For example, the Special Pesticide Review Division in EPA, which was responsible for considering the possible banning of a pesticide where there was some evidence of its being carcinogenic or causing other chronic effects, was abolished and its functions were placed in the division in charge of routine pesticide registration.[7] At Interior, the Heritage Conservation and Recreation Service, the federal unit in charge of outdoor recreation planning and historic preservation, was abolished and its functions were absorbed by the National Park Service.

Other organizational shifts within agencies were designed to weaken programs or to give more power to state authorities. For example, Interior's Office of Surface Mining reduced its field offices from 37 to 20 and replaced five regional offices with two technical service centers. As the Conservation Foundation has stated, this reflected a change in orientation "from a substantial federal regulatory role to one emphasizing cooperation with and assistance to state strip-mine control efforts."[8] At EPA, Gorsuch first abolished the Office of Enforcement, then reestablished it with a much smaller staff, and then reorganized it, all within the first 12 months of her tenure. In the spring of 1982 she replaced the top two enforcement officials, shuffled the office's division directors, and redefined the responsibilities of the office.[9] Not surprisingly the effectiveness of the office was reduced considerably: between June 1981 and June 1982, EPA cases referred to the Justice Department declined by 84 percent, compared with the previous 12 months, and civil penalties imposed by EPA dropped 48 percent.[10]

On a governmentwide level, a new system of cabinet councils was instituted. Five such councils were created (a sixth was added later). Each is nominally chaired by the president with the secretary of a department serving as chairman pro tempore. The Cabinet Council on Natural Resources and Environment was chaired by Watt. The council was quite active, having met 31 times in the first 16 months of the administration.[11]

According to an evaluation by one expert, the councils have been effective in reducing strains between the White House and the line agencies, in facilitating actions on second-level policy issues without compelling personal presidential attention to details, and in helping to keep the entire administration focused on the president's general agenda.[12]

The Cabinet Council on Natural Resources and Environment reduced the autonomy of EPA by subjecting some important issues, such as EPA's position on Clean Air Act Amendments, to critical review by Interior and other agencies before a final decision could be made. It is impossible to separate the institutional impact of the cabinet council on EPA from the fact that Gorsuch was a protégé and a great admirer of Watt. How much the council will influence EPA under another administrator remains to be seen.

The second major governmentwide change made by the administration was to increase significantly the influence of the Office of Management and Budget (OMB) over proposed regulatory actions. Executive Order 12291, signed by Reagan on February 17, 1981, requires that all major proposed rules be subjected to a "regulatory impact analysis"—essentially an analysis of the anticipated costs and benefits of the rule. The order gives OMB the power to review all proposed and final rules (whether major or not) and preliminary and final impact analyses before they are made public. The Congressional Research Service has noted that the executive order established "a formal, comprehensive, centralized, and substantively oriented system of control of informal rule making that is without precedent." [13]

The basic effect of Executive Order 12291 has been to give OMB, and thus also the White House, detailed control over all rule making by federal agencies (except the independent regulatory commissions). Jim Tozzi, the OMB official in charge of the review process, observed that "it has taken us nearly twenty years, through five administrations, to establish a central review office in OMB which has the authority to curtail the promulgation of onerous regulations." [14] Several consequences follow from this redistribution of authority: (1) regulations are likely to be more responsive to the policies and politics of the White House; (2) it takes much longer to issue a regulation; (3) responsibility for regulatory policy is divided and thus it is more difficult to know whom to blame or praise for the outcome; (4) those interests (usually business interests, at least in the Reagan administration) that have access to OMB have increased power over regulations;[15] and (5) the lack of accountability of OMB to Congress, the courts, and the public has become a more serious problem than before. The effects of the OMB review process are discussed at length in chapters 8 and 16.

The most widely publicized aspect of Executive Order 12291, the requirement that proposed regulations be subjected to a cost-benefit analysis, actually has had almost no impact on environmental policy aside from being part of the broader move to give more power to OMB. EPA already had become sensitized under previous administrations to the need to consider the costs of regulations and even before 1981 was quite sophisticated in conducting economic analyses. However, precise analyses of the benefits of proposed health and environmental regulations remain beyond the capability of state-of-the-art scientific and economic knowledge. Even some major costs, such as a regulation's effect on innovation or productivity, are essentially unquantifiable.[16] Thus the fundamental question of whether a proposed regulation is worthwhile is answered by judgment and politics, as it always has been.

The "New Federalism"

The Reagan administration continued a long Republican tradition by making efforts to shift responsibilities from the federal government to the states. The Republicans have favored such moves both because of a belief that "small" (state) government is inherently better than "big" (federal) government and because of their perception that political pressures are more likely to be favorable to Republican interests at the state than at the federal level. However, it is hard to avoid the conclusion that the Reagan administration used the shift of responsibilities to the states, at least in the environmental area, for another reason as well—as a way to eliminate particular functions altogether.

During the first three years of the Reagan administration, the great majority of state governments have been in deep financial trouble. Taxpayer revolts placed limits on the ability of states to raise taxes or pass bond issues. The near-depression economic conditions of the early 1980s sharply reduced state revenues while necessitating increased outlays for welfare and other service functions. Declines in gasoline sales reduced a major source of state revenue, while the gas "glut" weakened those states that derived significant revenue from oil and gas extraction. The changes in the federal tax code under Reagan adversely affected many states whose tax systems were based on the federal tax provisions.

Despite the states' financial plight, and despite a professed policy of giving them more responsibility, the administration pursued a policy of sharply cutting back on federal aid to the states.

The Congressional Budget Office reported that, in constant 1982 dollars, state water grants declined 53 percent between 1981 and the 1984 budget request. The comparable cut in air grants was 33 percent.[17] Similar, although somewhat less drastic, cuts were made in other assistance programs for state environmental functions.

These reductions significantly weakened the ability of states to implement their existing control responsibilities. In 1982 the average state depended on federal funds for 45 percent of its air pollution control budget and 46 percent of its water pollution control budget (excluding construction of waste-treatment plants).[18] While state grants were being reduced, EPA was trying to get the states to assume greater responsibility for pollution-control programs, both by delegating entire programs and by leaving to the states particular functions that had been carried out by the federal government. The premise of many of the most important pollution programs is that EPA will be able to certify the adequacy of state programs and then delegate responsibility for them. This is true, for example, of the National Pollution Discharge Elimination System (NPDES) permit program under the Clean Water Act and of the prevention of significant deterioration (PSD) program under the Clean Air Act. However, the reduction in federal grants has made it increasingly likely that either the states will not assume these functions, or, if they do, they will implement them poorly or not at all.

The Reagan administration has made a major effort to delegate programs to the states. According to the Council on Environmental Quality, "By the end of 1982 state governments had been delegated enforcement responsibilities for over 95 percent of applicable National Emissions Standards for Hazardous Air Pollutants, and over 90 percent of applicable New Source Performance Standards, up from 64 percent at the beginning of the year. In addition, of the 60 state and local agencies eligible to grant and enforce new source (air) permits, 48 had been delegated full or partial authorities by the end of 1982, up from 26 at the end of 1981." [19]

The Reagan drive to give regulatory responsibility to the states has created some backlash in the business community. Companies that have national markets do not look favorably on trying to cope with 50 different state regulatory schemes and perhaps numerous local regulations as well. Thus, when EPA decided not to issue noise regulations for motorcycles, the motorcycle manufacturers pleaded for a reversal of the decision, knowing that states and localities might try to fill the vacuum. Similarly, the chemical manufacturers, already faced with a number of state and local workplace chemical-labeling rules, have encouraged promulgation of a federal labeling rule that would preempt the local regulations.[20]

Given the political weakness and budget reductions at EPA, combined with the financial weakness of the states and the reduction in federal aid to them, the new federalism does not look promising. It is perhaps best understood as an attempt to reduce government power at all levels, rather than as an attempt to shift power from the federal government to the states.

The Effects on Policy Implementation

The Reagan administration brought a clear change in direction to environmental policy. In contrast to the general Carter policy—which called for protecting the environment while being aware of the economic costs to the private sector—the Reagan policy can best be summarized as reducing the costs to the private sector while being aware, sometimes, of the impact on environmental protection. The initial regulatory thrust of the administration succinctly captures the direction of Reagan policy—it was called the Task Force on Regulatory Relief. Regulations were perceived as burdens from which the public needed relief rather than as measures to protect the public.

The distinction between policy and implementation is arbitrary because in a very real sense the policy of an agency is what it does, not what it says. Although government officials may intend to make certain things happen and be frustrated by the conflicts and complexities of a seemingly intractable world, often the best gauge of what an official really intends is what actually happens as policy is implemented. Regardless of intentions, the skill of an official must be judged in part by the degree of success in converting policy into reality.

The most obvious gap between policy and implementation at EPA was Gorsuch's much publicized intent to bring "administrative efficiency" to the agency. She took over an organization that, although it suffered from numerous problems, was, in the opinion of many Washington observers, more efficient than most federal agencies. When she left, the agency was, in the opinion of incoming Administrator William D. Ruckelshaus, "on the verge of spinning out of control." [21] Agency employees were demoralized and many major programs were close to paralysis.

There are no objective measures available to describe the overall agency efficiency, but, from what this writer could judge, efficiency declined markedly between 1981 and 1983. It took longer than ever to get decisions made and routine rules approved. Communication among many agency programs ceased, and no effort was made to deal with chronic administrative problems such as contracting. All this is not surprising, given Gorsuch's operating style. She limited her contact almost entirely to a few trusted staff aides who themselves were mostly inexperienced in both administration and environmental policy. The deputy administrator, who in the past had been responsible for much of the day-to-day administration, was John Hernandez, a professor of engineering from New Mexico. Hernandez generally was excluded from the Gorsuch inner circle and limited his interest to some aspects of science policy and the agency's position on the Clean Water Act Amendments.

On paper the Gorsuch regime did achieve some administrative improvements, but often at a high cost in program content. The backlog of EPA reviews of state implementation plans under the Clean Air Act was reduced sharply, but at the cost of much less scrutiny of the plans. Similarly, although the pace of pesticide registrations was greatly accelerated, it was discovered that some of the EPA employees responsible for reviewing them were simply accepting the industry-submitted data as their own rather than subjecting the data to critical scrutiny.[22] The danger in doing this was highlighted by the finding in an internal EPA report that two-thirds of the test results from a major testing laboratory, whose data had been used in support of the

Figure 7-1 Civil Cases Referred by EPA to Justice Department

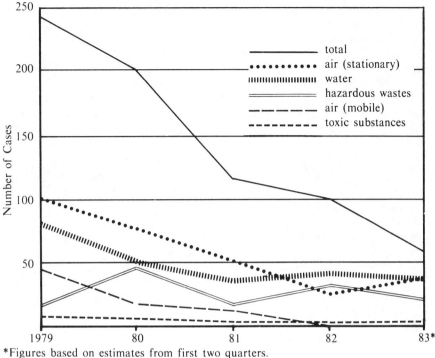

*Figures based on estimates from first two quarters.
Source: American Environmental Safety Council

registration of a large number of pesticides, were false and invalid.[23]

Enforcement, the cutting edge of implementation of the pollution-control laws, was in a state of confusion for most of Gorsuch's reign. As already noted, responsibility for enforcement was shifted several times. In 1980 EPA referred 200 civil enforcement cases to the Justice Department. In 1982 only 100 cases were referred *(see Figure 7-1)*. Between 1980 and 1982 the number of administrative enforcement orders issued by the agency declined by one-third. Air pollution enforcement orders plummeted to 23 in 1982 from 155 in 1980 *(see Chapter 9)*.

Other specific EPA programs and functions suffered the same fate as enforcement. All research projects not directly needed for immediate regulatory requirements were halted or were being phased out by 1983. As Robert V. Bartlett points out in Chapter 6, research at EPA steadily eroded, and by early 1983 "crippled" was the adjective most frequently used to describe the agency's Office of Research and Development.[24] Programs to monitor environmental conditions and trends were curtailed or eliminated. For example, the mussel-watch program, which provided the only data on organic chemical contamination of marine waters, was eliminated, and the inhalableparticulates network, which provided the only data on the type and amount of toxic substances breathed by the American public, was cut in half in 1983 and slated for elimination in 1984.

Dissemination of information by the agency was sharply reduced, a reduction that reinforced the agency's policy of minimizing citizen participation. In most of the individual programs, the opportunity for citizen input was formally or informally reduced. Funds for citizen education and citizen participation were eliminated not only in EPA but in the Department of the Interior and the Forest Service as well. At the top levels of the administration, Gorsuch followed Watt's policy of not meeting with environmental organizations.

The unfortunate consequences of EPA's implementation of its programs were starkly revealed in the 1983 investigations of the Superfund program. The basic implementation approach taken by the agency was first to negotiate with the relevant industries about recovering the costs of cleaning up abandoned hazardous waste sites and only after that to begin the actual cleanup. Thus, implementation was designed to delay the start of action to remove hazards, an approach that was compounded by internal dissension about the program, possibly politically motivated delays in cleaning up particular sites, and general administrative inefficiency.[25] The way in which Superfund was implemented triggered the events that led to Gorsuch's downfall.

Counterrevolution at EPA

By the fall of 1982 the impacts of the administration's policies on EPA were clear, and a growing number of Washington observers, especially on Capitol Hill, began to conclude that the administration's goal was not just to curb the agency or to change its policies, but rather to destroy it completely. It was a minority view, but all except the most ardent administration supporters had to concede that the future of the agency as an institution was being jeopardized by budget cuts, personnel departures, demoralization, poor management, and the isolation of EPA from all of its potential constituents, even the business community.

Institutional destruction is an unusual concern in Washington, so that the events that occurred in relation to EPA during the fall of 1982 and the following winter were news. The first major action was the vote by the full House of Representatives, on December 16, 1982, to cite Gorsuch for contempt of Congress, making her one of the highest ranking government officials ever subjected to a contempt citation. It now seems likely that Gorsuch withheld documents related to implementation of Superfund, the immediate cause of her citation, at the request of the Justice Department, which was looking for a test case on executive privilege.[26] However, her stormy history with the relevant House committees and her inability to compromise made the fight over the Superfund documents particularly vehement.

Gorsuch herself took the next step when, on February 4, 1983, she asked

Rita Lavelle, the assistant administrator in charge of hazardous waste and the Superfund, to resign. Lavelle refused but was fired three days later by the president. At this time, Lavelle was under investigation by two House subcommittees; one was considering charging her with perjury and the other was investigating a possible conflict of interest.

The Lavelle firing ignited the smoldering controversy into an inferno. Each day during February, the front pages of the *Washington Post* and the *New York Times* featured some new charge leveled against EPA. The number of congressional committees investigating the agency rose to six. On February 16, the *Times* called for Gorsuch's dismissal: "On becoming head of the Environmental Protection Agency, Anne Gorsuch inherited one of the most efficient and capable agencies of government. She has turned it into an Augean stable, reeking of cynicism, mismanagement and decay.... Mrs. Gorsuch is charged with protecting the nation's air, land and water from filth. Instead she has polluted the Environmental Protection Agency's reputation for impartial administration of science and law. Only with her departure can repair of the damage begin."

The White House, together with Gorsuch, took steps to try to limit the damage. On February 17, the president ordered a Justice Department investigation into the charges against Lavelle and other allegations of misconduct in the agency. On February 23, Burford (Gorsuch had married February 20 and changed her name accordingly) fired the agency's inspector general and the assistant administrator for administration. These steps only fanned the flames.

On March 1, Rep. John D. Dingell, D-Mich., wrote the president stating that he had evidence of wrongdoing and criminal conduct at EPA. The next day a *Times* editorial attacked the president: "The problem lies in the White House, which for two years has allowed Interior Secretary Watt and his protégé, Mrs. Burford, to maneuver around the laws protecting the nation's environment.... By maintaining her [Burford] in office, Mr. Reagan signals that he intends to maintain the policy of backdoor favoritism to industry and a stalemate of distrust with Congress."

Within the agency, the controversy brought all normal business to a halt. Guards were posted outside offices to prevent removal of documents, and a small army of FBI agents roamed the headquarters building conducting interviews as part of the Justice Department's investigation. The *Wall Street Journal* quoted a chemical company lobbyist's description of the agency: "There's a bizarre quality to the whole place. It's turned into a never-never land of rumor, innuendo and constant bureaucratic upheaval." [27]

On March 9, Burford submitted her resignation to the president, stating that she hoped it would "terminate the controversy and confusion that has crippled my agency." [28] Reagan accepted the resignation, praising her service as administrator; he expressed disappointment that "some persons" had "unjustly attacked" Burford and "made unfair judgements based upon allegations and innuendo alone." [29]

Burford's departure did not immediately quiet the agency's congressional critics. They shifted their fire to the remaining Reagan appointees. Charges of favoritism, conflict of interest, and perjury were leveled against a number of officials. On March 21 Reagan nominated Ruckelshaus, who had been EPA's first administrator, to succeed Burford. A few days later the White House accepted the resignations of five top agency officials who had been named in congressional charges. This left only three top appointees who had served under Burford, and two of them resigned shortly after Ruckelshaus took office. On May 18, 1983, Ruckelshaus was confirmed by the Senate and sworn into office by the president.

In retrospect, three explanations have been offered for the extraordinary chain of events at EPA. Each serves certain interests of those offering the explanation, but each also has some validity.

The first explanation, most frequently offered by environmentalists, is that the gap between the antienvironment views of the administration and the proenvironment views of the general public simply became too great to tolerate. The public was outraged at what was happening at EPA, and Congress, sharing the outrage and serving as the instrument of popular revulsion, spearheaded a campaign to bring the administration more into line with the popular will.

The second explanation—what might be labeled the Washington insider's explanation—is that the major cause of these events was the managerial, ethical, and, above all, political ineptness of Gorsuch and the other political appointees at EPA. Like a tragic figure from a classical Greek drama, Gorsuch, from her first day in office, began sowing the seeds of her own destruction. Each insult to Congress, each snubbing of an interest group, each refusal to listen or compromise formed a chain of events that could end only with the downfall of Gorsuch and her associates.

The third explanation, that of the Reagan administration, is that the EPA appointees were the victims of Democratic committee chairmen in the House and a liberal press corps. The House Democrats and the liberal press, especially the *Washington Post* and the *New York Times*, saw the changes in EPA as an opportunity to attack the president and to gain partisan advantage. They used any charges they could find to make the president's appointees appear corrupt and incompetent, and they were aided in their effort by information supplied by career EPA employees who did not support the president.

To a political scientist, two aspects of the EPA events are particularly intriguing. The first is the light that the events shed on the concept of an agency's constituency. Students in political science are taught that if an agency is to survive in a pluralist government with weak political parties, it must have support from nongovernmental groups in society. The nature of these groups and the strength and type of support that they give may vary widely, but without some kind of supportive constituency an agency cannot last. The EPA under Gorsuch, however, provided a unique case of a large and highly visible agency stripped of all constituency support. For a short while the president's support kept Gorsuch in office, but soon the lack of constituency resulted in a complete change of personnel and a sharp change in policy direction.

While the absence of constituency support for the EPA under Gorsuch was most apparent during the closing months of her tenure, this weakness was a factor almost from the beginning. The agency was not "captured" by the regulated industry interests, even though it attempted to mold its policies to satisfy the business community. The major industry groups were not particularly happy with the Reagan appointees to EPA from the start, and their disenchantment increased rapidly. After Gorsuch's first year in office, business interests feared that her political ineptness was working against them and that the inevitable backlash to her style and policies likely would result in stronger environmental regulation.

The second interesting aspect of the episode is what it shows about the mechanisms that the American polity has developed for changing major policy directions outside the electoral process. Many commentators noted the similarities between the Watergate events that led to the Nixon resignation and the events that led to Burford's—secrecy, shredding of documents, perjury, conflict of interest. The more important parallels, however, are in the process by which the protagonists lost their offices. In both cases, a symbiotic relationship between members of Congress of the party opposed to the president and the press created an issue that so dominated public attention and threatened to be so injurious to the party in power in the executive branch that finally the only course open was a major change in leadership.

It is very doubtful that what might be labeled the "no-confidence" process can be planned or intentionally triggered by any group or individual, because it requires action by too many independent parties. Rather, a set of conditions—publicly visible indications of illegal acts, an erosion of constituency support, a strong opposition in Congress, knowledgeable informants eager to talk to journalists, a visible target—are necessary to set the process in motion. Whether the process is healthy for American democracy is a matter that will not be discussed here, but it does seem that we have evolved a substitute for the parliamentary vote of no confidence.

Institutional Change and Environmental Policy

The institutional changes that took place at EPA in 1981 and again in 1983 were of a magnitude unusual in the American system. Several factors help to explain what made such changes possible.

EPA policy affects a broad range of interests. Pollution control regulations have an impact on nearly every sector of the U.S. economy, and pollution concerns thousands of organized groups and millions of individual citizens. Thus, changes in the political climate or relative political strength of different groups are likely to be reflected more in EPA policy than in the policy of many other agencies that deal with a smaller number of people and a narrower spectrum of interests. Political scientist A. Grant Jordan has pointed out a tendency in recent years for the constituency of federal agencies to become broader and less well defined.[30] EPA exemplifies this general shift from "iron triangles" to "elastic nets" as the characteristic configuration of the interest groups attentive to an agency's policies.

Reagan's election represented increased power for business interests and less power for environmental and consumer advocates. It signaled, at least for a time, a widespread sentiment against government regulation. These changes in relative power and perceived public opinion fueled Reagan's effort to launch a new policy cycle.

Both the Republican-controlled Senate and the nominally Democratic House gave general support to the Reagan changes, especially the budget cuts. Reagan also had a significant added advantage in making the EPA changes: his goals largely were negative—reduced budgets, curtailed programs, fewer regulations—whereas most of the traditional congressional checks on presidential power were designed to prevent presidents from taking positive actions. It is not easy for Congress to force executive agencies to use money they do not want or implement programs they do not support. Reagan was working *with* the bias of the system, a bias against positive action.

One can only speculate about the impact of the changes that have taken place. It is likely that the impact on policy and on the physical environment has been more incremental and can be reversed more easily than the impact on governmental institutions, which has been more radical and long term.

The broad policy mandates governing environmental policy have been left largely intact by the Reagan administration. During the first two and a half years of the administration, no environmental statutes were changed in any significant way, and most of the regulations implementing them were not changed drastically.

The impact on the physical environment is difficult to estimate because of the long time lag between governmental changes and the detection of physical impacts. If, for example, lax enforcement of the pollution-control laws actually has resulted in increased pollution, it will be several years before the data that would show such an increase are analyzed and made available. Some of the potentially most important impacts, such as increased disease from allowing the manufacture of high-risk chemicals, may never be detected, even if they did occur.

Some of the changes made by the Interior Department have more easily detectable and perhaps less reversible impacts. The accelerated leasing of public lands for oil, coal, gas, and mineral extraction could result in irreversible financial and ecological effects. To the extent that Watt's policies have led to the sale of valuable federal lands or the surrender of federal water rights, the lands will not be repurchased and the water rights will not be regained. The lack of money to purchase parklands will result in land-use changes that cannot be altered. The lack of funds for resource protection in the national parks may mean the loss of irreplaceable resources. The lack of support for historic preservation is likely to result in the irretrievable loss of some historic structures.

The institutional changes, especially at EPA, may be the most difficult impacts to reverse. The appointment of Ruckelshaus was a big step in restoring the agency's credibility, but a tarnished reputation takes a long time to restore. The de facto veto power over regulations that the administration gave to OMB means that EPA no longer fully controls its regulatory process, and the fact that OMB operates outside the due process and disclosure protections applicable to the regulatory agencies means that environmental regulations are still subject to charges that they were affected by unfair and covert influence.

The loss of many of the most senior and competent career personnel at EPA will not be rapidly remedied, as it can take years, even decades, to develop a cadre of capable and experienced people in an agency. The same applies to programs and institutions within the agency; for example, the development of a good laboratory or a smoothly running program can involve years of planning and work. The institutional damage done to EPA (as well as to CEQ and parts of Interior) between 1981 and 1983 was very great, and the reduction in governmental competence and capability will affect programs and performance for some time to come.

Notes

1. Richard P. Nathan, *The Plot That Failed: Nixon and the Administrative Presidency* (New York: Wiley, 1975).
2. Steven R. Weisman, "Reagan's Appointees Reflect the Process," *New York Times,* March 20, 1983.
3. Chester A. Newland, "The Reagan Presidency: Limited Government and Political Administration," *Public Administration Review* 43 (January/February 1983).
4. Kathleen A. Kemp, "The Regulators: Partisanship and Public Policy," *Policy Studies Journal* 11 (March 1983): 292.
5. Gary R. Covington, "The Council on Environmental Quality: A Prodigal Presidential Agency" (Paper prepared for presentation at the Annual Meeting of the Midwest Political Science Association, Chicago, April 21, 1983).
6. Dick Kirschten, "Administration Using Carter-Era Reform to Manipulate the Levers of Government," *National Journal,* April 9, 1983, 732-736.
7. U.S. Congress, House Committee on Agriculture, *EPA Pesticide Regulatory Program Study,* 97th Cong., 2d sess., December 17, 1982.
8. Conservation Foundation, *State of the Environment 1982* (Washington, D.C.: Conservation Foundation, 1982), 410.
9. *Washington Post,* June 23, 1982.
10. Howard Kurtz, "Since Reagan Took Office, EPA Enforcement Actions Have Fallen," *Washington Post,* March 1, 1983.
11. Newland, "The Reagan Presidency," 7.
12. Ibid., 10.
13. U.S. Congress, House Committee on Energy and Commerce, *Presidential Control of Agency Rulemaking,* 97th Cong., 2d sess., June 15, 1981, 70-73. For data on the results of the review process, see "Executive Order 12291 on Federal Regulation: Progress During 1982" (Executive Office of the President, Office of Management and Budget, April 1983, Mimeographed).
14. Jim Tozzi, deputy administrator for information and regulatory affairs, Office of Management and Budget, "A Note to the Regulatory Relief Community" (April 29, 1983, Mimeographed).
15. John Fialka, "Waiving the Rules," *Wall Street Journal,* June 6, 1983.

16. Daniel Swartzman et al., *Cost-Benefit Analysis and Environmental Regulations* (Washington, D.C.: Conservation Foundation, 1982).
17. Congressional Budget Office, *The EPA: Overview of the Proposed 1984 Budget* (April 1983, Mimeographed), 6.
18. National Governors Association, *The State of the States: Management of Environmental Programs in the 1980s* (Washington, D.C.: National Governors Association, 1982), 2.
19. Council on Environmental Quality, *Environmental Quality 1982* (Washington, D.C.: Government Printing Office, 1983), 75.
20. Martin Tolchin, "Industry Sees Dark Side of Regulation," *New York Times,* May 1, 1983.
21. *Washington Post,* May 28, 1983, 6.
22. Hearing before the House Committee on Agriculture, Subcommittee on Department Operations, Research, and Foreign Agriculture, *EPA Pesticide Regulatory Program Study,* 97th Cong., 2d sess., 195-197.
23. "The Murky World of Toxicity Testing," *Science,* June 10, 1983, 1130-1132.
24. Will Lepkowski, "Research at EPA: A Crisis of Bad Morale, Unhappy History," *Chemical and Engineering News,* May 9, 1983, 40-43.
25. *Air/Water Pollution Report,* May 23, 1983, 200.
26. See Philip Shabecoff, "EPA Chief Urges Opening All Files to Quash Dispute," *New York Times,* March 4, 1983.
27. Andy Pasztor, "Complex Cleanup," *Wall Street Journal,* April 29, 1983.
28. *Washington Post,* March 10, 1983.
29. Ibid.
30. A. Grant Jordan, "Iron Triangles, Woolly Corporatism and Elastic Nets: Images of the Policy Process," *Journal of Public Policy* 1, no. 1 (February 1981): 95-125.

8. DEREGULATION: THE FAILURE AT EPA

Richard N. L. Andrews

The history of recent American environmental policy is overwhelmingly a history of environmental regulation. Since the National Environmental Policy Act was passed in 1969, more than 20 major environmental regulatory statutes have been enacted into law. Equally significant regulatory laws intended to achieve other social purposes, such as occupational health and safety, consumer product and highway safety, and civil rights protection, also have been passed by Congress. These statutes in turn generated a decade-long outpouring of federal regulations—substantive, procedural, and administrative—that was unprecedented in U.S. peacetime history.

By 1980 two parallel trends in environmental regulatory policy had emerged, during both Republican and Democratic administrations. One was a growing commitment to "regulatory reform," which included efforts to use economic incentives to achieve regulatory purposes, increase regulatory oversight by the Executive Office of the President, and streamline and coordinate regulatory paperwork. Significant initiatives to these ends already had been undertaken by both the Ford and the Carter administrations. The other was a continued growth in the actual body of regulations, as the agencies gradually geared up to implement the full scope of their statutory responsibilities.

The times were favorable, therefore, for both the agencies and the regulated industries to digest their responsibilities, reassess those regulations that were unreasonable or ineffective, and adjust their initial responses to the laws into workable patterns of long-term compliance. Some reassessments already were scheduled, such as reauthorization of the Clean Air and Water Acts in the early 1980s. While other regulatory programs still were being phased in, Congress also was developing overall regulatory reform legislation, including proposals to strengthen both congressional and judicial as well as administrative oversight of proposed regulations.

Whoever won the 1980 presidential election, therefore, would have given serious attention to regulatory reassessment. A basic question that divided both the candidates and even the business community, however, was whether this reassessment should seek *stabilization* or *reversal*. Many companies had accepted and accommodated environmental goals as long as their competitors also had to comply and had invested in control equipment; for them, the preferred policy was simply the conservative goal of stabilization, making requirements and enforcement more predictable while weeding out inconsistent or unworkable provisions. Others, however—especially those that had not yet invested in compliance, along with some whose initial compliance investments may have been frustrated by later regulatory changes—chose to fight rather than comply and mounted a massive lobbying and advertising campaign against "government over-regulation." This latter group sought a fundamental reversal of the growth of business regulation in many substantive areas, including especially the environment.[1]

The Reagan administration came into office explicitly committed, as its highest domestic policy priority, to reversing the recent growth of the federal domestic programs and regulatory influence in American society. Environmental regulations were among those directly targeted for reconsideration, despite their general popularity and continuing political support. The administration also made a fateful initial commitment to pursue its deregulatory policy primarily through administrative means—such as appointing zealots to key positions, slashing budgets, expanding executive oversight authority, and unilaterally changing regulations—rather than through proposals to amend the regulatory statutes themselves. The results, after two and one half years, call into question both the legitimacy and the effectiveness of this strategy, even from the perspective of many people who agreed that vigorous regulatory reform was needed. This strategy has not achieved many reforms that were needed: in fact, by unnecessarily fanning partisan and ideological polarization, it has set them back. In the process it has caused serious damage to regulatory processes whose integrity and predictability are as important to businesses as to the general public.

The Deregulation Strategy

Within three weeks of Ronald Reagan's election to the presidency, he received a manifesto from his designated budget director, David A. Stockman, predicting a "Republican economic Dunkirk"—a preset trap leading to humiliating defeat—unless Reagan took swift and sweeping action to redirect federal regulatory policies. Stockman pointed to "over a dozen sweeping 1970s environmental, energy and safety statutes devoid of policy standards and criteria"; to a "vast tooling-up" by "McGovernite no-growth activists who assumed control during the Carter administration"; and thence to a "mindboggling outpouring of rulemakings, interpretive guidelines, and major litigation," all of them "heavily biased toward maximization of regulatory scope and burden," which was just reaching the stage where it would "sweep through the industrial economy with gale force." Stockman specifically attacked as examples EPA's proposed regulations for carbon monoxide, bus and truck noise, hazardous wastes, toxic chemicals, and industrial boiler emissions. He concluded that "unless swift, comprehensive, and far-reaching regulatory policy corrections are undertaken immediately, an unprecedented, quantum scale-up of the much-discussed 'regulatory burden' will occur during the next 18-40 months."[2]

Stockman's arguments were echoed by Reagan's transition team for business regulation—headed by Murray Weidenbaum, the economist who had led the attack against the expansion of business regulation—and they reflected Reagan's own prejudice that excessive environmental regulation was responsible for many of the nation's economic woes. Together these pressures simply rolled over the more moderate recommendations of Reagan's resources and environment transition team, even though the latter was led by experienced and distinguished Republican environmental leaders such as Russell Train and William D. Ruckelshaus.

One result was a green light for Stockman and Weidenbaum, with staff support by the Office of Management and Budget (OMB), to shape the administration's basic deregulatory policy and to target environmental regulations especially. Another result was simply to sweep aside both the recommendations and the values of knowledgeable Republican environmental leaders, including two former EPA administrators. This was a fateful policy choice, considering that those Republicans had set up the original environmental regulatory system and had run it for two of the three previous administrations; both knew its politics and problems far better than Stockman or Weidenbaum.

Methods: Administrative Tactics

To implement this policy, Stockman advocated "an orchestrated series of unilateral administrative actions to deter, revise, or rescind existing and pending regulations where clear legal authority exists." [3] He proposed an immediate moratorium on new regulations, mandatory use of cost-benefit, cost-effectiveness, and comparative risk analysis for all proposed regulations, and the use of OMB's power over agency budgets to shrink directly the size and influence of the regulatory agencies. By the middle of January 1981, OMB staff already had produced a "hit list" of some 242 regulations for possible reconsideration and a shorter list of 110 for early attention. Prominent on this list were EPA regulations affecting the auto, steel, and chemical industries. Proposals were being drafted for dramatic regulatory relief initiatives and for even more dramatic regulatory agency budget cuts. Political appointments to those agencies were being screened primarily for loyalty to the same policy directions.

The choice of unilateral administrative tactics clearly had features attractive to an incoming president seeking dramatic policy change, but it also had high costs both to regulatory predictability and to political legitimacy. It was the quickest way to achieve both the symbolic appearance and, to an extent, the reality of decisive policy change. It allowed the president to retain maximum control of the agenda and to claim maximum credit for the results rather than having to share the credit with his predecessors, the Congress, or other participants and interests in the regulatory process. It avoided the long gauntlet of agencies, constituencies, and congressional committees that would have to be run in order to change each particular regulatory statute. (Reagan could have sought a single overall regulatory reform statute, a subject Congress had in fact seriously considered in 1980, but did not.) Finally, it allowed him to focus all his legislative influence on budget and tax proposals, undiluted by other divisive issues.

However, this choice also neglected opportunities for statutory change in laws that were up for reauthorization at that time. It also seriously underestimated the need to establish legitimacy and build consensus for the particular policy changes the president wished to pursue and for which he ultimately would need broader acceptance by the Congress and public.

By the time Reagan took office in January 1981, his philosophy of government and his key policies concerning environmental regulation already were clearly set. Regulatory relief for business would take precedence wherever possible over particular regulatory objectives; environmental regulations would be especially targeted for reassessment; and unilateral administrative tactics would be the general approach to implementation. The primary authority to oversee implementation of these policies was lodged in the Office of Management and Budget (OMB). This too was a significant shift with mixed implications for public policy. It was assumed that regulatory change could be better achieved by "top-down" control through Executive Office agencies than by "bottom-up" initiatives in the regulatory agencies themselves—a debatable point.

Executive Implementation: Control by Oversight

One of Reagan's first acts as president was to create, on January 22, 1981, a Presidential Task Force on Regulatory Relief. Vice President George Bush was appointed chairman. Other members included the secretaries of commerce, labor, and the treasury, the attorney general, the OMB director (Stockman), the chairman of the Council of Economic Advisers (Weidenbaum), and the president's assistant for policy development. This task force was to review both proposed and existing regulations and to recommend changes to relieve businesses as well as state and local governments from federal regulatory burdens. Staff support was to be provided by OMB through its recently created Office of Information and Regulatory Affairs (OIRA), thus giving OMB the primary role in shaping the task force's agenda and output.

Regulatory Relief Task Force. Immediately the task force began compiling its own hit list of "burdensome" regulations. It began with the January list prepared by OMB (and in particular with some 30 to 72 regulations that had been formally proposed in the last few weeks of the Carter administration) and then the task force invited nominations by businesses, trade associations, state and local governments, and anyone else who might feel burdened by regulations. The largest number of requests received concerned EPA regulations. Among the particular environmental regulations singled out by the task force were all those affecting the auto industry, especially various air quality standards and gasoline lead limits; hazardous wastes; industrial pretreatment of waste-water discharges to public sewers; premanufacturing notification and other EPA regulations concerning manufacture and testing of new toxic chemicals; and pesticide registration. The most immediate product was a regulatory relief package for the auto industry—including 18 deregulatory actions by EPA and 17 by other agencies—responding to its economic distress in the face of domestic recession and effective foreign competition.

By December 1981, 91 existing regulations had been targeted for review. Sixty percent of those concerned health, safety, or environmental quality, most promulgated by EPA and the National Highway Traffic Safety Administration. By August 1983, when the task force declared its mission accomplished and disbanded, it had reviewed 119 regulations, nearly half of them from EPA and NHTSA; 76 of these had been revised or eliminated, including 17 completed and 5 more proposed for EPA. Three more were still under review.[4]

Regulatory Review. On February 17, 1981, President Reagan issued Executive Order 12291, "the support beam of his administration's framework for regulatory reform," in the words of a conservative commentator.[5] This executive order built upon previous requirements that agencies prepare "regulatory impact analyses" (RIAs) for all major regulatory proposals, but it went beyond them. Whenever an agency proposed any major new regulation, Reagan's order directed, its benefits had to be calculated in economic terms and balanced against its costs, and only regulations whose calculable benefits thus exceeded their costs should be issued—no matter that benefits to health and environmental quality might be difficult or even inappropriate to quantify in economic terms.

The executive order also gave unprecedented oversight authority to OMB to control the regulatory process through supervision of these analytical requirements. OMB not only would review all RIAs but also could demand RIAs for other proposed or existing regulations. OMB was given authority to delay publication of proposed rules in the *Federal Register* until they satisfied OMB, and no reviewable record of OMB's comments or the agency's response had to be kept. This new oversight process represented a direct White House intervention in the varied "balancing" judgments assigned by the regulatory statutes to the agencies.[6]

Budget and Staff Reduction. As discussed in Chapter 6, the Reagan administration also used draconian budget and staff cuts—initiated by Stockman and the OMB staff before agency administrators even were appointed—as a deliberate policy tool to reduce the influence of the regulatory agencies. Before Anne Gorsuch was even sworn in as administrator, EPA's staff had been cut by 11 percent, and a 12 percent cut had been targeted for its budget; a second 12 percent cut was proposed just 6 months later, and by the 1984 budget these reductions had grown to a staff reduction of 29 percent and a budget cut in real terms of 44 percent.

Reorganization. Reagan also effectively eliminated all other Executive Office mechanisms for regulatory policy making and consolidated these functions in OMB. He eliminated the Council on Wage and Price Stability, which had reviewed regulatory analyses under presidents Ford and Carter, and transferred its staff to OMB. He also abolished the Regulatory Analysis Review Group (RARG), a quasi-cabinet council somewhat similar to the Bush task force except that it also had as its members some regulatory agency heads. Third, he eliminated the U.S. Regulatory Council, the one forum in which the regulatory agencies themselves were induced to participate and to coordinate regulatory reforms.[7] Since the Council on Environmental Quality could not be abolished without congressional action, Reagan simply fired its entire staff and replaced them, after a budget cut of 72 percent, with a token staff of loyalist appointees who had little experience or influence.

While streamlining the Executive Office has merit in principle, Reagan's reorganization had an unfortunate effect on regulatory reform. The Executive Office is in a unique position to promote interagency coordination and other reforms aimed at eliminating the sometimes conflicting requirements of many separate laws. The abolishment of the Regulatory Council and RARG, however, destroyed the only two organizations in which these kinds of reforms were beginning to emerge. Only ad hoc OMB review of individual regulations remained.

From the perspective of institutional politics, OMB thus won a major victory, one coveted by some of its senior staff members for 20 years. But from the perspective of regulatory policy, this victory might well prove seriously counterproductive. OMB can now block regulatory proposals, but it has neither the authority nor the expertise to initiate better ones, nor to make other changes that would improve regulatory management within and among the regulatory agencies. In budget and now regulatory matters OMB stands inevitably in an adversarial rather than in a cooperative posture toward the agencies. It is thus a poor substitute for institutions, such as the Regulatory Council, through which the agencies might participate cooperatively in improving regulatory management.

Appointments. As noted in Chapter 7, most of Reagan's political appointees were inexperienced and were selected on the basis of ideological conformity. A key question to ask of this tactic—especially in light of subsequent events—is: why not a William Ruckelshaus from the start, or any of a number of competent appointees that Reagan had available from his transition team and other sources? The only likely answer seems to be that either Reagan, or the advisers who framed the appointment decisions to the regulatory agencies, *did not want* competent or experienced people in these positions. Experienced people were assumed to be "the enemy," sympathetic rather than opposed to regulation. Reagan and his advisers wanted people who either would deregulate vigorously or at least would follow orders—

people who were on "automatic pilot," so to speak. Experienced people would have independent access to their agencies' constituencies, independent ideas of how to manage their agencies and make regulatory decisions, and a strong likelihood of sympathizing with their career staffs on at least some issues. They also would have ties to the "issue networks" in each particular policy arena. At the least they would have slowed down the deregulatory campaign by more substantive analysis and more methodical procedure. Choosing inexperienced heads for the regulatory agencies thus appears to have been a deliberate tactic for pursuing uncritical deregulation, and for further consolidating regulatory control in the Executive Office and effectively in OMB.

In the thrill of victory and the rush of postelection events, ambitious presidential advisers, themselves inexperienced and newly come to great power, possibly never asked themselves the other question that remains unanswered: could agencies with complex legal and technical responsibilities in fact be adequately managed, let alone a radical agenda of lasting policy change be best achieved, by inexperienced ideologues? This question had special force in the regulatory policy area, where many decisions are assigned directly by statute to the agency head.

Administrative Implementation: Following Orders

In regulatory decisions the agency head's responsibility is not simply to implement the president's administrative priorities. The administrator also must make quasi-legislative and quasi-judicial judgments required primarily by statute and by judicial interpretation. Those judgments must be based upon a reviewable record of evidence and reasoning rather than simply a presidential policy preference. Each of the laws administered by EPA sets its own standards—some vague, some quite specific—by which the EPA administrator is to balance the various technical, economic, and other factors that are to enter into the regulatory decisions.

Every EPA administrator therefore has an assumed loyalty to the president, but a more fundamental and independent duty, once appointed, to carry out the regulatory responsibilities assigned directly by the statutes. As a practical matter, the agency head also must build and maintain a consensus on how the laws should be carried out among many constituencies: the White House for one, but also the agency's professional staff, the Congress, and the groups affected by the decisions, such as businesses, state governments, and environmental groups.

The early resignation of Anne Burford (formerly Gorsuch) as EPA administrator reflected in part a congressional vote of no-confidence in the broader budget and regulatory policies of the Reagan administration. But it resulted at least equally from a failure on her part to understand both the substantive role of a regulatory official and the broad-based consensus-building approach necessary to execute it.

Gorsuch's policy agenda for EPA included five objectives:

(1) providing a better scientific foundation for agency decision making;

(2) instituting regulatory reform measures to support the president's economic recovery program;

(3) eliminating backlogs and delays in many of the agency's major programs;

(4) strengthening federal-state-local relationships to support the president's New Federalism program;

(5) improving management and reducing budget at all agency levels.[8]

All these objectives directly affected the agency's regulatory programs. While several represented legitimate goals, their implementation raised serious questions of competence and judgment, and even charges of corruption within the agency, that led to a loss of legitimacy. Ultimately the administrator herself resigned under pressure, and all but one of the EPA's other top-level administrators were fired by Reagan.

Better Science

Science provides an essential foundation for EPA regulations, and over the years EPA has been criticized for basing some of its rules on inadequate scientific evidence. These criticisms focused in part on the precision and accuracy of basic data and in part on the quality and defensibility of scientific conclusions. Some criticisms had merit, although environmental standards inevitably are judgments based upon ambiguous evidence and arguable assumptions.

Gorsuch made two policy changes. Under her supervision, the agency required more detailed prepublication review, by senior administrators and by EPA's Science Advisory Board, of all internal and contract studies. Although in principle desirable, the reviews raised staff complaints of increased administrative delays and bottlenecks; also some changes in the membership of the Science Advisory Board appear to have been based on political considerations.

Gorsuch also tried to refocus EPA's research resources toward the narrow mission of regulatory support, reducing or eliminating support for studies of potential problems still unregulated (such as crop loss due to pollution and indoor air quality). At best such a policy might improve current regulations by shortchanging the future's; it also could be interpreted as a deliberate element of the deregulatory strategy, preventing new initiatives by withholding funds for research that might justify them.

Gorsuch also cut the overall research budget by more than 50 percent in real terms from 1981 to 1984 and the budget for independent research (such as by universities, where quality control and peer review are normally best) by two-thirds.[9] Her rationale for these cuts was an assertion that enough efforts were being completed so that research could be reduced. Clearly some projects were being completed, and some other past priorities deserved reassessment: many of the cuts fell on areas such as industrial technology development that might arguably be done as well by the industries themselves.

But in light of EPA's serious knowledge gaps in rapidly developing areas such as toxic chemicals, along with the agency's need to reassess early standards set on weak evidence, a serious commitment to improving EPA's science would have dictated simply a reallocation rather than a reduction of EPA's research budget. A more plausible explanation of Gorsuch's policy, therefore, is that her primary goal was not improving science, except where convenient and free of cost, but implementing the Reagan/Stockman policy of deregulation and domestic budget cuts.

Actual decisions also cast doubts on Gorsuch's commitment to using better science in regulatory judgments. Formaldehyde, for instance, was identified by peer-reviewed studies as a potential human carcinogen, and in May 1981 Gorsuch received a staff recommendation that it receive a priority assessment for potential regulation. In response, however, her deputy and assistant administrators (John Hernandez, Jr., and John Todhunter) held three secret "science court" meetings with industry scientists and lawyers and subsequently revised the summary of issues in the documents to support a decision not to regulate formaldehyde.[10] Regardless of the decision's merits, the use of secret meetings with industry spokesmen and of personal opinion to override and revise staff analysis hardly exemplifies good science or good regulatory procedure.

Other incidents raised similar questions about the agency's policies. Examples include the decision to lift EPA's ban on disposal of liquids into hazardous waste landfills (rescinded under pressure a month later), to use scientifically disputed assumptions systematically slanted toward less stringent regulation in evaluating potentially carcinogenic pesticides, and to delete from an EPA report, at the company's request, the identification of a Dow Chemical Co. plant as the source of Michigan dioxin contamination.[11] These decisions all displayed judgments that subordinated EPA's own scientific conclusions and other competing viewpoints outside the agency to the preferences of the regulated industries. Such judgments show neither good science nor good regulation.

Regulatory Reform

Under previous administrations EPA had pioneered regulatory reforms such as emissions trading and also had led interagency efforts toward regulatory coordination. EPA Administrator Douglas Costle, for instance, both proposed and eventually chaired the U.S. Regulatory Council in the Carter administration. EPA also played a prominent role in regulatory coordination at a technical staff level through the Interagency Regulatory Liaison Group. While such efforts were in part self-serving—seizing the initiative rather than leaving it to OMB and the White House staff—they also were valuable and legitimate steps on their merits.

To Gorsuch these reforms were "neither effective nor far-reaching in their scope" at their then-current stage of implementation. Instead of further developing them, however, she established her own reform agenda, redirected "to assist in supporting the president's economic recovery program." This agenda included centralized control over regulatory development, vigorous regulatory relief in response to task force requests, and streamlined reporting.[12] She also advocated substituting voluntary cooperation as much as possible for adversarial enforcement proceedings, and allowing state and local governments more flexibility to weaken federal water quality standards.

The Gorsuch record in pursuing this agenda is mixed. Its most beneficial effects were probably in paperwork streamlining, such as the 50 percent reduction in regulations governing grant requests for waste-water-treatment plants, and in a variety of minor regulatory changes generally regarded as cost saving and not obviously harmful.

Yet other actions appeared to subordinate the EPA's responsibilities to White House and business pressures for regulatory relief with more debatable consequences for the agency's statutory mandates. In at least some cases these pressures resulted in serious judgment errors.

At the request of representatives from the gasoline blending industry, for instance, the Bush task force and OMB persuaded EPA to relax its regulations limiting lead additives in gasoline, despite the well-documented evidence of automotive lead's serious effects on urban children. The health science and environmental communities reacted strongly to the proposal, and ultimately the standard was tightened rather than relaxed.[13]

A package of 18 regulatory relief measures was adopted to benefit the auto industry, including proposals to relax heavy-truck emission standards and average diesel particulate emissions. Technical changes also were made to allow more flexibility in application of air quality regulations. Several of these have since been challenged in court, and at least one has been reversed (and was on appeal as of this writing in late 1983).[14]

In the regulation of hazardous waste disposal, EPA abruptly lifted its ban on disposing liquids into chemical waste landfills—apparently to benefit, at least in part, a particular firm in Gorsuch's home state of Colorado, which reportedly had large volumes of these materials lined up and ready to dump in anticipation of the change. The agency reinstated the ban just a few weeks later, under fire from state governments, environmentalists, and even the disposal trade association. In response to task force requests concerning toxic substances, EPA adopted unenforceable voluntary testing and self-certification by chemical manufacturers as a substitute for rule making. Through a combination of budget and regulatory actions, EPA also eliminated all noise regulation.

Perhaps equally important as its actions were areas in which EPA did *not* act under Gorsuch. New regulations came slowly, if at all. By July 1982 EPA had adopted only three of twelve new source performance standards for air quality that had been proposed at the time Gorsuch took office, and it had proposed only one of eleven others that were technically ready for issuance. Similar patterns were evident in other program areas.[15] Responding to OMB pressures, EPA sought to delay indefinitely its regulations for toxic water pollutants discharged to public treatment plants; this action was reversed by court order as an illegal form of deregulation.[16] Most regulations that were issued weakened existing ones: reporting and insurance requirements for hazardous waste facilities were eliminated, for instance, and voluntary testing of toxic chemicals was substituted for EPA rules. Other problem areas deliberately were left unregulated on the grounds that evidence was not yet sufficient, yet at the same time the budget for research that might have been redirected to provide such evidence was being slashed instead.

Most seriously, EPA's own regulatory reform needs were left unmet. Some of EPA's basic statutes were excessively complicated, others lacked procedures for setting priorities, and all needed to be better coordinated to ensure a positive cumulative impact. Two basic statutes were up for reauthorization—the Clean Air Act and the Federal Water Pollution Control Act—and both laws provided rare opportunities for a skillful administrator to build consensus for reforms that required legislative action. These issues, however, required a commitment to good regulation rather than simply to deregulation, and they required consensus-building among the agency's many constituencies—businesses, Congress, state and local governments, environmental groups, the EPA's professional staff, as well as the administration—if they were to be solved. The EPA under Gorsuch not only failed to tackle these issues effectively but also seriously poisoned the atmosphere against the cooperation and consensus building that would be needed.

Finally, EPA's record in enforcement reflected, at the least, serious mismanagement, if not a deliberate attempt to weaken it. Gorsuch's stated position was that enforcement was a vigorous commitment wherever negotiation and voluntary steps were not sufficient to achieve compliance, and she asserted that enforcement steps would be taken whenever negotiation and voluntary actions did not result in compliance. EPA did obtain several highly-publicized voluntary settlements with industries, especially relating to cleanup of old hazardous waste dumps. (Some, however, led to charges of "sweetheart deals" and were made over the objections of EPA lawyers.) [17] But the enforcement budget was cut 26 percent from 1981 to 1983; the enforcement staff was reorganized every 11 weeks during Gorsuch's first year; the agency's output of civil cases and administrative orders dropped by more than 50 percent during that period; and Gorsuch herself reassured at least one company that it need not worry about enforcement against its violations of gasoline lead regulations. According to the General Accounting Office, EPA water-quality enforcement actions declined by more than 40 percent after a 1982 policy memorandum directing "nonconfrontation" settlements. In the same period, 82 percent of a random sample of major dischargers violated their permits at least once: nearly one-third of the violators were significantly in violation at least four months in a row, and 37 percent of the sample submitted incomplete reports.[18]

It is to EPA's advantage to foster voluntary compliance: it cannot take every violator to court, and a few difficult court cases easily can monopolize its resources. The legitimate voluntarism concept, however, depends heavily upon a credible enforcement threat, both to stimulate response and to assure firms that their competitors also must comply. The evidence does not appear to support Gorsuch's assertion of a vigorous commitment to maintain such a threat.

Elimination of Backlogs

A major point of pride to Gorsuch was her elimination of a wide range of backlogs and red tape in the agency's regulatory decision processes. Some of these represented clear improvements, although others were more form than substance. State implementation plans for air quality, for instance, had become encumbered by detailed EPA-approval procedures. Gorsuch reduced these by 90 percent, and court-ordered deadlines for issuing effluent guidelines were met for the first time. The backlog reduction in pesticide registration, however—from 785 applications to zero in two years—raised questions as to whether speed of decisions was being substituted for care in evaluation.[19] Moreover new backlogs in regulatory development were created by the use of centralized administrative control to block proposed new regulations mandated by statute.

Federal-State Relations

The return to the states of both regulatory authority and financial responsibility was a major Reagan administration theme. Gorsuch and her staff thus took considerable satisfaction in asserting that they had reduced administrative requirements that burden state governments and had delegated greater regulatory authority to states in many programs. Between 1981 and 1983 the number of states authorized to administer air quality deterioration prevention increased from 16 to 26, while those authorized to administer hazardous waste programs increased from 18 to 34. Three more states took over water quality permitting, and as many as 26 were expected to take over underground injection control programs in the near future.[20] EPA's general policy clearly shifted from a presumption against delegation to the states toward favoring it unless a clear deficiency was known.

Four serious problems, however, called into question Gorsuch's asserted success in this area. First, the effort to return responsibilities to the states was slowed by the nation's recession and by Reagan's deep budget cuts in federal aid to the states. Many federal environmental regulations already were being implemented primarily by state and local governments, supported by federal grants: more than 45 percent of their budgets for air and water quality, for instance, and more than 69 percent for hazardous wastes came from federal funds. These grants were expected to secure interstate benefits, since significant problems often cross state boundaries and therefore require federal attention. EPA's 1984 budget, however, would provide the states funds with less purchasing power than they had received ten years before. Gorsuch intended ultimately to reduce all these grants to zero. According to a survey by the National Governors' Association, most states could not make up a 20 percent reduction in federal support, and many asserted that they would consider eliminating, turning back, or proportionally reducing programs if federal funds were reduced or eliminated.[21] Such a result might, of course, be a fortuitous or even deliberate contribution to Reagan's goal of deregulation, but it was not consistent with the claim that these responsibilities would be better executed by the states.

Second, the delegation of some responsibilities to the states in fact *increased* the administrative burden on them, requiring them to do paperwork that had been done previously by EPA. In effect, then, federal budget reduction was being achieved at the expense of the states.

Third, the combined effect of delegating regulatory discretion to the states and reducing EPA's enforcement credibility left some states increasingly vulnerable to being played off against others with more lax standards. States always had complained publicly about EPA interference, but many also depended on EPA as a scapegoat for firm regulation of politically powerful local industries. Without federal requirements and EPA enforcement to support them, they could easily be intimidated by firms threatening to relocate elsewhere or to close marginal plants. Finally, despite their attacks on EPA, many industries in fact preferred uniform national requirements to 50 different state systems and continued to seek federal preemption of state rules in areas such as hazardous-waste shipping, chemical labeling, and pesticide marketing.[22]

It is doubtful that EPA's rosy progress reports to the White House reflected these more complex realities.

Management Improvement and Budget Reduction

Gorsuch constantly asserted that EPA could "do more with less." Without doubt EPA's management could be improved, and her streamlining of requirements and reduction of backlogs probably helped. But EPA was not managed badly to begin with, and beyond marginal belt tightening it simply was not credible that the agency could perform better with drastically reduced resources. If it could, why not save real money by doing so at the Pentagon, by cutting the Defense Department's budget? If national security is to be measured by budget increases, then so should environmental protection. Under Gorsuch's implementation of the Reagan/Stockman agenda, however, the agency's four major regulatory programs—air, water, hazardous wastes, and toxics—were cut by 44 percent during fiscal years 1981-1984, and federal assistance to the states under those programs was cut by 47 percent.[23] Such a policy could be interpreted only as a backdoor repeal of statutory responsibilities through administrative tactics, and as such it fundamentally corroded the legitimacy of the administration's program in the eyes of Congress and the public.

Policy Failure and Its Lessons

Ronald Reagan entered office with a ready-made and maturing conservative agenda for environmental reform. It was acknowledged widely that the laws, even if basically sound, were too complex to be well managed, either by

EPA or by its state and local counterparts; that some costly standards were based on inadequate scientific evidence; that federal and state roles needed to be clarified and simplified; that the joint effects of many regulations on the same industrial processes needed to be examined and rationalized; that priorities had to be set sensibly among hazards; and that flexible market mechanisms should be used more widely to achieve regulatory goals.

These ideas had reputable intellectual support as well as political acceptance—in varying degrees, to be sure—by most constituencies involved with environmental regulation. Key laws already were on the legislative agenda for reauthorization during Reagan's first term, and Congress's own discussion of regulatory reform as a whole was maturing. Reagan's own popularity, the Republican capture of the Senate, and the normal deference accorded a new president offered the most auspicious possible conditions for responsible initiatives to stabilize and improve the nation's environmental policies.

By early 1983, however, two years after Reagan's election victory, environmental regulation had become his single most total policy failure and his most glaring political embarrassment. The regulatory process and its public legitimacy had been seriously damaged, without even actually achieving much substantive deregulation. A bit of streamlining was accomplished, but the overall effort had received several direct rebuffs by the courts. Nothing close to a clear philosophy or effective program of overall regulatory improvement had emerged at either EPA or OMB. In the press, news accounts constantly juxtaposed two parallel trends: the spreading public concern about real environmental hazards, especially toxic contamination sites and spills, and the progressive destruction of EPA's credibility through scandal, internal mismanagement, budget cuts, and proposals to weaken or eliminate regulations.

Put simply, the administration's policy strategy for environmental regulation had failed: it had lost its legitimacy with most of its necessary constituencies outside the administration and even some inside. The administrator's departure, along with nearly all other senior EPA appointees, marked the administration's admission that some of the strategy's elements had failed; their replacement by William Ruckelshaus and a new team represented its attempt to correct the errors, or at least to mitigate the political damage.

What happened and why? Was the EPA debacle an indictment of Reagan's policy, of his administration's tactics, or simply of Gorsuch's implementation of them? How much difference might Ruckelshaus make?

Simplistic Ideology

A basic cause of EPA's failure was Reagan's own initial decision to use his presidency to implement a simplistic ideology rather than to govern. To govern requires constant balancing and bridge building among competing values, most of them legitimate and important to the broad mainstream of American citizens; environmental protection is unquestionably one of these. Deregulation and budget reduction are perennially popular slogans, long espoused by Reagan himself and advocated also by influential ideologues among his "kitchen cabinet" of close friends and advisers and by some corporate and trade association lobbyists. To implement them wholesale, however, was to ignore the government's legitimate and necessary roles in a complex, mixed public/private economy, as well as the widespread popular support for these roles despite rhetorical complaints. Reagan's rejection of the mainstream Republican environmental leaders' advice, and his pursuit of indiscriminate deregulation and budget cuts instead, was a fundamental judgment error. He rejected an agenda that reflected a conservative Republican philosophy yet benefited from widespread support for one that represented the unquestioning adoption of a radical right-wing wish list. Advocates of this course in the business community were themselves foolish and irresponsible to overreach as they did, as some within it have since pointed out;[24] but Reagan was even more so, to seek to impose ideological victory rather than to build on the broadening consensus for moderate conservative reforms. The politics of polarization invite response in kind, as the results have now demonstrated.

Reckless Tactics

Even a consensual policy can be derailed by poor implementation. The attempt to impose a divisive policy through unilateral administrative tactics was naive and reckless, philosophically authoritarian rather than 'conservative, and in practice not only ineffective but also seriously damaging to Reagan's chances for achieving success.

Executive oversight, for instance, is important for coordination among regulatory agencies, for developing consistent approaches and sensible priorities for regulation, and for involving the regulatory agencies themselves in better management. The Reagan administration, however, eliminated these sorts of coordination and used oversight only as an adversarial control instrument, freezing the agencies out of the executive office, blocking them through OMB, and pressuring them through the task force. This tactic may have stopped a few particularly onerous regulations, but it actually hampered the achievement of better regulatory management.

Cost-benefit analysis, similarly, is a valid and useful tool, if not pressed too far, for improving regulatory decisions. In principle value-neutral, its use in some form is intrinsic to any reasoned choice of regulatory decisions or priorities. It is required by several environmental regulatory laws already. Its implementation under Reagan's Executive Order 12291, however, tainted it with an obvious deregulatory bias and a hidden agenda of OMB control; and OMB in turn took only a reactive rather than a constructive leadership role. Even OMB's own use of economics was obsolete in single-mindedly emphasizing efficiency rather than multiple objectives. In practice it served as an unaccountable source of political pressure on the regulatory agencies; in the words of OMB's senior regulatory review official, "My staff and I have definite ideas as to what kinds of regulatory changes should be made and we fight for them."[25] While some proposals thus were stopped on grounds of costs exceeding benefits, OMB's ad hoc use of these arguments to deregulate increased public cynicism about the tool's neutrality. It also seriously reduced both the legitimacy and the accountability of regulatory decisions by introducing opportunities for political pressure, off the public record, through OMB.

Using drastic budget cuts as a deregulatory weapon was equally damaging. It was not credible on budgetary grounds, since the regulatory agencies are a minuscule element of the federal budget, dwarfed by social services and defense. Even within EPA, the budget for regulatory activities was much smaller than that for nonregulatory functions, such as construction grants. The effect of budget reductions on the EPA staff were inevitably divisive and demoralizing, and thus inimical to positive reform. The drastic EPA budget cuts contradicted anything Gorsuch might say about better science, more effective implementation by the states, or credible enforcement. They did subtler but more pervasive damage by destroying morale, threatening both the employees' personal security and the institutional goals to which they were loyal, and rendering them hostile to the administration from the outset. Knowingly or thoughtlessly, David Stockman set Anne Gorsuch up to fail.

Most foolish of all, perhaps, was Reagan's pursuit of ideology over competence in his appointment of regulatory officials. The legitimacy of every regulatory decision, and especially of deregulatory decisions, depends crucially upon both the analytical competence of its reasoning and the appearance and reality of evenhandedness in the ultimate judgment. All parties to regulation depend on this legitimacy, businesses even more than others since they are most directly affected by it. Despite the availability of talented and experienced Republican candidates, however, Reagan appointed an EPA administrator and senior subordinates who had little or no experience in management, no understanding of a regulatory administrator's duties, and obvious biases that undermined legitimacy. Even if Reagan believed Carter had favored environmental interests in his appointments, an equal but opposite error was not the answer. The business community loses, as well as the public, if competence and legitimacy are lost to either side. The attempt to achieve radical policy change by means of ideological loyalist appointees untainted by experience thus stands as probably the single most reckless tactic, and clearest failure, in Reagan's policy strategy.

Mismanagement

Despite these broader lessons, Gorsuch's own inexperience, biases, and authoritarian approach to management, and that of her subordinate appointees, also contributed significantly to the EPA's regulatory debacle. She and her senior subordinates, themselves presidential appointees, accepted and defended White House policies and tactics, and they made serious errors of judgment and management as well that ultimately proved their undoing. Handicapped from the start by White House goals and tactics and by their own inexperience, they conceived their roles as White House subordinates rather than as regulatory officials with independent responsibilities. They did not try to overcome these handicaps by learning the issues and seeking to build a consensus; instead they tried to redirect regulatory policy on their own, distrusting their own organization and ignoring constituencies with whom they expected to disagree. A more reliable prescription for failure would be difficult to suggest.

Ruckelshaus: Policy Reform or Damage Reduction?

William Ruckelshaus, EPA's first administrator, returned to the agency in May 1983 after easy Senate confirmation and a tumultuously enthusiastic welcome from the staff. He demanded and apparently received from the president commitments that he report directly to the president, that he have greater budgetary influence, and that the president would honor his recommendations for senior appointments at EPA. He already had proven his commitment to the agency, his ability to work with its professional staff and political constituencies, and his substantive appreciation of the technical and political issues involved in its decisions. He also was widely respected and had demonstrated under President Richard Nixon his personal willingness to resign rather than make unethical decisions.

Ruckelshaus entered office with a presidential mandate to restore public trust in EPA. Specifically, he was directed to improve management of the Superfund program, develop an acid rain policy, vigorously enforce the laws, and identify the federal and local governments' proper roles. As an outspoken advocate of balancing the social benefits of environmental rules against their economic costs, he supported the creation of a government-wide process for assessing and managing risks. In one early initiative he solicited local public opinion about a standard balancing the harmful effects of arsenic pollution from a smelter against potential economic losses if the plant closed. Immediate policy changes also included a Superfund budget increase, a decision to begin cleaning up hazardous waste dumps immediately rather than waiting to first negotiate settlements with the responsible industries, a review of federal and state enforcement roles, and a commitment to bolster EPA's research program. By November he also had reversed Gorsuch's initiative to weaken federal water quality standards, a significant policy signal on an important issue.[26]

The most important implication of Ruckelshaus's appointment, however, lay not in particular policy differences but in the basic attitudes he brought to environmental regulation. He insisted that public officials be judged on how they perform as public servants, rather than on which group—environmental or business—they represent, and he made clear his intention to hire as staff only "the best people" with "iron integrity."[27]

He asserted that the administration initially had misread its mandate by attempting to deregulate environmental and health regulations along with economic controls; while the procedures of social regulation needed reform, their basic goal did not.[28] An effective national regulatory program, according to Ruckelshaus, was a *necessity* for free enterprise and was far preferable to relying on voluntary compliance at the mercy of scofflaw competitors: "the only voluntarism at EPA is if the EPA voluntarily decides not to enforce the law." [29] Significantly, he made clear his commitment to administer and enforce the laws as written until and unless statutory reform occurred, rather than to undermine them by administrative tactics.

Ruckelshaus's appointment thus appeared to signify a rejection of Reagan's simplistic initial goals and tactics in environmental regulation, a concession to the continuing political importance of environmental protection, and a reacceptance of the moderate conservative regulatory reform agenda advocated by Reagan's environmental transition team.

The question that remained was how much of that agenda Ruckelshaus could implement both outside and within the Reagan administration. On the outside, the agenda, even in 1980, addressed controversial issues; but with the political momentum then available and Ruckelshaus's own stature and ability, he probably could have had a vast impact. In mid-1983, however, he had less than 18 months until the 1984 election, and he faced the added constraints of external polarization and internal organizational damage that had to be overcome before major changes could be attempted. Presidential campaign politics inevitably would color any major initiatives, and the opportunity for reasoned reform that existed in 1981 would be gone. Even with the best efforts, therefore, Ruckelshaus might only rebuild the momentum of policy consensus toward its 1980 point. Although he could initiate a few changes, they would not compare with what he could have achieved in four years.

On the inside, Ruckelshaus's appointment in itself did not remove the other powerful advisers who advocated continuing deregulation and budget reduction, opposed serious efforts to control environmental problems such as acid rain, and hoped that Ruckelshaus's appointment by itself would remedy the political damage caused by their earlier tactics. By December 1983 Ruckelshaus's recommendations on acid rain had been blocked in the cabinet, and his request to restore the budget to its 1981 level had been rejected by OMB. The extent of his effectiveness even within the administration thus clearly depended on how much continuing political pressure was generated in the public at large.[30]

It is unfortunate that much of the legitimate conservative agenda that Reagan's administration might have achieved thus appears to have been lost to bad judgments that easily could have been avoided and to continuing ideological rigidity. It is also tragic that so much damage was done in the process both to environmental protection and to the cause of regulatory reform itself.

Notes

1. Murray Weidenbaum, *The Future of Business Regulation* (New York: Amacom, 1980).
2. *National Journal,* December 20, 1980, 2188.
3. *National Journal,* January 31, 1981, 28.
4. Presidential Task Force on Regulatory Relief, "Fact Sheet: Year-End Summary of the Administration's Regulatory Relief Program," December 30, 1981; "Reagan Administration Regulatory Achievements," August 11, 1983.
5. Antonin Scalia, "Reagulation: The First Year," *Regulation,* January-February 1982, 19.
6. Executive Order 12291, February 17, 1981. For additional information, see V. K. Smith, ed., *Environmental Policy Under Reagan's Executive Order: The Role of Benefit-Cost Analysis* (Chapel Hill: University of North Carolina Press, forthcoming 1984).
7. A particularly important contribution of the Carter administration was the creation of a U.S. Regulatory Council to coordinate regulatory programs, eliminate duplication and gaps, produce a semiannual calendar of regulations in progress, and provide a vehicle for developing common policies on issues regulated by various agencies (for instance, chemical carcinogen regulation). This council had as its chairman the EPA administrator and included the heads of 36 executive branch and independent regulatory agencies. It appears to have been the only regulatory reform mechanism that addressed the substantive coordination of regulatory requirements across agency lines.
8. U.S. Congress, Joint Hearings, House Government Operations, Energy and Commerce, and Science and Technology committees, *EPA Oversight: One-Year Review,* 97th Cong., 2d sess., July 21-22, 1982, 332.
9. Data from American Environmental Safety Council. For additional information on science research budget, see *Science,* March 18, 1983, 1303; *Science,* March 25, 1983, 1404; and A. M. Gorsuch, *Setting EPA's Course for the Eighties: Directions of the U.S. Environmental Protection Agency During the Next Two Years* (Washington, D.C.: EPA, 1982).
10. U.S. Congress, House Committee on Science and Technology, Subcommittee on Investigations and Oversight, *Formaldehyde: Review of Scientific Basis of EPA's Carcinogenic Risk Assessment,* Hearing, 97th Cong., 2d sess., May 20, 1982.
11. U.S. Congress, House Committee on Agriculture, Subcommittee on Department Operations, Research, and Foreign Agriculture, *EPA Pesticide Regulatory Program Study,* Hearing, 97th Cong., 2d sess., December 17, 1982, 87; Joint Hearings, *EPA Oversight,* 521; Associated Press report, March 18, 1983; *Science,* September 2, 1983, 934.
12. A. M. Gorsuch, *Setting EPA's Course.*
13. U.S. Congress, House Committee on Government Operations, *Lead in Gasoline: Public Health Dangers,* Hearing, 97th Cong., 2d sess., April 14, 1982; Joint Hearings, *EPA Oversight,* 558-562; *New York Times,* February 19, 1982; *Washington Post,* August 11, 1982; *Washington Post,* August 16, 1982; *Science,* August 27, 1982, 807-808.
14. Joint Hearings, *EPA Oversight,* 541-552; *NRDC v. Gorsuch,* 51 *Law Week* 2113. For additional information, see Mark Green, "The Gang That Can't Deregulate," *The New Republic,* March 21, 1983, 16.
15. Joint Hearings, *EPA Oversight,* 541, 672-703.
16. Joint Hearings, *EPA Oversight,* 470-518; *NRDC v. EPA,* 683 F. 2d. 752 (3d

Circuit).

17. *Washington Post,* November 19, 1982, November 27, 1982, February 10, 1983.
18. C. Peterson, "EPA Enforcement Cuts Linked to New Violations," *Washington Post,* December 6, 1983.
19. A. M. Gorsuch, *Setting EPA's Course; Washington Post,* January 31, 1983, and February 1, 1983.
20. "On Delegation to States," *Environmental Forum,* January 1983, 9.
21. "The State of the States: Management of Environmental Programs in the 1980s" (National Governors Association, May 1982).
22. *New York Times,* May 1, 1983; *Washington Post,* April 7, 1983.
23. U.S. Congressional Budget Office, "The Environmental Protection Agency: Overview of the Proposed 1984 Budget," (Mimeographed).
24. B. Fielding, "The Environmental Interregnum — It's Over," *Environmental Forum,* June 1983, 10-15.
25. W. N. Grubb, D. Whittington, and M. Humphries, "The Use and Abuse of Benefit-Cost Analysis in the Federal Government: The Implementation of Executive Order 12291," in *Environmental Policy Under Reagan's Executive Order.*
26. *Washington Post,* March 23, 1983, April 30, 1983, May 23, 1983, May 28, 1983, June 15, 1983, June 23, 1983, June 30, 1983, July 14, 1983, November 1, 1983; *Inside EPA,* March 25, 1983.
27. *Washington Post,* March 23, 1983.
28. New York Times News Service, July 26, 1983.
29. *Washington Post,* June 3, 1983.
30. C. Peterson, "EPA Chief Asks Reagan to Restore Budget," *Washington Post,* December 7, 1983.

9. JUDICIAL OVERSIGHT
OF ENVIRONMENTAL DEREGULATION

Lettie M. Wenner

Since the ratification of the U.S. Constitution, federal courts have represented one forum where individuals and groups dissatisfied with the decisions of legislators and executive officers could go to have their grievances heard. It is not surprising, therefore, that environmental and conservation organizations have taken their unmet demands to the federal courts. Although these groups were successful in the 1970s with the legislative and, to a lesser degree, with the executive branches of government, they also looked to the courts to guarantee that laws passed by Congress were effectively enforced by the agencies entrusted with their implementation.[1] Opponents to environmental groups tried to block access to the judiciary by arguing that such organizations lacked standing in court because they could demonstrate no personal injury to themselves. However, the U.S. Supreme Court under Chief Justice Earl Warren in the 1960s had lowered the court-imposed, standing-to-sue barrier, thereby encouraging groups that could not prove economic injury to use the courts. The provision for citizen suits that Congress wrote into many environmental statutes in the 1970s also encouraged this trend.

Courts traditionally have been considered conservative institutions in the sense that their powers can be used easily to delay changes in the status quo. Equity remedies that courts possess (such as the injunction) have enabled them to stop temporarily actions taken by other officials while the fairness of these actions could be reconsidered. Early in the 1970s environmentalists were even able to postpone the development of Mineral King Valley next to Sequoia National Park in California through a court case that ultimately was unsuccessful.[2] Although the court never agreed that the valley should be preserved, the lawsuit effectively delayed development until the administration in power changed its policy controlling land development there. The courts rarely devise permanent solutions to environmental problems, but their capacity to delay the implementation of political decisions until the equity of the situation can be established sometimes reverses the outcome of an earlier decision.

This capability to delay the final decision regarding any controversy can cut in both directions. In the 1970s many industries used the delay mechanism of court challenges to postpone the inevitable day when pollution control regulations would apply to them.[3] Because the outcome of a court remand is usually to return discretion to the administrative agency in charge of implementing policy, use of the delay mechanism in the 1980s has often resulted in formerly ambiguous policies being changed into more developmentally oriented ones.

This chapter focuses on recent court decisions in environmental and natural resource disputes and on what their impact may be on policy implementation by the Reagan administration. Have the courts acted as a check on what has been called Reagan's "administrative presidency" or on the efforts of the Environmental Protection Agency (EPA), the Interior Department, and other agencies to "deregulate" the environment? Or do recent trends in litigation serve to enhance the discretionary powers of the administration? The first section of this chapter summarizes the general pattern of environmental litigation since 1970 to put recent trends in perspective. We then turn to analysis of recent judicial decisions on pollution and natural resource controversies, indicating how the courts have responded to regulatory initiatives by Reagan's appointees. This analysis is followed by a discussion of some important Supreme Court decisions handed down in 1983 and what their import may be for future environmental policy. Finally, some conclusions are drawn concerning the current status of environmental litigation.

Trends in Environmental Litigation: 1970-1982

Litigation under various environmental laws has been on the rise since 1970, both because of the number of environmental laws that were passed in the 1970s and because of the increasing level of information about these laws among all factions in environmental disputes. These legal conflicts generally fall into one of four modal types: (1) government enforcement actions against industry, (2) intergovernment disputes, (3) environmental complaints against government actions, and (4) business complaints about government actions.[4]

In industry-initiated cases government agencies are forced to play an environmentally conserving role in which they defend their own actions, as well as the legislation on which they base those actions, against industry arguments that they acted arbitrarily and capriciously. On the other hand, in cases initiated by environmental groups, government agencies assume a developmental role, often acting as surrogates for industry. In those cases they make arguments similar to those made by industry: that polluters need more time to clean up because of technical or economic difficulties and that limits cannot be set too high because they would strain the resources of industry. Government is thus placed in an ambivalent and shifting role in environmental litigation.

There has been a modest increase in government prosecutions since 1970, from about 25 cases a year in the early 1970s to a high of 55 cases in

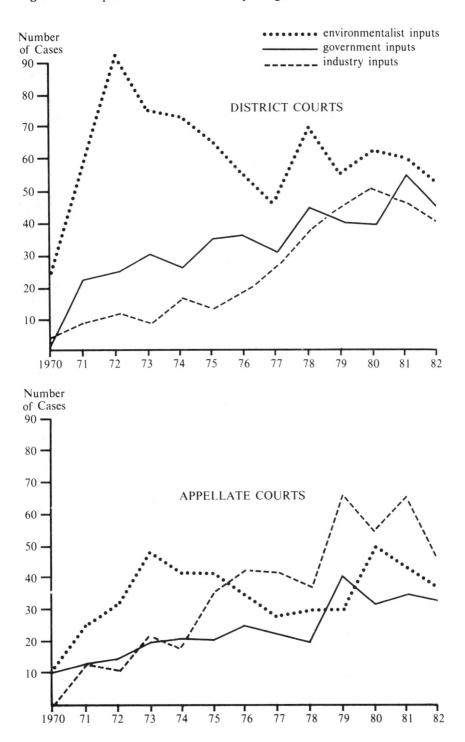

Figure 9-1 Inputs to Federal Courts by Litigant and Year

1981 *(see Figure 9-1)*. The number of government enforcement actions becomes less impressive when we consider that about half of these government cases represent intergovernmental disputes rather than government prosecutions of industry. In fact the vast majority of these are state-government-initiated cases in which the federal government is as likely to play an antienvironmental role as a proenvironmental one. Because of the many new laws passed in the 1970s under which the government could sue in the 1980s, the modest increase in enforcement actions is less than expected.

It may seem remarkable that government-initiated cases have not actually declined since the inauguration of the Reagan administration, given its desire to conduct environmental policy without confrontation with industry. However, most of the 1981 decisions and many of the 1982 ones were begun in the waning days of Jimmy Carter's administration, and such a pattern may yet emerge after all those cases have had a chance to clear the courts.

The government agency involved in such cases is crucial. Contrary to expectation, most government suits were not begun by the federal agency responsible for controlling pollution, EPA, or that responsible for managing natural resources, the Department of the Interior. State pollution control agencies brought more cases than any other group, and although the Reagan administration has reduced federal funding available to these pollution control agencies, some states have tried to fill the vacuum created by the administration's new policy of nonconfrontation with industrial polluters.

Other federal agencies that have not had their budgets so severely restricted as has EPA traditionally have been involved in pollution control litigation. The Army Corps of Engineers, for example, sues some landowners each year for filling wetlands or dredging waterways without Corps permits. The Coast Guard is active in prosecuting ship and barge owners for spilling oil into navigable waterways. While these cases may be locally important, they do not take on the importance of a federal suit against a major industrial polluter, and yet they constitute a significant portion of the government suits.

From 1970 through 1982 industry's complaints of government overregulation increased steadily. This increase was especially evident at the appellate court level, where the number of business-initiated lawsuits exceeded both government and environmental organizations' demands on court time every year after 1978. One reason for the intense use industry made of the courts of appeals rather than the trial courts is that many pollution control laws specify that objections to agency decisions must be made at the appellate level. Hence, like environmental groups, many industries made their first demand on the court system at the appellate level.

Environmental groups began more trial level cases than did industry through 1982, but at the appellate level industry had caught up to them by 1975. One reason environmental groups dominated the docket of the trial courts is that about half of their cases concerned the National Environmental Policy Act (NEPA), which provides that government projects that will have major environmental effects require environmental impact statements (EISs). Although commercial interests occasionally misuse NEPA to press economic claims, for the most part NEPA remains a law helpful to environmental interests. In the other half of their court cases environmental groups attacked government agencies for regulatory inaction, making the argument opposite the one business makes when it claims environmental laws and regulations are too severe. Like industry, environmentalists perforce must make many of the latter kinds of claims at the appellate level.

Government has maintained an impressive record in winning court decisions from 1970 through 1982 (62 percent of its cases), regardless of which role it played in any given case. Its margin of victory was most impressive (67 percent of its cases) when it was the plaintiff. This is most likely due to careful selection of cases to take to court, for the Justice Department is conservative in litigating environmental cases referred to it. There also appears to be a built-in advantage to being the initiator of a suit because of the ability to frame the question before the court.[5] Because government plays a proenvironmental role when it is plaintiff, government-initiated cases advance the environmental cause more than any other kind of case. Whatever the agencies' reasons for selecting a small number of cases to prosecute, it is certain that if the percentage of government prosecutions increased, the federal courts would produce results more favorable to the environmental cause.

Although their margin of victory was less impressive than when they were the plaintiff, government agencies also won the majority of cases in which they were the defendant. Their margin of victory tended to be about the same regardless of whether the challenge came from industry (63 percent) or environmental groups (62 percent). This may seem remarkable given the extensive resources available to industry for litigation as compared with those available to environmental groups dependent on public subscriptions. However, it seems less so considering the fact that environmental groups usually advocate strict adherence to the letter of the law, whereas industry often searches for wording in environmental control laws that will deflect or defer the general intent of the legislation.

The general pattern of environmental cases decided during the first two years of the Reagan administration seems remarkably similar to that established in the 1970s. Government prosecutions increased modestly throughout the period and did not diminish notably, even after the change in administration. Environmental groups turned to the courts early in the 1970s and increased their inputs only gradually even in the 1980s. Industry drastically increased its demands on the courts over the past decade, probably as a result of its investment in environmental law expertise. Government was the most successful of all three litigants, even after the change in administration. Courts tended to support the environmental and commercial interests about equally throughout both periods, despite the drastic change in administrative attitudes. Finally, it is important to note that three agencies in the Reagan administration have achieved great publicity for their avowed determination to adopt a prodevelopment stance: EPA, and the departments of Agriculture and Interior. It is with these three agencies that enforcement of the most important environmental legislation resides. Hence it is useful to consider in greater detail the pattern of cases in which they have been involved, both historically and in the early 1980s.

Environmental Protection Agency Cases

The modal type of case envisioned by environmental groups that were instrumental in passing laws in the 1970s was one in which government agencies would prosecute industries violating the law. This type of case, however, never became typical even during the heyday of enforcement of the laws. Upon coming to power, the Reagan administration made it clear by word and actions that it intended to prosecute even fewer cases than its predecessor had. In the first nine months, the Reagan Justice Department received only 50 charges of environmental law violations; of these only 12 came from the EPA after Anne Gorsuch (later Burford) became administrator and eliminated the enforcement division.[6]

According to congressional Democrats, EPA had averaged 200 referrals to Justice each year under the Carter administration.[7] The EPA was involved in only 123 of some 451 government suits completed in the federal trial courts from 1970 to 1982. Only 77 of these were against industry, and some were the equivalent of the water pollution cases begun by the Coast Guard against oil spillers.[8] Throughout the 1970s EPA averaged fewer than 10 cases a year against major industrial polluters, as for example when it sued Reserve Mining for polluting Lake Superior.[9] This contrasts sharply with the reported 200 referrals per year to the Justice Department under the Carter administration. It is, however, understandable that 20 times more cases are referred than are eventually adjudicated in court. The Justice Department functions as a gatekeeper, selecting some cases for litigation but dropping many others because of the department's limited resources or priorities that are different from those of EPA's attorneys. Filing a court case is often used as a threat to induce industry to bargain about compliance, and many cases actually initiated in court are settled long before they reach adjudication.

The few cases developed by EPA and prosecuted by the Justice Department that produced court judgments in 1981 or 1982 were begun, for the most part, in the Carter administration. Although some of these cases ended in favorable verdicts for government and the environment, many of them were settled by agreement between industry and government. One such case that actually produced a court record involved the Hooker Chemical Company, which was responsible for toxic wastes at Love Canal in New York. Hooker and EPA reached an amicable agreement after the new administration took office. Residents in the area, however, intervened to argue that the settlement would not guarantee a cleanup of the contaminated area, or their health and safety. The district court nevertheless deferred to the agency, saying that it had the requisite expertise and discretion about when to settle.[10]

Another case settled under EPA Administrator Gorsuch involved a toxic dump in Louisiana. This case would have gone unrecorded except that the judge was dismayed at the onus for the outcome of the case being cast on the court. He complained that both EPA and industry were using the court's acquiescence in their mutual agreement to keep the terms of settlement secret from the press and public, saying, "Rather than make a full and truthful disclosure to the public, the parties have chosen to blame a federal judge for their inability to now disclose information which the public and media seek." [11]

Much of the litigation with which EPA was involved in the first two years of the Reagan administration arose under the most recent pollution control laws: ones having to do with the control of toxic wastes. It was these most recent laws that the EPA under Gorsuch was responsible for interpreting. The Comprehensive Environmental Response Compensation and Liability Act (CERCLA) was passed in 1980. It created a Superfund from taxes on the petroleum and chemical industries to clean up abandoned toxic waste dumps that represent a current health hazard, but for which no responsible owners can be found. However, it did require the government to recover cleanup costs whenever possible. In 1982 the government launched a suit against a hazardous dump site that was leaching dangerous chemicals into the soil near the Delaware River in Pennsylvania. Yet, in the words of the court, EPA failed to use the section of CERCLA that was designed to help government recover costs from off-site generators of wastes:

> Astonishingly, the government here has chosen to ignore those provisions of the statute which give it clear authority to remedy the pollution problem at the Wade site and recover its costs from Gould and other off-site generators, and has instead chosen to sue under two different statutory provisions. [12]

The government based its case on the 1976 Resource Conservation and Recovery Act (RCRA) and on a different section of CERCLA having to do with imminent hazards from ongoing disposal of wastes. Because there was no ongoing disposal, the district court was forced to dismiss the case against the waste producer, although the judge clearly did not want to do so. As he observed, "it was because of RCRA's clear inability to address problems of past unsafe disposal practices that led to the 1980 CERCLA legislation." [13]

In another 1982 case, in North Carolina, EPA again used RCRA to apply to the leaching of toxic wastes into the ground water of an area near an abandoned dump. Like the court in Pennsylvania, the North Carolina court agreed with industry that RCRA does not apply to abandoned sites. The court then went on to discuss CERCLA, hinting that the government had filed under the wrong law, when it said, "The court feels that the Congress has provided a vehicle through which corrective measures can be undertaken." [14]

Three possible explanations exist for EPA's bizarre behavior in these cases: (1) EPA and/or the Justice Department wanted to expand the coverage of RCRA despite congressional policy in CERCLA; (2) government attorneys assigned to the cases were not fully conversant with the laws; or (3) the existing managers of EPA and Justice wanted to sabotage the effectiveness of the laws.

In the first two years of the Reagan administration, as in the past, EPA was involved in many more cases as defendant than as initiator of the lawsuit. The largest number of cases was initiated by industry against EPA's regulations and guidelines. Industry was determined to keep up the pressure on EPA, as well as to help mold the courts' interpretations of the newer laws. Many industry-initiated cases challenged EPA decisions made in the Carter administration about the Clean Air and Clean Water acts. Others, however, concerned the newer laws. For example, when EPA under Carter in 1980 interpreted RCRA to include mining wastes as solid wastes, the chemical industry objected, but it took until 1982 for the Circuit Court of the District of Columbia to uphold EPA's version of the law.[15]

Generally, the courts tended to uphold EPA's earlier regulations, but in at least some cases this outcome was due to the arguments of private intervenors, not to the government's attorneys.[16] However, in some instances the courts remanded a decision made by the Carter EPA to the agency for reconsideration. For example, in 1979 EPA published regulations that made it mandatory for smelters to continuously control their sulfur dioxide emissions unless they could show that the expense of such control technology would force the smelter to close.[17] In 1982, however, the D.C. Circuit ruled that the Congress had not intended that such a strict standard should be applied to smelters.[18] The court remanded the issue to EPA, and under the Reagan administration it seemed likely that an accommodation with industry soon would be reached.

Environmental groups sued EPA in the same manner as industry did but for the opposite purpose—to insist on firm application of the laws. One typical kind of case occurred when the Natural Resources Defense Council (NRDC) sued to force EPA to meet the deadlines written into legislation for setting effluent standards under the Clean Water Act.[19] Although this case ended when EPA agreed to issue the requisite regulations, EPA had failed to do so by 1982; NRDC had to return to court later to argue against a further extension of the government's deadline.[20]

In addition to riding herd on older laws' requirements, in the early 1980s environmental groups wanted to ensure that EPA-drafted regulations for the newer laws would protect the population against toxic substances. When he assumed office, President Reagan issued an executive order placing a freeze on the issuance of all new federal regulations drafted in the waning days of the Carter administration, pending the writing of regulatory impact statements (RISs).[21] Consequently, environmental organizations sued to force EPA to act on some of the suspended regulations, such as those governing the pretreatment of toxic wastes before industry could discharge them into municipal sewers.[22] They also sued to force EPA to begin the slow process of writing guidelines for new laws, such as CERCLA.[23]

In addition to its conflicts with environmental groups and industry, EPA was involved during the first two and a half years of the Reagan administration in some intergovernmental disputes with states and/or municipal governments. In some cases the states assumed a proenvironmental stance, as when Connecticut joined environmentalists in objecting to EPA's ratifying a New York plan to increase its sulfur emissions from utilities that would affect the quality of Connecticut air.[24] In a similar fashion Illinois joined the Environmental Defense Fund in arguing that EPA must meet the deadline written into the RCRA by promulgating standards for hazardous wastes.[25] In other cases the states represented an antienvironmental concern, as when New York got a federal judge in a New York district court to agree that EPA's restrictions against the dumping of sewage sludge into the Atlantic Ocean were too costly.[26]

Despite the change in policy toward the environment in the executive branch in 1981, the federal courts tended to find as often in favor of EPA discretion in 1981-1982 cases as they ever had. Hence, it did not appear that there would be any compensatory movement on the part of the courts to balance the new political tilt toward developmental values. Instead, the courts appeared as likely as ever to defer to expert administrative discretion in making decisions about regulations regardless of the self-consciously antiregulatory philosophy of the administrators. Nevertheless, demands by environmental groups continued during the Reagan administration because there was little for them to lose by taking the issue to court instead of simply accepting agency decisions.

Natural Resource Cases

Many of the most important court cases that were decided during the first two years of the Reagan administration dealt not with pollution control but with the use of natural resources. The latter reflected the conflict between energy conglomerates' desire to explore and develop minerals in publicly owned lands, and conservation organizations' desire to preserve a part of that public trust for future generations. Since the 1973-1974 energy crisis, all administrations have attempted to make the United States more energy independent by emphasizing the development of domestic sources. Many of these programs have included the intense exploitation of fossil fuel deposits in the public trust lands owned by the U.S. government: national forests, parks, monuments, wilderness areas, wildlife refuges, and other lands located mostly west of the Mississippi River, as well as the coastal zone (land lying immediately off our shores under both oceans). These public lands are managed either by the Forest Service in the Department of Agriculture or by the Department of the Interior through its Bureau of Land Management (BLM). This intensified effort to find and exploit mineral wealth on the public trust lands has led to increased involvement of the departments of Agriculture and Interior in environmental litigation.

A few cases during 1981 and 1982 represented government efforts to enforce regulations about strip mining on both public and private lands. All of these cases were started during the Carter years when the coal mining industry complained bitterly about the zealous enforcement of the Surface Mining Control and Reclamation Act (SMCRA). The courts in various parts of the country generally were willing to uphold these enforcement efforts despite varied industry defenses against them.[27] Most of the major cases in recent years have been initiated either by conservation groups and/or state governments trying to slow the Reagan administration's rush to lease mineral rights in all the public lands, or by industry seeking to speed that same process.

The Agriculture Department

In 1964 Congress passed the Wilderness Preservation Act, which charged the departments of Interior and Agriculture with the task of making an inventory of all public lands held in trust for the American people. Throughout the 1970s the Department of Agriculture worked to classify some 62 million acres of national forestlands either as wilderness or as open to exploration and development by commercial interests. The first Roadless Area Review and Evaluation study (RARE I) was completed by the Forest Service in 1972 but was declared incomplete by a federal court because it lacked an environmental impact statement (EIS).[28]

By 1977 the Forest Service had taken a second cut at dividing all its roadless areas into one of three categories: wilderness (15 million acres), further planning (10.8 million acres), and nonwilderness (36 million acres). A number of groups challenged this second effort (RARE II), including the state of California, the Natural Resources Defense Fund, and the Clear Creek Legal Defense Fund. The lumber industry intervened on the side of the government, showing its own satisfaction with the designation of the majority of roadless areas in the national forests as open to development.

The federal district court in northern California found that the EIS was deficient because it did not contain information about particular sites that would be turned over to timber development, nor had it given the public sufficient time to comment on the EIS. The court issued an injunction prohibiting any development of national forestland in California that would change the wilderness character of the areas until an adequate EIS was written, and the Ninth Circuit upheld that decision.[29] Both courts remanded the matter to the Forest Service to reconsider the procedure by which it had decided to designate most of the remaining roadless areas in the national forests as open to development. At the time the second decision was rendered, the lumber industry argued that the court's finding must mean that the 15 million acres designated as wilderness were open for reassessment also. However, the court disagreed with that interpretation, saying:

> California's complaint below urged only that the Forest Service's *Nonwilderness* designation failed to follow these procedures, limiting the scope of the litigation to this single area. Moreover, NEPA's central requirement is that agencies must take a 'hard look' at the *environmental* consequences of its proposed action. It is unclear why a more intensive review of the Wilderness designations' environmental consequences might have given the Forest Service reason to reconsider its Wilderness recommendations and allocate additional areas to Nonwilderness. [court's emphasis] [30]

Nevertheless, despite this clear judicial disavowal of the need to reconsider the areas that were selected to be preserved in the wilderness holdings of the national forests, the head of the Forest Service, John B. Crowell, Jr., formerly a corporate executive in the timber industry, argued that this decision gave the Forest Service the opportunity to go back over *all* the RARE II decisions made in the Carter administration and redesignate wilderness areas to nonwilderness, whether located in California or elsewhere.[31] Thus a judicial decision viewed initially as a victory for conservation groups to force the Forest Service to reconsider prodevelopment decisions in a limited geographical area was converted into an opportunity to reconsider all the compromises struck between industry and conservationists throughout the country in the 1970s. The courts' capacity to delay finalizing political bargains had indeed backfired on the groups that had hoped to use this weapon to their advantage.

The Interior Department

During the Carter administration, the Department of Interior launched an intensified effort to increase drilling for oil off U.S. shores, pursuant to the Outer Continental Shelf Land Act (OCSLA) of 1953 (amended 1978), to develop more domestic sources of oil. The National Wildlife Federation, together with the Eskimo village of Kaktovik and a local environment group, North Slope Borough, sued to slow this process off the shores of Alaska. A D.C. district court found the EIS written for these leases was inadequate because it did not consider sufficiently the impact on endangered species in the area.[32] The court sent the EIS back to be rewritten and admonished the Interior Department to administer all its leases for oil drilling in the Alaska area so as to protect the bowhead whale and to conform to NEPA.

However, by October 1980 the Circuit Court of the District of Columbia was ready to lift the injunction against Interior, to allow it to begin taking bids again for tracts off Alaska. The reason given for lifting the injunction was that the process of accepting bids for the tracts had no environmental impact. There would be time enough, the court argued, to write detailed EISs about particular tracts when the companies began their exploratory drilling. The court pointed out that it was the intent of the OCSLA to increase exploration for oil off the shores, not to inhibit it.[33]

There had been approximately a year's delay—most of 1980—while the issue was adjudicated, but the outcome was the same as originally decided by the Department of Interior: exploration was to be permitted in the fragile Beaufort Sea. Moreover, discretion was now placed in the hands of an administration more eager to develop natural resources in public lands than were the officials against whom the litigation was launched.

In 1981 the same type of issue was raised by the state of California against Interior's intensified leasing program under Secretary James G. Watt. Earlier objections to the national government's program to allow drilling off the California coast had been generally decided in industry's and the U.S. government's favor.[34] In 1981, after the Reagan administration began its campaign to lease offshore lands to the oil industry, California again filed suit against additional leasing. This time the district court in California, after throwing out claims based on OCSLA, the Endangered Species Act, the Marine Mammal Protection Act, and NEPA, accepted the state's objections based on the Coastal Zone Management Act (CZMA), which requires that the national government consult state authorities before doing anything that will affect the environmental quality of the wetlands in the state.[35] Later, however, the Ninth Circuit decided that Interior had not followed all the procedures OCSLA demanded and sent the five-year drilling plan back to Watt for reconsideration.[36]

In another round of suits, the district court issued an injunction against further leasing because of Interior's refusal to listen to the concerns of state government regarding the coast, and the Ninth Circuit partially upheld this decision. On January 9, 1984, however, the Supreme Court overturned the Ninth Circuit, saying that the act of leasing does not directly affect the coastal zone.[37] Thus the final outcome was to ratify Secretary Watt's choice of which areas to lease even under CZMA.

Industry, too, had increased its complaints against Interior before the advent of the Reagan administration, and many of these cases remained unresolved by 1981. One of Interior's important functions, aside from its management of the public lands, is administering the Surface Mining Control and Reclamation Act (SMCRA) through its Office of Surface Mining (OSM). Industry challenged nearly every regulation promulgated under this strip mining law during the waning days of the Carter administration, but most were upheld.[38]

In fact many regulations issued under SMCRA were rewritten to accommodate industry's demands as soon as James R. Harris, the new director of the Office of Surface Mining, took charge.[39] Environmental groups began challenging the new regulations almost immediately, but courts generally seemed willing to leave discretion about regulations to Interior. For example, in 1982 the D.C. Circuit court ruled that state plans could be ratified by the OSM as long as they were judged "no less effective" than federal ones. Under the Carter regulations, they were to be "no less stringent." [40] Now it is entirely up to OSM officials to determine whether control over strip mining should be turned over to the states for administration.

In the most bizarre of industrial cases against Interior in the early 1980s, the Pacific Legal Foundation and the Mountain States Legal Foundation sued the former head of Mountain States, James Watt, in his new capacity as interior secretary, to force him to open portions of wilderness areas to oil and gas exploration. The areas under dispute were similar to the RARE lands under the Forest Service's management that already had been the subject of litigation in *California v. Watt*. Many of BLM's public trust lands were in a "primitive" (roadless) state and hence were potentially designatable as wilderness areas. During the Carter administration some BLM lands had been selected for study for wilderness potential. If Interior recommended and Congress approved their designation, they might be made into wilderness areas. However, under the Federal Land Policy and Management Act (FLPMA) of 1976, these areas were open to exploration for valuable minerals until January 1, 1984. Under President Carter's secretary of interior, Cecil Andrus, no drilling or mining permits were issued for such areas in an attempt to preserve their wilderness potential until final congressional action was taken on them. In contrast, one of Watt's first actions on taking office was to attempt to open all these study areas to mining and drilling. This effort, however, led to a protracted conflict with the House Committee on Interior and Insular Affairs, headed by Rep. Morris K. Udall, D-Ariz., which forced Watt to withdraw some of these areas from exploration. Hence, a need was created for a suit to "force" Interior to reopen the lands to exploration. The administration clearly had no interest in defending such a case, and in fact the case might have been thrown out as constituting no controversy under the U.S. Constitution, given Watt's continuing identification with the interests represented by his former employer. However, intervenors stepped in to argue the conservation point of view: Representative Udall and other members of Congress, the Bob Marshall Alliance, the Wilderness Society, and the Sierra Club. (The last-named environmental groups often intervene in government/industry disputes to see that their interests are truly represented.) In this case the federal district court in Montana interpreted FLPMA to mean that the interior secretary has discretion in this policy area.[41]

At the end of 1982 an uneasy truce was worked out between Congress and the administration by which the latter agreed to stop issuing permits for drilling and mining in wilderness study areas. It was, however, breached immediately after Congress left for its Christmas break in 1982. Secretary Watt simply dropped hundreds of thousands of acres of roadless areas from study area classification and began issuing permits for drilling there.[42] Ironically, an oversight provision that Congress originally had imposed to prevent an overly zealous interior secretary from closing off too much area to exploration was converted by a comparatively more conservation-oriented Congress to prevent the now prodevelopment Interior Department from consigning all undeveloped areas to commercial use. The Sierra Club and several other conservation organizations filed suit immediately, and the courts were called upon again to referee the conflict between Congress and the executive branch over who has discretion under FLPMA about drilling and mining in wilderness areas. The Supreme Court, in a recent case, may have changed the ground rules under which this case will be decided *(see p. 196)*.

The Supreme Court's Role

Throughout the 1970s the Supreme Court, under Chief Justice Warren E. Burger (1969-), responded less favorably to demands made by environmental groups than did other federal courts. The latter were divided among themselves, with the eastern and middle western circuits more favorably disposed toward the environment than the western and southern circuits.[43]

The D.C. Circuit court came to be identified especially with environmental causes. Environmental groups brought as many cases as possible to that forum, whereas business groups made their demands in other circuits, such as the Fourth.[44] The Supreme Court under Chief Justice Burger not only took more cases from the more environmentally oriented circuits to review, but also overturned a larger percentage of them. Understandably, during the early 1980s environmental groups reduced the number of appeals that they made to the Burger Court, while industry and government increased theirs.

This antienvironmental stance of the current Supreme Court has been exemplified in recent years by a number of cases involving nuclear power. The controversies behind these cases began many years ago. Antinuclear groups initiated most of these cases in the D.C. Circuit, which agreed with them that the Nuclear Regulatory Commission (NRC) had given insufficient consideration to issues such as the costs and technical difficulty of disposing of radioactive wastes.[45] However, the Supreme Court overturned two antinuclear decisions in 1978 when industry appealed, and the Court remanded both cases to the D.C. Circuit court with instructions to give less scrutiny to the substantive judgments of expert agencies.[46]

The D.C. Circuit responded in 1982 by again labeling the NRC's actions as arbitrary and capricious and not in accord with NEPA.[47] Industry again appealed, and the Burger Court overturned this decision also in June 1983, instructing the D.C. Circuit to become more "deferential" toward administrative agencies and to accept all decisions made "within the bounds of reasoned decision making."[48] In a related case the Supreme Court also overturned the D.C. Circuit in April 1983, ruling that the NRC was not obligated to consider an antinuclear group's arguments that restarting an undamaged reactor at Three Mile Island, where a major accident had occurred in March 1979, would cause psychological damage to people living in the vicinity.[49]

The Supreme Court did make one decision widely perceived as detrimental to the nuclear power industry in 1983. It upheld the constitutionality of a California law that effectively stymies the siting of new nuclear plants in that state until the federal government solves the problem of disposing of nuclear wastes.[50] In so doing it rejected the industry's argument that the NRC has exclusive control over such plants on the ground that this state law is an economic regulation, rather than a health and safety measure that the federal government has preempted through the Atomic Energy Act. Because of the direction and tenor of other nuclear cases, however, this case should not be viewed as demonstrating any particular concern over nuclear hazards by the current Court. It is instead an example of the Burger Court's concern for the right of states to make crucial policy decisions rather than the federal government. A majority on the Court currently views the expansion of decision-making authority by the states in many policy areas as legitimate; the antinuclear interests simply received the benefit of this overriding concern.

Judicial deference to administrative discretion is another priority that the Burger Court apparently has developed in the last decade.[51] This tendency has been most apparent in cases concerning the NRC, but it can assist environmental regulatory agencies as well. When industry challenged the regulations of agencies such as EPA and OSM, the Supreme Court often upheld their technical expertise, although never so completely as it did the NRC's. For example, in 1980 a district court in Virginia delayed the enforcement of strip mining regulations because of a coal industry suit,[52] but the Supreme Court overturned that decision and upheld most of the regulations issued by the Carter administration under SMCRA.[53] Since that time, however, many of those regulations have been changed by the Reagan administration.

In one 1983 case involving consumer safety the Supreme Court refused to allow the Reagan administration to change regulations issued by its predecessor. In 1977 the National Highway Traffic Safety Administration (NHTSA) under President Carter issued a regulation requiring either air bags or automatic seat belts for new cars. In 1981 this regulation was withdrawn, but the Supreme Court ruled that this was an arbitrary and capricious decision because the new NHTSA administrator had given no consideration to requiring air bags in all new cars.[54] The Burger Court thus was faced with the reality that agency technicians could change their expert judgments with the political winds. This may have weakened the justices' willingness to rely on agency omnipotence, at least in the face of abrupt changes. It did not eliminate the possibility that the NHTSA could reach the same conclusion again and would be upheld by the courts because of an improved administrative record.

When courts defer to the discretion of agencies that are concerned about the public safety, the policy outcome is likely to be environmentally benign. In the current administration, in which agencies are more likely to respond to industry demands than to consumer or environmental ones, such judicial deference is apt to result in more developmentally oriented policies. Despite the air bag decision, the Supreme Court's tendency in the recent past has been to defer to agency expertise in cases in which public intervenors have objected to administrative actions. This is in line with the oft-stated ideology of the Burger Court, which maintains that too many social issues have been brought to the federal courts for settlement. This criticism is often voiced by conservative writers who were opposed to the social policy making of the former Warren Court (1954-1969), which tended to uphold the civil rights of politically uninfluential groups. The belief that public policies should be made by elected representatives of the people rather than by appointed judges, however, has been voiced by liberal writers from the time of Chief Justice John Marshall, when judicial oversight of legislative and executive actions was begun. The Burger Court's tendency both to order lower courts to defer to agency discretion and to uphold state governments in controversial policy areas may be interpreted as lending support to democratic modes of decision making. It also reduces the number of access points to government for groups that are not influential with a given administration.

In June 1983 the Supreme Court decided a landmark case that may have larger policy implications than any of those that directly concern environmental questions. In this case the Burger Court ruled unconstitutional a provision written into law enabling Congress to veto administrative actions taken by the agency charged with enforcing the law.[55] In so doing the Supreme Court opened to challenge as many as 200 federal laws by which Congress has attempted to control executive discretion through ordering agencies to report to congressional committees and receive their consent before implementing policies. One natural resource management law that may be subject to new interpretation under this court ruling is FLPMA *(see p. 193)*. Under FLPMA, the Department of Interior is obligated to report to Congress before designating public lands wilderness areas or opening them to development. Under the new Court ruling, the secretary of the interior may be freed of much of his obligation to seek congressional guidance before making major policy decisions concerning the disposal of large federal land holdings.

This Court ruling may cut in the opposite direction as well because many agency decisions designed to assist consumer and environmental groups may be stymied, as well as helped, by congressional action. What happens in these situations, therefore, depends on the values of, and constraints placed upon, the people holding executive and legislative offices. The distribution of power between executive and legislative branches is clearly subject to the political process. New legislation may be passed that will alter the balance. At the moment, however, the administration and the Supreme Court appear to agree on a number of issues, and President Reagan will appoint any replacements to that Court until at least January 1985.

Conclusions

The Supreme Court, although the final arbiter, is not the only decision maker in the federal judiciary. The Court can review only a minority of decisions made by even one circuit in any given year. Hence the federal circuits, which tend to be more favorably disposed toward environmental values, continue to wield some power. A comparison of environmental litigation before and during the Reagan administration indicates that, at least superficially, the kinds of cases have not changed. The same three major litigants—government, industry, and environmental groups—continue to make approximately the same number of demands. In fact many of the cases that cleared the courts in the first two years of the Reagan administration were initiated during the Carter regime, especially those begun by government prosecutors. Upon closer inspection of individual conflicts, it appears that the only litigant left to argue the environmental point of view in some lawsuits between industry and government were private intervenors who appealed cases lost by government.

Courts continued to support environmental causes at approximately the same level as they had in pre-Reagan years. They continued to defer to administrative expertise concerning environmental regulation despite some courts' recognition of the executive branch's hostility toward regulatory goals. Hence a considerable amount of deregulation has been accomplished by the executive branch from 1981 to 1983, despite the fact that there is little evidence that either Congress or public opinion was in substantial policy agreement with deregulation. Because of the courts' traditional deference to administrative agency decision making, legal cases could at most only delay some policy changes. In a few cases court delays may actually have changed an originally probusiness decision into a more environmentally damaging one by giving the administration a new opportunity to revise regulations.

Environmental groups, bereft of support at the administrative level, perforce have increased their demands on the courts. In some cases they have won delays in decisions; however, the upshot of many of these decisions has been to return discretion back to the very administrators in EPA, Interior, and Agriculture who made the initial antienvironmental decisions. In the long run this procedure cannot produce more environmentally benign results. At the moment, however, such groups can turn only to Congress or to the courts to delay or modify the current administration's goal of deregulating environmental policy in the United States. Many irreparable decisions have been made, especially in the natural resource management field, in which drilling and mining in wilderness areas already has begun. In the area of pollution control, the cleanup operation is likely to be substantially delayed. When it is renewed at some future date, inflation undoubtedly will have increased the ultimate cost to the taxpayer.

The Supreme Court in the 1980s gave clear signals to lower federal courts that they should restrain themselves when asked to review decisions made by federal administrative agencies. At the same time it reduced congressional oversight capacity toward the same agencies. In some policy areas the Burger Court also showed deference toward state governments in their competition with the national authorities. The judicial branch of the United States is the final arbiter of the balance of power between the states and the federal government, and between the executive and legislative branches of government. At the present time, the Burger Court appears to favor both state governments and the executive branch in their respective conflicts. What this will mean for environmental and natural resource policies clearly depends on the policy preferences of individuals occupying statehouses around the nation and serving in the major administrative agencies in Washington. In the early 1980s, with an administration unconcerned about environmental values and many state governments preoccupied with economic survival, this development does not bode well for environmental and conservation values.

Notes

1. See, for example, Joseph L. Sax, *Defending the Environment: A Strategy for Citizen Action* (New York: Knopf, 1971).
2. *Sierra Club v. Morton*, 348 F. Supp. 219 (1972).
3. Lettie McSpadden Wenner, *The Environmental Decade in Court* (Bloomington: Indiana University Press, 1982), 52-54.
4. The larger study on which this analysis draws was based on an analysis of nearly

2,800 cases adjudicated in federal courts from 1970 through 1982 (Wenner, *The Environmental Decade in Court*). Reports of these cases were obtained from the Bureau of National Affairs, *Environment Reporter: Cases, The Environmental Law Reporter,* and *Federal Supplement* and *Federal Reporter, Second Series.* Each case was coded according to date, location of court, circuit, type of case, litigants involved, outcome for each litigant, government agency involved, and laws invoked. Coding for outcome of cases was done on a scale of one to five, from complete loss to complete victory. A neutral outcome was coded three, and a mean score of three represented the same number of wins and losses.

5. See, for example, Marc Galanter, "Why the 'Haves' Come Out Ahead," *Law and Society Review* 9 (Fall 1974): 95-160; and Craig Wanner, "The Public Ordering of Private Relations: Winning Civil Court Cases," *Law and Society Review* 9 (Winter 1975): 293-306.
6. *New York Times,* October 15, 1981, 5.
7. *New York Times,* April 4, 1982, 4.
8. *U.S. v. Chevron Oil,* 9 ERC 1503 (1976).
9. *U.S. v. Reserve Mining,* 431 F. Supp. 1248 (1977).
10. *U.S. v. Hooker,* 540 F. Supp. 1067 (1982).
11. *U.S. v. Petro-Processors of Louisiana,* 548 F. Supp. 546 (1982).
12. *U.S. v. Wade,* 546 F. Supp. 785 (1982).
13. *U.S. v. Wade,* 546 F. Supp. 787 (1982).
14. *U.S. v. Waste Industries Inc.,* 18 ERC 1521 (1983).
15. *Chemical Manufacturers v. EPA,* 673 F. 2d 400 (1982).
16. *Appalachian Power Company v. EPA (Costle); Intervenor Natural Resources Defense Council,* 671 F. 2d 801 (1981).
17. *Federal Register* 42551 (1979).
18. *Kennecott Corp. v. EPA,* 684 F. 2d 1007 (1982).
19. *Natural Resources Defense Council v. Train,* 510 F. 2d (1975).
20. *Natural Resources Defense Council v. Gorsuch,* 685 F. 2d 718 (1982).
21. Executive Order 12291; 46 *Federal Register* 3193-3198 (1981).
22. *Natural Resources Defense Council v. EPA,* 683 F. 2d 759 (1982).
23. *Environmental Defense Fund v. Gorsuch,* 17 ERC 1172 (1982).
24. *Connecticut v. EPA,* 656 F. 2d 902 (1981).
25. *Illinois v. Gorsuch,* 530 F. Supp. 34 (1981).
26. *City of New York v. EPA,* 15 ERC 1965 (1981).
27. *U.S. v. Dix Fork Coal Co.,* 692 F. 2d 436 (1982); and *U.S. v. Log Mountain Mining,* 550 F. Supp. 811 (1982).
28. *Wyoming Outdoor Coordinating Council v. Butz,* 484 F. 2d 1244 (1973).
29. *California v. Bergland,* 483 F. Supp. 492 (1980); and *California v. Block,* 690 F. 2d 753 (1982).
30. *California v. Block,* 690 F. 2d 760 (1982).
31. "Administration Scraps RARE II," *Sierra* (March/April 1983), 11.
32. *North Slope Borough v. Andrus,* 486 F. Supp. 332 (1980).
33. *North Slope Borough v. Andrus,* 642 F. 2d 589 (1980).
34. *California v. Andrus,* 608 F. 2d 1247 (1979).
35. *California v. Watt,* 520 F. Supp. 1359 (1981).
36. *California v. Watt,* 668 F. 2d 1290 (1981).
37. *California v. Watt,* 683 F. 2d 1253 (1982); *New York Times,* January 10, 1984.
38. *In re Permanent Surface Mining Regulations,* 14 ERC 1083 (1980).
39. *New York Times,* September 12, 1983; January 21, 1983; and May 1, 1983.

40. *Sierra Club v. Wall*, 18 **ERC** 1565 (1982).

41. *Pacific Legal Foundation v. Watt*, 529 F. Supp. 982 (1981).

42. *New York Times*, December 18, 1982, 1.

43. Wenner, *The Environmental Decade in Court*, chap. 7.

44. Ibid., 128-143.

45. *Natural Resources Defense Council v. Nuclear Regulatory Commission*, 547 F. 2d 633; and *Aeschliman v. Nuclear Regulatory Commission*, 47 F. 2d 622 (1976).

46. *Vermont Yankee Nuclear Power Corporation v. Natural Resources Defense Council*, 435 U.S. 550 (1978).

47. *Natural Resources Defense Council v. Nuclear Regulatory Commission*, 685 F. 2d 459 (1982).

48. *Baltimore Gas & Electric Company v. Natural Resources Defense Council*, 19 ERC 1057 (1983).

49. *Metropolitan Edison Corporation v. People against Nuclear Power*, 18 ERC 1985 (1983).

50. *Pacific Gas and Electric Company v. State Energy Resources Conservation and Development Commission*, 51 LW 4449 (1983).

51. See, for example, Norman Vig, "The Courts: Judicial Review and Risk Assessment," in *Institutions and Technological Risk Control*, ed. Susan G. Hadden (Port Washington, N.Y.: Kennikatt Press, 1984).

52. *Virginia Surface Mining and Reclamation Association v. Andrus*, 83 F. Supp. 425 (1980).

53. *Hodel v. Virginia Surface Mining and Reclamation Association*, 16 ERC 1027 (1981).

54. *New York Times*, June 25, 1983, 1.

55. *Immigration and Naturalization Service v. Jagdish Rai Chadha et al.*, 51 LW 4907 (1983).

Part III

POLICY CHANGE:
SUBSTANCE AND IMPACT

10. ENERGY POLICY:
CHANGING THE RULES OF THE GAME

Regina S. Axelrod

The Reagan administration's energy policies represent a radical departure from those developed by previous administrations. Perhaps the most symbolic divergence concerns the Department of Energy. Established by the Carter administration, the Energy Department had been targeted for elimination by President Ronald Reagan. The Energy Department's demise would have limited effective action on energy issues in view of its role in analyzing, developing, and implementing policy. In any event the Reagan administration has not had an energy-supply crisis, such as an embargo, with which to contend. Perhaps such a situation requiring immediate action and the availability of strategic plans and coordinating mechanisms might have challenged the administration's complacency toward energy.

The Reagan administration adheres to the beliefs that it is best to keep the government out of the marketplace in general, and that market forces will produce the best energy policy. This has meant not only the immediate deregulation of oil and the gradual deregulation of natural gas prices (both begun in the Carter administration) but also a retreat from future planning and analysis, which would consider issues such as resource development, environmental impacts, and economic hardships caused by high energy prices.

The Reagan administration would like to transfer decision making on energy issues to the private sector, where—it is posited—individuals can act on behalf of their own interests. The free-market approach has become the administration's solution to all energy challenges, whether they involve supply-interruption crises or pollution resulting from increased fossil-fuel combustion.

The administration also has encouraged increasing the United States' energy supplies, tying such development to its economic recovery program. Energy Department Secretary Donald Hodel predicts an increase of one-third to one-half in electric-generating capacity by the year 2000. As inflation and unemployment diminish, capital will become available to support not only research and development (R & D) energy programs but also the development of oil and coal reserves. This emphasis on supply has been maintained without sustaining balanced support for programs begun during the Carter administration that were designed to encourage conservation and to develop solar or renewable energy sources.

The administration contends that bureaucratic reforms will make energy planning more efficient and more consistent with its program for economic growth. Nevertheless, the long-term consequences of this governmental retreat from managing complex energy and environmental issues will be profound. Analysis of the administration's programmatic goals and actions on energy issues demonstrates how bureaucratic shifts can effect substantial changes with minimal public attention.

This chapter examines energy policies that either immediately affect the environment or have the potential for long-term effects. For example, three-quarters of U.S. sulfur oxides and one-half of particulates, both of which pollute the air, come from fossil-fuel combustion. Other energy sources also affect the ecosystem. For instance, hydroelectric plants alter water pathways, disrupting fish life. Summarizing several of these interactive relationships will demonstrate the scope and complexity of the problem and help assess the significance of the Reagan administration's changes in energy policy.

One particular long-term effect of fossil-fuel use has been a persistent concern of the scientific community. Combustion technology is the largest single source of carbon dioxide, and it contributes to the production of the "greenhouse effect." As the atmospheric content of carbon dioxide increases, heat is trapped in the atmosphere. Scientists predict that an increase in the temperature of the earth's atmosphere could cause such dramatic climatic changes as the melting of the polar ice caps and the subsequent flooding of coastal areas. Since coal has more carbon than natural gas or oil, its increased use will result in greater production of carbon dioxide. It is feared that if we wait until climate changes actually occur, it will then be too late for remedial action.

Increased use of coal also results in greater emissions of trace elements, including lead, mercury, nickel, arsenic, and cadmium. These become toxic when leached into the ground water or absorbed into the food chain. Coal also contributes to increased airborne concentrations of polycyclic aromatic hydrocarbons and pyrobenzenes, both of which are carcinogenic. Coal mining presents the additional hazard of toxic-waste ponds. Strip mining for coal has aesthetic costs as well because industry resists land reclamation, which is both difficult and expensive.

Sulfur oxides, nitrogen oxides, and particulates, all byproducts of combustion, cause respiratory infections. The old, the young, and the chronically ill are especially vulnerable. These pollutants cause not only increased medical costs and death, but also the deterioration and corrosion of buildings, metals, art works, and highways as well as damage to property, crops, forests, and fish. The effects of acid precipitation, largely traceable to fossil-fuel combustion, now have been well documented *(see Chapter 11)*.

The development of synthetic fuels, which includes the extraction of oil from shale formations, production of liquefied coal and oil mixtures, and coal gasification, also present environmental problems. The retorting of shale (the process by which oil is obtained by subjecting shale to very high temperatures) produces tons of waste and can damage vulnerable aquifers through drilling or the leaching of toxic materials. Aside from water pollution, oil-shale production also contributes to air pollution by emitting nitrogen oxides, sulfur, hydrocarbons, ammonia, and hazardous trace metals. Synthetic products also contain toxic nitrogenic substances that make them difficult to handle and transport.

Even this brief survey of the short- and long-term environmental consequences of energy use demonstrates the wisdom of taking energy policy seriously. Consideration of such environmental impacts should be part of any effort to redesign national energy policy. It is cause for concern that the Reagan administration has not given more serious attention to the interrelationship between energy and environmental problems. A selected number of energy programs will be reviewed in the next section in order to illustrate how energy policy has changed since 1981, what particular strategies the administration has used to institute such changes, and, finally, how these policy changes may be expected to affect the United States' long-term environmental quality as well as its ability to plan for its energy future.

Analysis of Energy Programs

Government officials can have a significant impact on patterns of energy usage, which in turn affect the environment. This section, therefore, will provide an analysis of institutional changes, budgetary cutbacks, staff reductions, executive-legislative interactions, and administrative decision making. This analysis will help to explain the changes that have occurred during the Reagan administration, describe the likely long-range impact on the environment, and illustrate the ways in which the goals of U.S. energy policy have been altered.

Because of space limitations, more attention will be given to conservation and renewable energy programs than to programs concerned with conventional energy sources such as fossil fuels, synthetic fuels, and nuclear power. Although there have been substantial changes in these latter programs, conservation and alternative energy technologies are of greater interest for our purposes, because these more benign strategies offer greater potential for achieving an energy future that has the least adverse environmental impact.

Conventional Energy Sources

Fossil Energy R & D. The federal government long has been committed to supporting R & D for fossil fuels. Beginning in 1981, however, R & D funds for fossil energy have declined precipitously, with the Office of Management and Budget (OMB) pressing for even sharper cuts than those supported by the Energy Department. A budget of close to $1 billion in fiscal 1981 was cut by one-third by fiscal 1983, and the president requested only $138 million for 1984. While it was likely that Congress would restore some of these funds as it had in the past, these dramatic cuts severely affected program operations.[1]

Although the budget request for 1984 includes funds for additional analysis of the environmental impacts of fossil-fuel combustion, such activities have been reduced. The coal program was scheduled to suffer a 50 percent cut in 1984 if Congress did not restore funds.[2] The administration requested $4.3 million for petroleum R & D for 1984, which was $1.4 million less than the 1983 appropriation. There is a paucity of research on the environmental problems associated with synthetic fuels, especially fugitive emissions, scrubber efficiency, and sulfur dioxide control technology. Support for studies on environmental impacts, worker health, occupational and workplace safety, and health requirements for surface coal gasification and coal liquefaction has decreased substantially since 1982. Without basic environmental-impact data, it is difficult for government officials to set safe standards and support existing ones. Industry challenges the establishment of new standards and the existence of old ones based on lack of incontrovertible data. The unavailability of information makes decision making more vulnerable to political forces, which generally do not function on behalf of the public interest. And while the Energy Department would like industry to take on environmental research, there are no private sector commitments to do so.

The department also lacks a mechanism to make environmental criteria a part of its decision-making process. The Energy Department's Office of the Environment was dismantled early in the Reagan administration, and whatever clout that office had in evaluating the agency's decisions for their environmental impact was eliminated.

Coal. The United States has abundant coal reserves that could provide energy for hundreds of years. Coal supplied only 20 percent of U.S. energy needs in 1983, apparently leaving considerable room for growth. A substantial increase in its use, however, involves significant environmental risks because coal is a "dirty" fuel.

Utilities are by far the largest users of coal, and they account for approximately 60 percent of all manmade sulfur dioxide emissions in the United States. During the Carter administration the Energy Department recognized the environmental problems associated with continued or increased use of coal—such as acid precipitation—but the Reagan administration has not.

Domestic coal production increased to 824 million tons in 1981 from 599 million tons in 1973.[3] But the coal boom has slowed, and coal production in October 1982 fell by 18.8 percent from the year before. Similarly, domestic coal consumption declined from 733 million tons in 1981 to 707 million tons in 1982.[4] The glut of coal on the market has been attributed to the economic recession, environmental regulations, rising labor costs, foreign competition, the success of conservation efforts, and the cancellation of synthetic-fuels projects.

While the Reagan administration has not actively encouraged coal conversions by electric utilities, it would like to limit the barriers to increased coal production by modifying the Clean Air Act. Such a strategy would reduce the compliance costs of electric utilities, thereby stimulating the coal industry.[5] The administration also has advocated easing the implementation of the Surface Mining Control and Reclamation Act of 1977 and the Federal Coal Leasing Act Amendments of 1976. Congress passed this legislation to ensure that strip-mining companies adhered to environmental safeguards.

In addition, Reagan proposed that the number of inspectors in the Office of Surface Mining be reduced in fiscal 1982, but Congress refused on the grounds that reducing personnel in program offices is as injurious as cutting their budgets. The strategy at the Interior Department, which administers these laws, is to devolve these decision-making powers to the state level. The role of the federal government thus has changed from one of regulation and enforcement to one of providing technical assistance to states.

Oil Leasing. The drilling for oil in waters close to shore also poses environmental problems. Offshore drilling has resulted in devastating oil spills, changes in fish-migration and spawning patterns, damage to wildlife, major blowouts, and irreparable alterations to the coastline.

While total domestic production of crude oil has declined from 9.2 million barrels per day (bpd) in 1973 to 8.6 million bpd in 1981, the search for new supplies continues.[6] The total number of wells drilled was three times greater in 1982 than in 1973. Nevertheless, the Interior Department intends to increase offshore drilling by leasing tracts on both continental shores of the United States. For example, in 1981, Interior Secretary James G. Watt proposed leasing 50.1 million acres off Long Island, New York, Massachusetts, Rhode Island, New Jersey, Delaware, Maryland, Virginia, and North Carolina. Interior issued 30 percent more oil and gas drilling permits in 1981 and 1982 than during the final two years of the Carter administration and announced a new leasing program in 1982 that would make almost the entire outer continental shelf—approximately a billion acres—available from July 1983 to June 1987.

Synthetic Fuels. Synthetic fuels are fossil fuels whose form has been altered. A synthetic crude oil, for example, is derived from oil shale (found in rock formations) by heating it to a very high temperature through a process called retorting. Coal can be liquefied through crushing, heating, and pressurizing. Also, coal can be gasified by being subjected to steam under pressure at high temperatures. However, the process of making synthetic fuels requires huge amounts of energy and water, reducing the gains of creating an alternate form of energy. The environmental hazards occasioned by synthetic-fuels development include air quality deterioration, water contamination and waste, acid precipitation, disposal of tons of waste material from mining and processing (slag), and irreparable damage to land from mining operations.

Synthetic fuels development is expensive, and the product may not be price-competitive with oil or coal. Because it was argued that industry could not develop synthetic fuels without some federal insurance against market risks, the government stepped in. President Carter initially refused to empower the Energy Research and Development Agency to guarantee loans, but in 1977 support for synthetic fuels grew and so did promises of money. Funds for design work and a conditional loan guarantee were appropriated to cover the first year's construction costs. In 1979 the Energy Department received massive appropriations—especially when compared with those for conservation and renewable-technology programs—to establish a synthetic-fuels program.

The Synthetic Fuels Corp. (SFC) came into existence with the signing of the Energy Security Act of 1980, which provides for a multiyear budget appropriation from Congress. The appropriation was $20 billion for the first phase, 1980 to 1984, and $68 billion is in reserve for funding until 1992. The corporation may agree to loan and price guarantees, and to purchase commitments. The price guarantee would be used when product price risk was large; the loan guarantee would be used if the costs of either plant completion or of performance risk were considered substantial. Purchase agreements are not considered desirable by the SFC.

A government-sponsored synthetic-fuels program offered members of Congress benefits, such as jobs, if projects were developed in their districts or states. The program also offered an opportunity for reducing U.S. dependence on imported oil, a Carter administration goal. In addition, it had a national security dimension in that a developed synthetic-fuels industry would be a reliable supplier of fuel to the U.S. military.

It was not until Janaury 1982 that the corporation made its first decision to accept 11 projects for possible subsidization. Then, in a devastating move for the synthetic-fuels industry, Exxon Corp. in early 1982 abandoned its huge Colony Oil Shale Project in Colorado. By May 1982 disappointment had set in among synthetic-fuels supporters. President Reagan's position that energy decisions should be left to the marketplace, together with falling oil prices, adequate market supplies, high interest rates, and burdensome inflation, would leave the industry with poor market and financial prospects. Without government guarantees for their products or their loans, the private sector was unwilling to bear the risks of synthetic-fuels development. The original goal of 500,000 bpd was abandoned, and only two plants were under construction in late 1983 (Union Oil Co.'s oil-shale project in Colorado and the Great Plains coal-gasification plant in North Dakota). The $20 billion committed for the first round of projects was left largely unspent.

The Reagan administration had committed itself to helping the synthetic-fuels market by providing incentives to the private sector for development. SFC Chairman Edward Noble explained: "The Corporation is a catalyst for speeding development of a privately held, privately managed and, I hope, economically viable synthetic fuels industry." [7] Noble expressed the belief that this could only be done if industry could depend on stable government policies minimizing risks of long-term capital investments.[8] Nevertheless, this position was at odds with the Reagan free-market philosophy. How could the government subsidize synthetic fuels if the market provided insufficient incentives? It was difficult, especially in view of its arguments that conservation and renewables energy technology did not deserve government support. Until fall 1981 Reagan had wanted to eliminate SFC, but his advisers were divided on the issue. So, rather than take on a fight in Congress where an unusual coalition of conservative Republicans and liberal Democrats emerged to support the corporation, the president has not openly opposed synthetic fuels development.

During the Carter administration, the Environmental Protection Agency (EPA) developed criteria for synthetic-fuels development called "Pollution Guidance Documents" to guide federal and state permit writers. The documents were to advise on environmental effects, performances of control technology, and costs. The guidance documents appeared in draft form but were never issued by the Reagan administration. EPA under Reagan wanted more general documents, leaving the states with less information on which to base their air- and water-quality permitting decisions. Subsequently SFC published environmental monitoring guidelines in fall 1983, which attempted to give direction to project sponsors on data collection. However, the guidelines were ambiguous and gave SFC considerable discretion as there was no formal opportunity for public comment on the projects nor specific procedures for SFC decisions.

If synthetic fuel development does take place, will it be consistent with environmental protection and developed in a way that is compatible with the health and safety needs of the population? The absence of sound data and the Reagan administration's unwillingness to allocate resources to pursue questions such as these suggest reasons for doubt.

Nuclear Energy. Although President Carter supported nuclear power, funds were also available during his administration for outreach programs in conservation and renewable energy and for R & D technology in renewable, conservation, and fossil energy. He also offered a government commitment of continued support in these areas. Reagan, too, has spoken words that express a continuing supportive interest in the nuclear industry: "One of the best potential sources of new electrical energy supplies in the coming decades is nuclear power." [9]

The Reagan administration justifies its generous support of nuclear research and programs by maintaining that its economic recovery strategy requires reliable and increasing energy supplies. According to the administration, as the United States continues to rely on electricity, centralized nuclear power plants will best meet energy needs.

Ignoring trends that indicate a decreasing demand for electricity, the administration projects a "doubling of electric generation capacity over the next thirty years." [10] The Energy Department anticipates that nuclear power will provide 22 percent of our electrical needs by 1995. In order to revitalize the nuclear industry, the administration would like to streamline licensing procedures and complete the Clinch River Breeder Reactor, which was opposed by President Carter.

Hazards associated with expansion of nuclear power plants include: (1) contamination from low-level radiation (from uranium mining and plant leakages); (2) contamination from disposal of nuclear waste (since there are no permanent sites); (3) unlimited production of plutonium (sabotage, theft, and unauthorized weapons production); and (4) potentially the most serious, failure of control mechanisms that would result in catastrophic accidents such as core meltdowns. The Reagan administration has given little consideration to these serious problems. The Nuclear Regulatory Commission (NRC) has refused to consider long-term effects, such as cancer, and has maintained that each reactor should be built so that there is one chance in ten thousand of a core meltdown during a 40-year period. However, NRC studies also show that some plants currently fail to meet even *that* requirement.

In addition to unresolved questions about power-plant safety and evacuation plans, there remains the issue of where to dispose of spent fuel rods. This issue has been ignored by the nuclear industry, and no long-term plan for storage or disposal has been developed, necessitating emergency action as temporary sites become full. The 1982 Nuclear Waste Policy Act directed the Energy Department to locate repositories for high-level radioactive waste and spent nuclear fuel. Utilities now store 8,000 metric tons of radioactive waste and are expected to accumulate an additional 24,000 tons by 1990.[11] Repository operations were expected to begin by January 31, 1998.

The debacle at Three Mile Island in 1979 hurt the nuclear industry by alerting the public and political leaders to the potential for disaster. At the same time, nuclear plants under construction have been cancelled due to cost overruns, construction delays, faulty designs, and poor management. The nuclear industry, arguing that Reagan was not providing enough help, invested betweeen $30 million and $40 million in 1983 to alter the public's attitude toward nuclear power. A coalition of utilities and energy industries formed the U.S. Committee on Energy Awareness to accomplish this goal through media advertisements and commercials.

The Reagan administration, however, has not abandoned the nuclear industry. Energy Secretary Donald P. Hodel has said it is his objective to revitalize the nuclear industry and streamline licensing procedures. The balance in the Energy Department R & D budget has shifted since 1981, giving a greater portion to nuclear technologies at the expense of fossil, solar, and renewable energy sources, and conservation programs. The high costs associated with nuclear power have not prevented substantial government support, which was justified as in the national interest.

Alternative Sources of Energy

Solar and Renewable Energy. Although public opinion polls indicate that a majority of Americans still believe solar energy represents the preferred source of energy for the year 2000,[12] Reagan administration actions discourage the development and use of solar power and renewable energy sources. (The term *renewables* refers to production of energy through utilization of unlimited fuel sources, such as sun, wind, geothermal, small hydroelectric dams, and photovoltaics, which have little or no impact on natural ecological systems.)

Such a posture is contrary not only to sound environmental policy but also to national security interests. Solar and renewables involve fewer environmental hazards than conventional fossil fuels and nuclear power. In addition, by replacing some oil, they can "stabilize oil prices, improve the country's balance of payments and enhance national security." [13]

Solar and renewable energy technology R & D received encouragement and support during the Carter administration. The Reagan administration's position is that it will continue to provide a technical research base for utilization by the private sector through basic and generic research. Where industry perceives substantial investment risks, the government will support research if it has potential benefit to the nation. That is to say, when the market discourages research in technical advances because of high initial costs or risks, the government will provide assistance, short of commercialization.

The administration's ultimate goal is to transfer responsibility for developing and marketing solar and renewable technology to the private sector. This position is repeated in every section of the Energy Department's solar and renewable budget almost sentence for sentence: "The overall goal of the solar energy program is to provide the technological base from which private industry can develop systems for transforming direct sunlight and indirect solar resources into energy forms suitable for widespread use." [14] The Energy Department contends that the elimination of federal subsidies for conventional fuels and higher prices for energy will enhance the role of renewables.

The 1984 budget requests for solar and renewable energy show substantial decreases in and/or elimination of research programs. Table 10-1 shows that the hardest-hit programs were solar, $61.1 million to $21.9 million; alcohol fuels, $5.0 million to zero funding; wind energy, $31.4 million to $8.6 million; and international renewable energy, $10 million to zero funding. Congress responded by augmenting these figures, but the overall total for the 1984 budget authority still is less than for 1983. This represents a distinct departure from the Carter administration's pledge that 20 percent of U.S. energy would be generated by solar sources by the year 2000. Although Carter had requested $559 million for fiscal 1981 for renewables, Reagan requested only $86.6 million for 1984. In addition, Reagan cut consumer information programs and reduced staff at the Solar Energy Research Institute by one-third, only six months after he took office.

The Reagan administration justified these massive cuts by saying that the market would encourage solar and renewables research and production as decontrolled energy prices increased. However, even if prices stabilized—as occurred during the temporary oil glut of 1982-1983—environmental and health imperatives and long-term energy needs provided enough reason to pursue alternate energy technologies. Without federal support and encouragement, energy consumers will be uninformed about successful solar technology. States and municipalities with weak or no state laws regarding solar energy and with competing budget demands will be unable to build a solar and renewable future.

The Reagan administration's commitment to transferring technology to the private sector and to individual consumers can be judged by examining its implementation of the Solar Energy and Energy Conservation Bank Act of 1978. Administered by the Department of Housing and Urban Development (HUD), the Solar Energy and Energy Conservation Bank was designed to offer low-interest loans to states that would provide grants and loans for local projects. It had not begun operating when Reagan assumed office, and the new president refused to support its establishment, fired its planning staff, and declined to promulgate regulations.[15] Because the administration was ignoring a congressional mandate, a coalition of interest groups and cities sued HUD for impounding congressionally appropriated money. Under a federal district court order in June 1982, the president was obliged to put the bank into operation. Subsequently regulations were proposed, and HUD allocated $30.4 million to states, to be distributed as states completed agreements with HUD.

HUD's proposed regulations limited the use of bank funds to conservation measures and passive solar technology, eliminating support for active solar technology such as solar water heaters. HUD also refused to allow credit unions, city governments, and financial institutions to distribute funds (which critics say would have ensured wider distribution), proposing instead to give money to existing state programs. In sum, the administration's refusal to request new money for the Solar Bank in fiscal 1984 was an attempt to destroy a program established by Congress and upheld by courts.

Interest in solar energy still thrives, although it is less strong than if government encouragement had persisted. The number of passive solar homes and the number of buildings with active solar energy systems have substantially increased. According to the administration, the solar and renewables program has been so successful that it no longer needs government support. "Continued subsidies or regulations for those who otherwise would act to conserve or develop renewable resources is not necessary and not cost-effective," said Energy Secretary Hodel.[16]

Energy Conservation. Some experts think energy conservation is a painless remedy for energy and environmental problems. It allows consumers to save money that otherwise would be spent on energy and to spend it someplace else, thereby stimulating the economy. By reducing demand through conservation, the availability of supply increases. Fuel not used remains a resource for future use. Of even greater significance is that decreased energy consumption reduces adverse environmental impacts: the less fossil fuel burned, the fewer pollutants emitted into the air and water. Conservation buys time for the United States until environmentally benign energy sources are available.

The conservation industry is relatively new. Little public interest in conservation existed until the energy crisis during the winter of 1973-1974, when President Richard Nixon organized the Federal Energy Administration (FEA). FEA worked to develop a conservation program for buildings, to provide information on energy affairs to consumers, and to outline emergency measures to reduce demand. The Interior Department likewise was in-

Table 10-1 Department of Energy Renewable Energy Budget

(In millions of dollars)

	Carter Request 1/81	Reagan Request 9/81	Congressional Appropriations 12/81	Budget Authority:[1] 1982	1983	Reagan Request 1984	Budget Authority[1] 1984
Photovoltaics	161.6	54.1	78.0	75.0	58.0	32.7	50.4
Solar Thermal (including active and passive)	149.8	57.5	77.0	76.0	61.1	21.9	60.3
Biomass Energy Systems	55.5	18.0	20.5	20.5	16.0	17.3	—
Alcohol Fuels	32.6	8.8	10.0	10.0	5.0	—	28.4
Wind Energy Conversion Systems	73.6	18.3	35.4	34.4	31.4	8.6	26.5
Ocean Energy Systems	36.8	—	20.8	20.8	10.5	—	5.5
Renewable Energy Information	12.7	3.5	6.7	6.7	3.0	3.1	3.3
Renewable Energy International	13.0	8.8	4.0	4.0	10.0	—	.5
Program Support	—	—	4.0	3.5	1.0	—	.8
Solar Reserve Account	—	—	15.0	12.3	—	—	—
Program Direction (administration)	6.9	4.0	4.0	4.0	5.8	3.0	6.0
Total	558.96	170.1	275.4	268.2	201.94	86.6	181.7

[1] The actual amount appropriated by Congress, that is, the spending level.

SOURCE: *Congressional Budget Request FY 1984* vol. 2 (Washington, D.C.: Department of Energy, January 1983); *Inside Energy with Federal Lands*, February 7, 1983, 9; *Solar Lobby*, *Sun Times* (March-April 1982), 18; PL 98-50, 1984 appropriations bill.

structed to develop conservation programs. The conservation budget grew to $174.1 million in 1977 from $14.5 million in 1974, indicating both bipartisan congressional and administrative support. An Energy Department evaluation of conservation programs reported that the "national conservation program strategy that evolved was primarily one of trying to offset the disincentives to conservation which resulted from energy prices being kept artificially low through price regulations." [17]

In 1983, we used less energy per Gross National Product (GNP) dollar than we did in 1974. From 1960 to 1973 both GNP and energy consumption growth increased at proportional rates. From 1973 to 1980 the energy consumption rate increased at a lower level than the GNP rate, indicating a change in the historical pattern of U.S. energy growth keeping pace with GNP rates. From 1973 to 1980, energy consumption increased only four quads, from 76 to 80 quads. (One quad is equivalent to a quadrillion British thermal units, or BTUs.) This figure is "20 quads lower than it would have been had pre-embargo economic and fuel price trends continued unchanged." [18] Of this 20-quad reduction, half was attributed to a recession economy; the other 10-quad reduction resulted from improved efficiency (such as technical changes in residential and commercial sectors, and automobile fuel efficiency) and operational changes (including changes in habits such as car-pooling and lowered thermostats). These changes indicate that economic growth and energy conservation are no longer incompatible.

Also, as conservation has increased, the amount of oil imported has decreased from more than 8 million barrels per day in 1977 to more than 5 million barrels per day in 1981.[19] This represents almost a one-third reduction in oil imports.

Conservation was responsible for about 5 percent of the energy savings in 1980, which is equivalent to 0.67 quads, or a savings of $3.9 billion.[20] Moreover, the government has made back its investment in conservation in actual energy dollars saved. The observed reduction in energy per unit of GNP owing to investment in energy conservation may be even larger than currently measurable because of long-term pay off from continued R & D programs. It is estimated that for every dollar spent by the government in conservation, the private sector invests five. It is also estimated that business and residential tax credits have stimulated private sector activity in conservation technology.

If energy conservation has been one of the most successful efforts of the Carter and early Reagan administrations, then why has the Reagan administration tried so diligently to destroy these programs? The conservation budget is illuminating in this regard *(see Table 10-2)*. The $709 million appropriation for fiscal 1981, during the Carter administration, represents a peak in expenditures. The 1981 budget was in place when Reagan took office, but he attempted through a series of requests to Congress to spend less than the 1981 congressional appropriation. Congress allowed $67.7 million to be deferred to the 1982 budget. Reagan requested $171.6 million for 1982, but Congress allocated $384 million. For 1983, Reagan requested a budget of only $21.8 million, virtually eliminating every conservation effort, including

Table 10-2 Energy Conservation Budget

	Budget Authority[1] 1981	Budget Authority[1] 1982	*(In millions of dollars)* Reagan Request 1983	Budget Authority[1] 1983	Reagan Request 1984	Budget Authority[1] 1984
Buildings and Community System	91.33	47.66[2]	—	39.10	16.39	37.4
Industrial	69.61	28.85	—	27.90	10.63	33.7
Transportation	105.05	58.94	—	53.90	40.96	65.0
Multisector	26.47	16.47	17.54	12.73	3.10	12.8
State and Local	402.25	231.91	4.26	233.66	3.30	280.2
Energy Impact Assistance	10.00	—	—	—	—	—
Feasibility Studies	4.59	—	—	—	—	—
Total	709.30	383.84[3]	21.80	367.29[4]	74.38	429.1

[1] The actual amount appropriated by Congress, that is, the spending level.
[2] Includes monies not spent by Reagan in 1981.
[3] Includes $67,762 for deferrals from fiscal 1981 and $173,008 from transfers. This leaves $145,000 of actual new dollars from Congress.
[4] Includes $88,000 from transfers.

SOURCE: *Congressional Budget Request FY 1983* and *Congressional Budget Request FY 1984* (Washington, D.C.: Department of Energy), Office of Management and Budget; interior support tables, PL–98–146.

weatherization, assistance to state energy offices, appliance standards, the Residential Conservation Service, waste energy reduction, and building systems programs. Yet Congress restored the authorization level to $367 million. Similarly, in 1984 Reagan requested $74 million, and Congress saw fit to fund the conservation budget at a level of $429 million.

The Reagan administration claims that conservation is a success and, therefore, needs no further governmental direction. Congress, on the other hand, disagrees. It funded almost every program in energy conservation with resounding numbers showing its disdain for Energy Department attempts to dismantle congressionally mandated programs. By January 1983, it was clear that the administration, which had been trying to use the budgetary process as a key political tool for achieving its agenda, was no longer in charge of the energy budget.

The broad aggressive role of the Carter administration has been replaced by a policy of deregulation of the price of oil and natural gas to force higher energy prices, driving consumers toward conservation. It is projected that conservation technology will be taken up by industry when energy prices reflect real energy costs. Individual and business long-term investment in conservation will be encouraged by tax credits and accelerated depreciation, and by a general improvement in the economy due to inflation reduction measures, such as lower taxes and elimination of regulations. Most Energy Department programs, including conservation, have been oriented toward the future, have involved high-risk technology, and have provided planning assistance to state and local governments. "Research is planned and executed with a high degree of interaction with the private sector groups that will ultimately use the results of the reseach. In this way, relevance and rapid transfer of the results are assured." [21]

However, many of the advances in technology would not have been accomplished without government support. Private sector industry does not reap immediate benefits from advanced R & D in conservation, nor does it have the incentive to invest in information networks for the public sector. Because many private sector organizations' R & D budgets are becoming smaller and because there is a shortage of competent managerial talent in conservation, it is more likely that the private sector will not be capable of assuming these new responsibilities.

State and Local Conservation Programs. Federal support for state and local government conservation programs was included in the Energy Policy and Conservation Act of 1975 (PL 94-163) and the Energy Conservation and Production Act of 1976 (PL 94-385). The National Energy Extension Service Act of 1977 (PL 95-39) and the National Energy Policy Act of 1978 (PL 95-619) created additional programs.

State energy conservation grant programs began in 1976. In order to receive funding, states had to initiate eight conservation steps, including programs relating to lighting efficiency standards, thermal efficiency standards, mandatory right-turn-on-red traffic light laws, and public education on energy. Money was used to support state and local governments in

Table 10-3   State and Local Assistance Programs:
Energy Policy and Conservation Grant Programs

| | | | Budget Authority[1] (in millions of dollars) | | | | | Reagan Request |
1976	1977	1978	1979	1980	1981	1982	1983	1984
5.0	35.0	71.5	57.8	47.8	47.8	24.0	24.0	—

[1] The actual amount appropriated by Congress, that is, the spending level.

SOURCE: Office of State and Local Assistance Programs, Department of Energy.

developing plans that would "reduce projected 1980 energy consumption by 5 percent or more." [22] The budget levels for 1976-1984 are shown in Table 10-3.

Until 1980 presidential budget requests exceeded congressional appropriations. Although Reagan as of the end of 1983 had requested no funds for these programs since he entered office, Congress has continued to appropriate money, albeit at levels lower than during the Carter administration. While the states have developed their own energy offices to manage conservation programs, the federal government has provided continual assistance in the form of technical aid, training workshops, and energy information-sharing programs. Most states depend on federal money to support their energy offices, and the budget reductions have hurt these offices.[23] During 1980, the State Energy Conservation Program (SECP) saved about 3.1 quads or 4 percent of the actual 1980 U.S. energy consumption, according to reports by the states. The Energy Department estimates a slightly more conservative figure of 0.2 quads, which still amounts to a significant savings.[24]

Two other programs that deserve mention are the weatherization assistance and the schools and hospitals programs. The weatherization program provides states with funds to weatherize low-income households through subcontractors or community organizations. The results have been lower energy bills for 758,000 homes (a savings of 25 percent of the energy normally consumed in these homes) through 1981 and an estimated savings of 3 million barrels of oil annually.[25]

The schools and hospitals program gave grants to implement conservation measures and provide technical assistance to institutional buildings. The annual estimated savings is 17.8 million barrels of oil. More important, the long-range impact is lower energy bills and the creation of jobs in the construction industry. Government grants resulted in investment at twice the rate of government outlays.

As of the end of 1983, the president had asked for no funds to continue these programs. In 1981 Congress ignored the presidential request for a rescission, and the administration argued that monies to assist homeowners could be found elsewhere in federal block-grant programs or HUD low-income assistance programs to assist homeowners. But the president never introduced legislation to eliminate the weatherization program, perhaps because it was particularly popular in Congress.

The implementation of these and other state and local energy conservation programs also was hampered by personnel changes and sharp reductions in force (RIFs). The Office of State and Local Programs, successful in promoting and realizing conservation, had its supervisory staff completely replaced by the end of 1980. Most new employees had little experience in the programs and were therefore learning on the job. This instability affected the delivery of services to the states, which meanwhile were being forced to cut back their own programs. In the Energy Department's Office of Energy Conservation and Renewable Energy, there were 405 filled positions in 1981, 314 in 1982, an estimated 278 in 1983, and an estimated 123 in 1984. In state and local assistance programs, staff was reduced from 350 in 1980, to 180 in 1981, to 150 in 1982; in 1983 staff was reduced to 143, and a request was submitted for a mere 65 for 1984.[26]

The rapid attrition of staff made it impossible for many programs to continue functioning. Continual reorganizations and shifting of personnel left all but one division director, in conservation, new on the job. Of eight branch chiefs in 1982, only one had been on the job more than five months.[27] Between October 1, 1981, and February 2, 1982, the staff of the Building Energy and Research Office was reduced from 75 to 54.[28] In the Renewable Energy Office, staff levels fell from 247 in early 1981 to 194 after the fall RIF, and to 151 by November 1981.[29] Program directors complained that there were insufficient personnel to administer and monitor grants.

Because the administration's budget requests for some Energy Department programs were low compared with congressional appropriations for 1982 and because Congress was leery that personnel for some programs would be cut, the Final Supplemental Appropriations Act of 1982 established floors for staff reductions. It should be noted, however, that conservation, solar, and renewable programs fell below these minimum levels despite the legislation.[30] As of January 3, 1983, the Energy Department had 131 full-time employees in the Office of Conservation and as of December 29, 1982, 163 employees in state and local programs. The congressional legislation had established floors of 154 for conservation R & D and 180 for state and local conservation.

Appliance-Efficiency Standards. Consistent with its disregard for congressional support for conservation programs, the administration has engaged in a battle to thwart efforts to conserve energy by setting and labeling the efficiency standards for appliances. The 1978 Energy Policy and Conservation Act (PL 94-163), as amended by the National Energy Conservation Policy Act (PL 95-619), provided the basis for establishing appliance-efficiency standards that were to be completed by January 2, 1981. The Reagan administration failed to produce the standards until public interest groups took the Energy Department to court.

Although industry opposes standards in general, many companies prefer federal standards. (About 46 states have standards for some appliances.) The proposed federal standards were to apply to refrigerators, refrigerator-freezers, dishwashers, clothes dryers, water heaters, room air conditioners, furnaces, humidifiers and dehumidifiers, television sets, and kitchen ranges and ovens. Section 325(a)(1) of the act required the Energy Department to establish efficiency standards unless the agency determined "by rule either that a standard would not result in significant conservation of energy or that a standard is not technically feasible or economically justified." [31]

The Carter administration had suspended the process of analyzing the appliance market during the presidential transition period. On February 23, 1981, after Reagan had taken office, the Energy Department announced it would not issue any efficiency standards until it had fully reviewed comments received (during the 1979-1980 Carter period) on its notice of proposed rule making issued December 13, 1979. The Reagan administration's subsequent review and second round of public comment took one and a half years, whereupon the Natural Resources Defense Council and the Consumers Union sued the Energy Department for failure to meet the schedule stipulated by the National Energy Conservation Act. A settlement was agreed upon for promulgation of standards for all appliances (except home heating other than furnaces) by October 29, 1982.

On April 2, 1982, however, the Energy Department proposed that a standard for eight of the products would not be made because it "would not result in significant conservation of energy and would not be economically justified." [32] The October 29, 1982, court deadline passed, and on December 22, 1982, the Energy Department finally issued "no standard" standards for ovens/ranges and clothes dryers, meaning that there would be no federal standards. Federal standards supersede any existing or future state or local standards. The Energy Department did make provisions for states and localities to apply for a waiver of the "no standard" standard, to be issued within six months from the date of the submission of a petition. The Energy Department would adopt such a ruling if there were a significant state or local reason for adopting a more stringent standard than the federal one of "no standard," unless a burden on interstate commerce would result.

The Energy Department had promised to complete standards for six other appliances by April 30, 1983, as part of its court settlement with the National Resources Defense Council (NRDC) and Consumers Union. The department also had agreed to pay NRDC and the Consumers Union $10,000 in legal fees for their negotiating time. On August 30, 1983, it issued a "no standard" standard for the remaining appliances, and the matter was taken up in the federal courts as NRDC and the states of New York, California, Minnesota, and Texas filed suit against the Energy Department.

The apparent strategy of the administration in these actions has been to avoid executive responsibility for implementing congressional law. The creation of a "no standard" standard, however, was hardly the intent of Congress when it passed the Energy Policy and Conservation Act in 1978.

Setting efficiency standards for appliances was an attempt to eliminate the inherent inefficiencies of a free-market system. Almost half the products covered—for example, furnaces, washers, and air conditioners—are bought by contractors, leaving the consumer little discretion. Normally, such decisions are made more on the basis of cost than efficiency. Therefore, instead of developing efficiency standards for implementation, the Energy Department—after having been forced into court—simply concluded that no standards should be set according to its analysis of industry costs versus conservation benefits. The Energy Department thus has undermined the efforts of Congress to provide contractors, builders, and consumers with information on which to base their decisions at the marketplace.

Radical Versus Incremental Change

The administrative system and public policy process often have been criticized as ineffectual. Where government action is needed to address large or critical problems, the responses have been slow and change has been small or incremental. The Reagan administration not only has made some radical changes in the overall governmental mission in energy policy, but it also has used the administrative process to institute those changes in a political climate of opposition from Congress, public interest groups, and state and local governments. These changes are outlined below.

(1) The Reagan administration's energy policies have been made by OMB, not by the Energy Department or the White House. OMB reviews all proposed federal regulations and must approve them before they are promulgated. Beginning with Secretary James Edwards, Reagan's first Energy Department secretary, budget decision making was shifted from the Energy Department to OMB, which had the final word and from which there was no appeal. OMB's policy role coupled with its budget role has transformed it into a strong, centralized administrative unit for domestic policy.

(2) The New Federalism of the Reagan administration implies a greater role for the states in the establishment and implementation of policy. The administration has turned over programs to them, arguing that because states are closer to the people they will be more sensitive to their particular needs. However, states lack money and qualified personnel to take over federal functions and responsibilities. During the last decade the states and the federal government have developed working relationships on environmental and energy issues. But, in a short time span, the New Federalism has forced states "to choose between short-term economic gain and protection of irreplaceable resources." [33] Without federal standards, states are vulnerable to industry pressures and may be forced to relax existing regulations to keep industry from being lured away.

According to the Energy Department's Office of Policy, Planning, and Analysis, the New Federalism strategy would affect the role of planning.

> The Reagan administration is dedicated to free market principles so adjustments to future changes are not feared but are fully expected. This

approach recognizes the tremendous uncertainties underlying energy projections, and it gives fair warning that these projections do not constitute any sort of blueprint for the future that the administration is committed to pursue at all costs—least of all by direct governmental intervention.[34]

By taking this position, the administration suggested that because we rely on the market and because we cannot accurately predict market behavior, the government should not engage in planning activities. Carrying this logic further, because we do not plan, information is rendered less valuable. Consequently, the Energy Department's Energy Information Administration has cut back on collecting and disseminating information, issues few publications, and, indeed, now charges money for them. The department also has lowered the mandatory reporting requirements for electric utilities by 20 percent and reduced the number of utilities required to report. The department also sought to discontinue the Financial Reporting System, mandated by the DOE Organization Act of 1977, which produces a report on the financial activities of oil companies.[35] Fewer data are collected because less analysis is needed. Reliance on the free-market system diminishes the importance of analyses and projections. No government in recent times has sought to beat its opponents by declaring war on information.

(3) The Reagan administration's early proposals to dismantle the Energy Department, which were rebuffed by Congress, were consistent with its belief that the energy issue no longer required government management. Under the proposal, some government functions would have remained, such as weapons production, emergency planning, international trade, and some R & D, while the private sector would have handled commercialization of energy technologies. Key functions would have gone to the Commerce Department. The Interior Department would have received the management of federally owned energy reserves. Enforcement authority would have been transferred to the Justice Department. A new agency within Commerce, the Energy Research and Technology Administration, would have been established for energy R & D, uranium enrichment, and other defense-related activities. The proposal for reorganization had no provisions for conservation activities and no decision-making structure for consideration of environmental impacts. After a decade of the government's recognition of the interrelationship of energy and environmental issues, the breakup of the Energy Department would have meant that energy issues would be dealt with in piecemeal fashion and without the opportunity for comprehensive environmental review. Since the administration believes that energy is no longer a critical concern except for supply problems, and the market resolves such issues, the dismantling of the department would have dealt a final blow to official recognition that energy policy should be considered in the context of associated issues such as the environment.

Congressional approval was needed to dismantle the Energy Department, and the 97th Congress was not forthcoming with its support. Many in Congress suggested that only the federal government could attend adequately to energy issues and that dismantling the agency was an overreaction to the problems created by excessive energy regulations. However, Secretary Hodel said he viewed the agency "as an interim ... step along the way in the maturing of our national attitude toward energy. ... It should no longer be a separate Cabinet-level agency devoted only to energy." [36] Hodel also said that energy policy should be considered within the Commerce Department along with economic and trade policy.

(4) Instead of introducing legislation to repeal an energy program, the Reagan administration has resorted to zero budgeting. Most programs were continued only because Congress chose to ignore the Reagan budget requests. The administration has attempted to modify the effects of statutes through budget manipulation. Money appropriated by Congress has not been spent on time, and contract work has not begun on schedule. The repercussions of this are serious. A program officer, planning for the next fiscal year, must either plan for zero budget (given the Reagan budget request) or plan for a clandestine undisclosed amount (anticipating congressional support).

The Energy Department's program directors have been forced to act as if the 1983 zero budget was a reality and phase out programs until Congress comes to the rescue. This makes it difficult to keep staff, interferes with planning in the national laboratories, and interrupts long-term research projects. Moreover, if many programs are zero budgeted, Congress, lacking appropriate staff, will have difficulty judging the level of resources that should be replaced and ensuring that funds are being spent as appropriated.

(5) Reorganization of personnel or changes in agency tasks can have major impacts. Where grade structures have been lowered, forcing out long-term civil servants, personnel have been placed in positions above their level of experience, leaving viable programs in incompetent hands.

Under the Carter administration, the Office of Policy Planning and Analysis analyzed and evaluated programs and trends. It attempted to organize information and to propose new regulations. Because of the Reagan administration's emphasis on paring down regulations in an effort to get the government out of energy decision making, the role of the office has changed. According to administration philosophy, a free marketplace does not require analysis, and so the Office of Policy Planning and Analysis is now free to take on new and different tasks. For instance, when nuclear-waste legislation was passed by Congress and signed by the president on January 7, 1983, 60 people from the office were asked to devote time to its implementation. During the 180 days that followed, those who were once responsible for conservation and renewables were charged with the incongruous task of implementing nuclear-waste legislation. So, although personnel have been retained in this office, their duties have been changed.

Conclusion

Although some commentators have observed that the United States has no national energy policy, decisions nevertheless are being made that affect how we use energy and that pose significant environmental risks. Policies may be implicit, and refusal to act can be as effective as action.

The United States is facing two separate supply problems. One is short-range; the other, long-range. The former results from production or transportation factors, the latter from the inevitable scarcity of fossil fuels. Because conservation measures have helped reduce demand for electricity, the need for more power plants has become far less pressing. Industry dreams of hundreds of nuclear power plants scattered throughout the land that have been abandoned. The United States must develop an energy mix for the present that will result in patterns of energy consumption posing the least damage to the environment.

The impact of this administration's policy should not be underestimated. The professional civil service has suffered great losses. It will take many years to rebuild the government's analytic capacity because experts either have left the government or have been fired. Cutbacks in government R & D for conservation and renewable energy, and fossil fuel pollution control technologies will increase the leadtime for developing environmentally sound technologies in the private sector. These avenues of research are needed if long-term changes are to occur in patterns of energy usage. The devaluation of information and the reduction of data collection and analysis on the part of government give industry an unparalleled monopoly on basic data. The effect may be to transfer decision making to the private sector despite the fact that the public interest and national future are at stake.

The present administration has attempted to thwart the intent of major environmental and energy legislation through administrative actions. Overwhelming evidence exists that Reagan's programs for energy and the environment will strengthen the political leverage of already powerful industries at the expense of the public interest. The destruction of programs and the federal government's virtual inattention to the complex interrelationship between energy and environmental issues will have a profound effect on our precarious future.

We need a comprehensive energy policy that enables us to fuel our society in the next century without destroying our environment. Our government has a constructive role to play in creating the economic and political conditions necessary to ensure that decisions on energy policy will incorporate environmental values. Otherwise, we can not look forward to a society, or even a world, capable of sustaining human life.

Notes

1. *Congressional Budget Request FY 1984*, vol. 6 (Washington, D.C.: Government Printing Office, January 1983), 13; *Inside Energy with Federal Lands*, January 10, 1983, and January 31, 1983; and PL-394, the Interior and Related Agencies Bill, December 30, 1982.
2. *Congressional Budget Request FY 1984*, vol. 6, 15, 112.
3. Energy Information Administration, *Monthly Energy Review*, December 1982, DOE/EIA-0035, 60.
4. Energy Information Administration, *Quarterly Coal Report*, April 1983, DOE/EIA-

0121, 27.

5. James B. Edwards, energy secretary, "Seminar on Utility Finances" (Speech delivered before the U.S. National Committee of the World Energy Conference and the Edison Electric Institute, October 28, 1981).
6. *Monthly Energy Review,* December 1982, 32, 56.
7. Edward E. Noble, chairman of the board, U.S. Synthetic Fuels Corporation, statement before hearing of the Senate Committee on Energy and Natural Resources, 97th Cong., 2d sess., February 10, 1982.
8. Edward E. Noble, statement before joint hearings of the House Committee on Science and Technology, subcommittees on Energy Development and Applications and on Investigations and Oversight, 97th Cong., 1st sess., July 27, 1981.
9. Statement by the president, Office of the Press Secretary, White House, October 8, 1981.
10. *Congressional Budget Request FY 1984*, vol. 2, 95.
11. *New York Times,* January 16, 1983.
12. *Sun Times* (Washington, D.C.: Solar Lobby), 9.
13. *Reagan and the American Environment* (San Francisco: Friends of the Earth, 1982), 77.
14. *Congressional Budget Request FY 1984* vol. 2, 15.
15. *Reagan and the American Environment,* 68.
16. *Inside Energy with Federal Lands,* December 6, 1982, 5.
17. "Report to Congress," *Sunset Review: Program by Program Analysis*, vol. 2 (Washington, D.C.: Government Printing Office, 1982), 183.
18. *Energy Use from 1973 to 1980: The Role of Improved Efficiency* (Oak Ridge, Tennessee: Oak Ridge National Laboratory, 1982), 37.
19. James B. Edwards, secretary of energy (Speech before the National Association of Towns and Townships, Washington, D.C., September 11, 1981).
20. *Sunset Review,* 185.
21. *Congressional Budget Request FY 1984*, vol. 7, 15.
22. *Sunset Review,* 212.
23. Jack N. Barkenbus, "Federal Energy Policy Paradigms and State Energy Roles," *Public Administration Review* 5 (September/October 1982): 415.
24. *Sunset Review,* 215.
25. Ibid.
26. *Congressional Budget Request FY 1984*, vol. 7, 12, 61.
27. Memorandum from John P. Millhone, director, Building Energy, Research and Development, to Joseph Tribble, assistant secretary for conservation and renewable energy, and Maxine Savitz, deputy assistant secretary for conservation and renewable energy, February 8, 1982.
28. Ibid.
29. Memorandum from Robert San Martin, deputy assistant secretary for renewable energy, to Joseph Tribble, assistant secretary for conservation and renewable energy, December 1, 1981.
30. PL 97-257, Sec. 303. According to the legislation, in the Office of the Assistant Secretary for Conservation and Renewable Energy, there could be no fewer than 352 employees; no fewer than 154 could be assigned to conservation R & D, and 180 to state and local conservation. For the Office of the Assistant Secretary of Fossil Energy, a floor of 754 was established, of which no fewer than 150 could be assigned to headquarters, 280 to the Pittsburgh Energy Technology Center, and 250 to the Morgantown Technology Center. The minimum was set at 450 for the Economic Regulatory Administration.
31. *Federal Register* 7 (December 22, 1982): 57199.
32. Ibid., 57200.

33. Robert Flacke, commissioner of the Department of Environmental Conservation in New York State, "Letters to the Editor," *New York Times,* October 4, 1982.
34. Department of Energy, Office of Policy, Planning and Analysis, "Energy Projections to the Year 2000," July 1982 Update (Washington, D.C.: Government Printing Office, August 1982), 1-1.
35. *Inside Energy with Federal Lands*, March 14, 1983, 3.
36. *Inside Energy with Federal Lands*, December 6, 1982, 7.

11. REVISING THE CLEAN AIR ACT: LEGISLATIVE FAILURE AND ADMINISTRATIVE SUCCESS

Richard J. Tobin

In late 1970 Congress passed the most comprehensive environmental law in the nation's history with unanimous approval in the Senate and only one dissenting vote in the House of Representatives. The Clean Air Act Amendments were significant because of their emphasis on the protection of the public's health. The law required the Environmental Protection Agency (EPA) to define the levels of air quality necessary to protect the public's health and welfare. If control technologies were not available to meet these levels, Congress nevertheless expected industry to develop them in time to meet the mandated deadlines. According to the Senate's report on the law, companies either would have to meet the levels or be forced to shut down.[1]

During the 1970s Congress gradually receded from its uncompromising position and subsequently revised the law several times. The most significant revisions occurred with the passage of the Clean Air Act Amendments of 1977. These amendments introduced substantive changes, but the major thrust of the 1970 legislation was left largely intact. The goal remained that of reducing air pollution to acceptable levels.

Substantial progress was made in achieving this goal in the 1970s. Emissions of particulates, for example, composed of dust and other particles resulting from fuel combustion and industrial processes, declined by more than 30 percent between 1970 and 1980. Levels of sulfur dioxide, a gaseous product of fossil-fuel combustion, declined by nearly one-quarter over the same period. The average number of days in which all major pollutants taken together created "unhealthful" or "very unhealthful" levels of air quality also decreased. These improvements were evident in most American cities.[2]

By 1980, therefore, the United States was making progress, yet much remained to be done. Residents of many metropolitan areas still suffered from frequent exposure to unhealthy levels of air pollution, and progress had not been uniform. In addition, research had demonstrated the need for increased attention to problems such as acid precipitation and potentially carcinogenic air pollutants.

227

Few people deny the need to achieve acceptable levels of air quality, but considerable doubt exists about the strategies designed to achieve these levels. In fact, the federal clean air program is one of the nation's most controversial environmental laws. During his 1980 presidential campaign, Ronald Reagan cited the program as a prime example of misguided priorities and overregulation and indicated that, if he became president, the clean air program would be revised as an important part of his efforts to deregulate the American economy.

Causes for Concern

Before examining Reagan's statutory and administrative efforts to revise the federal clean air program, it is first useful to explore some of the major criticisms directed at it by those who are subject to its provisions.[3] This review adds perspective to the proposals for change and provides some explanation for Reagan's efforts to revise the program.

Whether composed by business or public officials, any catalogue of complaints about the clean air program is voluminous. Among those subject to its regulation, for example, complaints are likely to be directed at problems in implementing the provisions of the 1977 amendments and at the costs and consequences of compliance.

The 1977 Clean Air Act Amendments comprise one of the most detailed environmental laws ever written. More than 180 pages in length, the amendments are three times longer than the 1970 legislation. The 1977 law is not only long but complex as well. As an illustration, disagreement exists on such seemingly elementary issues as what constitutes a source of air pollution and the definition of clean air. During the 1970s, EPA issued such definitions, in the form of air quality standards, for seven pollutants—ozone, airborne lead, hydrocarbons, carbon monoxide, sulfur dioxide, nitrogen dioxide, and total suspended particulates. Doubt exists, however, about whether several of these standards are medically appropriate or scientifically defensible.[4]

Critics add further that Congress intended state and local governments to have primary responsibility for the prevention and control of air pollution. Despite this intent, many people claim that EPA has become too involved with local enforcement issues or has delayed ceding to state air pollution control agencies the power to implement their own programs. Under the law, states must develop comprehensive implementation plans outlining controls to be imposed in order to achieve the national air quality standards for each regulated pollutant. EPA approval is required for each state implementation plan as well as for each subsequent modification. This approval process is often a source of delay and friction between the states and EPA. In one case in the early 1970s, for example, EPA found unacceptable the state of California's plan to reduce automobile pollution in the Los Angeles metropolitan area. As a result of a court suit, EPA developed its own plan, but it was one in which local preferences and political realities were completely ignored. According to the EPA plan, the total number of vehicle miles traveled in Los

Angeles between May and October would have to be reduced by more than 80 percent. To accomplish this, gasoline would have to be rationed six months of every year. The plan eventually was dropped because of widespread opposition and doubts that it ever could be implemented. California's case provides one example of friction, but state officials also complain about changing federal requirements, inadequate EPA guidance, and inconsistency among the agency's ten regional offices. Once a state submits a plan to EPA for approval, lengthy delays usually follow. Until EPA initiated new procedures in 1981 to expedite review of plan revisions, routine changes took approximately 14 months to process.[5]

Other provisions of the law stimulate still more opposition. For areas of the country not meeting the air quality standards, the 1977 law forbade the construction of major sources of air pollution after mid-1979 unless existing sources reduced their emissions to accommodate the new source. This requirement may have discouraged some companies from considering new construction (or modifications of existing plants) in certain parts of the country, particularly the industrialized East and Midwest. Construction in most "clean air" areas is possible, but prospective developers must demonstrate that their projected emissions will not seriously jeopardize existing levels of clean air. The cleaner the area, however, the less additional pollution is allowed. The result, some claim, is a restriction on industrial siting and development, especially in the West. In situations where construction is allowed, the time necessary to receive a permit can exceed one year.

The procedural and substantive requirements associated with the 1977 amendments are not limited to stationary sources. One study found that automobiles are subject to *hundreds* of federal air quality regulations.[6] In some cases these regulations make it difficult to comply with the requirements of other federal laws. For example, emission control devices often reduce fuel economy (in addition to raising prices). Furthermore, many critics consider it irrational to require all autos to meet the same emission standards regardless of their location, whether it be rural Iowa or downtown Chicago.

Regulated industries also complain that the costs of compliance with the clean air program are too high or are altogether neglected in the legislation. Considering the costs of control alone, an impressive case can be made. Each year the President's Council on Environmental Quality (CEQ) estimates the value of the incremental pollution-abatement expenditures that have been made in response to federal environmental legislation. In every year between 1972 and 1979, funds devoted to the abatement of air pollution exceeded the combined total for all other categories for which estimates are made (noise, pesticides, solid wastes, drinking water, toxic substances, land reclamation, and water pollution). Estimated cumulative expenditures for the control of air pollution also are expected to be higher than for any other category through 1988 *(see Table 11-1)*.

Critics find the costs of compliance especially intolerable because they often see little relation between these costs and the resulting benefits. They cite regulation of emissions from automobiles as a leading example. Several provisions of the law, such as those related to the setting of air quality standards, preclude consideration of costs, implying that, whatever the ultimate costs, Congress has found them acceptable before the fact. Critics respond that this blindness to costs causes consumers to pay for some entirely unnecessary pollution controls.

This list of complaints is not meant to be exhaustive, but rather to illustrate that, by the end of 1980, a significant body of grievances had developed, and a large number of people were calling for change in the program. Reagan included himself in this group. From his perspective the Clean Air Act Amendments of 1977 provided an ideal place to begin a comprehensive deregulation of American society. The amendments' financial authorization would expire on September 30, 1981, at the end of the fiscal year.[7] Congress thus would be considering revision to the law and likely would seek some direction from the White House. In addition, many of Reagan's aides believed that revision of the amendments would allow Reagan to seize the initiative on regulatory reform, fulfill his campaign promises to reduce excessive government regulation, and demonstrate that the perverse inefficiencies of regulation could be eliminated without abandoning desirable goals.

Reagan's landslide electoral victory was seen as a mandate to proceed. If any doubts remained about his intentions, they were dispelled when David Stockman, an ardent opponent of government regulation and Reagan's nominee to head the Office of Management and Budget, released a planning document a few weeks before the inauguration. No better opportunity existed for deregulation than the Clean Air Act Amendments of 1977, which represented, in Stockman's words, "staggering excess built upon dubious scientific and economic premises." Of the 14 specific changes Stockman recommended in the planning document, half involved changes in the clean air law.[8]

Pursuing the Mandate

Reagan's election was not the only indication that changes in the clean air program might occur. The election of a Republican majority in the Senate, assuring Republican control of all committee chairmanships, could only help the reform efforts, or so many people believed. In the House of Representatives, Michigan Democrat John Dingell would serve as chairman of the Committee on Energy and Commerce, which would have responsibility for considering changes in the clean air program. Although presidents usually cannot depend on their partisan opponents for support for their proposals, Dingell would be a likely exception. Beginning in 1955, Dingell had represented a portion of Detroit that includes more than a dozen automobile manufacturing plants as well as the headquarters of the Ford Motor Co. In short, the political climate for change appeared ideal, and Reagan would have his choice of approaches. He could seek substantive reforms through Congress and the legislative process or procedural and administrative change through EPA.

Table 11-1 Incremental Pollution Abatement Expenditures, 1973-1979, and Estimated Cumulative Expenditures, 1979-1988[1] (billions of dollars)

	1973	1975	1977	1979	Cumulative 1979-1988
Air Pollution	$3.6	$ 9.0	$12.2	$22.3	$299.1
Other Sources of Pollution[2]	2.7	5.4	7.1	14.6	219.4
Total	$6.3	$14.4	$19.3	$36.9	$518.5

[1] The amounts represent expenditures made pursuant to federal environmental laws beyond those that would have been made in the absence of such laws. The amounts include capital costs and operation and maintenance.

[2] Includes noise, pesticides, radiation, solid wastes, drinking water, toxic substances, land reclamation, and water pollution.

Source: Annual reports of the Council on Environmental Quality, 1974, 1976, 1978, 1980.

Seeking Legislative Change

Many people expected the Reagan White House to lead a well-organized effort to revise the clean air law. Indeed, the Reagan administration began its term in January 1981 with the expectation that it surely would achieve far-reaching legislative changes. In spite of the administration's initial optimism and continuing opposition to the law, after three years in office Reagan had not achieved any of his legislative goals. At midterm the *Wall Street Journal* noted that the political climate had changed so much that the administration clearly was on the defensive and willing to delay attempts at change in order to avoid the adoption of amendments that would strengthen the law.[9]

What happened to cause such a dramatic change in perspectives? No single answer exists, but an explanation can be found in a series of related factors. These include a misreading of public opinion, unrealistically expecting Congress to be receptive to proposals for comprehensive change, and having difficulty in developing and presenting proposals for legislative change. A brief examination of the administration's efforts in Congress demonstrates how these factors operated to discourage change.

Ordinarily, when presidents seek changes in legislation, they take the initiative by developing detailed draft bills, which friendly members of Congress then introduce for the administration. This was exactly what many members expected the Reagan White House to do soon after taking office, especially in view of the authorization deadline of September 30.

Knowledge of the deadline and of the consequences of inaction had prompted committees in the House and Senate to have their own review of the existing law well under way. Many of the necessary oversight hearings had been completed in 1980, so most of the major issues already had been identified. In addition, as part of the 1977 amendments, Congress had created the National Commission on Air Quality (NCAQ) to make a bipartisan, comprehensive assessment of air pollution control and the effects of the 1977 law. When the commission issued its report in March 1981, it took note of past progress but urged that control of air pollution be considered "a continued national priority" requiring "continued substantial investments" through the 1980s because of the severity of the pollution that remained. The report concluded that the existing law did not need the fundamental change that Ronald Reagan had called for during his campaign for the presidency. In contrast, the commission stated that the law was sound and needed only refinement.[10]

These developments suggested at least two conclusions. First, the imminence of the September 30 deadline meant that time for consideration of major changes in the law would be limited, particularly given the president's wish to occupy Congress with tax and budget matters. Second, the NCAQ's report indicated that major changes might not even be necessary.

This view was anathema to opponents of the law, including many in the new administration who sought to fulfill campaign promises by rewriting the law completely. If they were to prevail, however, they would have to develop proposals in time for Congress to consider them at an early stage of the legislative process. Lengthy delays could well be fatal. In short, a sense of urgency existed among those in Congress who favored massive change.

This sense of urgency did not translate into an effective strategy for revision. Several examples illustrate the point. After promising that it would quickly provide Congress with proposed revisions in the law, the administration delayed on several occasions. As a consequence, when officials from EPA testified at congressional hearings in the spring of 1981, they could not speak conclusively because the administration had not yet defined many of its positions. So unsure was EPA on some issues that its officials actually declined to testify at certain hearings. The agency's problems also were compounded because Anne Gorsuch was not confirmed as the agency's administrator until several months after Reagan became president.

The administration's efforts at revision suffered further when drafts of possible changes fell into the hands of the press or of unsympathetic members of Congress in late May and early June 1981. The drafts called for things such as the elimination of national air quality standards, the application of cost-benefit analysis to the setting of standards, the elimination of federal sanctions for localities not achieving standards, and elimination of the requirement that pollution-control devices on automobiles be maintained in proper working order. Other parts suggested that EPA's enforcement of the law should be discretionary, that limits for automobile exhausts be relaxed, and that polluted areas be allowed to assess their own progress in abating air pollution.[11]

The drafts contained lists of possible options without indicating which ones might actually be recommended to Congress, but this did not prevent critics from reacting sharply and negatively. In an effort to counter criticism, the administration stressed that the drafts were the work of low-level bureaucrats and that neither Gorsuch nor the White House had reviewed them.[12] Regardless of the claims, however, the administration had suffered substantial damage, and this before its formal proposals had even been released.

The administration suffered a second jolt in mid-June when the *Harris Survey* released the results of a nationwide poll. Thirty-eight percent of the respondents believed that the Clean Air Act Amendments should be made stricter, and another 48 percent wanted the law kept substantially as it was; only 12 percent wanted it to be weakened. Nearly eight of ten respondents thought that federal air pollution standards were either "just about right" or "not protective enough." In summarizing his findings, Louis Harris observed that the "uncompromising attitude on the part of Americans concerning pollution clean-up could spell trouble for the Reagan administration..." (*see Chapter 3*). [13]

Whether due to the adverse reactions to the leaked proposals, a recognition of widespread public support for the clean air program, or the administration's apparent inability to decide precisely what it wanted, the White House abandoned its plan to provide the Congress with specific proposals for change. Instead, in early August 1981, the administration issued 11 "basic principles" that would guide efforts to change the law. As Reagan would later observe, the principles reflected needed changes that were essential to the success of his program for economic recovery.[14]

In spite of the importance the president attached to the principles, many were deliberately vague and offered limited guidance. All were cast in a positive tone, and nothing was said overtly about relaxing or revising the law in such a way as to impair air quality. As an illustration, the first principle called for continuing "steady progress toward cleaner air." Other principles stated that laws and regulations "should be reasonable" and related to "economic and physical realities," that air quality standards "should be based on sound scientific data" (but not subject to cost-benefit analysis), and that states "should be accorded a full partnership" in implementing the clean air laws. The administration added that emission standards for automobiles "should be adjusted to more reasonable levels," that research on acid precipitation should be accelerated, that rules be changed to allow new electric power plants to burn more coal, and that a more effective program for the control of hazardous air pollutants should be established.[15]

One might expect that the principles' seeming blandness would not spark much criticism, but such was not the case. The Sierra Club declared that the Reagan administration had launched a "massive 'big-lie' campaign to lull Americans into believing [the] Clean Air Act is safe, while it pursues [a] back-room strategy to worsen air quality."

In addition to the adverse reaction that the principles generated, they also had an effect on the prospects for achieving revisions of the sort the president desired. By failing to provide specific proposals in a draft bill, the administration and EPA relinquished an opportunity to play an influential role in the revision process. Without its own bill, the administration had nothing with which it could lobby or negotiate. The absence of a bill also meant that the administration would not be able to depend for support on traditional party loyalties among Republicans in Congress. These members could vote according to their conscience or the views of their constituents without having to vote against a presidential initiative.

That the administration was willing to accept these possible consequences was ironic. Ceding the initiative reduced the chances that Reagan would achieve the reforms he wanted. Equally significant, the actions were at odds with his subsequent claim that change in the clean air law was his "top priority in the area of regulatory reform." [16]

In the absence of an initiative from the president, proponents of change in the House of Representatives eventually introduced their own bill—HR 5252—in December 1981. Its sponsors, who included John Dingell and several other Democratic and Republican members of the House Committee on Energy and Commerce, labeled their proposal a moderate compromise. It attracted support from the Business Roundtable, the National Association of Manufacturers, the U.S. Chamber of Commerce, the Motor Vehicle Manufacturers Association, and, most important, from the Reagan administration. Environmental groups immediately called the proposal a "dirty air" bill, claiming that it would double automobile emission standards, extend the deadline for meeting the national air quality standards by as much as 11 years, and allow substantial increases in pollution near national parks and wilderness areas. Environmentalists also criticized HR 5252 because it did not address the problem of acid precipitation and because it would maintain what the NCAQ had called inadequate provisions covering hazardous air pollutants.

Debate on the bill was bitter and highly contentious in Dingell's Committee on Energy and Commerce. Moreover, Dingell's coalition could not control the outcome of several key votes, and, because the 1977 law would remain in effect unless changed, his opponents openly favored delay. As a result, a revised clean air bill did not emerge from the committee in either 1981 or 1982, so the full House of Representatives had no bill to consider when it adjourned in late 1982.

In the Senate the members of the Committee on Environment and Public Works reached agreement on a bill, largely because most of them believed that significant revision was unnecessary. When the committee finished its work in August 1982, it recommended to the Senate by a 14-1 vote that several adjustments be made to update the law, that most of the existing automobile emission controls be maintained, that EPA increase its control of hazardous air pollutants, and that action be initiated to address the problem of acid rain. Ironically, a Republican-controlled committee had proposed a relatively stringent bill, completely rejecting the president's call for wide-ranging change. Like the House of Representatives, however, the Senate also adjourned without taking any action on a revised clean air bill.

The 98th Congress: Still Trying

President Reagan used his State of the Union message in January 1983 to call for congressional passage of "a responsible Clean Air Act." [17] By this time, however, the prospects for success along the lines he desired had dimmed considerably. The November election had brought many new Democrats to the House of Representatives, and these tended to be more liberal and more proenvironment than the individuals they had replaced. In the Senate the election brought in only a few new members, but changes in the composition of the Committee on Environment and Public Works seemed to strengthen the hand of those in favor of a stringent law. The relative standing of lobbying groups also affected the prospects for change. Environmentalists perceived themselves to be in a strong position, and many of them believed that any congressional revision would provide opportunities to strengthen the 1977 amendments. In contrast, industrialists and others critical of the amendments found themselves on the defensive. Much had changed in two years. Industry occupied a weakened position, with its lobbyists predicting that they were unlikely to recover from their defeats of 1981 and 1982.

Anne Gorsuch's problems at EPA culminated in her departure from the agency and delayed the administration's efforts in Congress. Meanwhile, the Reagan White House had still not decided on an appropriate overall strategy. In Congress there was little pressure for immediate action. No comprehensive proposals had been introduced in the House of Representatives by mid-1983, and no timetable for action could be discerned.

For many people there appeared to be advantages in delay, and speculation was widespread that since a comprehensive bill had not passed in 1983, then the matter would have to wait until after the 1984 presidential election. If this proves to be the case, Reagan will have failed to fulfill one of the key promises of his 1980 campaign. He will also have provided a salient illustration that apparent electoral mandates are often no match for stiff congressional opposition, particularly when an administration lacks a well-conceived legislative strategy.

Implementing the Clean Air Act

If the Reagan administration faced frustration in Congress, it still had the opportunity to achieve reform through EPA's interpretation and implementation of the existing clean air amendments. Opportunities for reform along these lines were many: the amendments are vague and frequently provide the agency and its administrator with a broad range of discretion. The administrator can decide, for example, which air pollutants should be regulated and how strictly. Similarly, the administrator can establish deadlines, grant waivers from these deadlines, and determine what constitutes compliance with regulations. In short, the complexity of the amendments and the need for literally hundreds of implementing regulations provide any administrator with wide latitude. The agency's flexibility in administering the amendments suggests that Reagan's failure to obtain statutory reform might not be indicative of the prospects for achieving his policy goals through the administrative actions of EPA.

The administration initiated its efforts in the latter area in April 1981, when EPA, at the request of the vice president's Task Force on Regulatory Relief, issued a statement listing 18 actions it intended to "implement in an effort to reduce the regulatory burden on the motor vehicle industry." [18] According to EPA, these actions would save the industry over $800 million and consumers over $4 billion through 1986, "without significantly affecting air quality." The announcement suggested that the actions were mundane, straightforward, and highly desirable, but this was far from obvious. Many of the proposals were intended to relax, revise, delay, or eliminate regulations that the Carter EPA had already justified. The auto industry had appealed to the Carter administration to consider most of the changes that the Reagan administration later proposed, but nearly all of them were rejected. From the perspective of the environmentalists, the Reagan administration's responsiveness to the automobile industry represented a "regulatory cave-in" that could not be justified on grounds of either health or economy. Citing EPA's own data, one former official of the agency argued that several of the proposals would cause a net increase in both air pollution and consumer costs.[19]

Lead-in-Gasoline Regulations

Any controversy that developed as a result of the initial proposals was minor compared to what followed. In August 1981, the vice president's task force asked EPA to reconsider its regulations governing the amount of lead that refiners are permitted to add to gasoline. Leaded gasoline boosts octane ratings and thus engine performance. When lead enters the body, however, it can cause blindness and mental retardation, especially among children. Such adverse health effects have been identified even in cases where blood-lead levels are only marginally elevated.

EPA's initial regulations had specified that large refiners could add no more than 0.8 grams of lead per gallon to gasoline. In October 1980 this was lowered to 0.5 grams per gallon.[20] The 1977 amendments exempted small refiners from these low levels until October 1, 1982; in the interim, they could add as much as 2.65 grams per gallon, depending on their size. Firms failing to meet these requirements could be fined up to $10,000 per day.

The task force asserted that small refiners would face enormous capital costs if forced to comply with the 0.5 level. With economies of scale it is less expensive for large refineries to produce gasoline containing low levels of lead than it is for small refineries. Moreover, said the Reagan administration, the lower level might be too stringent "in light of declining demand for leaded gas and new evidence on [its] health effects." [21] Accordingly, EPA was directed to explore "quick relief" for small refiners and to consider relaxing or rescinding the rule.

When EPA issued its proposed revisions in February 1982, the agency announced that it was seeking public comment on a wide range of alternatives, including maintaining the existing standard, relaxing it incrementally, or adopting different standards for urban and rural areas. In addition, EPA proposed that the deadline of October 1, 1982, for small refiners be postponed indefinitely. The latter group considered this a great victory, asserting that it would prevent many refineries from going out of business "without reason and without environmental benefit." [22]

The controversial nature of the proposed revisions prompted Congress to become involved and to question EPA's objectivity. Rep. Toby Moffett, a Democrat from Connecticut and chairman of the Subcommittee on Environment, Energy, and Natural Resources, called an oversight hearing on EPA's lead-related activities on the day before EPA was to hold its own public hearings. Moffett disclosed that Gorsuch had met with representatives from the Thriftway Co., a small refinery located in New Mexico that sought a waiver from EPA that would permit it to exceed the legal limits for adding lead to gasoline. Gorsuch reportedly indicated that such a request might soon be unnecessary in view of her plans to abolish or revise drastically the lead rules. Consequently, she allegedly encouraged Thriftway to ignore the lead requirements and said that EPA would not enforce them. When asked for written assurances, Gorsuch supposedly told Thriftway's lawyers that such assurances were not needed because they "had the word of the EPA Administrator." [23]

In addition to publicizing Gorsuch's discussions with Thriftway, Moffett released EPA records showing that its officials had held 30 meetings with representatives of the lead and petroleum industries before announcing the proposed revisions. In contrast, the agency's officials had not discussed the proposals with public health officials or sought recent medical information on the health effects of lead.

At EPA's hearings in mid-April, many medical experts argued against any relaxation of the standards; only those representing the lead industry challenged their testimony. Thus, both sets of hearings suggested that if the agency opted for relaxation it could anticipate complaints that it had acted unfairly and without full consideration of available medical data. When EPA did act in mid-1982, however, it startled both the petroleum industry and the environmental and public health community. Stating that "a relaxation of the standard for lead in gasoline would be counterproductive to the alleviation of this serious national problem," the agency withdrew its earlier proposal and announced that it intended to tighten the lead rules, which it did in October 1982.[24]

Under the new rules the total amount of lead entering the atmosphere would have to be reduced by over 30 percent by 1989. To achieve this reduction, the EPA narrowed the distinction between large and small refiners. The latter cried foul, claiming that the new rules would compel them to close about 25 refineries and idle millions of dollars worth of equipment. Several lawsuits protesting EPA's actions quickly followed, but the suits were unsuccessful in causing the agency to reverse its decision. In early 1983 EPA further offended the small refiners by initiating an enforcement action against Thriftway for violations of lead-in-gasoline rules in 1981 and 1982.

Motor Vehicle Regulations

The outcome of the debate over the lead rules was not what the Reagan administration had intended originally, but this was not the case for several of its other proposals. Many of these had first been identified in April 1981, but EPA was obliged to take action on each of them separately by revising existing regulations. Two brief examples indicate how the agency proceeded.

In 1980, after public hearings, the Carter EPA set standards to limit the emissions of diesel particles from automobiles and light trucks. The standards would be effective for the 1982- to 1984-model years; for vehicles manufactured thereafter the standards would be more stringent. EPA's action was noteworthy because diesel-powered vehicles produce 30 to 100 times more particles than gasoline engines equipped with catalytic converters. In addition, diesel particles tend to be very small, with the result that they remain in the air for weeks and can penetrate deep into human lungs. Far more important, the particles contain carcinogenic substances, can aggravate asthma and chronic bronchitis, and can irritate the eyes, nose, and throat. So serious is the potential for harm that the Council on Environmental Quality has declared that "an increase in human cancers could occur from large-scale use of light-duty diesel vehicles." [25] Nevertheless, citing a lack of appropriate technology, the Reagan EPA proposed a two-year delay—until the 1987-model year—for imposition of the standards originally scheduled to affect the 1985 and later model years. [26]

The Carter EPA had also proposed diesel-particle standards for heavy-duty trucks in January 1981, with the expectation that these would be finalized in mid-1982. Reagan's EPA missed that target date, letting it be known that it did not expect to issue final regulations for heavy-duty diesel engines until the end of 1984. This delay came despite a report from the National Academy of Sciences emphasizing that more stringent "control of heavy-duty diesel emissions should be a high priority." [27]

In a second case, the Carter EPA had adopted regulations requiring heavy trucks to control 90 percent of their emissions of carbon monoxide, beginning with 1984-model years. The Carter administration had concluded that the regulations were highly cost-effective, technologically feasible, and necessary to reduce a growing pollution problem in urban areas. The NCAQ supported EPA's judgment, noting that truck manufacturers could install technological controls already developed and in use. The commission added that if the 90-percent control requirement for carbon monoxide was relaxed or repealed, then additional areas of the country would be in violation of the national air quality standards for that pollutant. These conclusions persuaded the Senate Committee on Environment and Public Works to include in its proposed revisions to the clean air law a section specifically prohibiting EPA from changing the standards. Despite the support for the standards, EPA announced in late 1982 a one-year delay in the requirement's effective date, "to avoid imposing additional costs on the manufacturers of heavy duty vehicles." [28] The agency also said it was considering a new standard, perhaps one that would double the allowable emissions of carbon monoxide.

Hazardous Air Pollutants

President Reagan's desire to change the 1977 clean air law and EPA's efforts to relax or revise the regulations by which it is implemented suggest an obvious disenchantment with this legislation. This disenchantment caused many people to wonder how faithfully the Reagan EPA would implement the requirements of the existing law, since these would remain in effect until changed. During her tenure as head of EPA, Gorsuch frequently stated that her task was to obey congressional mandates to protect the environment and that she was fully committed to doing so. Equally important, Gorsuch continually emphasized that her agency would be able to improve the nation's environmental quality with reduced resources. How well did she and her agency succeed?

One way to answer this question is to examine the extent to which the Reagan EPA has met the deadlines for regulatory decision making that the 1977 amendments imposed. Such an examination provides an indication of the Reagan administration's success in implementing the Clean Air Act Amendments and, perhaps, a measure of the administration's substantive commitment to its goal of a healthy environment.

Before examining the issue, however, a major caveat should be introduced. When Congress establishes deadlines in environmental laws, it often underestimates the magnitude of the task at hand and the amount of time required to assemble the scientific and technical evidence needed to justify regulatory action. Consequently, it is not uncommon to miss congressionally mandated deadlines regardless of which party controls the executive branch. Nonetheless, for the Reagan EPA in particular, meeting deadlines provides a test of its claim that it could effectively implement environmental laws despite diminished resources. One issue is especially worth examining because it reflects a priority that Gorsuch established during her first year as EPA's administrator. This issue is the development of regulatory standards for so-called hazardous air pollutants.[29]

These pollutants are the most serious and potentially the most detrimental because they "can cause, or contribute to, an increase in mortality or an increase in serious irreversible, or incapacitating reversible illness." [30] The 1977 law required EPA's administrator to identify and list such pollutants and to propose emission standards for them within six months of their formal listing. Final standards must then be issued within another six months unless the administrator concludes in the interim that the pollutants are not actually hazardous. In setting an emission standard, EPA must include "an ample margin of safety to protect the public health"; the agency cannot consider the costs of compliance, however high.

These requirements have caused substantial problems for EPA. Some hazardous air pollutants can be carcinogenic at *any* level of exposure; thus strict interpretation of the law would prohibit any emissions whatsoever and thereby eliminate all risks linked to exposure. At first glance this may appear desirable until it is realized that coal-burning and nuclear-powered utilities, steel making, petroleum refining, and synthetic organic-chemical manufacturing all emit some small amounts of airborne carcinogens. Faced with the prospect of massive economic dislocation associated with strict interpretation of the law, EPA took the position in the 1970s that Congress had not realized or intended the full consequences of implementation.[31]

This perspective was that of an agency reluctant to regulate. As the NCAQ noted in 1981, EPA preferred to avoid listing an air pollutant as hazardous unless there was "almost irrefutable scientific evidence of harm with which to justify agency action." [32] By 1977, EPA had listed and established emission standards for only four hazardous air pollutants—asbestos, beryllium, mercury, and vinyl chloride—and then only as a result of legal pressure from environmental groups. In addition, the agency had listed benzene as hazardous but had not yet issued emission standards for it.

In its review of the Clean Air Act in 1977, Congress found this pace to be intolerable and made it clear that it expected the pace of regulation to quicken considerably. Congress also specified four additional substances—arsenic, cadmium, radioactive pollutants, and polycyclic organic matter—that it required the EPA to consider for regulatory action. As a result of congressional prodding, EPA listed radionuclides as a hazardous air pollutant in late 1979 and inorganic arsenic in mid-1980. According to the timetable established in the 1977 law, emission standards for the two pollutants should have been issued no later than one year after their listing. However, EPA took no action on either pollutant in the first two years of the Reagan administration. The agency finally proposed standards for the two pollutants in 1983, acting only after federal courts compelled it to do so. It was ironic that the federal courts had to become involved. Gorsuch had made the regulation of hazardous air pollutants one of her priorities and had once stated that it would be difficult to regulate such pollutants more slowly than the Carter EPA had done.[33] Despite this emphasis and her earlier claims that reduced budgets would not reduce the EPA's capacity to implement the law, EPA officials found themselves telling a federal judge that the agency had missed deadlines for action on radionuclides because of limitations on staff and budget.[34]

Before President Carter's term ended in January 1981, EPA had proposed four emission standards for several sources of benzene, a potential cause of leukemia and a product of coke ovens, petroleum refineries, and fumes from gasoline at service stations. The Reagan administration's initial estimates in April 1981 for the issuance of final regulations on benzene were identical to those made during the closing days of the Carter EPA three months earlier. These estimates indicated that all four standards would be finalized by January 1982. Two years later, however, none was; in fact, the Reagan EPA decided to withdraw three of the four proposed standards for benzene, asserting that they were unnecessary, despite the agency's earlier statements that the standards were needed to protect the public's health.

As a last example, the Carter EPA had projected that acrylonitrile and coke oven emissions would be listed as hazardous air pollutants during the first five months of 1981. They were not and, by late 1983, the agency no longer was estimating dates for action on acrylonitrile, preferring only to say that a listing date was simply "indeterminate." For coke-oven emissions the Reagan EPA delayed the expected date for final action until December 1984. Similarly, the Reagan EPA provided no indication of when or even if it would act on cadmium or polycyclic organic matter. By early 1984, in addition, the EPA also had not revealed its intentions with regard to dozens of additional "priority candidates" for possible regulation that the agency had been studying at least since the late 1970s.[35]

New Source Performance Standards

When industrialists are seeking potential sites on which to build, states often offer many incentives in order to attract the development. To prevent the states from using lax air pollution controls as an incentive, Congress decided on the establishment of "new source performance standards" (NSPSs) at the federal level. Briefly, such standards require certain new major stationary sources of air pollution to meet federally prescribed limits on emissions. If a company wishes to build a new petroleum refinery or steel mill, for example, federal NSPSs usually are required regardless of the state or site selected. In determining what the standards should be, EPA can consider costs, energy requirements, and other environmental effects of the controls.

Before the 1977 amendments were enacted, the EPA had established NSPSs for 24 categories of air pollution. Not satisfied with this pace, Congress required EPA to identify by August 1978 all categories that eventually would need NSPSs, and then to issue final standards for one-quarter of these categories by August 1979, for three-quarters by August 1980, and for the remaining categories by August 1981.

One year late, in August 1979, the EPA issued a list of categories, in priority order, that would require performance standards. When Gorsuch became head of EPA in May 1981, action had been completed on 37 of 98 categories. Gorsuch told Congress that completion of the work on the NSPSs would be one of her priorities. The agency's budget proposal for fiscal year 1982 indicated that 14 new standards would be issued in that period and another 15 in the next. The projections were unduly optimistic; the Reagan EPA has missed every goal and deadline it established for itself in April 1981. As an illustration, the Reagan EPA originally estimated that final standards for 13 NSPSs proposed during the Carter administration would be issued no later than February 1982. The first ones were not issued until April 1982, and the average delay for the 11 that were eventually issued by December 1983 was nearly 14 months. The standards that the Reagan EPA had not completed by that date involved source categories ranked as the most important on the agency's own priority list.

In addition to the standards that the Carter EPA had proposed, the agency's technical staff developed another 11 that were ready to be proposed in January 1981. For the eight of these for which the Reagan EPA subsequently made projections, it said that all would be formally proposed by

April 1982, and that final standards would be issued no later than May 1983. Again, every projected deadline was missed. By the end of 1983, only six of the eight standards had been proposed, and none had been finalized.

The Case of Acid Precipitation

The previous sections have shown the Reagan administration to favor deregulation to the point of neglecting statutory deadlines for the establishment of new regulations. Both its actions and its inactions have been consistent with the president's philosophy that the role of the federal government in the making of environmental policy should be diminished. Thus it is interesting to examine how the Reagan administration has addressed one environmental problem—acid precipitation—that probably requires substantially greater federal involvement.

Acid precipitation is formed when emissions of sulfur oxides (primarily from coal combustion) and nitrogen oxides (primarily from motor vehicle exhausts) react with water vapor in the atmosphere to form sulfuric and nitric acid. Rain or snow containing these chemicals can be as acidic as vinegar, and acid precipitation has been linked to damaged crops and forests, decreased soil fertility, sterilized lakes, and corroded metals. Areas that are especially sensitive to precipitation containing nitric acid include the West Coast and the Rocky Mountains in Colorado. Precipitation containing high levels of sulfuric acid affects much of the northeastern United States and eastern Canada. The Canadians assert that thousands of their lakes are now empty of fish and that tens of thousands more are at risk because of acid precipitation. So severe is the problem to Canadians that most consider acid precipitation to be their country's most serious and pressing environmental problem. They look to the United States for relief because about half of Canada's problem with acid precipitation originates in the United States. Many government officials in Canada consequently consider the problem to be the most serious irritant in relations between Canada and the United States. Concern about acid precipitation is not limited to Canada. In an environmental message to Congress in 1979, President Carter labeled acid precipitation as "a global environmental problem of the greatest importance." [36]

Despite Carter's assessment, resolution of the problem may be difficult for several reasons. First, sulfur dioxide, and, therefore, acid precipitation, are products of coal combustion. Such combustion can be reduced, but that would conflict with the government's policy, which every president since 1973 has supported, to increase substantially the amount of coal burned in order to reduce dependence on imported oil. Increases in the use of coal could lead to a doubling in consumption between the mid-1970s and 1990. Unfortunately, much of the increased consumption has and will come in the Midwest, where locally mined coals tend to have relatively high sulfur levels.

Second, the Clean Air Act requires that states ensure compliance with national air quality standards within relatively small air-quality-control regions, some of which contain only a few counties. One simple way to achieve compliance under these circumstances is to build very tall stacks that will disperse pollutants widely enough to ensure that they will not be registered within the air quality control region in which they originate. This approach was popular in the 1970s, when more than 425 stacks exceeding 200 feet were built. Electric utilities are responsible for two-thirds of all these stacks and for 96 percent of those more than 500 feet. The tallest stack is nearly one quarter of a mile high.

Although tall stacks can solve local problems, they increase regional ones. Pollutants emitted high into the atmosphere tend to be more persistent, are more likely to be transformed into acid precipitation, and are more likely to be transported farther away, often traveling hundreds of miles. States or Canadian provinces downwind from tall stacks or major sources of pollution thus suffer damage that they have no effective way of preventing. Many people believe that the inability of individual states to address the problems of acid precipitation and long-range transport of air pollution requires a federal role in coordinating and implementing appropriate responses.

Third, the costs of an effective abatement program are likely to be high. One association of electric utilities has estimated that if controls were imposed, electric bills in Ohio, Indiana, and Illinois would increase by 50 percent. Overall costs for a control program have been placed at more than $100 billion, although estimates vary widely.

These problems did not deter the Carter administration from declaring that immediate action on acid precipitation was necessary. Douglas Costle, EPA administrator during the Carter years, stated in early 1980 that the time had come "to make the transition from research to action" even though knowledge about acid precipitation remained incomplete.[37] One of these actions was the signing of a Memorandum of Intent on Transboundary Air Pollution between Canada and the United States in the summer of 1980. In the memorandum both countries recognized acid precipitation as a "serious problem" and agreed that negotiations between them on a cooperative agreement on transboundary air pollution would begin no later than mid-1981. The countries further agreed to "develop and implement policies, practices and technologies to combat acid precipitation's impact."

As a result of these actions, a growing concern about the problem, and pressure from the Canadians and many state officials in the Northeast, acid precipitation was a priority item on the government's environmental agenda when Reagan became president. Although this may have been the case in January 1981, the Reagan administration's actions through early 1984 suggested that acid precipitation was not considered an issue in need of immediate attention.

One way to get a sense of the Reagan administration's stance on the problem is to examine the views of the president's key advisers. A sampling of statements from some of Reagan's aides clearly places them among those who do not believe the problem to be of outstanding importance.

James Watt, Reagan's first secretary of the interior: ". . . every year there's a money-making scare. This year it's acid rain."

James B. Edwards, Reagan's first secretary of energy: "I don't want to stop acid rain, because 99.9 percent of all rain is of an acid nature. In some areas it's good for crops ... and a little acid helps to neutralize the soil."

James F. McAvoy, a Reagan adviser on acid precipitation: "... the harbingers of doom are now telling us that acid rain is 'poison from the sky.'" "What has become so critical about the phenomenon as to generate the attention it is now receiving? For what reason have inflammatory and irresponsible headlines about acid rain appeared in the press?" [38]

These comments suggested that the Reagan EPA would be unlikely to adopt an activist approach toward acid precipitation. Indeed, its consistent position under Gorsuch and during the initial months under William Ruckelshaus was that efforts to control acid rain would be premature in the face of so many scientific uncertainties. To remedy these uncertainties the Reagan administration has provided increased funding for the study of acid precipitation and has called for an accelerated research program. During Gorsuch's tenure as EPA's head, however, the agency took the position that more would have to be known about the causes of acid precipitation—how it is formed, the relation between emissions and deposition, the nature of its effects, and the feasibility and potential economic effects of possible controls—before regulatory action could be considered or justified. To critics who said enough was known already, Gorsuch posed a rhetorical question: "Will the basis for future measures to control acid deposition be blind groping in response to political passions or the result of rigorous scientific analysis, judiciously applied?" [39]

In short, the Reagan administration has believed that regulatory action is premature, but other groups have disagreed. The National Academy of Sciences released a report in late 1981 urging prompt action to control acid precipitation. As the report noted, "continued emissions of sulfur and nitrogen oxides at current or accelerated rates, in the face of clear evidence of serious hazard to human health and to the biosphere, will be extremely risky from a long-term economic standpoint as well as from the standpoint of biosphere protection." [40] The Senate Committee on Environment and Public Works also disagreed with the administration's position. In its 1982 proposed revisions to the Clean Air Act Amendments, the committee members voted unanimously to require sizable reductions in emissions of sulfur dioxide in 31 states. Within the Reagan administration, the EPA, the Council on Environmental Quality, and the departments of State and Energy all opposed the provision.

Although the Senate provision never became law, the administration still had to contend with Canada and the issues raised in the 1980 Memorandum of Intent. Discussions between Canada and the United States began in June 1981 but soon came to a stalemate. So little progress had been made after two years of talks that the Canadians began to doubt whether the discussions were worth continuing. Rejecting the Reagan administration's contention that more research was necessary, the Canadian delegates responded that the balance of existing evidence "is the most compelling evidence for immediate action in public policy that we have ever encountered." [41]

The administration's unwillingness to commit itself to any substantive response was not the only source of irritation to the Canadians. In the Memorandum of Intent both countries had agreed "to promote vigorous enforcement of existing laws and regulations" as these require limitations on emissions. In spite of this commitment, the Reagan EPA agreed in its first year to permit 13 states to increase their allowable emissions of sulfur dioxide by more than one million tons a year. A second problem arose when scientific panels from two countries working in accordance with the memorandum finished their preliminary reports. The Canadian government asked the Royal Society of Canada to review these reports and, in turn, requested the Reagan administration to allow the National Academy of Sciences to participate in the review with the Royal Society. The administration refused and decided to cut off government funding of any further work by the academy on acid precipitation.

Questioning the objectivity of the National Academy, the White House announced that the administration would select and supervise its own scientific review group. In defense of this procedure, White House officials stated that the move would enhance the review's credibility and accelerate its completion. Critics charged that the action had simply politicized the review.

In the third action, the Justice Department declared in early 1983 that two Canadian films on acid rain that were being widely shown in the United States constituted "political propaganda." Citing the Foreign Agents Registration Act of 1938 the Justice Department stated that future audiences would have to be informed that the films were the products of foreign agents attempting to influence U.S. policy making.

Acid precipitation received still more attention during the months of May and June, 1983. When William Ruckelshaus became EPA's new administrator in May, Reagan listed acid rain as one of the areas he wished Ruckelshaus to address as soon as possible. Ruckelshaus initiated a comprehensive review of the administration's policies, but most remaining doubts about the need for controls were erased with the release of two reports in late June. In the first report, from the scientific panel the White House itself had established, the conclusions were unequivocal. The panel called for immediate action: "If we take the conservative point of view that we must wait until the scientific knowledge is definitive, the accumulated deposition and damaged environment may reach the point of 'irreversibility.' " In a report financed internally, the National Academy of Sciences reported a direct, linear relation between acid precipitation and emissions of sulfur and nitrogen oxides.[42] Lack of evidence supporting such a relationship was one of the key arguments that the administration had used to justify its opposition to a control program.

Whether these reports and others that will follow will cause the Reagan administration to support comprehensive regulatory controls for acid precipitation is not at all certain. The economic costs of such controls would be high, long term, and most likely to fall on large and politically important states such as Ohio, Indiana, and Illinois. Just as the Carter administration had been reluctant to impose controls to limit acid rain in 1980, a presidential election year, so, too, would Reagan, or any other Republican candidate, be unlikely to find short-term political value in proposing any costly and comprehensive control program. At the same time, however, presidential inaction calculated to avoid offending voters in the Midwest can offend New Englanders. Senators and representatives from the latter region, Democrats and Republicans alike, tend to be strong proponents of immediate action to limit acid precipitation. Additionally, the region's voters are increasingly making acid rain a political issue and demanding that public officials address it.

These problems suggest some of the difficulties that William Ruckelshaus faced in his efforts to prepare an effective strategy for controlling acid precipitation. He originally had intended to recommend a strategy to the president by September 1983. Ruckelshaus was unable to do so, however, because of significant opposition from senior administration officials, including David Stockman. By early 1984 the administration still had not developed a program, and further delay was the best that Ruckelshaus could promise.

Conclusion

A consistent theme of the Reagan EPA is that improved levels of environmental quality can be achieved through the application of efficient management and a "reasonable" approach to regulations and their implementation. It is unclear whether this goal has been achieved. Levels of air quality are related not only to the stringency and effective enforcement of government regulations, but also to the level of the nation's economic activity. Air quality tends to deteriorate as factories increase production and as the economy improves. Conversely, air quality usually improves during recessions or periods of economic decline such as occurred in 1981 and 1982. The Reagan administration's early record may thus show notable improvements in air quality. It is questionable, however, whether these improvements can be credited to the administration's efforts.

Over the longer term, the results are less likely to present a favorable picture. During its tenure the administration supported no major initiatives to control air pollution. Equally important, the administration's opposition to regulation may have a detrimental long-term effect. In the absence of regulation or other incentives to abate pollution, polluters rarely have cause to control their emissions. Furthermore, an obvious reluctance to require abatement signals to polluters that the government does not deem a problem to be serious. Such signals can be highly undesirable when the air pollutants are hazardous or when the consequences of inaction, as with acid precipitation, are enormously damaging and potentially irreversible. Unfortunately, the examples of acid precipitation and hazardous air pollutants are only illustrative. The Reagan administration has used scientific uncertainty as a pretext for delaying or forestalling action on indoor air pollution and on the increase of carbon dioxide in the atmosphere. These areas may not need immediate government action, but the potential for future harm at least justifies increased research funding, something the Reagan administration has opposed.

The administration's record may also have had detrimental procedural effects. In 1980, knowledgeable environmentalists agreed with ardent critics of the Clean Air Act Amendments that the law would benefit from revisions designed to improve its effectiveness and reduce its economic costs. The NCAQ, for example, while noting that the law was essentially sound, still recommended over 100 changes affecting nearly every part of the law. One can only speculate whether an approach to revision of the law different from that of the Reagan administration could have brought about a suitable compromise acceptable to environmentalists and industrialists alike. Nonetheless, it does appear that Reagan's approach has polarized competing groups. By taking extreme and politically untenable positions, the administration has encouraged those in favor of the law to defend it staunchly or to support equally extreme positions. As President Reagan discovered in his efforts to revise the law, the result is a deadlock in which each side views the motives of the other with increased suspicion.

While the president faced frustration in the legislative arena, EPA's implementation of the Clean Air Act since 1981 shows clearly the many opportunities for change that exist in the administrative arena. The administration's successes in this arena indicate that a president committed to far-reaching environmental deregulation can accomplish many of his goals, including many that run counter to the law's intent, without congressional consent or statutory change. To the extent a president faces resistance to statutory change, as Reagan has with the Clean Air Act Amendments, the temptation to avoid Congress and to rely on administrative interpretation builds. Whether this is desirable depends on one's preferences. On the one hand, an uncooperative Congress can be accused of sabotaging a president's electoral mandate. On the other, however, EPA's implementation of the clean air program during the Reagan administration suggests that important environmental policies are highly vulnerable to administrative change. Such change can occur largely outside the public's view and despite widespread popular and congressional support for the policies in question. Over the longer term, continued reliance on administrative interpretation without statutory change could signal a gradual decline in Congress's traditional dominance of environmental policy making. If dominance shifts to the executive branch, the long tradition of bipartisan support for clean air programs can also decline.

In sum, for an environmental program as important and as costly as the Clean Air Act Amendments, the Reagan administration may well have staked out the least desirable course of action and may thereby have affected adversely the debate over clean air for many years to come.

Notes

1. U.S. Congress, Senate Committee on Public Works, *National Air Quality Standards Act of 1970,* 91st Cong., 2d sess., 1970, 3.
2. Council on Environmental Quality (CEQ), *Environmental Quality 1981* (Washington, D.C.: Government Printing Office, 1982), 25-33.

3. The reader should not get the impression that only dissatisfaction with the program exists. Many people are highly satisfied with it, but they are not the ones calling for major changes in it.

4. Lester B. Lave and Gilbert S. Omenn, *Clearing the Air: Reforming the Clean Air Act* (Washington, D.C.: Brookings Institution, 1981), 16, 31. EPA revoked the standard for hydrocarbons in December 1982 after concluding that they did not affect human health.

5. CEQ, *Environmental Quality 1981,* 37, and National Commission on Air Quality (NCAQ), *To Breathe Clean Air* (Washington, D.C.: Government Printing Office, 1981), 101.

6. Melissa Merson, "Environmental Regulation of the Automobile," *Environment Reporter: Monographs,* December 17, 1982, 1.

7. If no action were taken by the deadline, the existing law would remain in effect provided Congress approved a bill to authorize expenditures for implementation.

8. *Washington Post,* December 14, 1980, C5; *Los Angeles Times,* February 18, 1981, sec. 1, 17.

9. *Wall Street Journal,* February 18, 1983.

10. NCAQ, *Clean Air,* 1-4. As the commission report noted, "During the 1980s millions of people will continue to live in areas exceeding healthful levels" of air quality.

11. *Washington Post,* May 26, 1981, A1; June 20, 1981, A3; June 24, 1981, D7; *Environment Reporter: Current Developments,* June 26, 1981, 275.

12. *Washington Post,* July 3, 1981, 30; *Environment Reporter: Current Developments,* June 26, 1981, 275.

13. Louis Harris, "Substantial Majorities Indicate Support for Clean Air and Clean Water Acts," *The Harris Survey,* June 11, 1981.

14. *Air/Water Pollution Report,* October 5, 1981, 385.

15. Environmental Protection Agency (EPA), "Environmental News," August 5, 1981.

16. *Air/Water Pollution Report,* October 5, 1981, 385.

17. *Washington Post,* January 26, 1983, A12.

18. *Federal Register,* April 13, 1981, 21628.

19. David G. Hawkins, "A Review of Air Pollution Control Actions under the Reagan Administration as of July 1982" (Natural Resources Defense Council, Washington, D.C., 1982, Mimeograph).

20. Although the limit was 0.5 grams per gallon, EPA actually had allowed large refiners to add as much as 0.549 grams per gallon because, when rounded, that amount "equals" the required level. *Washington Post,* May 27, 1982, A25.

21. Presidential Task Force on Regulatory Relief, *Reagan Administration Achievements in Regulatory Relief: A Progress Report* (Washington, D.C., August 1982), 27.

22. *Environment Reporter: Current Developments,* February 26, 1982, 1358.

23. U.S. Congress, House Committee on Government Operations, *Lead in Gasoline: Public Health Dangers,* 97th Cong., 2d sess., 1982; Eliot Marshall, "The Politics of Lead," *Science,* April 30, 1982, 496.

24. *Federal Register,* August 27, 1982, 38078. EPA announced the final regulations on October 28, 1982, only a few days before the fall congressional elections. Some journalists contended that the timing of the announcement was meant to affect voters' impressions of the Reagan administration and Republican candidates. See *New York Times,* November 11, 1982, D13.

25. CEQ, *Environmental Quality 1980,* 213.

26. The U.S. Supreme Court refused in November 1981 to review General Motors' claim that the 1985 standards were inappropriate. In contrast, the next month the National Academy of Sciences' National Research Council issued a report indicating that the standards were too ambitious. See Eliot Marshall, "Safe to Delay 1985 Diesel Rule, Study Says," *Science,* January 15, 1982, 268-269.

27. Hawkins, "Air Pollution Control," E3.

28. U.S. Congress, Senate Committee on Environment and Public Works, *Clean Air Act Amendments of 1982*, 97th Cong., 2d sess., 1982, 80.

29. U.S. Congress, House Committee on Appropriations, *Department of Housing and Urban Development: Independent Agencies, Appropriations for, Part 3*, 97th Cong., 2d sess., 1982, 78.

30. P.L. 95-95, Section 112 (a) (1).

31. NCAQ, *Clean Air,* 79. Despite EPA's position, Congress had realized that plants might be required to close if they could not achieve the applicable emission standards for hazardous air pollutants. See U.S. Congress, Senate Committee on Public Works, *A Legislative History of the Clean Air Amendments of 1970*, 93rd Cong., 2d sess., 1974, 133.

32. NCAQ, *Clean Air,* 77.

33. *Environment Reporter: Current Developments,* January 29, 1982, 1274.

34. *Sierra Club v. Gorsuch*, 18 *Environment Reporter: Cases*, September 30, 1982, 1549.

35. For a list of these "priority candidates," see NCAQ, *Clean Air,* 78. Many of these substances already have been regulated under the Clean Water Act.

36. *Weekly Compilation of Presidential Documents*, August 6, 1979, 1371.

37. Douglas Costle, "Acid Rain: The Time to Act is Now" (Washington, D.C.: Government Printing Office, 1980).

38. The quotations from Watt and Edwards are found in Russell W. Peterson, "Laissez-Faire Landscape," *New York Times Magazine,* October 31, 1982, 55. McAvoy's comments are cited in the *Washington Post,* June 16, 1981, A4, and the U.S. Congress, House Committee on Interstate and Foreign Commerce, *Acid Rain,* 96th Cong., 2d sess., 1980, 42.

39. Anne Gorsuch (Speech delivered to the Greater Pittsburgh Chamber of Commerce, Second National Symposium on Acid Rain, Pittsburgh, Pa., October 6-7, 1982).

40. National Academy of Sciences, National Research Council, *Atmosphere-Biosphere Interactions: Toward a Better Understanding of the Ecological Consequences of Fossil Fuel Combustion* (Washington, D.C.: National Academy Press, 1981), 3.

41. Robert Slater, assistant deputy minister of the Canadian Environmental Protection Service (Speech delivered to the Greater Pittsburgh Chamber of Commerce, Second National Symposium on Acid Rain, Pittsburgh, Pa., October 6-7, 1982), 10.

42. *New York Times,* June 28, 1983, A14; June 30, 1983, A16.

12. PRESERVING THE CLEAN WATER ACT: THE APPEARANCE OF ENVIRONMENTAL VICTORY

Helen M. Ingram and Dean E. Mann

The process of amending the Clean Water Act (CWA) has not generated anywhere near the level of controversy as the Clean Air Act (CAA) has during the Reagan administration. The lower political profile of water pollution, however, reflects neither agreement about policy nor the success of water-pollution controls. Despite some notable examples of improved water quality, there have been few advances in lowering levels of conventional pollutants since 1977. Moreover, toxic substances are becoming a serious problem, and fears are growing that they are contaminating ground-water and drinking-water supplies. The level of controversy may be low only because none of the participants perceives any gains to be made by widening the conflict.

Industry has quarrels both with the general philosophy and with specific provisions of the CWA but has not found the CWA's effluent-discharge permit system unduly burdensome. Furthermore, the federal government foots much of the bill for municipal waste-treatment plants, easing some of the pain of compliance.

Environmentalists find some encouraging signs in the modest progress in water quality. Despite a substantial increase in the Gross National Product (GNP) during the 1970s, the nation's water in 1983 was found to be not declining in quality by conventional criteria. Most polluters have applied for and received permits. The water-pollution problem is such that doing better would require changing targets and perhaps developing new approaches. Yet environmentalists have been too preoccupied with administrative and budget battles to formulate bold new initiatives in water policy. At the same time, they have greeted modifications suggested by the Reagan administration with a sense of déjà vu. The same strategies were found wanting in the late 1960s, so that responding to them now has seemed to move the program backward, rather than to correct errors.

This chapter examines the vexing issues of water-pollution control and weighs the implications both of Reagan administration changes and of

251

keeping to the unaltered course set by the Clean Water Act of 1972. Finally, it questions whether either of these two approaches does enough to produce clean water.

How Clean Is Our Water?

The CWA envisioned zero discharge of pollutants into the nation's waters by 1985 and an interim goal of "fishable and swimmable" waters by 1983. Measured by these criteria, the existing state of water quality in 1983 is disappointing, although exact measurements are not being taken. U.S. Geological Survey monitoring stations were set up to collect different types of data in different locations, so that data from different states are not compatible. What data do exist suggest that little or no real improvement has taken place in the levels of dissolved oxygen, fecal coliform, suspended solids, total dissolved solids, and phosphorus. Slight gains in some pollutants must be balanced against losses in others. For instance, the quantity of dissolved oxygen, which is necessary for fish and other aquatic life to survive, has improved especially in the Northeast and in the South Central and Great Plains states. But there has been virtually no abatement in the level of bacterial pollution during the last seven years. It also appears that the situation of total dissolved solids (inorganic salts and other substances that are dissolved in water) is deteriorating.[1]

There is scattered evidence that water quality in some places is improving. The aging process of lakes Ontario and Erie has slowed and fish have reappeared. Poor water quality in the Potomac River is no longer a disgrace to the nation's capital, and Ohio's Cuyahoga River has not recently burst into flames as it did in the 1960s. The Westfield River in Massachusetts and the Penobscot River in Maine have shown dramatic improvements in quality.[2] However, these examples of success are far too isolated for us to deduce a positive trend.

At the same time that water quality has been holding its own against conventional insults, new kinds of violations have emerged. Heavy metals and other contributors of toxic pollution have become commonplace in lakes and rivers, especially in the Northeast and Middle Atlantic regions. Groundwater contamination is becoming a serious problem throughout the United States, as salt water, microbiological contaminants, and toxic chemicals intrude, perhaps irreversibly, upon water supplies that are as yet largely untapped but that may be essential in the future. The problem is most acute where ground water is currently an important source for municipal water supplies. In Tucson, Arizona, for example, 55 drinking-water wells have been closed because of traces of trichloroethylene (TCE), a carcinogenic substance.

Environmentalists and the Reagan administration interpret the data about water quality very differently, although neither believes that the record, in light of the circumstances, is all that bad. Environmentalists point out that our GNP has grown in real terms by about 40 percent since 1970. Fifty-seven million acres of new cropland are being farmed, and 20 to 30 million acres of land have been converted to urban uses over the last decade. Both types of shifts result in increased pollution. Holding our own in water quality is thus a noteworthy accomplishment.[3] Rather than change the CWA, environmentalists believe the nation should go on to address emerging problems.

The Reagan administration believes that environmental progress has been made but at too high a price: water-pollution regulations have eroded the federal system and encroached upon decision-making power better left to state and local governments; environmental regulations have damaged the economy; industry has borne undue burdens; the water act's technology-based standards are inefficient; and cleanup dollars are not being used to best advantage. Ways need to be found—so the Reagan administration asserts—to lower these costs of water-pollution control.[4]

The costs are undeniably high. According to Commerce Department figures, federal government expenditures on water-pollution abatement and control increased from $861 million in 1972 to $5.6 billion in 1980.[5] Other data indicate that water-quality protection accounts for as much as 60 to 70 percent of state and local spending on environmental programs.[6]

The Water Pollution Control Federation reported in May 1983 that $37 billion had been spent to construct water-pollution control facilities since passage of the CWA, amounting to $19 per year per person. Estimates of the cost of future construction vary, but the federation reports an Environmental Protection Agency (EPA) estimate of $57 billion by the year 2000—or $118 billion if the nation decides to treat storm water and to build the necessary collector sewers for it.[7] Other estimates are even higher.[8]

Clean Water Act Strategy and Its Critics

The extent to which the nation's waters have been cleaned up relates to the policy strategy of the CWA. The key elements of this strategy include technology-based standards, construction grants, discharge permits, concentration on point sources, and a strong federal presence. Each part of the act's strategy and several associated issues, including the Corps of Engineers' permit program and ground-water contamination, will be discussed below. Further, the difficulties that have emerged and that have been pointed out by two authoritative bodies created for the purpose of evaluating water policy will be noted. The National Water Commission (NWC) published its report on general water policy in 1973, and the National Commission on Water Quality (NCWQ) in 1976 put out a report designed to provide guidance for "mid-course corrections" in the CWA. The Reagan administration has proposed its own modifications, which environmentalists have generally resisted.

Technology-Based Standards

The CWA ignores the quality or uses of the receiving water into which pollution is discharged. The decision in favor of technology-based standards was based on a thorough disillusionment with the receiving-water standards provided for in legislation passed by Congress in 1965. The 1965 standards had allowed for the classification of streams receiving effluents and established different gradations of cleanliness. Environmentalists came to believe that statutes simply were reclassifying dirty streams downward instead of cleaning them up.

The CWA requires that every polluter upgrade its effluent in stages, installing the best practicable control technology (BPT) everywhere by 1977 and the best available control technology (BAT) by 1984. Although this approach has advantages, not the least of which is the symbolic assurance that the "best" controls are being required, it may not result in water quality improvements commensurate with the effort. In writing effluent guidelines, EPA must rely on industry consultants who are informed about the technical and economic feasibility of various controls. Accordingly, critics have charged that BPT often is determined by what large, progressive firms in an industry already are doing. The result is hardly burdensome to industry. A Resources for the Future economist estimates that the annual cost of the act averages well under 2 percent of each firm's sales.[9] At the same time, BPT does not pressure industries to continually do better.

More importantly, installation of BPT and eventually BAT may not be related to cleaning up bodies of water and arguably is quite inefficient. Water has a natural assimilative capacity, in that certain bacteria in water can break down organic wastes into constituent chemical parts. How great that capacity is varies with temperature, the speed of the water's flow, and other conditions. Requiring uniform technology means treating some wastes that the stream actually could handle. Furthermore, streams may be contaminated by sources completely unrelated to those controlled by BPT. Under these circumstances, industry outfalls may be required to discharge water that is actually cleaner than the receiving stream, and the cleanup effort is more or less wasted.[10] Because technology-based standards fail to take into account the condition of receiving water, policy evaluators such as the General Accounting Office have said that cleanup efforts "cost more than necessary, and accomplish much less than expected." [11]

The National Water Commission was unequivocal in its opposition to technology-based standards in its 1973 report. The commission argued that the receiving-water approach contained in the 1965 law was beginning to bear fruit and that the value to society of improving water quality should be defined in a functional and dynamic manner: "Water is polluted if it is not of sufficiently high quality to be suitable for the highest uses people wish to make of it at present or in the future." [12] The commission argued that the technology-based policy would be excessively costly, force increased pollution onto other media such as air and land, and ignore the natural capacity of water to cleanse itself. Pure or natural water was considered unattainable because it would never be possible to control all discharges, particularly those from nonpoint sources. Also, pure or natural water existed almost nowhere and was unnecessary for most purposes.

The NCWQ concluded in 1976 that, although the technologies existed to achieve the total elimination of discharges into the nation's streams, those technologies were "generally prohibitively costly, energy-intensive, and create large quantities of residuals that must be disposed of in some way other than into the water." [13] The commission urged paying greater attention to conservation and reuse of water, while trying to "restore and maintain the physical, chemical and biological integrity of the nation's waters" through a receiving-water strategy.

Sen. Edmund S. Muskie, D-Maine, perhaps the principal political agent in the passage of the CWA, took issue with these conclusions. He argued that the NCWQ ignored the unsatisfactory experience under the 1965 law, assumed unsatisfactory performance of the 1972 law without adequate evidence, assumed costs that were not demonstrable, and ignored the evidence of improvements resulting from application of the 1972 act.[14]

Despite more than a decade of experience with technology-based standards, this same battle continues, with the Reagan administration again urging a return to receiving-water based standards and the environmentalist groups vigorously defending the existing approach.

The administration would like to take into account the different characteristics of water bodies in setting standards and sees no reason why water-quality standards everywhere should be the same. The quality of receiving water might well vary according to water use and local preference.[15]

Although environmentalists concede some difficulty with BPT and BAT, they are unwilling to consider adopting ambient and varying standards. They note that implementation would require monitoring and modeling capabilities that may not exist. Laboratory tests may not reflect the "interactive, cumulative, and synergistic effects" of pollutants in the actual stream conditions. There is concern that switching would render useless much of EPA's work in the last five years, and that the change would be costly and burdensome.

Construction Grants Program

A central strategy of the CWA for cleaning up the nation's waters was the upgrading of municipal waste-water treatment plants to so-called secondary treatment, which removes approximately 95 percent of pollutants. More than $30 billion has been disbursed under a program in which the federal government funded up to 75 percent of the eligible costs of a waste-treatment project, and the local community, usually with state assistance, paid the rest. Funds have been apportioned to states according to a congressional formula, with each state setting its own project construction priorities.

Despite very large expenditures, the program has run into real trouble. The program's costs have been enormous, and the need for more funds continual. A 1980 EPA survey recorded $120 billion in remaining sewage construction needs. Funding and construction have lagged, and in 1977 the deadline for achieving secondary treatment had to be extended to 1983. In addition, the priorities set by states bore little relation to cleanup needs, and municipalities contributing the most to pollution often were given lower priority for construction grants than other municipalities.

Although construction grants funded waste treatment, the CWA failed to address a very significant problem for municipal water pollution, that of combined storm drains and sewers. Rainstorms in combined systems often flood out municipal treatment plants, dumping thousands of gallons of raw sewage into rivers. Modifying such combined systems would cost additional billions and tear up streets in major cities for years.

Other failures of omission have plagued the CWA's construction grant program. The federal government has paid 75 percent of the costs of building waste-treatment plants, but none of the operation and maintenance costs. The result is that cities have built Cadillac projects without the funds or technically qualified operators to maintain them, and some plants operate substantially below design capacity.

Environmentalists and the Reagan administration differ sharply over whether the problems of the waste-treatment grant program call for the federal government to do more or less. The administration obviously has opted for less and at a slower funding pace. Funding of the program expired in October 1981, and a special $2.4 billion special appropriation, termed minimal by environmentalists, did not pass until February 1982.

Rather than considering the option of federal funding for plant operation and maintenance, EPA is trying to place the responsibility at the local level. According to the Council on Environmental Quality's 1981 annual report,

> EPA's role has shifted from a "hands on" project management function to that of providing program guidance, oversight, and evaluation. Strong, well organized local operating agencies are the key to improved plant operation and maintenance.[16]

In spring 1981 Congress accepted changes proposed by the Reagan administration in the grants program.[17] The compliance date for secondary treatment was extended to 1988, and state and local governments both were given more flexibility in determining cleanup priorities. The modifications in legislation emphasized the need to redirect grant funds to projects that will improve water quality most significantly. The federal share of funding was scheduled to be reduced to 55 percent in the year 1985, and project eligibilities also were to be reduced. These legislative changes also presented the administration with the opportunity to alter EPA rules and regulations, as we will discuss later in the chapter.

Discharge Permits

Under CWA, every public and private facility that discharges wastes directly into U.S. waters must have a permit. National Pollutant Discharge Elimination Systems (NPDES) permits are issued by an EPA regional office or by one of the 33 states with EPA-approved permitting programs. The job of issuing permits has been one of staggering proportions. More than 64,000 NPDESs have been issued. Numbers alone do not tell the whole story, however. For the system to work, permit writers must have a high level of expertise, and permit holders must be monitored to determine compliance. Budget and personnel cuts at the state and federal levels hurt the permit system, since the system's success depends on enforcement actions against polluters violating their permits. Environmentalists have criticized EPA for too many negotiated settlements and lack of vigor in pursuing litigation.

The administration would like to relax the permit system and introduce what it calls innovation. It proposes to extend the term before renewal is required for industrial permits from five years to ten. EPA has initiated a general permit that would cover categories of polluters who discharge the same types of wastes within a designated geographic area and warrant similar pollution measures.[18] EPA also has attempted to apply to water pollution the "bubble" concept that the Reagan administration supports so strongly in air pollution. The bubble policy releases existing plants from pollution controls at one or more effluent outfalls in exchange for compensating increases in controls at other emission sources. In guidelines for permit writing published in July 1982, EPA developed an intraplant bubble approach for the iron and steel industries.[19] The multiple-plant water bubble approach has evoked special interest among top EPA policy makers because of its potential for offering large cost savings to industry, presumably without resulting degradation to water quality.

Nonpoint Sources of Pollution

The CWA recognized that a significant percentage—perhaps even the preponderance—of pollutants entering the nation's fresh water come from nonpoint sources: agricultural, storm-water, and building-site runoff. Urban runoff often is the major source of certain toxins, particularly in highly industrialized cities.[20] More than half of the discharges of suspended solids, fecal coliforms, nitrates, and phosphates are nonpoint.[21] The NPDES system could not control such pollution; therefore, it was necessary to establish a mechanism of land-use planning and control. Section 208 of CWA provided such a mechanism. It directed the states to develop areawide waste-treatment plans emphasizing the need to identify nonpoint sources and to develop regulations and land use measures to control them. EPA, however, emphasized point-source control, and the states were pleased to avoid the politically perilous step of imposing new building and zoning requirements.[22]

There were reasons other than political expediency for avoiding such action. Data on the problem usually were lacking: the control mechanisms were either not available or extremely costly; and EPA lacked both authority and resources to monitor effectively and to enforce the necessary "best management practices." Funds to support 208 planning always were in short supply both for states and for local planning agencies. Moreover, the CWA strategy assumed an institutional capacity to make areawide and regional plans and decisions, which neither existed nor was adequately fostered by the legal and financial support of EPA's 208 authority.[23]

Section 208 planning never was robust, but it fell on especially hard times at the end of the Carter administration and during the Reagan administration. The Council on Environmental Quality (CEQ) reported in 1980 that progress in control of nonpoint-source water pollution was "negligible." [24] The reasons were clear: 208 plans were not binding, and both the principal agents of nonpoint-source pollution—urban runoff and agricultural runoff—were difficult to control.

But ignoring nonpoint-source water pollution does not make it go away, and the Reagan administration, apparently recognizing that, has revived interest in land-use planning. In mid-1983 it was reported that EPA was moving (under some pressure from states) to develop a policy for significant action on quality goals. In keeping with administration philosophy, the Reagan program would emphasize coordination, information gathering, monitoring, and technical guidance, leaving to the states the responsibility for setting priorities. Environmentalists were pressing for far more ambitious programs. One version was found in an amendment to the CWA proposed in 1983 that would (1) require the states to develop plans to remedy pollution from nonpoint sources and to implement such plans in four years; (2) require EPA to develop plans if the states failed to do so; (3) authorize $150 million for cost sharing with the states on plan implementation; and (4) allow downstream states to ask EPA to require that upstream states develop plans compatible with their own.[25] Given the historic opposition to such federal involvement in land-use decisions, the prospects for adopting these proposals seemed dim.

Controversy Over the 404 Permitting Program

Since the passage of the Refuse Act in 1899, the Army Corps of Engineers has had responsibility for issuing permits for dredging and filling operations that might affect the navigability of waterways. This permitting process did not extend to most wetland areas, including salt marshes and freshwater streams and their tributaries. Passage of the CWA appeared to extend the corps' authority to the "waters of the United States," thereby extending its control over dredging and filling activities.

The corps' interpretation of the new statute at first was extremely restrictive, largely corresponding to its authority under the Refuse Act. Only a federal court decision[26] led the corps to adopt a broader interpretation of the law, one that some feared would lead to federal involvement in every farming and ranching operation.[27] A more temperate view finally emerged from corps policy making, reflected in standards that emphasized biological productivity, aquatic sanctuaries, drainage and flushing properties, and erosion and flood control. Its ultimate jurisdiction covered 25,000 miles of waterways, 3 million miles of lake shoreline, 30,000 miles of canal shoreline, and 148 million acres of wetlands, a substantial proportion of which were in Alaska. Given the staggering scope of responsibility, the corps moved to restrict the scope of its activity, exempting routine operations on farms and ranches and providing general permits for continuing operations, such as beach erosion control, structures on the outer continental shelf, and minor road-crossing fills.

The 404 permitting process remains a controversial item on the water-quality agenda. The corps continues to press for changes in the law and regulations, seeking to limit the review period, increase delegation of authority to the states, define more narrowly the scope of its authority over certain wetlands, and increase the use of general permits.

Environmentalists are vigorously opposing such changes both in Congress and in the courts. They argue that the corps' proposals are evidence of a serious underestimation of the value of wetlands, that they load the decision-making process in favor of development, and that they are based on an exaggeration of the costs in time and money involved in the permitting process. Environmentalists cast doubt on state capacity to undertake management of the permitting process—an argument corroborated by the reluctance of most states to assume the authority they currently have because of the cost burden. EPA and Fish and Wildlife officials have expressed similar opposition to the corps' proposals. The National Wildlife Federation and other environmental groups have challenged the corps' efforts by suing to prevent issuance of six nationwide blanket permits and to prevent the granting of state-program general permits that arguably extend beyond the law.

Ground-Water Quality

Half the nation depends on ground water for drinking and other residential uses; as a result, Congress has called repeatedly for additional strategies to deal with the problems of ground-water pollution. The federal government already plays a major role in protecting ground water through water-quality planning, regulating toxic-waste disposal, protecting drinking water, controlling solid-waste disposal, and restoring safe ground-water conditions through the Superfund legislation, which finances toxic-waste cleanup. Nevertheless, this network of legislation does not constitute a coherent approach to protecting aquifers from temporary and sometimes permanent contamination from animal and chemical wastes, pesticides, and salinity. To express its concern for the problem, EPA in 1980 prepared a ground-water protection strategy in which the agency also recognized the exceptionally sensitive political issue of state versus federal authority over water resources, especially ground water.[28] The strategy proposed no new laws; rather, it emphasized support for state-developed strategies, setting priorities for various classes of water and minimum national standards for selected high-priority problems, and coordinating federal program activities. EPA recognized the "fierce competition for resources in state governments and a major management challenge facing state officials" but nevertheless concluded that the states should assume primary responsibility for planning and management.[29]

The proposal languished at the end of the Carter administration, and consideration of further federal involvement in ground-water management has been difficult during an administration dedicated to protecting state prerogatives. EPA worked for two years to prepare a draft policy statement, which as of late 1983 had yet to achieve official endorsement. The proposed statement called for the states to take the lead, for improved federal coordination and support of research, and for improved data collection; yet it also made clear that state action was voluntary.[30] An EPA source called the proposed statement "mild," while an Environmental Defense Fund source called the draft policy "so insipid as to be virtually useless." The spokesperson called for federal policy to prevent degradation and to provide a process for cleaning up existing contamination.[31] Nevertheless, the statement was blocked by the cabinet council on the environment because James G. Watt, interior secretary at the time, feared federal intervention in state prerogatives and the Office of Management and Budget resisted another environmentalist "raid on the Treasury." It was suspected that Watt was further concerned that a strong national policy on ground-water pollution could stymie his efforts to increase coal and gas production on federal lands.[32]

A Strong Federal Presence

The CWA emphasizes the role of the federal government; it places the authority for establishing BPT and BAT firmly in the hands of EPA, replacing the ambient water standards previously set by states. The federal goals of fishable/swimmable water and, ultimately, zero discharge of pollutants are uniform and national under CWA. Uniformity of standards was very important to environmentalists in supporting the act; as a spokesperson of Friends of the Earth expressed it, uniformity was necessary to protect the states from industry pressure. Otherwise, "the polluters will walk all over them." [33]

The devolution of power to state and local governments is a keystone of Reagan administration environmental policy. CEQ's annual report for 1981 states that

> state and local environmental officials are aware of the complexity of considerations surrounding water pollution control decisions and are held directly responsible for the outcome of those decisions. Given adequate guidance and technical assistance, these officials are the most appropriate persons to make local pollution control decisions.[34]

Some state and regional officials strongly support reducing the federal presence. Leo Weaver of the Ohio River Valley Water Sanitation Commission likened the pre-Reagan EPA-state relationship to that of parent and child or master and serf.[35]

Environmentalists object that state and local preeminence in water pollution was tried previously and failed. State and local governments were running well-established water-pollution control programs before the federal government stepped in. In the early years of federal government involvement, strong attempts were made to keep control at the state and local levels. The preamble of the 1956 Water Pollution Control Amendments promised "to recognize, preserve, and protect the primary responsibility of the States in controlling water pollution." [36]

Table 12-1 Evolution of Federal Presence in Water Pollution Policy

Legislation	*Federal Role*	*State Role*
Water Pollution Control Act of 1948	Do research Make loans to states	All decision-making authority
Water Pollution Control Act Amendments of 1956	Permanent authority to become involved in water pollution policy Make grants to states Hold conferences on interstate pollution	All decision-making authority Financial responsibility shifted in part to federal level
Federal Water Pollution Control Act of 1961	Make larger grants to states Federal jurisdiction extended to navigable waters	All decision-making authority Financial responsibility further shifted away from states
Water Quality Act of 1965	Federal government set water quality standards on interstate waters Federal government could set standards if states failed to act	States lose power to decide whether to set standards States must establish water quality standards and adopt plan for enforcement
Clean Water Restoration Act of 1966	Federal financial responsibility extended Enlarged power to set regulations and initiate court action	States lose some standard-setting power Financial responsibility shifted heavily to federal level
Water Quality Improvement Act of 1970	Federal government regulates oil spills	No change
Clean Water Act of 1972	Federal standards and deadlines Federal guarantee of permit system	States reduced to implementation authority
Mid-course corrections of 1977	Larger federal role in toxics	States given more authority in grant program

Table 12-1 traces the slow, step-by-step transfer of decison-making authority in water-pollution policy from the states to the federal government. The first national water-pollution legislation in 1948 involved the federal government simply in a research and grant-giving capacity. By 1965 the federal government was requiring states to set ambient water quality standards. Finally, with the Clean Water Act of 1972, the federal government took over responsibility for setting standards and guaranteeing enforcement. States were reduced to playing a role in implementation. Dissatisfaction with what states were accomplishing pushed Congress to take each successive step in establishing a dominant federal presence. The 1977 amendments to the CWA did return some authority to the states: construction-grants project review was altered to give states more responsibility, and a portion of grants funds was allocated for state management activities. At the same time, the 1977 amendments also gave preeminence to the federal government in determining effluent limits based on BAT for 129 priority toxic pollutants.

Political Environment for Policy Change

Despite the fact that the policy strategies set forth in the CWA are neither clearly successful nor agreeable to all interested parties, the political outlook for overt and authoritative change in water-pollution policy during Reagan's first term was far from favorable. The central elements in the issue are set forth below.

The administration's legislative agenda placed the process of amending the Clean Air Act (CAA) ahead of the task of modifying the CWA. Administration officials and Congress both became bogged down in the battle over air amendments. By the time it became clear that the Clean Air Act was not going to be changed radically, the opportunity to alter the CWA fundamentally had all but disappeared.

It already has been noted that industry never has displayed as strong hostility to the CWA as to the CAA. This is not to say that industry has been uncritical. Paul Oreffice, a representative of Dupont, stated at the 1982 annual meeting of the Chemical Manufacturers Association that

> according to research done by the Department of Commerce, the nation spent $112 billion on water quality from 1972-1979. Forty-two percent of that amount came from tax dollars and the remaining fifty-eight percent came from industry. With the condition of the national and world economies, we need to get more out of every dollar of national income.[37]

Most criticisms have been directed toward particular inefficiencies as industry sees them, such as the pretreatment rules, which will be discussed subsequently.

The public supports the CWA. Whatever view they take of the law's accomplishments, Americans do not want to see it weakened. A Harris Poll undertaken between June and November of 1982 found that an overwhelming 94 percent of Americans believed that the CWA should be kept intact or made even stricter. It is interesting to note that this same poll found that only

17 percent of those interviewed predicted that their local water bodies would be less polluted 10 years hence. The public seems to be focusing more strongly on efforts than on results.[38]

Few strengthening amendments appear feasible. Changes that might make the CWA more effective would require much more money and/or many more basic changes in approaches. In a time of recession and budget deficits, it has been nearly impossible to enlarge domestic budgets. Formulation and passage of innovative legislation typically require united support from the administration and Congress. Many experts have argued that a river-basin approach giving regional authorities the power to levy effluent fees would be an improvement. However, with environmentalists out of power at EPA, the opportunity to build support for new initatives is limited. Environmentalists are distracted by other battles, including defending EPA from budget and personnel cuts. Furthermore, they disagree among themselves about the best course of action.

Constructive legislative change has been blocked by polarization. The rhetoric of James Watt and Anne Gorsuch has so alienated environmental forces that they have reacted with suspicion to most administration suggestions for change. They fear that the so-called innovative ideas the administration says will lead to greater efficiencies are in fact intended to serve polluting interests and to weaken the impact of landmark environmental legislation such as the CWA. Environmentalists worry that any admission of weakness in legislation will invite wholesale dismantling of the regulatory mechanisms that have taken so much time and effort to set up. Under William Ruckelshaus's direction at EPA, rhetoric has become more moderate, but at the close of 1983 a political environment for significant change in the CWA did not exist.

Reagan's Legislative Proposals

In 1982 then EPA Administrator Gorsuch signaled to Congress that legislative changes to the CWA were not high on the administration's agenda. She wrote that the CWA was "fundamentally sound as it stands without need for major or extensive revision at this time," adding that the administration's suggestions for modifications would be limited to "a few areas where obvious statutory problems have emerged." [39] On May 26, 1982, Gorsuch sent to Congress a wish list of changes. The package of amendments was almost three months late, which all but assured that the 97th Congress, in an election year, would not have time to consider the amendments and the reauthorization of the CWA before the Christmas break. The targets for action were not the essential elements of CWA strategy as described above. Instead, the administration focused upon specific provisions that its industrial constituency, particularly chemical manufacturers, had found bothersome.

Altering Pretreatment Requirements. The so-called pretreatment rules in the CWA and the 1977 amendments require industry to remove toxic substances before they are discharged into the sewer system. The administration's proposals would have made pretreatment standards optional so long as cities did something to prohibit toxic discharges from passing through or disrupting their sewer facilities.

Industrial toxic substances can pose significant problems to municipal waste treatment. Community plants are designed to treat common residential wastes. Toxic wastes often pass right through waste-treatment plants, causing the same health and environmental damage as if they had been dumped directly. In addition, highly contaminated industrial wastes can interfere with the sensitive biological processes that treat residential sewage, and they can cause waste-treatment plants to do a less than efficient job on all wastes. In some cases industrial wastes corrode pipes, cause explosions, and knock out plants. Toxic chemicals concentrate in the sludge from plants, making sludge disposal more difficult.

EPA got off to a slow start in implementing the pretreatment rules, and little happened for the first decade. Finally, in 1980 EPA began to set standards and establish ground rules for the program. Cities adopted schedules to meet federal requirements by 1983. Almost as soon as the program got under way, the Reagan administration issued its first deregulatory hit list and another year's delay ensued. EPA undertook a lengthy study addressing questions such as whether cities can handle the job without federal help and initiative and whether regulations should focus solely on the water-quality impacts of toxic discharges, ignoring the sludge disposal problems.[40]

Managers of large public treatment facilities stated that implementing mandatory industrial pretreatment standards would be excessively burdensome for them. Kenneth Kirk, assistant executive director of the Association of Metropolitan Sewage Agencies, which represents 100 of the largest municipal treatment agencies in the United States, has stated: "Sorting out the different effluents to monitor and track to establish removal credits would become a nightmare. The cities don't care who is discharging what. They just treat it all."[41]

Industry supported reconsideration of pretreatment. Roger Strelow of the Business Roundtable has said, "The basic problem is that you have a statutory scheme that doesn't work. It is a total flop. The environmentalists just want to get on with it. But we say mandatory pretreatment will end up wasting money without any demonstration of need."[42]

The Reagan administration's approach was to allow waivers of enforcement of categorical pretreatment standards as long as the local agencies could demonstrate that water quality would not decline and that they had the capacity to monitor effects. John W. Hernandez, Jr., former deputy administrator of the EPA, summed up the Reagan administration's position on pretreatment: "What we are trying to do is improve the management of a very complex part of the Clean Water Act by allowing both municipalities and industry to act in a more cost-effective way. Also, we want to relieve the EPA of some of the regulatory problems we otherwise would continue to have."[43]

Environmentalists strongly disagreed with the position taken by industry, municipalities, and the administration. They contended that industry should be held responsible for cleaning up its own wastes rather than be able to run them through municipal systems at considerable risk to those systems. Furthermore, environmentalists maintained that toxic substances should be handled with extreme care. According to James T. Banks of the Natural Resources Defense Council, "Sludge is the linchpin of the program. But there is no data on how dirty our municipal sludge is or how dirty it can be. So if we don't know what we're doing, we would be better off to pretreat as much as possible." [44]

Extended BAT Deadlines for Industrial Toxics. The administration proposed to extend the BAT compliance deadline for industrial treatment of toxics from July 1, 1984, to July 1, 1988. The compliance deadline for "best conventional technology" (BCT) to treat nontoxic industrial pollutants also would be extended to July 1, 1988, to bring industry into parity with municipalities, which were granted a five-year extension in 1981 to meet CWA standards of BPT. In addition, the deadline for EPA to issue effluent guidelines for BAT and BCT would be extended to July 1, 1988.

The 1977 amendments to the CWA required industry to install BAT by July 1, 1984, to mitigate point sources of pollution where toxics were being discharged directly into public waters. EPA was given responsibility for developing BAT discharge guidelines for 34 categories of industries.[45] However, as in its handling of the pretreatment standards, EPA has been very slow to produce the BAT discharge guidelines; it had written only one by the spring of 1982. It is worth noting here that, in 1981, the first year of the Reagan administration, EPA cut the budget for the Effluent Guidelines Division, maintaining that work on the guidelines was virtually complete.

Industry, particularly chemical manufacturers, has pushed hard for the extension of the BAT requirements, many of which it has called unnecessary. Hernandez stated: "It is not possible for industry to meet guidelines by the 1984 date. Industry does not know what it has to do. It is just common sense to extend the date." [46]

Some environmentalists objected vociferously to the proposed four-year BAT compliance extension. A Natural Resources Defense Council spokesperson was quoted as saying, "For each year that BAT regulations are delayed, EPA has estimated that over one hundred million pounds of toxic chemicals will be discharged into the nation's waters." [47] This postponement nevertheless appears to be one of the less controversial issues in the debate over amendments to the act.

Extending Other Deadlines. The administration also proposed to extend the term of NPDES permits from five years to ten. This provision would give industry greater security in that, once a firm had satisfied permit requirements, it would not have to deal with bureaucracy for 10 years. However, environmentalists objected that this would prevent more stringent controls from being imposed for a decade and slows progress toward clean water.[48] Nevertheless, there appears to be considerable consensus on the need to extend the permit period. In 1982 about 35,000 permits already had run out and were extended simply on their existing terms until the future requirements could be settled by Congress.

As a particular aid to industrial builders of new plants, the administration proposed that new source performance standards (NSPS) would apply to a plant only if construction begins after the final NSPS rule is issued. Industries have complained about rule changes in the middle of the game. Environmentalists, on the other hand, saw stringent rules for new industries as a way to make giant strides in cleaning up water. It is much more difficult to retrofit old plants.

Enforcement and Exemptions. Other proposals would have given the EPA administrator greater discretion in levying civil penalties for noncompliance and exempting dams and military facilities from water-pollution requirements.

Reaction to Reagan's Legislative Proposals

If the administration hoped to avoid contention by proposing relatively marginal changes to the CWA, the strategy failed. Neither industry nor environmentalists were satisfied. Industry was disappointed that the administration had backed away from a waiver of BAT and had opted simply for extending deadlines. Former Deputy Administrator Hernandez admitted that, because BAT was a nationwide standard, there probably were cases in which treatment was being applied simply for treatment's sake, with no substantive improvement in water quality. He stated, however, that "EPA could not measure the need for a change in BAT at present." [49] Industry spokesmen expressed a preference for a one-year authorization so that the BAT-waiver issue could be further debated. Thus, although industry and larger municipalities viewed the administration's pretreatment proposals as a step in the right direction, the step simply did not go far enough for them.

The reaction of environmentalists was anything but favorable. Fran Dubrowski of the Natural Resources Defense Council said that the legislative proposals, coupled with the EPA's administrative actions, "amount, to a major overhaul of the Clean Water Act." [50] Members of environmental groups were urged to contact legislators to prevent clean water from going "down the drain."

Sen. John H. Chafee, R-R.I., in July 1982 hearings before an environmental subcommittee, made it clear that he had little sympathy for an overhaul of CWA. He stated: "Over the past decade, thanks to federal laws, our rivers, harbors, bays and estuaries have become cleaner. In individual 'hot spots' there is work still to be done, but nationally the trends are encouraging. The effort begun in 1972 to control pollution at the point of discharge, rather than through subjective judgment of how much pollution a waterway can assimilate, is being carried out successfully." [51]

The administration's amendments failed to pass Congress in 1982, which was not surprising given their late introduction in an election year and the lack of enthusiasm with which they were received. Instead, Congress continued the program for another year at the same level of funding. The starting point for debate in 1983 was the bill Chafee introduced on February 3. From the environmentalists' perspective, the bill fell "short of what is needed," but rejected "damaging changes proposed by the Reagan administration." The Chafee bill extended industry BAT deadlines for three and a half years, compared with the administration's five-year proposed extension. It also would require states to maintain water-quality standards that might be allowed under some EPA rule changes, which will be discussed below.

Administrative Actions

However much Congress can do to protect water quality programs and budgets, each administration retains considerable leeway to act on its own. In October 1982 the Reagan administration attempted to accomplish through regulation at least part of what it had failed to do through legislation. It promulgated a new set of rules that revived the importance of state-set ambient water-quality standards and reduced the federal presence in decision making. The 1981 amendments to the construction grants program had been intended to cause states to forge a stronger link between the siting of treatment works and the overall improvement of water quality. As part of this plan, Congress had asked states to revise their water-quality standards by 1984. State water-quality standards, which were so important before the passage of the CWA in 1972, had continued to exist but had been much less significant than the uniform national technology-based standards. The new EPA rules upgraded the role of ambient water-quality standards and provided states with more flexibility in setting standards for particular water bodies. EPA's approach to the iron and steel industries provides an example of relaxed rules. As a result of agency actions, costs to industry of controlling pollution were reduced substantially since the agency issued new effluent guidelines in spring 1981.

The reaction of state officials to the rule changes was mixed. There was universal agreement that increasing state responsibility and flexibility was an empty gesture unless the federal government continued to supply states with adequate financial resources. State officials deplored the unsuccessful attempt on the part of Reagan's budget cutters to reduce the grants funding to states by 20 percent. Some state officials welcomed the reduction in the strong federal presence implied in the rules changes. They felt that in the past the EPA had been too rigid and had imposed needless economic hardships upon states. States, they believed, were better able than the federal government to make site-specific decisions about desirable levels of water quality. Other state officials were less enthusiastic.

Clint Whitney, the executive director of the California Water Resources Control Board, expressed the sentiment of the more skeptical state officials:

> Frankly we see this as a retreat in the federal commitment that was made in 1972 for a federal presence in our water pollution control program.

We in California have effectively used EPA as somewhat of a gorilla in the closet, if you will, and we've exercised our choice as to standards in California, and we believe other states should exercise their choice as well. The present regulations allow us to do that. On the other hand, when we've had a tough time exercising a choice for a higher quality standard, we've pointed to the gorilla in the closet.[52]

Environmentalists reacted negatively to the rules changes, fearing that states simply would use the new flexibility to downgrade water quality. A spokesperson for the Environmental Defense Fund stated:

Well, I think the bottom line of the new rules is going to be that this so-called increased flexibility—a magic term thrown around that sounds politically attractive—is going to make it easier for some states to say, "Well, a body of water is polluted, we're not going to try to clean it up," or perhaps, that "a body of water is too polluted, but we don't want to put too much pressure on some industry that we're trying to attract to come into this region to comply with the best possible rules to control their effluent discharges." [53]

Such environmentalist concerns found their way into John Chafee's legislative proposals, which would prevent states from downgrading their water quality standards from what they were in January 1983.

The Reagan administration's preference for reducing the federal role in water quality was expressed in budget actions. Between 1981 and 1983, funding for water-quality programs at the EPA was cut by more than 40 percent, and the administration requested further cuts in its fiscal 1984 budget. That budget request proposed to cut water-pollution grants to the states by $30 million, or 55 percent. Clearly, despite the congressional commitment to protect the CWA, the administration could and did do a great deal to reduce the federal presence in water-pollution policy.

Events under Ruckelshaus's Leadership

William D. Ruckelshaus has supported strongly the Clean Water Act and has backed away from changes in the law and regulations suggested by his predecessor. Within a few weeks of taking office, he had asked for the resignation of a number of top officials, including Frederic Eidsness, who had headed the water program under Gorsuch. In testimony before a Senate subcommittee, Ruckelshaus conceded that waivers permitting some municipalities to exempt certain industries from pretreatment requirements would be an administrative headache. In consequence, the pretreatment provision that had initially been so strongly backed by the Reagan administration was dropped.[54]

Furthermore, Ruckelshaus made significant revisions in water-quality rules proposed in October 1982 by Gorsuch. These revisions make it much more difficult for states to relax their standards. The rules retain, with limited exceptions, the nondegradation policy intended to protect pristine waters. Reportedly, Ruckelshaus had to face down opposition from the Office of

Management and Budget on the rules changes, and environmental groups praised the reversal as a significant victory.[55]

At the adjournment of Congress in 1983, an amendment to the CWA had not yet become law. However, the position of Ruckelshaus made it unlikely that any substantial dismantling of the legislation would occur. An industry spokesman dissatisfied at what congressional committees were willing to consider stated, 'We are disappointed that they have chosen to ignore virtually every significant issue our group identified." [56] Environmentalists undoubtedly would see retaining the CWA, problems and all, as further evidence of success.

The victory, perhaps, was more illusion than reality; it did not advance the cause of water-pollution control, but merely kept it from falling back.

Conclusion

The CWA of 1972 was a bold and innovative attempt to make waters everywhere clean enough for fish and swimming by 1983 and to accomplish zero discharge everywhere by 1985. It departed substantially from the past in the size and nature of federal commitment. The key elements of the strategy chosen to clean up water included technology-based standards, construction grants, discharge permits, concentration on point sources, and a strong federal presence. Broad policy changes often encounter unexpected negative consequences and problems of implementation, however, and the CWA was no exception. In the decade following the passage of the act, the elements of the cleanup strategy were found wanting.

The most serious charge to be leveled against the CWA is that waters are not cleaner than they were in 1972. Little or no improvement has been measured overall in the amount of conventional pollutants, and toxics problems have become worse. Furthermore, ground water, on which many cities depend for drinking water, is being degraded, so far without a strong, coherent federal government defense. No effective way has yet been devised to deal with nonpoint sources of pollution, even though they contribute more than half of the problem. The CWA lacks the authority to require the land-management practices that would be necessary in order to reduce such pollution.

The preoccupation of environmentalists with preventing damage to the CWA has come at the expense of concentrating on needed improvements. The Watt/Gorsuch rhetoric so alienated environmentalists that they found any policy modifications coming from the administration unacceptable. We have argued here that the administration's proposed changes were not, in fact, fundamental. At the same time, environmentalists and their congressional allies have been so consumed with battles in the legislative and administrative trenches that, until Ruckelshaus's appointment, they have had neither time nor energy to formulate substantial perfecting amendments of their own. As a result the nation is likely to continue under much the same regulatory regime in water pollution, flaws and all.

Notes

1. Conservation Foundation, *State of the Environment 1982* (Washington, D.C.: 1982), 97.
2. Council on Environmental Quality, *Environmental Quality 1981* (Washington, D.C.: Government Printing Office, 1982), 52.
3. Conservation Foundation, *State of the Environment 1982*, 99.
4. *Environmental Quality 1981*, 75.
5. Commerce Department, Bureau of the Census, *Environmental Quality Control: Government Finances, Fiscal 1980.* (Washington, D.C.: Government Printing Office, 1982), v.
6. *Environmental Quality 1981*, 308.
7. Water Pollution Control Federation, *A Decade of Progress: America's Quest for Clean Water* (Washington, D.C., December 1982).
8. See, for example, "Cleaner Air and Water: Can We Afford 690 Billion Dollars?" *U.S. News & World Report*, February, 28, 1983, 27.
9. Henry M. Peskin, "Preserving Illusions—The Clean Water Act After Ten Years," *Resources* 72 (February 1983): 12.
10. A. Myrick Freeman, "Air and Water Pollution Policy," in *Current Issues in U.S. Environmental Policy*, ed. Paul R. Portney (Baltimore: Johns Hopkins University Press, 1978), 51.
11. Stephen J. Lyton, "GAO Study Says Effort to Clean Potomac Wasted," *Washington Post*, January 7, 1982.
12. National Water Commission, *A Water Policy for the American People* (Washington, D.C.: Government Printing Office, 1973), 70.
13. National Commission on Water Quality, *Report to the Congress* (Washington, D.C.: Government Printing Office, 1976), 30.
14. National Commission on Water Quality, *Report to the Congress*, 44.
15. *Environmental Quality 1981*, 85.
16. Ibid., 77.
17. Municipal Wastewater Treatment Construction Grant Amendments of 1981, Public Law 97-117.
18. *Environmental Quality 1981*, 82.
19. *Environment Reporter*, July 23, 1982, 343-416.
20. Peskin, "Preserving Illusions," 12.
21. Freeman, "Air and Water Pollution Policy," 52.
22. Kathy Barton, "The Other Water Pollutant," *Environment*, June 1978, 12-20.
23. Terry D. Edgmon, "Areawide Environmental Management or Myth of the Region? Implementing 208," *The Environmental Professional* 1, no. 3 (1979): 199-205.
24. Council on Environmental Quality, *Environmental Quality 1980* (Washington, D.C.: Government Printing Office, 1980), 133.
25. *Western Water Newsletter*, July 15, 1983, 1.
26. *Natural Resources Defense Council v. Callaway*, 392 F. Supp. 685 (1975).
27. Congressional Research Service, *Wetland Management* (Prepared by the Environmental and Natural Resources Policy Division, Library of Congress, for the Senate Committee on Environmental and Public Works, July 1982).
28. Environmental Protection Agency (EPA), Office of Drinking Water, *Proposed Groundwater Protection Strategy* (Mimeographed, November 1980).
29. EPA, *Proposed Groundwater Protection*, III-15.
30. *Environment Reporter*, October 29, 1982, 907-910.
31. *Environment Reporter*, May 13, 1983, 94.
32. Cass Peterson, "Watt Said to Block New Policy for Water Safeguards," *Washington Post*, February 18, 1983, A4.

33. George Alderson, legislative director of Friends of the Earth, before the Senate Committee on Public Works, Subcommittee on Air and Water Pollution, *Water Pollution Control Legislation*, 92d Cong., 1st sess.

34. *Environmental Quality 1981*, 86.

35. MacNeil-Lehrer Report, *EPA Muddy Waters*, October 29, 1982.

36. U.S. statutes at large, vol. 70, preamble.

37. Paul Orrefice, "Toxic Water Pollutants: Microbes Can Do the Job," *The Journal of Commerce*, June 3, 1982.

38. "New Harris Poll Finds Overwhelming Support for Clean Water Law," *Conservation Report*, December 15, 1982, 1.

39. James T. Banks and Frances Dubrowski, "Clean Water: Act III," *The Amicus Journal* (Spring 1982): 25-30.

40. Kathy Koch, "Administration Proposals to Revise Clean Water Act Delayed by Objections," *Congressional Quarterly Weekly Report*, April 17, 1982, 874.

41. Kathy Koch, "Congress to Review Clean Water Legislation," *Congressional Quarterly Weekly Report*, Jan. 23, 1981, 124.

42. Lawrence Mosher, "Environmentalists, Industry Left Cold by EPA Bid for New Pretreatment Rules," *National Journal*, June 12, 1982, 1060.

43. Ibid., 1058-1061.

44. Ibid.

45. Ibid., 1061.

46. Kathy Koch, "Congress to Review Clean Water Legislation."

47. William Chapman, "Environmental Groups Assail EPA on Its Clean Water Proposals," *Washington Post*, April 9, 1982.

48. L. Tangley, "Water Pollution Law to be Reviewed," *Science News* 121 (June 19, 1982): 406.

49. "EPA Supports Utility Wishes on Thermal Pollution Mitigation Requirements," *Conservation Report*, July 15, 1982.

50. Koch, "Congress to Review Clean Air Legislation," 124.

51. John Chafee, "Good News," *The Amicus Journal* (Spring 1982): 32.

52. MacNeil-Lehrer Report, *EPA Muddy Waters*.

53. Ibid.

54. "Panel Would Retain Strict Water Rules," *Washington Post*, June 23, 1983.

55. Cass Peterson, "EPA to Keep Water Quality Goals Strong," *Washington Post*, November 1, 1983.

56. *Washington Post*, June 23, 1983.

13. DEFUSING THE TOXIC TIME BOMB: FEDERAL HAZARDOUS WASTE PROGRAMS

Steven Cohen

From mid-1981 until early 1983, Congress, the bureaucracy, and the environmental community battled with political appointees in the Environmental Protection Agency (EPA) over the nation's hazardous waste policy. In late 1982 EPA Administrator Anne McGill Gorsuch (later Burford) was cited for contempt of Congress for refusing to give congressional committees access to hazardous waste enforcement files. In February 1983 EPA hazardous waste chief Rita Lavelle was fired by President Ronald Reagan. Finally, in March 1983 the agency's top administrator bowed to the wishes of the White House staff and resigned, paving the way for the return of moderate Republicans to EPA's leadership.

From the moment that Gorsuch and Lavelle were confirmed in office, EPA's hazardous waste program was thrown into turmoil. Environmental professionals in the agency were astounded by the inexperience, incompetence, and ideological fervor of the agency's political management. Lavelle's immediate predecessor—excluding interim appointments—as hazardous waste chief was Eckhart C. Beck, an environmental professional who had previously been a state environmental official, an EPA deputy assistant administrator, and the administrator of EPA's Region II. Beck's predecessor was Thomas Jorling, a former member of the staff of Sen. John Sherman Cooper, a Republican from Kentucky, and a major drafter of the 1972 Federal Water Pollution Control Act. In contrast, Lavelle had worked in public affairs for California government and industry. Her understanding of the federal government and hazardous waste management was extremely superficial. Most of EPA's other political appointees were equally inexperienced. The few who were experienced and worked closely with the agency's career professionals did not remain in office for very long.

Hazardous waste policy posed a particularly vexing problem to the Reagan administration. The administration was ideologically committed to scaling down environmental programs, but it was clear that the public wanted action on hazardous waste, a newly discovered environmental danger that

273

required immediate attention. The administration's approach differed for each component of EPA's hazardous waste program:

- The highly visible government-sponsored hazardous waste cleanup program (Superfund) was allowed to grow, though at a relatively slow pace.
- The program requiring private parties to clean their own waste sites was slowed to a crawl.
- The low-visibility program regulating the transport, storage, and disposal of hazardous waste was cut back and significantly slowed down.

As soon as the Reagan administration's intent to cut back became obvious, the environmentalist counterattack began. EPA staffers leaked reams of material to Congress, the media, and the environmental community. Congress began a long series of oversight hearings. Nevertheless, for a year and a half EPA careerists found their professional world turned upside down. Draft regulations were rewritten by industry lawyers. Corporate access to the agency increased, while environmental groups were shut out. Vital research programs were curtailed or eliminated. Senior career managers were transferred without cause or justification.

Initial efforts to call attention to EPA cutbacks were largely unsuccessful. However, in autumn 1982 the administration made a critical error. The president refused Congress's request for hazardous waste enforcement files, claiming executive privilege. This focused media attention on the issue, eventually resulting in Gorsuch's contempt citation. A second major error was made when a bureaucratic power struggle was made public. Gorsuch had accused Lavelle of going over her head to Edwin Meese, counselor to the president, and asked for the hazardous waste chief's resignation. When Lavelle refused to resign and had to be fired by Reagan, the issue became a front-page drama. By the time the curtain fell, Gorsuch, Lavelle, and the entire political management of EPA had been swept out of office.

While the issue that stimulated this conflict makes less dramatic reading than front-page news, hazardous waste remains America's most pressing environmental problem. This chapter looks behind the headlines and analyzes the federal government's two major programs addressing the hazardous-waste issue: the Resource Conservation and Recovery Act (RCRA) and Superfund. RCRA, which is designed to "prevent future Love Canals," establishes a system for managing today's hazardous wastes. Superfund provides government with a means of rectifying past mistakes. The chapter describes these programs, analyzes EPA's progress in implementing them, and assesses the Reagan administration's impact on EPA programs.

The Nature of the Problem

Every time we wrap a slice of cheese in plastic wrap, purchase a nylon backpack, or drink coffee from a styrofoam cup, we are contributing to this nation's hazardous waste problem. We all use and benefit from goods that, when manufactured, create toxic wastes as unused byproducts. The production of plastics and synthetic chemicals increased dramatically after World

War II. Goods previously made of wood, wool, and cotton were replaced by those made of plastic, polyester, and similar substances. These synthetic materials lasted longer than "natural" materials, and for a time were less expensive.

A huge amount of hazardous waste already permeates our ground and water, and the amount being generated now is staggering. In 1980 EPA estimated that Americans produced more than 57 million metric tons of hazardous waste per year. In 1983 the Office of Technology Assessment set this figure at 255-275 million metric tons.[1] According to Stephen Plehn, then director of EPA's Office of Solid Waste, "Over 750,000 businesses generate hazardous wastes, and over 10,000 transporters move them to treatment or disposal at over 30,000 sites. Up to 50,000 sites have been used at some time for hazardous waste disposal." [2]

In 1980 EPA estimated that approximately 90 percent of the nation's hazardous waste was disposed of by environmentally unsound methods.[3] Estimates of the total number of waste sites vary. During the legislative debate over Superfund in 1980 EPA projected a total of 30,000-50,000 sites and estimated that between 1,200 and 2,000 of these sites posed serious threats to human health and the environment. Superfund requires waste-site owners to report their sites to the government, and as of March 1983 EPA had received notification of 14,000 sites. If we add to this number an estimate of truly abandoned (buried or forgotten) sites, nonreported sites, and municipal or county landfills, it is possible that there are close to 30,000 sites. EPA has collected extensive data at about 800 waste sites, and early in 1983 published a list of the nation's 418 most serious dumps.

Hazardous materials also are released by spills that occur during chemical production or transport. Unlike dump sites, most spills are cleaned up rapidly and with little fanfare. In some cases, however, spills receive considerable public attention, particularly when whole communities are evacuated to protect public health. Most often it is the private sector, occasionally under government supervision, that undertakes the cleanup, as Henry Van Cleave, head of EPA's Environmental Emergency Response Division, explains:

> The common conception of cleaning up hazardous material spills is one of government specialists rushing to the rescue. In fact, 93 percent of the responses to such environmental emergencies are taken care of by the industrial concerns directly involved. The majority of the problems are eradicated quietly and efficiently long before they become a source of public concern.[4]

In 1980 EPA estimated that more than 70,000 different chemicals were being manufactured in the United States, and approximately 1,000 new chemicals were added to that total every year.[5] As we deplete natural resources, we tend to create synthetic substitutes, adding to the volume of chemicals transported. In the absence of a positive program to prevent spills it is likely that their number will increase.

Hazardous Waste as a Political Problem

When the country's mass environmental movement began in the late 1960s, it focused on visible sources of environmental pollution. Solid waste or "land pollution" was not a major item on the political agenda. Slowly, a number of scientists, bureaucrats, and environmentalists began to understand that the least visible of the nation's environmental problems might be the most serious.

In the 1970s hazardous waste was considered part of the larger problem of solid waste and recycling. Thus, attention was directed at legislation that would regulate the manufacturing, not the disposal, of these substances. The most important of these laws was the Toxic Substances Control Act (TSCA). When the Resource Conservation and Recovery Act was debated in 1975-1976, it received very little public or media attention.

All this was to change with the Love Canal crisis. In 1977 an unusually wet spring thaw caused highly toxic chemicals to escape from a dump built in an abandoned canal in Niagara Falls, New York. Toxic wastes contaminated private homes and an elementary school and eventually resulted in the evacuation of several hundred residents. The events at Love Canal, and the discovery of thousands of similar sites around the country, placed hazardous waste high on the national political agenda.

The waste-site issue is tailored to the U.S. federal political system. The effects of dump sites are intense, local, and normally concentrated within single legislative districts. Hazardous waste dumps frequently stimulate citizen activism.[6] Localized controversies can be ignored by other political systems but require rapid response in the United States.

Love Canal helped to make hazardous waste cleanup a political necessity. The need for action was demonstrated again in late 1982, when massive dioxin contamination was discovered at Times Beach, Missouri. After considerable delay, and immediately following the firing of Lavelle, Gorsuch announced that EPA would use $30 million from Superfund to buy all the homes in Times Beach.

Eventually, the issue of toxic and hazardous waste became so important that, when Reagan appointees appeared to be mishandling the cleanup program, public pressure forced the president to bring in a whole new team to manage EPA. For the first three months of 1983, the *Washington Post* and the *New York Times* featured a nearly unending stream of front-page stories about EPA and hazardous waste. By the time Reagan appointed William D. Ruckelshaus to be EPA administrator, hazardous waste had become a major national political issue and the preeminent environmental problem of the 1980s.

Hazardous Waste as an Implementation Problem

Managing America's hazardous wastes is an extremely difficult task. The effects of chemical waste on human health and the environment are poorly understood. Many firms are involved in the generation, transport, and disposal of hazardous waste, and government often has a difficult time regulating the activities of large and diverse groups. Although technology is available for safely treating and disposing of hazardous waste, government has not yet convinced industry to utilize this technology. Finally, cleaning up hazardous-waste dumps is a relatively new activity for government, and new organizational capacity and technology must be developed before cleanup programs can succeed.

Synthetic chemicals can be hazardous, but they too are used widely and are integral to our economy. The public is afraid of these substances but uses them every day without realizing it. Americans never have been asked to pay the true costs of using chemicals—a sum that would include the price of disposing of hazardous waste. Until recently chemical companies were not asked to devote resources to managing hazardous waste. Clearly, if hazardous wastes are to be properly managed, a significant number of behaviors must be changed. Engineering these changes is a major challenge faced by government in the mid-1980s.

The federal government has responded to this complex problem with the RCRA and Superfund programs. RCRA requires the federal government to formulate rules for handling and disposing of hazardous waste. States are expected to ensure that these rules are obeyed by private parties within their borders. The major incentive that a corporation has for spending money to comply with RCRA is fear of punishment.

Through the Superfund program, the federal government has provided $1.6 billion to help pay for cleanup of waste dumps. However, estimates of the resources needed to clean up all of America's serious dump sites range from $30 billion to $50 billion. Although some money will come from voluntary and enforced private cleanup, nowhere near enough money is likely to be provided.

To sum up: the tools available for implementing federal waste-management programs are cumbersome and do not provide the resources needed to stimulate widespread changes in behavior. Although public support and media attention are focused on the hazardous waste issue, this attention has proven fickle in the past and should not be counted on in the future. The difficulties of implementation make it unlikely that the public will be satisfied with the pace of action. Given the complexity of the problem, the corporate stake in minimizing waste-disposal costs, public expectations, and the problems normally associated with starting any new governmental program, it would be surprising if any federal hazardous waste program achieved early success.

Regulating Hazardous Waste: RCRA

When the Committee on Interstate and Foreign Commerce reported RCRA to the floor of the House in September 1976, it noted:

> The overriding concern of the Committee . . . is the effect on the population and the environment of the disposal of discarded hazardous wastes—those

which by virtue of their composition or longevity are harmful, toxic, or lethal. Unless neutralized or otherwise properly managed in their disposal, hazardous wastes present a clear danger to the health and safety of the population and to the quality of the environment.[7]

Congress eventually approved a law that was both ambitious and complex. Title III of RCRA gives to the federal government the authority to regulate hazardous waste. RCRA requires EPA to determine which wastes are hazardous. Section 3001 requires EPA to develop criteria for defining wastes as hazardous, and to publish those criteria along with a list of hazardous substances. Section 3002 stipulates that EPA must develop standards for record keeping, container labeling, and waste containers, and that it must create a manifest system to track hazardous waste from generation to disposal.

Section 3003 also regulates the transportation of hazardous waste. It requires transporters to participate in the manifest system, accepting the waste manifest from the generator and ensuring its receipt by the disposal, treatment, or storage firm. Additionally, they must take the hazardous waste shipment to a permitted facility. RCRA mandated that EPA issue regulations implementing all these provisions by March 1978.

Section 3005 of RCRA requires operators of hazardous waste treatment, storage, or disposal facilities to obtain permits before accepting shipments of hazardous waste. EPA was given until March 1978 to establish regulations defining appropriate methods of waste handling and disposal. A related provision gives to EPA the authority to delegate hazardous waste regulation to states willing to enforce standards equal or superior to federal standards; another establishes criminal and civil penalties for violators of hazardous waste regulations. When RCRA was reauthorized in 1980 the penalties established in 1976 were increased substantially.

Finally, Section 7003 of RCRA gives EPA the authority to sue waste-facility owners whose operations present an imminent and substantial danger to public health or the environment. The 1980 revisions to RCRA strengthened this provision by allowing the government to sue where threats to health or the environment *might* occur. In the original 1976 statute the government had to prove that health or environmental damage already was occurring.

RCRA under the Carter Administration

EPA, like the rest of American society, was slow to understand the hazardous waste problem. The agency's technical staff and field personnel initially were unable to convey the seriousness of the situation to senior management. During 1977 and 1978 hazardous waste was not a high-level priority in the agency. Inadequate resources were allocated to the office responsible for promulgating the RCRA regulations. As a result, the regulations implementing RCRA's sections 3001-3004 were not even proposed until December 1978 and were not issued as final until February and May of 1980.[8]

The RCRA regulations proposed in 1978 were attacked strongly by both industry and environmentalists. Suits by environmental groups resulted in a court-ordered timetable for promulgating RCRA rules. EPA, however, was not able to meet the judicially imposed schedules. Although political caution was certainly one factor, the sheer complexity of the regulatory task also must have contributed to the missed deadlines.

Although far behind schedule, the Carter EPA eventually did promulgate RCRA regulations. Those issued in February 1980 established a manifest system to track hazardous waste from "cradle to grave." The May regulations delineated the specific chemicals and the type of waste generators covered by RCRA.

Environmentalists were not happy with the results. They believed that the 1980 final regulations were weaker than the draft regulations EPA had proposed in 1978. A Sierra Club publication noted that, with the 1980 regulations in place, ". . . advocates of strong [hazardous waste] controls felt that significant portions of the problem remained unregulated by the EPA." [9]

While environmentalists and EPA technical officials argued for stronger controls, the chemical industry fought for fewer regulations and weaker controls. During the middle of this political storm, EPA's leadership battled with the Office of Management and Budget (OMB) and obtained increased funding for hazardous waste programs in President Jimmy Carter's proposed budget for fiscal 1981. In that budget the Carter administration proposed a 47 percent funding increase and a 91 percent staff increase over the previous fiscal year. After congressional consideration, RCRA's budget was increased from $47.4 million to $106 million for the fiscal year.[10] In the tight 1981 budget, RCRA's funding increase must be seen as evidence of a significant upgrading of the program's priority and stature. In fact, by the end of fiscal 1981 RCRA funding had risen well above $106 million, to a total of nearly $150 million.[11]

Formal rules and regulations are an important symbol of bureaucratic intent, but resource allocations more concretely demonstrate administrative priorities. The Carter administration's proposed 1981 budget clearly indicated that hazardous waste regulation was off the "back burner." Had Carter won reelection, there is little doubt that the level of effort devoted to controlling hazardous waste would have been increased. However, on January 21, 1981, Ronald Reagan became president, and for the next two years RCRA implementation followed a different course.

RCRA Under Reagan

While the Carter administration managed to divert resources to RCRA during a tight budget year, the Reagan administration had other priorities. Reagan's budget for fiscal 1982 proposed a 23 percent cut in RCRA spending, to less than $120 million.[12] In addition, a governmentwide hiring freeze had a dramatic effect on efforts to increase staff in the waste program.

In the first months of the Reagan administration EPA's RCRA regulations came under sustained attack by industry, the White House, and

OMB. The administration's criticism of RCRA was part of a larger effort to curb what Reagan and his people termed "regulatory excess" throughout the federal government. Utilizing new authorities from Reagan's Executive Order 12291 on regulatory reform and from the Paperwork Reduction Act, OMB challenged EPA's RCRA regulations. Specifically, OMB attacked the reporting requirements included in the "cradle-to-grave" waste-tracking system and criticized the high costs of implementing EPA's waste-disposal standards. An OMB evaluation paper written in early 1981 proposed that EPA begin a "major revision of the RCRA regulations." [13] According to OMB, the RCRA rules were "the most complex set of regulations in recent history . . . [and would] lead to a range of inanities and a degree of silliness that could eclipse the early days of OSHA." [14] In response EPA moved to reduce the reports and other paperwork required under the RCRA regulations.[15]

During Gorsuch's tenure, the EPA attempted on a number of occasions to relax the RCRA rules. Virtually each time, public opinion and political pressure forced EPA to retreat to previous policy. The most striking example of this pattern concerned EPA's May 1980 RCRA regulations prohibiting the disposal of liquid wastes in landfills. The Chemical Manufacturers Association and other industry group interests lobbied EPA to modify this ban. On February 25, 1982, EPA suspended the ban for 90 days and proposed that landfills be allowed to utilize up to 25 percent of their capacity to store liquid waste. The public was provided no opportunity for comment on this proposed regulation.

As soon as the ban was suspended, EPA found itself under attack by states that already had begun to prohibit liquids in landfills. Additional criticism came from environmentalists and a new trade association. The Hazardous Waste Treatment Council asked EPA to reinstate the liquid waste ban, noting that

> the burden of lifting all requirements in this situation penalizes companies who have attempted in good faith to comply with the requirement. . . . Removing the restrictions against landfilling also destroys immediately incentives to more effectively dispose of, treat, or destroy these containerized liquid hazardous wastes.[16]

On May 17, 1982, EPA reinstated the ban. Rep. James J. Florio, a Democrat of New Jersey who was a longstanding proponent of stringent hazardous waste regulation, observed that allowing liquid wastes in landfills "was the most glaring and outrageous example of EPA's inactivity in this area." Florio suspected "a conspiracy with the chemical industry" and estimated "that over 220,000 gallons were dumped every day during that open period." [17]

Although Representative Florio's suspicions of conspiracy have not as yet been proven in court, a controversy involving former EPA consultant James Sanderson suggests that Florio's concern may have been well founded. While Sanderson served as a close aide to Gorsuch, he also represented the Illinois company, Chemical Waste Management (CWM). CWM operated a landfill southeast of Denver, Colorado, that directly benefited from the relaxation of the liquid-waste ban. During the period between February 25 and May 17, 1982, CWM buried 1,500 barrels of liquid waste in its Denver landfill.[18]

The RCRA program was not dismantled during Gorsuch's administration; regulatory efforts were modified significantly and directions were changed, but increments of progress can be charted. The issue is whether "increments of progress" are an adequate response to the hazardous waste problem. I am convinced that a much larger program and more dramatic progress were urgently needed. While the nation was fast recognizing the dimensions of the hazardous waste problem, the EPA was treating hazardous waste regulation as an unfortunate imposition on the private sector. RCRA's operating budget was slashed from close to $150 million in fiscal 1981 to $100 million in fiscal 1982; it was further reduced to $87 million in fiscal 1983.[19] A delicate effort to build an institution capable of coordinating and implementing complex legislation was seriously disrupted. Grants to the state government organizations responsible for implementing RCRA also were reduced dramatically, impairing institution building at the state level.

Finally, the most significant damage to the federal hazardous waste program may not have occurred in regulation development or bureaucratic institution building, but in the minds and perceptions of private-sector managers. While Gorsuch and Lavelle ran EPA's hazardous waste program, many regulated industries did not behave as if breaking RCRA rules would result in severe punishment. Without the threat of enforcement a regulatory program is purely symbolic. Enforcement stimulates private companies to allocate resources to analyze and act on regulatory requirements. Under Gorsuch and Lavelle a waste company was being economically rational if it chose to ignore RCRA, since its chances of getting caught were minimal.

Although it is difficult to chart precisely the degree of damage done to the federal hazardous waste program between 1981 and 1983, it is clear that under the management of Ruckelshaus and his assistant administrator for Solid Waste and Emergency Response, Lee Thomas, the program slowly began to revive. Career professionals in EPA's Office of Solid Waste began the tedious task of rebuilding their battered morale and damaged organization. Nevertheless, valuable time had been lost. As the mid-1980s approach, hazardous waste management is plagued by technical uncertainty, institutional disarray, and a potentially massive price tag. It is by no means certain that the United States has either the will or the capacity to manage its hazardous garbage. The importance of that task becomes apparent when we examine the costs of cleaning up our past mistakes.

Cleaning Up Hazardous Wastes: Superfund

The Love Canal drama of working-class families forced by chemical contamination to evacuate their homes transformed the problem of hazardous waste from one dealing with a form of garbage disposal to a crisis of "toxic time bombs." Land pollution, or solid waste management, was the last environmental issue addressed in the United States. Yet as we learned more about the dimensions of the problem, it became apparent that a major program would be needed to rid the nation's land and water of toxic chemicals.

In spring 1979 the Carter administration proposed a comprehensive, billion-and-a-half-dollar program to clean up chemical dumps and spills. Carter's EPA proposed to raise most of the money for the program from a tax on oil and chemical companies. The Superfund fee system is based on the principle that the polluter pays. It is both a regulatory program, requiring private parties to clean their own hazardous wastes, and a direct-action program, giving EPA the money and authority to clean up rapidly hazardous spills and sites.

A multifaceted piece of legislation, the Superfund proposal required consideration by congressional finance, environment, and transportation committees. Throughout 1979 and 1980 the Superfund bill slowly progressed through the legislative process. It was actively opposed by the Chemical Manufacturers Association (CMA), which asserted that EPA had overstated the size of the waste problem. A lame duck session of Congress held after the Republican electoral victories in November 1980 finally enacted Superfund. A compromise was reached when environmentalists realized that the change in administrations and Senate leadership would soon weaken their position, and when the Reagan transition team recognized the immediate need for some sort of cleanup statute. As finally enacted, the legislation was considerably weaker than that approved by the Senate Environment and Public Works Committee in mid-1980. Funding for compensating human victims of toxic-waste contamination was eliminated, and the private sector liability section was weakened. The original Superfund proposal would have made it easier for government to sue private parties to force cleanup.

Nevertheless, on December 11, 1980, President Carter signed into law the $1.6 billion Superfund bill—formally titled the Comprehensive Environmental Response, Compensation, and Liability Act of 1980 (CERCLA). The fund was financed by $1.38 billion in taxes levied on chemical feedstocks and crude oil and by $220 million in general appropriations. Tax collection under CERCLA was expected to cease in 1985 or temporarily be suspended if the unobligated balance in the trust fund exceeded $900 million.

According to then EPA Assistant Administrator Eckhart C. Beck, the philosophy behind the program was to be one of "shovels first, and lawyers later." Where private parties responsible for dumping could be found, the government would require them to clean their own sites. But when a hazardous waste site truly was abandoned or when the private party refused to respond, Superfund would enable the government to move swiftly in order to protect public health and the environment.

It is difficult to compare Superfund under Carter, who was already a lame-duck president when the legislation was enacted, with Superfund under

Reagan. It is clear, though, that a hazardous waste program was given higher priority during the Carter administration than during the first two years of the Reagan presidency. EPA under Carter developed and fought for the Superfund legislation and managed to stretch existing authorities and resources to begin working on the problem. Using authority under section 311 of the Federal Water Pollution Control Act, EPA transformed its oil-spill cleanup program into a small environmental emergency response program. The agency established a National Hazardous Waste Enforcement Task Force, which utilized enforcement authority under RCRA and the Federal Water Pollution Control Act to prosecute illegal waste dumpers. Finally, in March 1980, EPA began advance planning for the proposed Superfund program.[20] EPA was determined to begin action the moment that increased funding and broader authority were made available.

Superfund Under Carter: The Original Plan

Assistant Administrator Beck's assertion that Superfund would be a program of shovels first and lawyers later represents the Carter EPA's view of Superfund. Although EPA wanted private parties to clean up their own waste sites, Beck and other agency officials assumed that private cleanup would be obtained only if corporations feared the costs and consequences of government cleanup.

The ad hoc and tortuously convoluted governmental response to Love Canal had convinced the Carter administration that legislation was needed to: (1) provide funds and authority for rapid waste-site cleanup; (2) allow response regardless of the environmental resource under threat; and (3) begin to address the national waste cleanup problem.

The framers of the Superfund legislation understood that a total national cleanup program would cost between $30 billion and $60 billion, and that it was likely that Congress would provide EPA with only a fraction of the resources required. Congress specified that the federal authority to collect taxes from industry to fund the cleanup program would end in 1985, in order to assess the equity of the tax structure and make any necessary changes. Given the interim nature of the tax, the legislation included a number of provisions to gain the maximum cleanup for the minimum federal outlay.

The first of these provisions required cost-effectiveness. Congress instructed EPA that a "long-term remedy," which the legislation called for, need not be a total site cleanup, and that costs were to be carefully considered in designing cleanups. Although the fund allowed for restoring damaged natural resources, priority was given to containing the threat to human health and the environment. Second, the act set a six-month, one-million-dollar limit on emergency, or so-called removal, actions. This ensured that the dictate of cost- effective response would not be subverted by labeling long-term cleanups "emergency actions" —for which there was little time for cost analysis. Third, Superfund required states to share in the costs of all long-term, or remedial, cleanups. It was hoped that this provision would stimulate states to develop their own response capability. The time-funding limit on emergency actions ensured that most of Superfund's dollars could be obtained only if the states contributed some dollars of their own. Fourth, the act required EPA to publish a list of the nation's worst waste sites and to focus cleanup programs on those sites, ensuring that scarce funds would be devoted to the sites posing the greatest threat to human health and the environment.

The fifth and most important "leveraging" element of CERCLA was its liability provision. The Superfund statute allows the federal government to require private parties to mitigate releases of hazardous materials at sites for which they are responsible. If the private party refuses to respond or does not respond quickly enough, EPA has the power to clean the site itself and sue the responsible party to recover the costs. CERCLA also permits the courts to assess damage fines of up to three times the costs of cleanup. This regulatory component of Superfund was a critical piece of the overall Superfund strategy. If these threats were made credible by a few well-publicized examples, corporations throughout the country would begin cleaning up their own sites. By so doing corporations would avoid negative publicity, triple damages, and government interference in business operations. The bulk of Superfund dollars would be used for truly abandoned sites where no responsible party could be found, or where the responsible party could not afford to pay. Some abandoned-site cleanup would be financed by response funds recovered and damages assessed against financially viable responsible parties that resisted cleanup orders.

Clearly, this strategy involved a substantial use of federal authority. It assumed that an adversarial relationship between government and industry initially would be unavoidable. Congress and EPA assumed that all things held equal, industry would rather not spend its money cleaning up waste sites and that EPA could best encourage private cleanup by convincing industry that the alternatives were far worse. Once industry became convinced that EPA would use the "stick" of enforcement when needed, the agency then might offer the "carrot" of a cooperative relationship.

Government was attempting to modify corporate behavior, yet arbitrary and capricious exercise of government authority would be checked by EPA's tradition of acknowledging the power of corporate America and the need to be reasonable when regulating. In addition, agency planners recognized that endless conflict would not clean up waste sites. The initial Superfund strategy assumed a mix of confrontation and cooperation with industry; confrontation would be used—in part symbolically—to obtain cooperation.

Superfund Under Gorsuch and Lavelle

During the first two years of the Reagan administration Superfund was managed by EPA Administrator Gorsuch and Assistant Administrator Lavelle, who made substantial changes in the strategy that had been developed by Carter's EPA. Gorsuch reorganized the Office of Enforcement, dividing Superfund enforcement between the Office of Waste Programs Enforcement under Lavelle and the Office of Legal Enforcement Counsel under an associate administrator. Within EPA, morale was lowered and organizational effectiveness impaired. Outside EPA, the dissolution of the Enforcement Office communicated to the regulated community the symbolic message that EPA enforcement efforts would be relaxed.

Along with reorganization the agency adopted a policy of cooperation, rather than confrontation, with regulated industries. Conflict with industry was considered counterproductive, likely to result in extensive litigation and delay. According to then Assistant Administrator Rita Lavelle:

> Industry has probably the most important role in managing and disposing of hazardous waste. . . . First, private sector technical initiatives are being used to clean the sites. Second, where appropriate, private sector generators are "stepping up to the table," assuming their responsibilities and bringing about timely resolution of the problems.[21]

Gorsuch advocated a nonconfrontational approach to regulated industry. This approach grew out of the administration's sympathy for the very real challenges faced by the U.S. chemical industry, and Gorsuch and Lavelle's apparent belief that industry was willing to act in the public interest. The negotiated settlements that looked like "sweetheart" deals to Congress and the media were considered concrete environmental results by EPA management. In late 1982 Gorsuch announced that she did not believe there would be "a need for continuing the [Superfund] program beyond 1985" and reported that in addition to money spent by the government, the chemical industry had spent "$120 million to clean up America." [22] Lavelle, referring to the agency's success in raising funds through negotiated settlements, noted that "litigation in the same cases would still be underway with no income realized." [23] The emphasis, of course, was on money, not on cleanup.

Environmentalists complained that under the nonconfrontational negotiating strategy, funds were raised before the true costs of cleanup could be determined. They also objected to settlements where EPA gave away its right to bring further enforcement actions at negotiated sites. They complained that EPA was engaged in a private negotiation process that excluded public participation.

Despite the very real appearance and possibility of impropriety between EPA and the chemical industry, the fact remains that nonconfrontation was the agency's publicly defended and vigorously articulated strategy for securing private cleanup. The shovels-first, lawyers-later strategy was replaced by one of lunch now, lawyers maybe, but shovels never. Extended negotiation was added to the existing cleanup options of direct or judicially enforced response. Gorsuch explained this strategy in testimony during the fiscal 1984 appropriations process:

> The purpose of prelitigation negotiation is to encourage cooperative responsible parties to cleanup sites. Cleanup resulting from negotiation and settlement is likely to occur more quickly than cleanup resulting from litigation. . . . Negotiation can be particularly effective before litigation begins. The threat of litigation or administrative orders during prelitigation negotiations gives the federal government valuable leverage, because settle-

ment would allow private parties to avoid the great expense and adverse publicity involved in litigation. This leverage is sacrificed if the federal government automatically files cases before it begins negotiations with responsible parties. In addition, filing lawsuits before negotiations even begin alienates potentially cooperative responsible parties.[24]

Although some environmentalists and members of Congress labeled this strategy a perversion of legislative intent, the Gorsuch-Lavelle approach was consistent with the president's antiregulatory ideology and was supported genuinely by some political appointees at EPA. Even those EPA officials who did not believe that nonconfrontation was a viable strategy recognized the political power of industry in the Reagan administration and acknowledged the difficulty of coercing industry in that environment.

Although Gorsuch avoided confrontation with industry, she appeared to invite it with Congress. In late 1982 and early 1983 Congress became impatient with the pace of EPA's Superfund response and enforcement effort. Impatience turned into rage when Gorsuch, under orders from the president, refused to provide documents requested by Congress. Eventually she was cited for contempt of Congress and, along with Lavelle and nearly all of EPA's political appointees, was forced from office. It is too soon to tell what type of enforcement policies will be adopted by the EPA under Ruckelshaus, but clearly political reality in the mid-1980s requires an active and highly visible hazardous waste enforcement program.

Cleanups Under Gorsuch

Despite the failure to implement the comprehensive design of Superfund, some progress in starting the program was made between 1981 and 1983. Under Gorsuch and Lavelle, the agency used resources in the CERCLA trust fund to inventory, analyze, and occasionally respond to releases of hazardous materials. After the agency's political leadership was replaced in spring 1983, EPA's Office of Emergency and Remedial Response (OERR), the line organization in charge of Superfund's fund-financed response program, proposed initiatives to accelerate the program's implementation. This document reviewed the program's status and included two types of projections: the first projected program accomplishments if procedures developed under Gorsuch and Lavelle were continued and the second projected accomplishments if new procedures were adopted. The OERR document noted that

> the Superfund program has been severely criticized for failing to move rapidly to address the problem of abandoned hazardous waste sites. The initiatives described in this briefing [document] will significantly increase Superfund program activity over the next two years.[25]

The staff analysis proposed five sets of initiatives: (1) streamline Superfund rules and standard operating procedures; (2) improve relationships with the states; (3) clarify the role of enforcement in the overall Superfund program; (4) respond to releases of hazardous materials at federal facilities; and (5) improve management and regional/headquarters relations.

Table 13-1 Projections of Completed Remedial Activities, Fiscal Year 1981-1982

	Accomplishments under current[1] policy	Projected through fiscal 1985 under current policy	Projected through fiscal 1985 under initiatives
Planning	23	177	243
Cleanup Actions	2	15	43

[1] As of April 1983.

Source: Internal EPA Briefing Package, Office of Emergency and Remedial Response, April 1983.

Superfund staff argued that under Gorsuch and Lavelle the agency had adopted unnecessary policies that had delayed program implementation. One such policy required that states not only contribute funds to pay for cleaning up waste sites (as required by statute) but also that they pay some of the costs of the *planning*. States hard hit by the recession of 1981-1983 had difficulty raising planning funds, and even though several hundred million dollars sat in the trust fund, cleanups were delayed while states searched for money.

Tables 13-1 and 13-2 chart actual and projected Superfund accomplishments. Table 13-1 reports and projects completed long-term, or remedial, cleanups. Planning for 23 long-term cleanups, and implementation of 2 of those, had been completed by April 1983. OERR staff projected that if existing policies were continued, EPA would be able to plan 177 and complete 15 long-term cleanups by the end of fiscal 1985. If the initiative package was adopted by EPA's new management team, Superfund staff projected that they could plan 243 and complete 43 long-term cleanups in the same time period.

The document made similar projections for Superfund's short-term cleanup, or removal, program *(see Table 13-2)*. Between January 1981 and April 1983 EPA had completed 18 initial remedial actions (IRMs), 6 planned removals, and 107 immediate removals. If the existing policies were retained, total accomplishments would approximately double by the end of fiscal 1985. The OERR initiative package proposed that the arcane (and nonstatutory) distinctions between classes of short-term cleanup be abolished. (Under Lavelle, short-term cleanups were divided into "planned removals" and "immediate removals." This division was not required by Superfund and resulted in increased planning and red tape—hence slower cleanups.) Instead removals would be defined as CERCLA had defined them—short-term cleanup requiring less than one million dollars and six months to complete. If these distinctions and other policies designed to limit use of removal authorities were ended, EPA staff projected that almost 100 additional short-term cleanups (a total of 347) could be completed by the end of fiscal 1985.

The OERR initiative package, coupled with a request by Ruckelshaus for an additional $100 million from the trust fund in fiscal 1984, indicated that the Reagan administration finally recognized the political (if not environmental) dangers of delaying waste-site cleanup.

Reagan's Hazardous-Waste Policy

Without question, the federal government's effort to manage and clean up America's hazardous wastes suffered significant setbacks during Gorsuch's tenure. Reagan administration political appointees attempted to fold hazardous waste cleanup and regulation into their governmentwide effort to reduce regulation. Hazardous waste was a poor candidate for deregulation since in most respects hazardous waste already was deregulated—with devastating effects on environmental quality. It appears that Reagan officials misunderstood the nonregulatory nature of hazardous waste cleanup programs. For the most part, cleanup programs resemble police and fire rather than regulatory programs; environmental emergency response receives a level of public support equivalent to that enjoyed by the more traditional emergency services.

Gorsuch and her management team underestimated this support. In congressional testimony subsequent to the administrator's resignation, EPA career employees testified that Gorsuch and Lavelle had deliberately delayed and limited the program. Superfund Director William Hedeman stated that he had witnessed an "implicit policy to curtail the progress of the program." [26] Hedeman asserted that EPA's political appointees had slowed Superfund spending to demonstrate that the program was not needed.

Under Ruckelshaus, Reagan administration hazardous waste policy began to turn around. Presidential power and administrative discretion temporarily had "rewritten" federal hazardous waste law, but congressional oversight and public opinion forced a return to the original policies. Despite this turnaround, vital time had been wasted and some of the damage was expected to take a long time to repair. EPA's hazardous waste organization lost the momentum it had gained in the late 1970s. After things had quieted down, EPA hazardous waste staff could be seen wearing teeshirts referring to their former administrator that stated: "I survived the acid reign of the ice queen." No doubt, these "survivors" will be slow to take initiative and will continue to be sensitive to the political ramifications of their actions.

Hazardous waste policy under Reagan illustrates both the extent and limits of presidential power to make dramatic changes in government operations. For a year and a half EPA officials were able to circumvent congressional intent and public opinion as they redirected the waste programs. Had these officials not made a series of errors that focused media attention on their actions, hazardous waste policy might never have been turned around. The key to controlling abuses of administrative discretion is to publicize excesses. Unfortunately, the activities of government are too

Table 13-2 Projections of Completed Removal Actions, Fiscal Year 1981-1985

	Accomplished under current[1] policy	Projected under current policy	Projected through fiscal 1985 under initiatives
Immediate Removals	107	211	
Planned Removals	6	13	
Initial Remedial Actions	18	29	
Total Removal Actions	131	253	347

[1] As of April 1983.

Source: EPA Briefing Document, Office of Emergency and Remedial Response, April 1983.

numerous and complex to consider this type of control practical.

Even if the Reagan administration had not attempted to redirect federal hazardous waste policy, EPA would have faced substantial challenges in its effort to manage the nation's hazardous waste. The concluding section of this chapter reexamines federal hazardous waste policy and addresses two difficult and fundamental questions. Does EPA have the authority, resources, and organizational capability to solve the nation's hazardous waste problem? What can be done to manage America's hazardous waste?

Comparing the Problem to the Solution

Can RCRA and Superfund clean up today's hazardous waste and prevent tomorrow's? In March 1983 Congress's Office of Technology Assessment (OTA) issued a report entitled *Technologies and Management Strategies for Hazardous Waste Control*, which concluded:

> Newly established Federal regulations for hazardous waste facilities may not effectively detect, prevent, or control hazardous releases.... Data inadequacies conceal the scope and intensity of hazardous waste problems.[27]

Although RCRA should, in theory, prevent hazardous materials from being released into the environment, the regulatory process it establishes is too cumbersome. Its mix of reporting requirements, landfill procedures, and transportation requirements asks more of waste companies than they can give. EPA's reaction to this problem has been to relax the program's requirements. I believe that a more fruitful approach would be to charter a new set of private or quasi-public corporations to handle hazardous waste. These companies would begin as small demonstration projects and eventually would grow to cover the entire nation. The federal government could provide special loan, grant, and incentive packages to new organizations, which would be required to document and demonstrate their adherence to strict waste-handling standards. These organizations would be regulated public utilities with a monopoly on waste handling in a given location. Special tax credits and deductions would be given to disposal companies that developed and adopted new technologies and that could demonstrate they ran environmentally sound facilities. Similar benefits could be provided to waste generators that were able to reduce their hazardous waste. In addition, the federal government could begin a crash program to develop and research hazardous waste treatment technologies. In essence, hazardous waste handling is too complex to regulate and too dangerous to leave to the marketplace.

The costs of the program outlined above would be high in the short run, but far less than the long-run costs of cleaning up hazardous materials released from unsound facilities. Funds for the program could be generated by an excise tax on plastic products or through an increase in the Superfund tax on oil and chemicals.

Superfund itself will need to be dramatically expanded if the nation's hazardous waste sites are to be cleaned. As tables 13-1 and 13-2 indicate, only a small fraction of the nation's hazardous waste sites will be addressed under the CERCLA legislation. Stronger enforcement, and a great deal more money, will be needed if significant cleanup progress is to be made. Funding also will be needed to compensate the human victims of chemical contamination. Several pieces of legislation addressing victim compensation were introduced in Congress in 1983.

Substantial resources must be devoted to researching and developing waste cleanup and treatment technology because at this point we really do not know how to clean up a hazardous waste site. Every Superfund cleanup is an experiment, a prototype. Finally, we must conduct a comprehensive inventory of the nation's hazardous waste sites. Superfund files contain information on more than 15,000 waste sites, but many EPA professionals believe that additional sites exist.

We have taken the first halting steps to establish a system for managing our toxic wastes. Yet much greater strides must soon be taken if we are to defuse the toxic time bomb and preserve our lands and waters.

Notes

1. Environmental Protection Agency, *Everybody's Problem: Hazardous Waste* (Washington, D.C.: Government Printing Office, 1980), 8; Office of Technology Assessment, *Technologies and Management Strategies for Hazardous Waste Control* (Washington,

D.C.: Government Printing Office, 1983), 8.

2. Environmental Protection Agency, *Groundwater Protection* (Washington, D.C.: Government Printing Office, November 1980), 8.

3. EPA, *Everybody's Problem,* 15.

4. "Emergency Response by Industry and Government," *EPA Journal* 8 (July-August 1982): 28.

5. Congressional Quarterly, *Environment and Health* (Washington, D.C.: Congressional Quarterly, 1981), 27.

6. ICF, "Analysis of Community Involvement in Hazardous Waste Site Problems: A Report to the Office of Emergency and Remedial Response, U.S. E.P.A." (Washington, D.C.: ICF, 1981).

7. U.S. Congress, House Committee on Interstate and Foreign Commerce, "Resource Conservation and Recovery Act of 1976: Report of the Committee on Interstate and Foreign Commerce, U.S. House of Representatives on HR 14496," 94th Cong., 2d sess., September 9, 1976, 3.

8. Samuel Epstein, Lester O. Brown, and Carl Pope, *Hazardous Waste in America* (San Francisco: Sierra Club, 1982), 227. Regulations pertaining to sections 3002 and 3003 were issued in February 1980, while regulations dealing with sections 3001, 3004, and 3005 were issued in May 1980.

9. Epstein, Brown, and Pope, *Hazardous Waste in America,* 244.

10. Kathy Koch, "Carter Environmental Budget Stresses Chemical Clean Up," *Congressional Quarterly Weekly Report,* February 2, 1980, 315.

11. *Inside EPA, Special Report,* March 13, 1981.

12. Ibid.

13. *Inside EPA, Special Report,* April 24, 1981, 3.

14. *Inside EPA,* April 10, 1981, 1.

15. *Inside EPA,* July 3, 1981, 1.

16. *Inside EPA,* March 15, 1982, 2.

17. Lawrence Mosher, "Who's Afraid of Hazardous Waste Dumps? Not Us Says the Reagan Administration," *National Journal,* May 29, 1982, 957.

18. *New York Times,* February 26, 1983.

19. *New York Times,* March 6, 1983.

20. For a complete description of this process, see Steven Cohen and Marc Tipermas, "Superfund: Preimplementation Planning and Bureaucratic Politics," in *The Politics of Hazardous Waste Management,* ed. James P. Lester and Ann O'M. Bowman (Durham, N.C.: Duke University Press, 1983).

21. "An Interview With Rita Lavelle, Assistant Administrator for Solid Waste and Emergency Response," *EPA Journal* 8 (July-August 1982): 3.

22. *Inside EPA,* December 24, 1982, 27.

23. "An Interview With Rita Lavelle," *EPA Journal,* 4.

24. Draft testimony for the fiscal 1984 budget hearings (Washington, D.C.: EPA, February 1983).

25. Environmental Protection Agency, *Superfund Initiatives* (Internal Briefing Book, Office of Emergency and Remedial Response, Washington, D.C., May 1983).

26. *New York Times,* April 9, 1983.

27. Office of Technology Assessment, *Technologies and Management Strategies for Hazardous Waste Control,* 8.

14. SAGEBRUSH REBELS IN OFFICE: JIM WATT'S LAND AND WATER POLITICS

Paul J. Culhane

"Interior Secretary James Watt has developed an unofficial seal for his office—one with the Interior Department's buffalo facing right.
"The department's official seal depicts a buffalo, facing left."

Dallas Times-Herald
April 2, 1982

More than any other individual, James G. Watt came to symbolize the Reagan administration's record on natural resources and environmental policy making. As interior secretary, he was responsible for many (but not all) of the key natural resources agencies in the federal bureaucracy. In any administration, the interior secretary competes for the role of chief resources policy spokesman with other high-level officials—the administrator of the Environmental Protection Agency (EPA), the chairman of the Council on Environmental Quality (CEQ), the secretary of energy, and others. Most often, the interior secretary emerges as the principal spokesman, and Jim Watt (as he prefers to be called) had a firm grip on this role since he assumed the chairmanship of a cabinet natural resources and environment council early in 1981.

Jim Watt was a natural product of that part of the Reagan constituency that is most involved in environmental politics. During the "environmental decade" of the 1970s, conservation groups used a wide range of tactics to substantially alter the course of federal land and water policies.[1] The disaffection of traditional beneficiaries of federal land and water policies grew throughout the decade, culminating in the "Sagebrush Rebellion." Principally an effort by some western states to claim title to federal lands, this rebellion was fueled by resentment in certain western circles over President Jimmy Carter's "hit list" of water projects slated for deauthorization. Jim Watt, many of his fellow appointees to key resource agency posts, and Ronald Reagan (by his own proclamation) all are "Sagebrush Rebels." Their stated policy agenda in 1981 was to undo or reverse a laundry list of conservationist policy gains from the 1970s.

What environmentalists bemoan as the "ravaging of the West" has not, however, occurred. Cabinet secretaries, bureau chiefs, and presidents cannot easily bend a complex policy arena to their will.[2] As we shall see in the following pages, Jim Watt and the Reagan administration struggled with the legacy of past history in water and land policy, with often bitter opposition from interest group constituents of federal resources policy, with skilled and powerful coequal policy makers in Congress, and—ironically enough—with inopportune market conditions. This combination stymied implementation of much of the administration's rhetoric regarding public lands policy. Moreover, in the water policy arena—environmentalist criticism notwithstanding—Reagan administration policy even had a certain conservationist slant.

Jim Watt and Interior Politics

Jim Watt was a flamboyant character during his three years in office. In a remarkable two-day span in January 1983, for example, he condemned Indian reservations as "an example of the failures of socialism" and then compared his environmentalist critics to Nazis and Bolsheviks. Earlier, in a January 1982 speech, Jim Watt quipped that "I never use the words Republican and Democrats—it's liberals and Americans." In his final joke in September 1983 he lauded the equal-opportunity makeup of his recently appointed Linowes Commission, which was set up to study his controversial coal-leasing policies, as having "every kind of mixture you can have—I have a Black. I have a woman, two Jews, and a cripple."[3] Such outspokenness, along with an easily drawn face (bald pate and large glasses), made him a favorite of editorial cartoonists. President Reagan, whose campaign rhetoric on the environment included the misstatement that most air pollution is caused by plants and trees, reportedly agreed with almost all of Jim Watt's views and publicly supported his policies up to the very end of his tenure. The president's only public rebuke of Jim Watt followed the secretary's cancellation of a proposed Fourth of July concert in Washington, D.C., by the Beach Boys, whom Watt deemed less wholesome than his choice, entertainer Wayne Newton. President and Mrs. Reagan, familiar with old southern California entertainers, presented Secretary Watt with a statuette of a bullet hole in the foot.

Despite all this levity, Jim Watt was no clown. In an administration in which lack of Washington experience has seemed a major qualification for appointment to out-of-favor agencies, Jim Watt, 45, boasted a high level of experience and knowledge. He had served on the staff of Sen. Milward Simpson, a Republican of Wyoming, from 1962 to 1966 and then worked as a natural resources lobbyist for the U.S. Chamber of Commerce. During Richard Nixon's administration, Watt served first as deputy assistant secretary of the interior for water and power resources and later as chief of Interior's Bureau of Outdoor Recreation. President Gerald R. Ford appointed him to the Federal Power Commission in 1975. From 1977 to 1980,

Watt was president of the Mountain States Legal Foundation, an industry-supported public interest law firm set up as a counterweight to the influential environmentalist law firms founded in the early 1970s.[4] His résumé reveals that Jim Watt has participated actively in interior policy making throughout his professional life.

In view of his background, Jim Watt's flamboyant behavior should be recognized as one component of the Reagan administration's strategy for natural resources policy making. New administrations that come to Washington planning to significantly alter some domestic policy understand, or soon learn, that established *subgovernments,* or *iron triangles,* pose a major barrier to nonincremental policy change. These terms refer to the intricate network of relationships and accommodations among a bureau, its interest group clienteles, and the congressional committees that control its budget and statutory authorities.[5] These forces usually are more compelling than the mood of a new administration because (1) the actors in subgovernment politics share a common understanding of policy issues; (2) congressional committees normally control the legislative process; and (3) interest groups provide the public support needed by bureaus and, in many cases, congressional committee members. The Reagan administration prepared to battle federal iron triangles as part of its strategy to radically alter a wide range of domestic policies.[6]

The term *iron triangle* suggests relative homogeneity within the groups at each point of the triangle. The realities of natural resource politics, however, are more complex. In virtually every land or water policy arena one finds at least two opposing blocs of clientele groups, and the strengths of these blocs became fairly balanced during the 1970s.[7] These blocs have different allies among congressional committee members. In general, environmentalists' most powerful congressional allies are in House committees, particularly the House Interior and Insular Affairs Committee, chaired by Rep. Morris K. Udall of Arizona; the Public Lands Subcommittee, chaired by Rep. John F. Seiberling of Ohio; and the Interior Appropriations Subcommittee, chaired by Rep. Sidney Yates of Illinois. Traditional resource industry clients, on the other hand, have major allies in the Republican-controlled Senate, particularly in the Energy and Natural Resources Committee, chaired by Sen. James McClure of Idaho.

During the 1970s environmentalists firmly established themselves as members of natural resources subgovernments. They gained regular access to local-level resource decision makers through agency public participation programs and through the National Environmental Policy Act (NEPA) process, which requires public review of environmental impact statements (EISs) written for major federal decisions significantly affecting the environment.

The movement of northern, liberal, and urban members (such as Seiberling, Yates, and Udall) into committee chairmanships provided environmentalists with powerful, responsive allies in Congress. On the judicial front, liberalization of the legal doctrine of "standing to sue," together with court enforcement of NEPA's requirement for EIS writing, gave environmentalists powerful tools for opposing many resource developments *(see Chapter 9)*.[8] Finally, during the Carter administration, environmentalists achieved "establishment" status as political appointees. Among the highest ranking of the dozens of Carter's environmentalist appointees were Rupert Cutler, of the Audubon Society, as assistant secretary of agriculture supervising the Forest Service and the Soil Conservation Service; Gus Speth, of the Natural Resources Defense Council (NRDC), as chairman of CEQ; and Robert Herbst, of the Izaak Walton League, as assistant secretary of the interior for fish, wildlife, and parks.

On becoming interior secretary in 1981, Jim Watt tried to fracture Interior subgovernments. Industry access to Interior policy making remained good or improved. For example, the National Public Lands Advisory Council, appointed in February 1982, included ten industry representatives, eight professional or local government supporters of industry viewpoints, a zoo curator, an outdoor reporter, and no environmentalists. All things being equal, of course, industry access to policy making is commonplace and perfectly in accord with the norms of Washington politics.

However, Jim Watt went to unusual lengths to exclude environmentalists from Interior subgovernments. Late in 1981, the secretary instructed Interior political appointees that they and careerist Interior officials should not meet with environmental group leaders and lobbyists. Three months later, Jim Watt directed departmental officials not to meet with congressional committee staffers, the key day-to-day communication links in subgovernments. This ban was explicitly intended to hamper staffers' ability to prepare members for committee hearings and seemed chiefly directed at the House Interior Committee. Interior also reportedly applied indirect pressure through its industry clients on Washington lobbyists and consulting firms with Democratic or environmentalist ties.[9] In addition, the administration attempted to trim environmentalists' access to local policy making by incrementally revising regulations in such a way as to restrict or eliminate public participation in selected programs.[10]

Jim Watt's hardball politics were risky. His rhetoric and tactics generated aggressive counterattacks. Environmental groups vociferously petitioned for his removal and tried to make his record a partisan voting issue *(see chapters 2 and 3)*. The secretary was subjected to a gauntlet of congressional investigations. In 1982, for example: (1) the House Energy and Commerce Committee, chaired by Rep. John D. Dingell of Michigan, cited Watt for contempt of Congress when he refused to provide subpoenaed documents for a hearing on Canadian energy issues; (2) a congressional General Accounting Office (GAO) investigation charged him with spending departmental funds for personal airplane travel; and (3) Sidney R. Yates's House Interior Appropriations Subcommittee threatened to dock his salary by $8,842 for using the Carter-Lee Mansion in Arlington National Cemetery to hold Republican Christmas parties. In hearings, the interchanges between Jim Watt and members became uncivil, sarcastic, and highly personal.[11]

Most important, Jim Watt's behavior threatened the normal comity of Washington government. An appointee should not arrange to damage the careers of out-of-office partisans with whom he disagrees, because he too will someday be out of office. He should not slur citizens with whom he disagrees, because he must appear responsive to his agency's entire public. He is expected to be polite—indeed deferential—to Congress, because he is, by both law and common understanding, a subordinate of Congress as well as of the president. Jim Watt's behavior fell outside these unwritten rules of politics in a moderate, civil democracy.

Jim Watt paid the price for such behavior in the fall of 1983. The proverbial "informed administration sources" had rumored his imminent firing since late 1981. His September 21, 1983, joke to the U.S. Chamber of Commerce about the membership of the Linowes Commission provided the rallying point for the secretary's diverse opponents. President Reagan declared the matter "closed" a week after the incident, but Jim Watt continued to twist in the political winds. More than a dozen Republican senators, clearly concerned about the dangers of running for reelection with the controversial secretary still in office, called for his resignation. With the Senate leadership predicting lopsided passage of a Sense-of-the-Senate resolution demanding his dismissal for "conduct unbecoming a Cabinet officer," Jim Watt resigned on October 9, 1983.[12]

Public Lands Management

Most of the fireworks surrounding Jim Watt erupted because of his public lands policies. Three of the four public lands agencies in the federal government—the Bureau of Land Management (BLM), National Park Service, and Fish and Wildlife Service—are part of Interior. BLM manages the largest amount of land of the four, 254.9 million acres; the Park Service and Fish and Wildlife Service manage 68.5 million and 82.9 million acres, respectively, with large majorities of each agency's acreages located in Alaska.[13] The fourth agency, the Forest Service in the Agriculture Department, manages 189 million acres but is the largest of the four agencies in terms of budget and personnel. Even though the Forest Service is not an Interior bureau, Jim Watt was able to influence national forest management both formally and informally. BLM and another Interior agency, the Minerals Management Service, administer mining claims and mineral leases (such as coal, oil, and gas leases) on all federal lands, including those managed by the Forest Service. (The Minerals Management Service was established in February 1982, following a major Interior Department investigation of ineffective oil royalty administration by its predecessor, the Conservation Division of the U.S. Geological Survey. The Forest Service participates in mineral leasing decisions affecting its lands through a clearance procedure designed to protect surface resources.) Jim Watt also chaired the cabinet-level Council on Natural Resources and Environment, and John Crowell, the assistant secretary of agriculture in charge of the Forest Service, was a team player who shared Jim Watt's views on public lands issues.

The Sagebrush Rebellion

Jim Watt's stormiest battles were over the Forest Service and BLM. These two agencies' missions allow a wide and often conflicting range of "multiple uses" —timber production, wilderness preservation, livestock grazing, outdoor recreation, mining, and other miscellaneous uses. As environmental regulations, wilderness designations, and recreation uses of BLM and Forest Service lands increasingly interfered with traditional consumptive uses, resentment on the part of these agencies' industry clients fueled the Sagebrush Rebellion.

The purists among the Sagebrush Rebels advocate "privatization," asserting that BLM and Forest Service management is economically inefficient and that the agencies' lands would be better managed in private ownership.[14] The Sagebrush Rebellion began in June 1979, when the Nevada state legislature passed a bill claiming title to federal public lands in the state. This audacious piece of legislation was the most recent in a string of efforts by western (and particularly Nevada) stockmen to gain control over public domain lands.[15] The 1979 Nevada legislation did not·pose a particularly serious legal threat. The state's legal argument is premised on the notion that Nevada once had a right to all federal lands within its borders and that this right was somehow abrogated.

This argument, however, has no factual basis. During the nineteenth century the federal government granted public domain lands to states, and Nevada received sections 16 and 36 in every township when it entered the Union. In 1880 Nevada wisely traded its title to 3.7 million largely unsurveyed acres (98 percent of its grant lands) back to the federal government in exchange for 2.06 million acres of surveyed land of the state's choosing. The state then transferred almost all of this 2.06 million acres into private ownership. In its Statehood Act and in the 1880 land trade, Nevada explicitly relinquished all claims to federal lands.

While the Nevada Sagebrush Rebellion bill has little legal merit, it remains a powerful statement of the disaffection in some western quarters with federal land management policies. A number of other western states passed Sagebrush Rebellion laws similar to Nevada's. In addition, western members of Congress introduced legislation providing for the transfer of BLM and Forest Service lands to the states, which are presumed to be more supportive of development-oriented uses.[16]

If the Sagebrush Rebellion was chiefly a symbolic affair, the federal appointments of Jim Watt and other Sagebrush Rebels should have undermined the rebellion. Two of the key legislative sponsors of the Colorado Sagebrush Rebellion bill, Robert Burford and Anne Gorsuch, became BLM chief and EPA administrator, respectively, in the Reagan administration. (Robert Burford was to marry his longtime friend Anne Gorsuch at the height of the scandal that resulted in her resignation.) These officials' policies presumably would eliminate the grievances underlying the proposed transfer of BLM and Forest Service land to state governments.

This point of view, however, neglects the influence of those actors in the

Reagan administration with an ideological commitment to privatization. Their stance was not mollified by the appointment of a Jim Watt. Steven Hanke, a senior economist on the staff of the Council of Economic Advisers, enunciated these actors' fundamental axiom early in the Reagan administration:

> Private property is always more productive than public property. It is . . . false, contrary to the belief of most sagebrush [rebellion] supporters, that a transfer of public lands from federal to state ownership would improve productivity. The *only* way to improve the productivity and efficiency of public lands is to privatize them.[17]

The privatization advocates consequently support the transfer into private ownership of essentially all BLM and Forest Service lands.

The administration responded to this argument with an "asset management program," in which a White House task force received a mandate to sell off "surplus" federal lands. Despite fears that this task force might engage in a wholesale disposal of public lands, its efforts to date have met with little success. The task force found that many parcels of surplus federal lands are difficult to sell for both economic and political reasons. The initial inventory, for example, contained an eight-acre parcel of submerged mud owned by the Corps of Engineers at the end of a Seattle, Washington, canal. In addition, both the Forest Service and BLM manage a large amount of acreage located in scattered, small tracts that are not individually large enough or close enough to other federal lands to manage efficiently. Federal land managers have wanted to sell tracts like these for years, but have been unable to do so.

Public lands are generally the lands no one wanted. Most of BLM's holdings in the West have very low grazing potential, and most national forest land has fairly low timber production potential. From 1804 to 1976, the federal government attempted to dispose of public lands through a variety of homesteading, land grant, and land sales and exchange programs. Its failure to divest itself of surplus lands was not a matter of policy, but principally a matter of economics. Users typically found it then and now much more efficient to lease public lands than to own those lands and pay property taxes on them. This is the reason why private parties, for more than a hundred years, passed up opportunities to acquire public lands.

Political considerations also make it difficult to sell substantial amounts of public lands. On the one hand, environmentalists see public lands not as a bundle of insufficiently profitable commodities, but as an aesthetic and recreational heritage of every American citizen. A wide spectrum of editorial opinion concurs. Moreover, since the 1950s, environmental groups have lobbied for programs to preserve wilderness and recreational values and to protect soil and water conditions on public lands. Privatization would undo three decades of their best work.

On the other side of the political fence, Jim Watt's constituency does not consistently support privatization. The administration promoted the asset management program as a way to raise revenues and lower the federal debt. Achievement of this goal would entail land sales at a fair-market price. A fair-market price could be obtained only through competitive bidding. But western ranchers, who have leased federal land for decades to provide the range acreage needed for their livestock operations, could not support a fair-market auction for two reasons. First, they would run the risk of being outbid for the nearby public lands upon which their livestock operations depend. Second, most western ranches are very marginal agricultural businesses that cannot afford the capital and property-tax costs of a fair-market price.

The would-be beneficiaries of privatization insist on some form of preemption sales. Public range lands would be offered for sale only to ranchers who customarily use particular grazing allotments. Such a restriction of the number of potential buyers would, under basic economic theory, result in below-market-value sales. The "privateers," furthermore, propose a sales price equal to the capitalized value, at one percent real interest, of the grazing fees paid by a rancher for a federal range permit.[18] Federal grazing fees are fairly low—so low, in fact, that the value of the below-market grazing fee is translated into a significantly inflated capitalized value of a stockman's ranch. Because of the low level of grazing fees, the capitalized-fee-value proposal would guarantee an even lower sales price for public lands.

Jim Watt thus found himself caught on the horns of a dilemma. His constituency could support privatization only if public land sales took place on a preemption, below-market-price basis. But this approach ran counter to administration rhetoric, which stressed revenue generation and faith in free-market forces. Moreover, preemption sales would face intense criticism as, to quote a National Wildlife Federation bumper sticker, a "sagebrush ripoff." Finally Congress, particularly the House committees in the Interior subgovernment, would not approve a massive public land sale program. The Federal Land Policy and Management Act (FLPMA) provides, for example, that public land sales in excess of 2,500 acres are subject to a legislative veto.[19]

As a result of these economic and political problems, privatization has been a flop. The program envisioned sales of tens of millions of acres, with annual receipts of $4 billion. However, through June 1983, sales totaled a mere 4,600 acres, worth only $4.8 million. In July 1983, Jim Watt, realizing that the program was a political liability in the West for President Reagan, pulled Interior lands out of the asset management program. Depending on the level of appropriations, BLM will probably be able to offer only about $150 million worth of scattered tracts for sale in fiscal 1984. And only 6 million acres of small, scattered tracts remain on the Forest Service's asset management inventory; this land is merely listed as under "further *study*" for possible sale, since the Forest Service has no statutory authority to sell land.[20]

Wilderness Wars

Wilderness issues evoke more passion among public lands interest groups than any other issue. The Wilderness Act of 1964 defined a wilderness area as "undeveloped federal land retaining its primeval character and influence, without permanent improvements or human habitation, which is managed so as to preserve its natural conditions."[21] The act designated a small number of areas as initial units of the wilderness preservation system and instructed the Forest Service, National Park Service, and Fish and Wildlife Service to review all roadless areas under their jurisdiction for possible congressional designation as wildernesses. In two bitterly controversial "roadless area review and evaluation" (RARE) processes, during 1972-1973 and 1978-1979, the Forest Service examined potential wilderness areas (in 1978-1979, 2,919 areas comprising 62 million acres) across the entire National Forest system. Under FLPMA, the BLM will complete a review of 24 million acres of wilderness study areas by 1986. The Alaska National Interest Lands Conservation Act of 1980 also designated a large amount of federal lands as wilderness. As of December 1982 the wilderness system consisted of 258 designated wildernesses covering 79.8 million acres; 56 million acres of this total are in Alaska.[22]

Wilderness and Mineral Leasing. Jim Watt's most bitter policy conflicts involved mining and oil and gas leasing in wilderness areas. The Wilderness Act contains a provision allowing mining claims and mineral leasing to continue in wilderness areas through December 1983. The mining industry has been most interested in oil and gas exploration in the "overthrust belt," a geological province lying mostly under national forest land throughout the Rocky Mountains. Since BLM administers mining claims and mineral leases, this issue falls under the jurisdiction of the interior secretary. Since 1964, a succession of interior secretaries had followed an informal policy of not approving mineral leases in wildernesses. Jim Watt's Mountain States Legal Foundation successfully sued Interior over this policy in 1980.[23] With Jim Watt appointed interior secretary and the 1983 deadline for issuing mineral leases fast approaching, the mining industry was anxious to reverse Interior's longstanding freeze on wilderness leasing.

Relying on the court decision in the suit he had filed against his predecessor, Jim Watt began to do just that in 1981. However, Interior's processing of wilderness leases ran into a congressional brick wall. The entire 22-member California Democratic delegation protested loudly when the Forest Service recommended approval of 14 oil and gas leases in the Ventana wilderness along the Big Sur coastline, and the *Republican* Wyoming congressional delegation revolted against proposed oil and gas exploration permits on 92,000 acres in the Washakie Wilderness. The biggest fight, however, involved the Bob Marshall Wilderness in western Montana.

The one-million-acre "Bob" is named for the Forest Service official who founded the Wilderness Society. In May 1981, as the Forest Service was processing oil and gas lease applications, the House Interior Committee used an obscure "emergency" provision of FLPMA to order Secretary Watt to withdraw the entire Bob Marshall wilderness from mineral leasing. Jim Watt protested that the order was unconstitutional but nonetheless executed the withdrawal. A display of dazzling legal maneuvers followed: (1) Mountain States Legal Foundation and the Pacific Legal Foundation, another industry-supported group, sued Jim Watt, claiming the Bob Marshall withdrawal was unconstitutional; (2) the U.S. Department of Justice refused to defend Secretary Watt but challenged the standing-to-sue of Mountain States and Pacific; (3) a Pacific Legal Foundation attorney tried to finagle Jim Watt into undermining the government's legal strategy; and (4) the Sierra Club Legal Defense Fund, Wilderness Society, and Bob Marshall Alliance were appointed "defendants" to argue Jim Watt's case in support of the House Interior Committee's order. In a complex opinion, the court upheld the constitutionality of the Bob Marshall withdrawal order.[24]

Following the Bob Marshall affair, Rep. Manuel Lujan, Jr., of New Mexico, the ranking Republican on the House Interior Committee, introduced legislation banning all mineral leasing in wilderness areas. Lujan was furious over BLM's issuance of oil and gas leases in the Capitan Wilderness, which is located in his district. In November 1981, in the face of the Lujan bill and the withering crossfire from local congressional delegations and aroused preservationist groups, Jim Watt abandoned his direct tactic of issuing mineral leases in wilderness areas.[25]

In February 1982 Jim Watt orchestrated an attempt to defuse the wilderness controversy. Appearing on NBC-TV's "Meet the Press," he grandly proposed a moratorium on all mineral leasing in wilderness areas until the year 2000. However, the proposal turned out to be, in the words of the Sierra Club's John McComb, a "Trojan horse." [26] The scheme would have granted the president broad discretion to open wildernesses to mining upon a finding of "urgent national need." It would have released a wide range of wilderness study areas to immediate commercial uses. Finally, the proposal would have reversed the strategic advantage of preservation advo cates, whose tactics promised to stymie wilderness leasing through 1983, when the Wilderness Act's permanent termination of mineral leasing and mining claims would take effect. Under Watt's scheme, the December 31, 1983, termination would become only temporary until the year 2000, when the entire question of wilderness mining would be resurrected again.

The House bill that resulted from Watt's proposal, HR 6542, permanently withdrew wildernesses from mineral leasing, but rejected all administration- and industry-supported provisions that might have facilitated wilderness mining. The Senate Natural Resources Committee blocked this bill, but Sidney Yates's House Interior Appropriations Subcommittee attached riders to the fiscal 1982 supplemental and fiscal 1983 appropriations bills that prohibited Interior from processing mineral leases in wildernesses through September 1983. In the face of these reverses, Jim Watt abandoned his policy in December 1982.[27]

The "Release" Issue. While Jim Watt and Congress dickered over mining in existing wilderness areas, the really crucial wilderness policy issue took a back seat. As noted above, the Forest Service conducted two rounds of RARE studies during the 1970s, and BLM has studied wilderness areas since the passage of FLPMA in 1976. All reasonable parties in the process recognized that a minority of areas in the RARE and BLM inventories would actually be designated as wildernesses. The Forest Service's RARE II, for example, apportioned its 62 million roadless acres into 15.4 million acres of recommended wilderness, 36 million acres for multiple use management, and 10.6 million acres for further study.

The legal guidelines governing wilderness reviews prohibit most commodity uses of a wilderness study area before Congress makes a final determination. This ban artificially restricts many national forests' annual allowable timber harvest, so the forest products industry in particular wants nonwilderness areas released to multiple use management. But wilderness proponents essentially have held the "release" issue hostage to obtain favorable decisions on wilderness designations.

The Reagan administration, with Assistant Secretary of Agriculture John Crowell serving as point man, complicated the issue. Early in the 97th Congress, Crowell supported a bill that would have immediately released to multiple use all nonrecommended areas in the RARE II inventory, and set a deadline for congressional designation of recommended wilderness. Environmentalists' allies in the House, particularly Representative Seiberling, found the bill unacceptable, and it failed to move.

Congressional attention gradually focused upon individual bills that resolved all Forest Service wilderness recommendations within a particular state. However, serious legislative disagreements arose, particularly between Representative Seiberling and Senator McClure, over both the details of release provisions and the amounts of wilderness to be designated. As a result, the three major state wilderness bills (those for California, Oregon, and Wyoming) died in December 1982.[28]

An appellate court decision at the end of 1982 disrupted the state-by-state approach to wilderness legislation. In *California v. Block,* the Ninth Circuit held that the Forest Service's RARE II EIS was legally insufficient in its examination of California areas recommended for nonwilderness.[29] The court's opinion effectively invalidated the RARE II nonwilderness recommendations nationwide, except in the four states with completed RARE II wilderness legislation.

As a "solution" to the problems posed by the California decision, Assistant Secretary Crowell proposed another wilderness review—RARE III—that would take place as part of the Forest Service's ongoing land use planning process and presumably significantly decrease the amount of recommended wilderness. Crowell also proposed to allow multiple use in the areas RARE II recommended for nonwilderness. Environmentalists, knowing the latter part of this proposal could not withstand litigation, quickly extracted a pledge from the Forest Service that any uses in RARE III areas would be subject to an appeals process. Thus, in effect, a freeze on development would apply to RARE III areas. Given that a RARE III planning process would take years, Crowell's proposal would appear to undercut the forest products industry by significantly postponing the release of nonwilderness areas. However, Crowell clearly intended by this gambit to pressure Congress into a faster resolution of the state-by-state wilderness designation and release bills. As of the end of 1983 it was too early to tell whether Crowell's plan would work or whether more years of dicey wilderness disputes lay ahead. The history of this issue since 1964 suggests the latter.

Minerals Managing: Overleasing and Underprotecting

Jim Watt has been embroiled in other extremely controversial mining issues. Convinced that his predecessor had unduly hampered energy development by slowing down the leasing of energy minerals and overregulating mine operations, he aimed to radically increase the availability of federally owned coal, oil, and gas and to reduce environmental regulations that the mining industry claimed hindered coal extraction.

Oil and Gas Sales. Of all public land uses, oil and gas development of the outer continental shelf (OCS) returns the most revenues to the federal treasury. These submerged lands off the U.S. coast are leased by BLM. In 1982, 2,672 OCS leases were in force, covering 12.8 million acres. OCS oil and gas leases comprise only a fraction of all federal mineral leases (135,785 leases on 175.6 million acres), but they contribute more than four-fifths of the mineral receipts from public lands—$6.2 billion in 1982.[30]

OCS leasing was subjected to extensive litigation during the 1970s, including two precedent-setting NEPA cases. Most suits involved state and local government complaints about the onshore socioeconomic impacts of oil and gas drilling.[31] These controversies led to 1978 amendments to the OCS Lands Act and to a plan, released late in the Carter administration, for an orderly expansion of OCS leasing. When Jim Watt took office, he proposed to offer for lease, over a five-year period, 875 million acres of OCS lands— virtually all U.S. OCS lands—and to lease more than four times more acreage *annually* than had been leased during the entire 28-year history of the OCS program. Reaction to this policy, especially on the part of state governments, was perfectly consistent with the history of OCS policy making during the past decade. The state of California, joined by NRDC, hauled Jim Watt into court under the Coastal Zone Management Act and obtained an injunction against OCS Sale #53 in the Santa Maria Basin. Then California and NRDC, joined by the state of Alaska, brought suit, claiming the entire revised leasing program violated the OCS Lands Act, and they won again. Next, California sued Jim Watt over OCS Sale #68, obtaining yet another injunction.[32] Some prudent oil industry leaders feared that the scope of Jim Watt's OCS policy would so tie up Interior in injunctions that less, rather than more, OCS leasing would take place.

Actually, economic realities have hindered OCS leasing more than has political opposition. Jim Watt embarked on his OCS leasing policy at the same time as the world oil market began to experience a glut and a consequent softening of oil prices. OCS development is a very expensive business, not only in terms of lease payments to the federal government, but also in terms of the high cost of exploration work at sea. Thus, industry's actual bidding at OCS auctions generally fell disappointingly short of Interior's goals. In two major 1983 offerings, for example, Interior expected $8.4 billion in bids, but received only $5.6 billion.

Jim Watt also planned to step up onshore mineral leasing and claimed great success in this effort. But his claim was deceptive. To be sure, as of September 1982, 146 million acres of public lands were under oil and gas leases, as compared with an average of 90 million acres during the Carter administration. And Interior appeared to be leasing at an even higher rate during fiscal 1983. (More than 95 percent of public land mineral leases are for oil and gas.) But this increase only continued an already existing trend: the Carter administration figure had climbed from a Nixon-Ford administration level of about 65 million acres.[33] Also, acreage-under-lease figures lose significance when we consider that actual development takes place on only a small percentage of the leases in force. (The low federal lease fee—one dollar per acre per year—encourages speculative lease holding rather than diligent development.) Finally, following a major breakdown in lease administration, BLM suspended its oil and gas lottery, which accounts for the bulk of onshore leases, in October 1983.

Coal Leasing. Similar problems beset Jim Watt's policies on federal coal leasing. Interior attempted to significantly increase the amount of coal under lease at a time when coal demand was depressed and the coal industry had a huge backlog of unmined coal. As of 1983 18.6 billion tons of federal coal were under lease, while annual coal production from federal lands averaged only 82.9 *million* tons during 1977-1980, before the slump in demand. Moreover, western states resent Jim Watt's accelerated coal-leasing policy because (despite the administration's states-rights' rhetoric) it undercut the regional coal teams, joint federal-state panels that attempted to mitigate the socioeconomic effects of coal development on local communities.

A particularly difficult controversy arose after the 1982 auction of 1.5 billion tons of coal in the Powder River Basin of Montana and Wyoming. Because of a change in Interior's bidding rules, this sale netted only $55 million, which a GAO audit later charged was $100 million below fair market value. In the wake of this fiasco, the House Interior Committee issued an FLPMA emergency order barring Interior's planned Fort Union coal sale. Announcing that the order was unconstitutional, Jim Watt proceeded with the sale—which received very low bids, averaging only a penny per ton (less than a third the amount of the Powder River sale). The day after the sale, Federal District Judge Louis Oberdorfer enjoined consummation of the sale pending resolution of all constitutional issues. Then Congress, led by Representative Yates, attached a rider to an Interior appropriations bill that prohibited further coal leasing (as well as some significant oil and gas leasing) until a commission had reviewed Interior's coal program.[34] It was this Linowes Commission that provided the subject of Jim Watt's final, fatal "joke."

Strip-Mining Regulation. In the realm of federal regulation of mining operations, Jim Watt's major contribution was the gutting of the Office of Surface Mining (OSM). OSM, an Interior bureau established to implement the Surface Mining Control and Reclamation Act of 1977, regulates strip mining on both federal and nonfederal lands. Rather than try to have the law amended, the Reagan administration chose to undermine its implementation in four ways. First, James Harris, a former state legislator who led Indiana's challenge against federal strip-mining controls, was appointed director of OSM. Second, OSM's budget was cut and its staff slashed from 1,001 to 628 people. Third, OSM was reorganized to eliminate field enforcement offices. Fourth, Interior rewrote OSM's regulations to allow the states to administer strip-mining controls and eliminate specific federal standards on mine design.[35]

Jim Watt may have wrecked OSM as an enforcement agency, but environmentalists were determined to defend OSM's regulations. The National Wildlife Federation sued OSM to force an EIS on the revised strip-mining regulations. Then the federation and other environmental groups sued OSM twice more, once during the preparation of the EIS and once after the filing of final regulations. OSM's regulations thus lay in legal limbo: it had not negotiated agreements allowing states to issue strip-mining permits, and, thanks to the reorganization, it operated with inadequate staff. So coal companies' mining plans became rapidly backlogged awaiting approval, and environmentalists challenged several major plans that were approved. The frustrated mining industry's "regulatory reform" turned into a morass of regulatory delay.

Multiple Use Management

Mining and wilderness designation, though important, directly affect only a minority of Forest Service and BLM lands. The traditional commodity uses of most of these agencies' lands are timber production and livestock grazing. Under the multiple use principle, both agencies attempt to manage their lands so as to obtain an optimum balance of logging and grazing with other uses. By protecting soil and watershed conditions, they ensure that all uses can be sustained over the long term. Jim Watt's agenda included a number of ideas for changes in the Forest Service's and BLM's mainline programs. Actual policy changes to date, however, have generally been fairly arcane and less bitterly controversial than in other areas of public lands management.

Planning and General Land Management. The BLM and Forest Service have both devoted a great deal of work over the past decade to land use planning. The National Forest Management Act of 1976 governs the Forest Service planning process as well as a number of important forestry policies. BLM has worked with two principal planning processes: a comprehensive land use planning process mandated by FLPMA, and a specialized grazing allotment planning process governed by a settlement of a 1974 suit, *NRDC v. Morton*.[36] Reagan appointees Robert Burford at BLM and John Crowell at Agriculture have tinkered with these planning processes, but their changes have involved technical matters such as the nature of public participation required in planning and the biological-growth-potential standard for timber harvesting. By and large, these key agency policy-making processes have continued on their own momentum from the Carter years.

Obscure policy changes can nonetheless have significant effects, as three examples demonstrate.

First, the Reagan administration incrementally shifted priorities within the budget requests of public lands agencies from conservationists' programs to resource development accounts. For example, the Forest Service budget request for fiscal 1983 contained increases of $6.5 million for minerals management and $29.9 million for timber sales administration but decreases of $7.7 million for soil and watershed protection and $18.7 million for land acquisition. Similar shifts appeared throughout the 1982 and 1983 budget requests of all the public lands agencies.

Second, in 1981 and 1982 Deputy Director F. Eugene Hester of the Fish and Wildlife Service used his agency's annual planning-programming-budgeting procedures to increase economic development uses of wildlife refuges. Hester's directives, combined with subtle legal reinterpretations by the Interior Department solicitor's office, resulted in several 1983 proposals for oil and gas drilling in wildlife refuges.

Third, BLM director Burford issued an administrative directive allowing stockmen to file for water rights on public lands. Given the complexities of western water law, this directive would transfer effective leverage over federal grazing allotments from BLM officers to those ranchers holding water rights. Arcane as it may seem, therefore, Burford's action authorized a form of backdoor privatization of substantial amounts of BLM rangelands.[37]

The Timber Bailout. The major forestry issue during the Reagan years fits into the same pattern seen in Jim Watt's minerals policies. Since the 1960s, the bottom-line issue in Forest Service timber policy has involved the amount of timber to be sold annually. The forest products industry has been rapidly converting old-growth private forests into managed commercial forests. However, since it takes decades to regenerate a forest after logging, the industry faces an impending gap during which it will be unable to meet lumber demand using timber from industrial forests. Increased industry timber purchases from the Forest Service may not be possible, however, since the Forest Service follows a "nondeclining even-flow" policy. That policy limits national forest timber sales to a level that can be maintained perpetually at a constant or increasing level.

Assistant Secretary of Agriculture John Crowell, a former executive for Louisiana-Pacific Co. (one of the largest purchasers of national forest timber), argues that the Forest Service should double its annual timber sales from about 12 billion board feet—the level during recent years—to 25 billion board feet.[38] But Crowell does not have discretionary authority to implement this notion quickly. Individual national forests' annual allowable harvests are governed by the timber management components of NFMA planning processes, which are under way now but will require several years to complete. Moreover, substantial commercial forest acreage is tied up in RARE wilderness study areas.

Most important, Crowell did not take office at a propitious time for doubling national forest timber sales. Several years ago, forest products firms engaged in a bidding war to ensure steady supplies of timber for their mills. Then high interest rates brought housing construction to a standstill and the bottom fell out of the timber market. By mid-1981, the forest products industry panicked because its expensive federal timber could only be logged at an enormous loss. By April 1982 the Forest Service estimated that it would face a backlog of 40 billion board feet of sold but uncut timber.

Therefore, John Crowell, manager of one of the deficit-ridden federal government's better cash crops, had to propose a policy, in his words, designed "to reduce excessively high bidding for [federal] timber." [39] The Forest Service only had administrative authority for temporary solutions to the forest products industry's problems (such as short extensions of contract periods). Releasing timber purchasers from overbid contracts required legislative relief. The principal forestry issue in Congress during 1982-1983 thus became consideration of a timber bailout bill. Sen. Mark O. Hatfield of Oregon, the state in which overbidding posed the worst problems, sponsored the main bill, which would have allowed purchasers to cancel up to 40 percent of their contracts; also, it would have extended contract periods and made other concessions.

Timber bailout legislation, however, caused a major rift within the forest products industry. Timber operators in the South opposed Hatfield's bill because they believed it would give their competitors in the Pacific Northwest an unfair economic advantage. The South is especially well represented in the Senate Agriculture and Forestry Committee, chaired by Jesse Helms of North Carolina. Helms blocked the timber bailout bill throughout 1982 and 1983.

The overbidding fiasco has undercut Crowell's policy of increasing Forest Service timber sales. At the same time as Crowell attempted to persuade Congress to fund a huge increase in timber sales, he also had to convince Congress to release timber operators from contracts contributing to a 33-billion-board-feet backlog of uncut timber. Critics of Forest Service timber management practices (notably Rep. James Weaver of Oregon, the forestry expert on the House Interior and Agriculture committees) used the contradictions in these policies to block sales increases.

The National Parks

Jim Watt's policies for the national park system complemented the administration's "privatization" program regarding BLM and Forest Service lands. Privatization advocates argue that the federal government should acquire no more private land. As noted earlier, Jim Watt served in the Nixon administration as director of the Bureau of Outdoor Recreation. The principal function of this agency was to administer the Land and Water Conservation Fund (LWCF), a separate account in the federal budget funded by receipts from oil and gas leases. The major use of the LWCF in recent years has been to purchase land for authorized additions to the national park system, although half the fund is earmarked for grants to state and local government parks. Jim Watt served notice that sentiment would not rule his decisions when, among his first acts as secretary of the interior, he abolished his old bureau, which had been renamed the Heritage Conservation and Recreation Service (HCRS) during the Carter administration, and transferred its functions to the Park Service. The demise of HCRS (pronounced "hookers" in the trade) was little lamented, but Jim Watt also proposed—ostensibly to help balance the federal budget—not to spend any LWCF money.

Jim Watt's proposed freeze of the LWCF was influenced principally by one of the lesser known interest groups in public lands management. The National Inholders Association is composed of private landowners whose property is located within the authorized boundaries of federal land units— national parks, national forests, and the like. Some property owners whose land is acquired for public projects inevitably accumulate a list of grievances against the government agency involved. The Park Service can afford to be patient and cooperative in dealing with landowners, but those who want to retain their family land may still harbor resentment. National Inholders Association members are just such aggrieved property owners. Charles Cushman, an intense man regarded by environmentalists and many Park Service professionals as an unreliable character, heads the association.[40] Cushman's former lobbyist, Ric Davidge, was appointed as an aide to assistant secretary Ray Arnett, and Davidge became the person in Interior chiefly responsible for park policies.

Jim Watt's freezing of the LWCF came at a particularly difficult time for the Park Service. The national park system had expanded exponentially from 24.4 million acres in 1971 to 68.5 million acres in 1982. New Alaska parks accounted for the largest part of this increase, but during the 1970s Congress also authorized a number of new parks in the lower 48 states, especially in the East and near urban areas. The LWCF enabled the Park Service to acquire 1.4 million acres between 1965 and 1981, but a very large backlog of inholdings still remained. Jim Watt's refusal to buy these inholdings in a timely manner would make land acquisition all the more expensive in the future and greatly inconvenience those landowners who wished to sell to the Park Service. He also ran the risk that developments might take place on inholdings that would diminish park values. Past problems on inholdings have included clearcut logging, strip mining, and residential subdivision development.

Jim Watt claimed to be a friend of the parks, and indeed the Park Service's budget did not suffer as much as did many other agencies'. However, his budget priorities were unusual. The Park Service believes its major problems involve (1) the difficult staffing problem of fulfilling general management planning requirements and adapting to the police problems caused by increased visitation, while still maintaining its ranger-naturalist image; (2) the wide variety of threats to park natural and cultural resources emanating from outside many parks; and (3) difficulties with private concessionaires who operate hotels, tours, and other services inside the parks.

The secretary, however, seized upon a GAO study that asserted park sewers, roads, and other structures were deteriorating. So Jim Watt proposed to spend $105 million from the LWCF for sewers and structures. He also told park concessionaires that, if they had any problems with a person in the Park Service, he would eliminate either the problem or the person. Congress refused to accede to Jim Watt's program, however. It appropriated $227 million for the LWCF in 1982—which Jim Watt dawdled in spending—and cut his sewers-and-structures restoration program to $76 million.

Water Resources Development

The Reagan administration's approach to federal water resources policy has differed markedly from its public lands policies. Water policies have not generated nearly the level of bitter political controversy to date as have wilderness designation and mineral development issues. Rather, the administration has tried to reform water resources programs that have stagnated for a variety of political, economic, and practical reasons.

New water project authorizations have been essentially frozen since the hit list affair early in the Carter administration. To shake up water project policy making, Carter had targeted 18 water projects for "zero-budgeting." Contrary to the conventional wisdom that presidents cannot control such congressional "pork barrel" decisions, Carter actually rallied sufficient congressional support to have half these projects deleted from the fiscal 1978 appropriations bill.

Congress has authorized no new water projects since this shake-up. Major actions proposed by the Corps of Engineers, Bureau of Reclamation (BuRec), and Soil Conservation Service (SCS) have declined between 67 percent and 79 percent from the agencies' peak, pre-Carter years.[41] Also, the agencies have been saddled with different types of projects. The corps' workload now includes a higher proportion of dull operation and maintenance actions, as opposed to new projects. The SCS workload contains a lower proportion of small watershed projects, its bread-and-butter program.

Opposition to federal water projects is often based less on environmentalism than on economics. Local project beneficiaries regard a federally funded water project as a "free good," and members of Congress traditionally have considered it part of their job to deliver these goods to their constituents. However, the benefits derived from water projects are often open to dispute. Take, for example, the discount rate (a surrogate for the interest rate on the capital invested in the project) used in calculating a project's benefit-cost ratio. Many current projects have discount rates as low as 3.2 percent—hardly realistic in an era in which the prime rate fluctuates between 12 percent and 16 percent. To introduce some economic realism into water project decision making, the Carter administration proposed that state or local government sponsors pay a 10 percent share of water project costs. If a project was really necessary or beneficial, it was reasoned, sponsors would willingly share in its cost.

Coming on the heels of the hit list, Carter's cost-sharing proposal struck beneficiaries as another intolerable attack on water resources development. Opposition was especially bitter in the West, with its complex water politics.

The Colorado River basin provides an excellent example.[42] A complicated series of interstate compacts, court decisions, international treaties, water claims, studies, and plans has been enacted from 1922 through the 1970s regarding the Colorado. As a result, water users in California, Arizona, Nevada, Utah, Colorado, New Mexico, and Wyoming, plus Mexico and, most recently, Native American tribes all have valid, legal rights to Colorado River water. In order to enable these claimants to use their water, BuRec has been building dams and other projects in the Colorado River basin since the 1940s. However, the sum of the existing water rights and uses of the Colorado is substantially greater than the annual flow of the river. Southern California is currently using more than its allotted share because other users do not have projects in place to make use of their water. These other users, particularly in Arizona and Colorado, want BuRec projects built so that they can use the water rights to which they have been entitled for decades. Water rights are the keys to present agricultural and future energy development in the region.

Since resentment over the hit list fueled the Sagebrush Rebellion, Jim Watt and his fellow rebels had to try to undo the Carter shake-up in water resources development. In its first year, the Reagan administration floundered somewhat in the water policy arena while Jim Watt conducted a reorganization of water resources agencies. Perhaps his best decision in office (in this author's view) concerned BuRec. The Carter administration had changed the bureau's name to the Water and Power Resources Administration (WPRS, pronounced "woopers"). Jim Watt, to almost universal applause, immediately changed its name back to Bureau of Reclamation, the name it had used since 1902. Watt also arranged to have the Water Resources Council, an independent planning agency, abolished and its functions transferred to a new Office of Water Policy in Interior. Shuffling boxes around on organization charts, however, cannot substitute for a real policy.

The Reagan administration faced a difficult water policy predicament. Its constituents clamored for resumption of new projects, but hard realities and the administration's ideology made water projects difficult to support. While cutting the federal budget and facing a ballooning federal deficit, could the administration afford a new round of expensive water projects? Especially, could it afford them when the process of water project authorization and funding provides the classic example of a federal "pork barrel" program— "waste and abuse" in the Reagan rhetoric?

The administration's solution, first floated in 1982, was a comprehensive cost-sharing program under which beneficiaries of new flood control or water supply projects would contribute 35 percent of project costs (an increase from the heinous Carter proposal of 10 percent). Water project beneficiaries, knowing they could choose between 35-percent cost sharing or no water projects, accepted the policy in principle. Environmentalists and other critics, who had long nattered about water project economics, roundly applauded the proposal.[43] Based on the new cost-sharing policy, the administration proposed 13 new water project authorizations for fiscal 1984, the first since 1976.

The 35-percent cost-sharing policy did not really solve the administration's predicament, however. William Gianelli, the assistant secretary of the Army who supervises the corps, had strongly supported the proposal. The corps, one of the most politically skilled agencies in the federal bureaucracy, was well prepared for the new policy with a set of projects that could be authorized on a cost-share basis. Interior's BuRec and Jim Watt, on the other hand, were not enthusiastic supporters of cost sharing. Western water beneficiaries cannot afford to pay such a high proportion of the costs of irrigation projects. So, even though his cabinet council on natural resources approved cost sharing, Jim Watt knew cost sharing was no solution to his constituents' water project problem. The 13 new starts are Gianelli's corps projects.

The administration's water policy review, however, breached the dam that held back new water projects. In August 1983, the House Public Works Committee reported out an omnibus rivers and harbors bill containing a surprising 278 new water project authorizations—that is, over an order of magnitude more than recommended by the administration. This bill's cost-sharing provisions also fell far short of the administration's proposals (setting the stage for a conceivable Reagan veto of a bill containing new water projects). This House bill failed to move throughout the remainder of the 1983 session, however.

Conclusion

Jim Watt's record as chief steward of the nation's water resources and public lands has been more complex than the one suggested by environmentalists' and cartoonists' caricatures of "the famous wilderness rapist and despoiler of our precious natural heritage." By any reasonable standard, he and his colleagues have accomplished some good. It is hard to fault several of his reorganization decisions—particularly those involving HCRS, the Minerals Management Service, and the Water Resources Council. Moreover, the Reagan administration's cost-sharing proposals would, if implemented, add an important and welcome element of economic rationality into water resources development policy making. Even though Jim Watt was a lukewarm supporter of cost sharing, as chairman of the cabinet natural resources council he nonetheless deserved credit for allowing proponents of the policy to give the concept a try.

However, for the most part, Jim Watt and his colleagues have taken profoundly nonconservationist policy stances. Environmentalists grow numb at the thought of an administration that not only does not support more wilderness, but wants to open existing wildernesses to full-bore mining; that supports the concept of selling upwards of 343 million acres of BLM and Forest Service land to the lowest bidder; that wants to auction off almost every acre of OCS oil and gas tracts and federal coal lands in the midst of an oil glut on the world market and a backlog of unmined coal; that would rather build sewers in National Parks than fulfill the government's program of completing acquisition of parklands.

Some of Jim Watt's policies may have so undone programs and past accomplishments that it will take years for conservationists to rectify the Watt era. Certainly the secretary's rhetoric and personnel actions affected the morale and institutional competence of several Interior bureaus. As noted earlier the Reagan administration decimated OSM. Park Service professionalism has been badly shaken by another Interior "reorganization," which involved the demotion of the service's top three officials in Alaska and the replacement of virtually the entire Park Service directorate with people who are not park professionals. A comparable reorganization of BLM's directorate, and the firing of careerist state directors Robert Buffington (Idaho) and James Ruch (California), have caused similar concerns about the politicization of BLM.[44]

But economic realities or institutionalized political opposition have stymied most of the Reagan administration's radical schemes. In a number of the cases discussed above, inopportune market conditions and/or longstanding economic facts of life demonstrated that Jim Watt's policies rested on a very shaky rational-technical foundation. These conditions were exacerbated in an administration whose political rhetoric stressed budget-balancing and the strengths of the free market, but whose constituency was composed of business groups rationally seeking advantages for themselves. Thus, for example, John Crowell, former businessman and believer in the free market, found himself in an awkward position when he tried to simultaneously support a doubling of Forest Service timber sales *and* a bailout of backlogged, overbid timber contracts. One policy helped the federal budget; the other harmed it. One trusted the rationality of the free market; the other involved federal intervention to rectify a market failure. Jim Watt's faith in full-bore leasing of federal energy minerals fell flat when energy companies failed, in the midst of a supply glut, to pay the huge sums necessary to buy leases. Finally, the "asset management" and privatization advocates, despite their firm faith in the rationality of private entrepreneurs, seemed to have forgotten that the present pattern of public land ownership stems from more than a century of rational private-market decisions not to acquire the often-marginal lands managed by the BLM and Forest Service.

Natural resources subgovernments also regularly blocked Jim Watt's policies. The administration knew it would face significant political opposition to its radical land policies, it knew who the opposition would be, and it adopted direct tactics to try to undermine these opponents. Conservationists in Congress and environmentalists, however, were not buffaloed by Jim Watt's Interior Department. Like any new administration, the Reaganites faced a legacy of statutes, procedures, and court precedents that provided powerful tools to interests who knew how to use them. When Interior proposed to expand OCS leasing into sensitive tracts off the California coast, for example, the state found a judge and a few statutes whose fine print had been violated, and then sued Jim Watt, and sued him, and sued him again. More important, the House Interior Committee and the House Interior Appropriations Subcommittee repeatedly refused to support Jim Watt's legislative initiatives and used FLPMA emergency orders, appropriations riders, and other methods to hamstring Jim Watt.

Perhaps Jim Watt's tenure in office will be remembered most for the illegitimacy of his interior subgovernment politics. These last three years have not been politics-as-usual at the Interior building. The Carter administration had nudged the normally stable pendulum in this policy arena toward the environmentalist direction. Jim Watt tried to kick it back hard and far in the opposite direction, and in doing so polarized and embittered interior politics to an extraordinary degree. His unpopular policies and his highly visible verbal pratfalls ultimately proved so intolerable as to elicit a Senate "no confidence" motion. President Reagan chose his close friend and quiet troubleshooter, William P. Clark, as Jim Watt's successor. Clark had been deputy secretary of state and director of the National Security Council. He had no experience in natural resources management. Doubtless Clark will not continue Jim Watt's tradition of flamboyant public gaffes, but by all indications he is likely to continue Jim Watt's and Ronald Reagan's resource policies.

Notes

1. For a mid-decade overview of these changes, see Paul Culhane, "Natural Resources Policy: Procedural Change and Substantive Environmentalism," in *Nationalizing Government: Public Policies in America*, ed. Theodore Lowi and Alan Stone (Beverly Hills, Calif.: Sage, 1978), 201-262.

2. For a general theoretical treatment of the political environment of executive officials, see Herbert Simon, Donald Smithburg, and Victor Thomson, *Public Administration* (New York: Knopf, 1950), especially chapters 18 and 19; Francis Rourke, ed., *Bureaucratic Power in National Politics* (Boston: Little, Brown, 1978); Thomas Cronin, *The State of the Presidency* (Boston: Little, Brown, 1975).

3. "Watt's Indian Remarks Met by Calls for His Scalp," *Chicago Tribune*, January 20, 1983; "Watt Links Environmental Zeal, Nazism," *Chicago Tribune*, January 21, 1983; "Watt Sees Respite After Year of Fighting Conservationists," *New York Times*, April 15, 1982, 14; "President Is 'Steamed' about Watt," *Chicago Tribune*, September 24, 1983, 1.

4. "Interior Department: Religious Fervor," *National Journal*, April 25, 1981, 720-722.

5. Among the best recent studies of subgovernment politics is Randall Ripley and Grace Franklin, *Congress, the Bureaucracy, and Public Policy* (Homewood, Ill.: Dorsey Press, 1980). The concept, under the synonym "subsystems," was originated by J. Leiper Freeman, *The Political Process* (New York: Random House, 1955).

6. Timothy Clark, "The President Takes on the 'Iron Triangles' and So Far Holds His Own," *National Journal*, March 28, 1981, 516-518.

7. For two studies that document the balancing of public lands and water resources constituencies, see Paul Culhane, *Public Lands Politics* (Baltimore: Johns Hopkins—Resources for the Future, 1981); and Daniel Mazmanian and Jeanne Nienaber, *Can Organizations Change? Environmental Protection, Citizen Participation, and the Corps of Engineers* (Washington, D.C.: Brookings Institution, 1979).

8. These developments are described in Culhane, "Natural Resources Policy," in *Nationalizing Government;* and in the NEPA symposium issue of *Natural Resources Journal* 16 (April 1976). "Standing-to-sue" refers to the criteria accepted by the federal courts for allowing interest groups to file lawsuits against federal agencies' decisions.

9. "Watt Wants No Meetings with Environmentalists," *Chicago Tribune,* December 2, 1981, 4; "Watt Bans His Staff from Briefing Congressional Aides," *Chicago Tribune,* February 5, 1982; "Democratic Lawyers Finding Interior Cold," *New York Times,* February 2, 1982, 10.

10. See, for example, Friends of the Earth et al., *Indictment: The Case Against the Reagan Environmental Record* (Washington, D.C., March 1982).

11. Philip Shabecoff, "House Panel Finds Watt in Contempt," *New York Times,* February 26, 1982, 1; James Coates, "Watt's Too Much at Home on the Range, Congress Probers Say," *Chicago Tribune,* October 17, 1982; "Watt Facing Pay Cut over Debt to U.S.," *Chicago Tribune,* October 20, 1982; "Watt Is Target of Hill Fire," *Chicago Tribune,* March 23, 1982.

12. "Watt Quits Post; President Accepts with 'Reluctance,'" *New York Times,* October 10, 1983, 1, 14. The controversy over Watt's "joke" was a major front-page and editorial-page story from September 24 through October 10, 1983. For examples of earlier rumors of "imminent" firings, see "Regardless of How Watt Fares, Reagan Ready to Drop Him," *White House Weekly,* January 11, 1982, 4; "Stockman, Watt, Donovan Reportedly Face Ax," *Chicago Tribune,* August 29, 1982.

13. Culhane, *Public Lands Politics,* 44. BLM's acreage is an estimate of the agency's holdings after all Alaska land transfers. More than three dozen agencies manage federally owned acreages that are much smaller than those of the four main agencies.

14. The best known academic representatives of this point of view are Steven Hanke of Johns Hopkins University and John Baden of Montana State University. See, for example, Richard Stroup and John Baden, *Natural Resources: Bureaucratic Myths and Environmental Management* (Cambridge, Mass.: Ballinger, 1983). For a good example of the stern criticism of this point of view among resource management academics, see Wilderness Society, *Federal Land and the U.S. Economy* (Washington, D.C., conference proceedings, November 1982).

15. William Voigt, *Public Grazing Lands* (New Brunswick, N.J.: Rutgers University Press, 1976).

16. H.R. 3655 and S. 1245, 97th Cong., 1st sess.

17. Quoted in Gordon Lee, "What if the Government Held a Land Sale and Hardly Anybody Showed Up," *National Journal,* September 25, 1982, 1630. Also see the sources in note 14, above. An interesting and thoughtful variant on the privatization argument can be found in Marion Clawson, *The Federal Lands Revisited* (Baltimore: Johns Hopkins—Resources for the Future, 1983). Also see *Conservation Foundation Letter,* April 1982 and May 1982.

18. *Public Land News,* April 29, 1982, 1-2. The best coverage of the privatization issue generally can be found in volumes 7 (1982) and 8 (1983) of *Public Land News.*

19. 43 U.S.C. 1713. Note, however, that in *Immigration and Naturalization Service v. Chadha* (U.S., No. 80-1832, June 1983) the U.S. Supreme Court recently held legislative vetoes to be unconstitutional; "Supreme Court, 7-2, Restricts Congress's Right to Overrule Actions by Executive Branch," *New York Times,* June 24, 1983, 1. The Court clearly understood that its ruling in *Chadha* would also

affect FLPMA. However, the Court arguably also invalidated the entire statute, which would remove *any* authority for public land sales.

20. "Privatization Board Heads Down Tube," *Public Land News*, August 4, 1983, 2-3; "Watt Removes Land from Sale by Government," *Chicago Tribune*, July 28, 1983.

21. 16 U.S.C. 1131(c). For a history of wilderness programs, see Craig Allin, *The Politics of Wilderness Preservation* (Westport, Conn.: Greenwood Press, 1982).

22. Council on Environmental Quality (CEQ), *Environmental Quality—1982* (Washington, D.C.: Government Printing Office, 1983), 256; Culhane, *Public Lands Politics*, 59-60. For an example of the visibility of the wilderness issue, see the cover story "Battle Over the Wilderness," *Newsweek*, July 25, 1983, 22-30.

23. *Mountain States Legal Foundation v. Andrus,* 499 F.Supp. 383 (D.Wyo., October 1980).

24. *Pacific Legal Foundation v. Watt,* 529 F.Supp. 982 (D.Mont., December 1981); 539 F.Supp 1194 (D.Mont., June 1982). Also see Lawrence Mosher, "Wilderness System Is Under Seige by Oil, Gas, Mineral, and Timber Industries," *National Journal*, November 21, 1981, 2076-2080; "Bob Marshall Wilderness Withdrawn," *Public Land News*, May 28, 1981, 1-2; "Skirmishes Continue over 'Unlocking' Existing Wilderness Areas," *Public Land News*, September 17, 1981, 4-5; and Jim Robbins, "Battle for 'The Bob,' " *Living Wilderness* (Winter 1981): 19-25.

25. "Compromise Heads Off Ban on Wilderness Oil and Gas Activity," *Public Land News*, November 26, 1981, 1-2. Specifically, Interior agreed not to issue any wilderness mineral leases until June 1982.

26. "Watt Does Turnabout on Wilderness Mining," *Chicago Tribune*, February 22, 1982, 1, 6; "Watt Stirs Pot with Wilderness 'Mining Ban' Bill," *Public Land News*, March 4, 1982, 1-3.

27. Wilderness withdrawal legislation was covered in virtually every issue of *Public Land News* during 1982; see especially "Wilderness Leasing Ban in Appropriation," *Public Land News*, November 25, 1982, 7. Also see Philip Shabecoff, "Watt to Halt Energy Leasing in Federal Wilderness Areas," *New York Times*, December 31, 1982, 1, 5.

28. *Public Land News* covered the "release" issue regularly throughout its 1981 and 1982 volumes. See, in particular, "California, Oregon, and Wyoming Wilderness Bills Fail," *Public Land News*, January 6, 1983, 7-8.

29. *California v. Block,* 690 F.2d 753 (9th Circ., October 1982). Assistant Secretary Crowell's "RARE III" response to *California* has been covered in virtually every 1983 issue of *Public Land News*.

30. Bureau of Land Management, *Public Lands Statistics, 1982* (Washington, D.C.: Government Printing Office, 1983), 114-119, 182.

31. See Culhane, "Natural Resources Policy," in *Nationalizing Government*, 234-236; Lawrence Mosher, "Tough Issues, Tough Style Could Lead to Backlash Against Watt," *National Journal*, December 5, 1981, 2144-2148; Richard Corrigan, "The Green Wave," *National Journal*, February 27, 1982, 287; and Lawrence Mosher, "Despite Setbacks, Watt Is Succeeding in Opening Up Public Lands for Energy," *National Journal*, June 11, 1983, 1230-1234.

32. *California v. Watt,* 683 F.2d 1253 (9th Circ., August 1982); *California v. Watt,* 668 F.2d 1290 (D.C. Circ., October 1982); *California v. Watt,* 12 ELR 21045 (C.D. Cal., June 1982). In July 1983, however, the D.C. Circuit reversed its earlier decision, holding that Interior's errors had subsequently been corrected; 13 ELR 10243 (August 1983). And in January 1984, the U.S. Supreme Court

reversed the 9th Circuit's decision in the first *California v. Watt* case.

33. BLM, *Public Lands Statistics,* for 1982, 1981, 1980, 1979, 1978, 1977, 1974, 1971, and 1969; table numbers differ slightly from year to year.

34. Watt claimed the order was an unconstitutional legislative veto under the *INS v. Chadha* decision; see note 19. "Watt Defies Congress, Auctions U.S. Coal," *Chicago Tribune,* September 15, 1983, 1, 7; "Judge Blocks Watt's Coal-Leasing Move," *Chicago Tribune,* September 17, 1983, 1, 6; "House-Senate Panel Calls for Watt Restrictions," *Chicago Tribune,* October 1, 1983, 5.

35. Lawrence Mosher, "Regulatory Striptease," *National Journal,* May 5, 1981, 971-973; *Public Land News,* March 18, 1982; *Public Land News,* April 15, 1982; *Public Land News,* March 3, 1983.

36. *Natural Resources Defense Council v. Morton,* 388 F.Supp 827 (D.DC, December 1974).

37. Forest Service, "Actions on Budget Estimates for Fiscal Year 1983," *Friday Newsletter,* February 22, 1982; "Wildlife Refuges Are Urged to Increase Economic Uses," *New York Times,* August 18, 1982, 12; "U.S. May Lose Control of Western Rangeland," *New York Times,* February 14, 1983, 1, 6.

38. Lawrence Mosher, "The Nation's Ailing Timber Industry Finds It Has a Friend in Washington," *National Journal,* July 11, 1981, 1237-1241.

39. Agriculture Department, "Changes Proposed for National Forest Timber Sales," press release, January 15, 1982. *Public Land News* has covered this issue regularly from October 15, 1981, through mid-1983; see especially the March 4, 1982, and April 29, 1982, issues.

40. The most detailed information on Cushman and the Inholders Association can be found in Chuck Williams' exposé, "The Park Rebellion," *Not Man Apart* (June 1982). For other environmentalist reviews of Watt's park policies, see Robert Cahn, "The National Park System," *Sierra* (May/June 1983): 46-55; and the special issue, "The National Parks," *Wilderness* (Spring 1983).

41. Based on the author's compilation of EISs filed annually, 1970-1982, by the three agencies as reported in EPA, "Cumulative Index of Environmental Impact Statements" (Washington, D.C., EPA Office of Federal Activities, computer printout, January 14, 1983). Some of the decline in EIS filings can be attributed to old, pre-1970 projects whose EISs were filed in the early 1970s.

42. For a still-fascinating introduction to the Colorado River issue, see Owen Stratton and Phillip Sirotkin, *The Echo Park Controversy* (Syracuse, N.Y.: Inter-University Case Program Monograph #46, 1959). On the complexities caused by recent Native American water claims, see Peter Ognibene, "Indian Water Rights Clouding Plans for the West's Economic Development," *National Journal,* November 30, 1982, 1841-1845.

43. Peter Ognibene, "Selling Water Users in the West on Sharing Reclamation Projects Cost," *National Journal,* August 14, 1982, 1421-1425; Lawrence Mosher, "Water Torture," *National Journal,* July 23, 1983, 1559.

44. On the Park Service, see Cahn, "The National Park System," *Sierra:* 49-51. Regarding BLM, see "BLM Reorganization Puts 'Scare' into the Troops," *Public Land News,* August 6, 1981, 4-5; "Buffington Out in Idaho," *Public Land News,* November 12, 1981, 6-7; and, on the Ruch affair, *Public Land News,* February 17, May 26, June 23, and August 4, 1983.

15. THE WORLD ENVIRONMENT: REVERSING U.S. POLICY COMMITMENTS

Lynton K. Caldwell

During the early 1980s the government of the United States under President Ronald Reagan undertook a reversal of national policy that can fairly be described as extraordinary. Appointees of the president sought to disengage the United States from international environmental policy commitments. Attempts were made to undo official involvement in programs and agreements in which the United States had often been an initiator. Prior commitments seemed to be contradicted in a series of policy decisions that in effect removed the United States from a leadership role in world environmental affairs. Yet actual circumstances were not as simple as appearances. There were significant differences of opinion among Reagan appointees concerning the role of the United States in international environmental affairs; not all opinions were negative, nor were all appointees willing to concede a loss of leadership. The Reagan record in international environmental policy has reflected the distribution of decision making within the administration more than an explicit and deliberate policy for the environment.

The nearest approach to a general policy for international environmental affairs articulated by Reagan appointees has been greater reliance on market forces and less reliance on international expenditures and regulations in coping with environmental problems. It is an extension of the Reagan domestic program. The Reagan administration would doubtless be willing to lead other nations in this direction, but the governments of those nations appear unwilling, or perhaps unable, to follow.

On environmental issues in international conferences and in meetings of the General Assembly of the United Nations, the United States stood alone or nearly alone against the rest of the world. On matters of international environmental policy the Reagan administration, by the end of its first two years in office, had often isolated the United States not only from the nonaligned and developing countries but also from the nations of the European Community and from Canada. Writing in *Europe, Magazine of the European Community,* Erwan Fouere reported that the international

319

implications of U.S. environmental policy were causing increased tension as the United States and Europe followed increasingly divergent paths.[1] Environmental quality was growing rapidly as a political issue in Europe and continued to be given a higher priority by the American public than by the Reagan administration.[2]

The generally negative appearance of the Reagan administration toward international environmental cooperation was extraordinary not only for its frequent reversal of well-established positions, but equally for its erratic character and for the lack of any significant advantage to be gained thereby for the nation or the administration. Even persons who wanted to think well of the administration too often regarded official explanations for its positions as inadequate. More candid statements, often reflecting industrial or trade association viewpoints, were widely regarded as wrong in relation to the policy issues addressed and the long-term national interest. Explanations tended to be specious, invoking fiscal and philosophic rationalizations to cloak particular economic interests. Often, as in the presentation by Environmental Protection Agency (EPA) Administrator Anne Gorsuch (later Burford) to the United Nations Environment Programme (UNEP) commemoration of the 10th anniversary of the 1972 United Nations Conference on the Human Environment, preference was expressed for private initiative and the free market in dealing with environmental problems.[3]

If a real reason for the contradictory and often counterproductive stance toward international environmental cooperation can be identified, it must be heavily weighted by the oversimplified and underinformed perspective of the president and his closest advisers on the state of the world and modern society, and the tendency in the White House to delegate decisions on environmental issues to subordinates, with little specific policy guidance. The prepresidential public career of Ronald Reagan gives no indication of a predisposition for or against international environmental cooperation. The policy positions taken by members of his administration appear to be largely fallout from domestic interests and issues. To a large extent, foreign policy has reflected domestic politics, and world environmental affairs are no exception.

Three considerations, essentially domestic in origin, appear to have influenced Reagan's environmental policies abroad. The first was a desire to obtain advantage wherever possible for American economic interests—thus the administration's reluctance to cooperate in the international regulation of deep-sea mining and of commerce in hazardous substances. The second was an ideological bias against any increase in U.S. financial contributions to intergovernmental agencies generally, and especially to those in which the Soviet Union and "nonaligned" nations were prominent. As with domestic budget cuts affecting environmental programs and agencies, the actual dollar amounts were seldom significant in relation to the federal budget. The third was a preference for reliance upon market forces as a corrective to environmentally harmful practices. This last consideration was not peculiar to the Reagan people, having been advocated for many years by a number of very reputable political economists, notably those associated with the public choice/property rights school of thought.[4]

This is not to say that public choice economists necessarily endorsed the economic theories of Ronald Reagan, called "Reaganomics" by the news media. But there was a convergence of opinion from several sources and for diverse reasons that government was an inefficient and irresponsible custodian of the nation's natural resources and public services. A logical extension and corollary of this reasoning was that international, multigovernmental programs could be expected to multiply the inefficiencies of national governments. From this viewpoint, the mechanics of the market provided a more equitable and responsive way of serving the preferences of individuals than programs or services administered through governments or intergovernmental agencies. The nearest approach to an official statement on this premise was expressed by EPA Administrator Gorsuch on May 11, 1982, in a "Plenary Statement" to the Session of a Special Character held by the United Nations Environment Programme in Nairobi. She declared:

> Many of our actions have failed to take advantage of the natural corrective measures that can work through market forces—if governments allow them to operate. Too frequently, we responded with alarm to pessimistic projections—squandering scarce resources on inappropriate measures—rather than devoting those resources to the careful study of practical and effective ways in which we might improve our world.[5]

The viewpoint is not unreasonable in principle; but in a world in which the capabilities of a private, nongovernmental sector are in most national states minimal, the prescription is unrealistic. The mechanics of the market can hardly work in the absence of an effective market economy.

On environmental and public health and safety matters, it was the position of the Reagan administration that the United States should not extend its policies and regulations to other nations through export controls. Its view of international cooperative efforts generally was strongly colored by its perception of the interests of American business abroad and by the increasingly isolated position of the United States in the General Assembly of the United Nations. Absence of a comprehensive, consistent guiding policy for the United States on global environmental cooperation resulted in ad hoc decisions on specific issues, often weighted by the predilections of lower level decision makers with little or no prior experience in public or international affairs.

International Environmental Policy, 1965-1980

As background against which to evaluate the policy changes initiated by the Reagan administration after 1980, the position taken by the United States during the preceding four presidencies will be summarized.

Under the administrations of Presidents Lyndon B. Johnson, Richard Nixon, Gerald R. Ford, and Jimmy Carter, environmental and foreign policies were strongly influenced by an upper-class, notably eastern, elite that regarded environmental concerns as important and international in character. For example, Laurance Rockefeller, a moderate Republican, played a prominent advisory role in both the Johnson and the Nixon administrations. Environmental policy makers such as Christian Herter, Jr., in the Department of State, or Russell Train in the Council on Environmental Quality (CEQ) and the EPA, were well informed regarding the international character of many environmental problems and understood the necessity for international cooperation on a wide range of issues. The National Park Service, the Fish and Wildlife Service, and, belatedly, the Agency for International Development developed international programs and cooperative projects, especially following the 1972 United Nations Conference on the Human Environment in Stockholm.

How high a priority international environmental concerns received from the pre-Reagan presidents is conjectural. More important was a generally sympathetic policy position that pervaded the higher levels of their administrations. Official support was not equally strong on all international environmental cooperative efforts. But between 1965 and 1980 the United States asserted a leadership position on many issues (for example, international protection of whales and other endangered species). Some specific examples illustrate the leadership role of the United States in international environmental cooperation during these years.

In 1965, during the Johnson administration, a White House Conference on International Cooperation recognized the connection between international development programs and growing global environmental problems. Preparatory to this meeting a National Citizens Commission recommended formation of a United Nations Agency for Marine Resources, a World Institute of Resource Analysis, a U.N.-sponsored International River Basin Commission, and a Trust for the World Heritage in Natural and Scenic Areas and Historic Sites.[6] And on June 4, 1968, President Johnson called for Soviet-American cooperation in forming, with other nations, an International Council on the Human Environment.[7] Environment became one of the principal concerns of a newly established North Atlantic Treaty Organization (NATO) Committee on Challenges of Modern Society. On December 3, 1968, the United States supported Resolution 2398 of the U.N. General Assembly calling for a world conference on the human environment.

These international actions continued the cooperative posture previously taken by the United States on most international environmental issues by adhering, for example, to the Antarctic Treaty of 1959 establishing the south polar region as an international scientific reserve and to the 1967 Treaty on Principles Governing the Activities of States in the Exploration and Use of Outer Space Including the Moon and Other Celestial Bodies. Throughout the 1960s and 1970s the U.S. government and many nongovernmental organizations continued to support a codification of international law for the oceans and an international regime for the high seas and deep-sea bed beyond the jurisdiction of coastal states. At the 1967 annual meeting of the American Association for the Advancement of Science, Sen. Claiborne Pell, a Democrat from Rhode Island, told a symposium that an international ocean space treaty that would cover both the sea bed and the sea itself was urgently needed, and he advocated placing ocean resources under the jurisdiction of the United Nations.[8] Until the policy turnabout of the Reagan administration in 1981, the U.S. government continued to support a U.N.-sponsored Law of the Sea Treaty.

A generally positive role in international environmental affairs continued during Nixon's presidency. The United States, which took a leading role in the 1972 United Nations Conference on the Human Environment in Stockholm, was an early and generous contributor to the United Nations Environment Fund that supported the United Nations Environment Programme (UNEP), established in December 1972 by the U.N. General Assembly. The United States gave diplomatic support to several major post-Stockholm treaties, including the Convention on Prevention of Marine Pollution by Dumping Wastes and Other Matter (1972), the Convention on Protection of the World Cultural and Natural Heritage (1972), and the Convention on International Trade in Endangered Species of Wild Fauna and Flora (1973). President Nixon's preoccupation with political survival during the last months of his administration and the environmental indifference of President Ford did not significantly affect the environmental policy positions or commitments of the United States abroad. Its generally positive role was strengthened during the administration of President Carter, who was the first presidential candidate to make environmental protection an explicit campaign issue.

Three events in particular indicated the Carter commitment to international environmental cooperation. The first was Executive Order 12114 (January 9, 1979), which clarified the application of the National Environmental Policy Act (NEPA) of 1969 to the activities of U.S. government agencies abroad.[9] Under the terms of NEPA, Congress declared it national policy to "prevent or eliminate damage to the environment and the biosphere," and to "recognize the worldwide and long-range character of environmental problems and, where consistent with the foreign policy of the United States, lend appropriate support to initiatives, resolutions, and programs designed to maximize international cooperation in anticipating and preventing a decline in the quality of mankind's world environment." Federal agencies with major overseas programs had tended to resist NEPA requirements, such as the preparation of environmental impact statements (EISs), arguing that the act applied only within U.S. territorial jurisdiction. Executive Order 12114 reaffirmed the obligation of the federal agencies to observe the requirements of NEPA wherever their actions occurred—even within the territorial jurisdiction of other states.

The second event was the Carter Executive Order 12264 (January 15, 1981), which concerned the export of hazardous substances banned or significantly restricted in the United States. This order was a response to complaints from concerned citizens and some governments in developing countries that agricultural chemicals, pharmaceutical products, and assorted synthetic commodities that were considered too dangerous to be freely sold or distributed in the United States were being "dumped" abroad. The Carter order would have restricted this flow of dangerous or toxic materials and required vendors to notify the governments of receiving countries of the risks associated with specific products. The Carter order was applauded by public health, environmental, and foreign policy groups in the United States as an act of environmental good neighborliness.

The third event was the *Global 2000 Report to the President: Entering the Twenty-First Century*. The study that produced this report was organized by the Department of State and the CEQ at the request of the president. Preparation of the report occupied three years following Jimmy Carter's announced intention in his environmental message to the Congress (May 2, 1977) to obtain a study of "the probable changes in the world's population, natural resources, and environment through the end of the century." The three-volume report was released in the summer of 1980 and was largely obscured by the rhetoric of the 1980 electoral campaigns and a national preoccupation with the troubles of the domestic economy.

The conclusions of *Global 2000* were consistent with previous studies and modeling simulations of global trends undertaken during the 1970s. In brief, the *Global 2000 Report* found:

> ... Environmental, resource, and population stresses are intensifying and will increasingly determine the quality of human life on our planet. These stresses are already severe enough to deny many millions of people basic needs for food, shelter, health, and jobs, or any hope for betterment. At the same time, the earth's carrying capacity—the ability of biological systems to provide resources for human needs—is eroding. The trends reflected in the Global 2000 study suggest strongly a progressive degradation and impoverishment of the earth's natural resource base.
>
> If these trends are to be altered and the problems diminished, vigorous, determined new initiatives will be required worldwide to meet human needs while protecting and restoring the earth's capacity to support life. Basic natural resources—farmlands, fisheries, forests, minerals, energy, air, and water—must be conserved and better managed. Changes in public policy are needed around the world before problems worsen and options for effective action are reduced.[10]

The pessimistic tenor of the report and its call for worldwide cooperative effort did not make good presidential campaign rhetoric. Its message was not what the American voter wanted to hear. The Carter campaign proceeded as if the report had never existed. To the Reagan people the report was unacceptable, their reactions coinciding largely with the progrowth, antienvironmentalist perspectives of the American Enterprise Institute, the Heritage Foundation, and the Hudson Institute. Objections to *Global 2000* (not only those of Reaganites) were (1) that the threatening trends detailed in the report were either exaggerated or imaginary, (2) that the world was becoming richer not poorer, (3) that the report discounted human ingenuity to solve problems through technological innovation, and (4) that the report favored increased governmental and international planning and control in derogation of the free enterprise system—that great engine of freedom and prosperity which, unfettered, could meet the needs that really mattered to people.

Policy Making in the Reagan Administration

Against a historical background of generally sustained cooperation on international environmental matters, the Reagan administration assumed command and promptly began a reversal of policies, some of which had been in place for as long as two decades. Before turning to the specific actions taken by the Reagan people to undo what they regarded as environmental policy errors of the past, we will consider certain characteristics of the Reagan administration previously described in this volume, with particular reference to international environmental affairs.

Neither President Reagan nor his closest advisers appeared to understand or to be greatly interested in the scientific basis of environmental policy. Ad libitum remarks by Reagan frequently revealed his innocence in issues involving the physical and biological sciences. Thus, the president was poorly prepared to evaluate issues such as acid rain, endangered species, or the export of toxic chemical products.

His political debts to western land and natural resource development interests were paid by deference to their wishes in appointment of the secretary of the interior. One of Ronald Reagan's closest advisers and strongest supporters was Republican Sen. Paul Laxalt of Nevada, whose outlook was essentially regional and development oriented, and who brought James G. Watt to Reagan's attention. With the exception of James L. Buckley in the Department of State, there was no person of political prominence in the administration who was generally identified as having an interest in environmental affairs or any connection, formal or informal, to nongovernmental environmental organizations. The president's tendency to delegate policy matters in which he lacked personal knowledge or interest left environmental affairs in general, and their international aspects in particular, in the hands of diligent appointees bent on undoing the work of "forty years of bad government." Yet there was no presidential policy proscription against international cooperation on environmental matters.

Environmental Quality 1981, a report prepared for the president by the CEQ, promised a reevaluation of federal environmental programs that would be shaped by several principles, including:

- balancing costs and benefits
- allowing the marketplace to work
- decentralizing government responsibilities, and
- continuing global cooperation

What these principles meant in practice depended upon who applied them. "Continuing global cooperation," for example, might mean nothing more than intent to observe prior treaty commitments. The first three years of the Reagan administration revealed a pattern of inconsistency. The authors of *Environmental Quality 1981* took a more positive approach toward international cooperation than was evident at upper levels elsewhere in the administration, especially in the Office of Management and Budget (OMB). It seems clear that A. Alan Hill, chairman of the CEQ, took the principle of global cooperation seriously.

In addition to a presidential tendency to delegate decision making on low-priority issues, the Reagan administration regarded the United Nations system with dislike and intergovernmental organizations generally with suspicion. Administration appointees tended to regard U.N. agencies as subverted by communism and socialism and as hostile to market economy, free enterprise, and the United States. Rhetoric in the U.N. General Assembly and in numerous U.N. conferences tended to be hostile to the United States in general and to Reagan principles in particular. Constructive work in many of the U.N. programs and specialized agencies was often obscured by the political maneuverings of socialist and Third World (that is, the poorer nations') delegations. Administration resentment of a perceived anti-American bias in U.N. organizations was reflected in official notice, late in 1983, to withdraw United States membership from United Nations Educational, Scientific, and Cultural Organization (UNESCO).

The foregoing characteristics of the Reagan administration go far to explain its generally negative appearance on international environmental issues. Negative positions were taken on new international initiatives, and retreat from prior commitments undertaken or threatened on economy-related environmental issues (for example, on U.S. exports); simultaneously international cooperation was generally (although erratically) permitted to continue when there was no conspicuous conflict with high-level administration ideology. The negative actions were featured by the news media, but the positive measures received little publicity and were not widely known.

Public perceptions of the Reagan international environmental policies were shaped by the conspicuous acts of Reagan appointees in the U.N. General Assembly, at the third U.N. Law of the Sea Conference, and in the 10th anniversary session of the United Nations Environment Programme. With the exception of his signature on a commendatory letter to the voluntary, nongovernmental International Union for Conservation of Nature and Natural Resources, the president's personal statements indicated a lack of interest in environmental issues. Efforts by leading environmental groups to establish communication with White House staff (for example, with Edwin Meese III, counselor to President Reagan) were ineffective.[11] Consequently, hostilities worsened between the Reagan people and environmental organizations, which by mid-1983 had identified Reagan rather than his lieutenants as their principal adversary. Whether the appointment of a new secretary of the interior and the departure of Edwin Meese from the White House would administration policy on environmental affairs was conjectural early in 1984; but some observers saw a more positive position emerging.

An International Environmental Indictment

In the *Washington Post* on April 25, 1983, staff writer Cass Peterson summarized the case against a Reagan administration that was alleged to be indifferent-to-hostile toward international cooperation in environmental protection: "Since Ronald Reagan became president, the United States has blocked, damaged or destroyed numerous international environmental efforts in a sometimes clumsy campaign to remove regulatory obstacles, domestic or international, from the paths of commerce." The article echoed an indictment prepared and published during the preceding year by 10 environmental and conservation organizations. The indictment was introduced by the assertion that

> President Reagan has broken faith with the American people on environmental protection. During his first 14 months in office, he and his appointed officials have simply refused to do the job that the laws require and that Americans expect of their government—to protect the public health from pollution and to use publicly owned resources and lands for the public good.[12]

With specific reference to the international environment, the indictment detailed 10 charges of executive malfeasance or nonfeasance. It largely concerned issues domestic in character. Only one page was given to international matters, but here the environmental organizations found "a few bright spots."

In retrospect, however, even the bright spots showed an uncertain luster. The administration was commended for taking an "excellent position" at the July 1981 meeting of the International Whaling Commission. Executive action in this instance was consistent with the official position of the United States after the United Nations Conference on the Human Environment in 1972, but, of course, the United States had no economic interest in whaling to defend. Nevertheless, the administration might have taken a neutral position or undertaken to bargain with Japan (one of the principal whaling states) for quid-pro-quo concessions in matters closer to the objectives of the Reagan economic program. So credit was given for positive action in the protection of whales.

A second bright spot, an interagency cosponsored conference in November 1981 on conserving the earth's biological diversity, is less clear. The conference had been planned for some months before Ronald Reagan assumed office. There would have been little advantage to the administration in stopping it. No influential business interest or economic group publicly opposed the effort, although the subject did hold implications for agribusiness, notably concerning the dissemination of patented germ plasm for hybrid plants, and efforts by James L. Buckley in the Department of State were necessary to keep the conference from being derailed.[13]

A third alleged bright spot was the Interagency Global Issues Working Group, established in September 1981 to discuss coordinated response to the population, resource, and environment issues raised by *Global*

2000. But to what purpose was this effort undertaken? Some observers regarded the working group as a good-faith effort to explore the policy implications of the report. But others, including persons within the administration, believed that the "coordinated response" sought by the White House staff was intended to be a refutation of the report. The latter assessment seems a more plausible explanation of the administration's tolerance of the effort. In contrast to Reagan's unofficial and often ad hoc philosophizing on the fallacies of environmentalism, *Global 2000* could be regarded, at least by implication, as serious and considered criticism of free market tendencies, economic growth, and the American way of life. It was an official publication of the U.S. government and as such required a response from an administration committed to a different view of the probable future. The CEQ was ostensibly the lead agency to coordinate the interagency analyses of the report, and CEQ Chairman Hill apparently intended the effort to be objective. But there was the Cabinet Council on Natural Resources and Environment to be reckoned with, whose chairman, James G. Watt, was the administration's most conspicuous "antienvironmentalist."

The anomalous handling of *Global 2000* within the Reagan administration illustrates the consequence of policy delegation and divided counsels on matters in which the president had no great personal concern. Ideological budget cutting stripped the CEQ of resources to undertake significant independent investigations. Hill, owing perhaps to his earlier California association with Reagan administrators, had been able to prevent a subordination of the CEQ to Reagan's principal environmental lieutenant, Secretary of Interior Watt. But Hill's moderation and independence tended to distinguish him within the administration. The EPA was more closely aligned with the antienvironmentalist staff associated with Watt and the Cabinet Council on Natural Resources and Environment. The principal EPA officer for international affairs was Richard Funkhouser, who was on the record as opposing *Global 2000*.[14]

Antienvironmentalists within the EPA appear to have contrived an arrangement whereby the interagency review of *Global 2000* would be undertaken by Julian Simon and Herman Kahn with funding provided by the Heritage Foundation. The outcome of such a review by outspoken opponents of the report was easily predictable. Whatever claim the administration might have to objectivity in consideration of the report would be lost. Alan Hill was unwilling to participate in turning a serious and critical study into an ideological exposé. Meanwhile, staff to the Cabinet Council on Natural Resources and Environment and EPA head Anne Gorsuch initially obstructed any objective review from within the government. In consequence the Heritage Foundation funded Simon and Kahn to produce their dissection of *Global 2000* without an official imprimatur.[15]

At a meeting of the Global Tomorrow Coalition (of environmental and futures organizations) in Washington on June 2, 1983, CEQ Chairman Hill reported briefly on progress of the interagency study, emphasizing the need for better forecasting of trends—a requirement that since 1970 had been implicit in Section 204 of NEPA. In his address Hill set forth the philosophic position underlying the administration's specific actions concerning international environmental issues. Arguing that America retained leadership in global environmental affairs, he declared:

> While there is general agreement on our basic objectives, there is a lesser degree of consensus on the best way to achieve those objectives. I'm concerned that a few believe the *only* path to a quality environment is by massive intervention by a powerful government. Our administration believes there's a better way, and that asserting America's leadership requires consideration of those concepts.
>
> We clearly stated our belief in the *Global Environmental* principles adopted by the Administration last year. In that document we said, "Individual ownership of property, free and well-developed markets in products and capital are powerful incentives for resource conservation." This principle is "the better way." [Hill's emphasis] [16]

With the change of command at EPA following the resignations of Administrator Anne Burford (formerly Gorsuch) and International Affairs Office Director Richard Funkhouser, and with the publication under other auspices of the Simon-Kahn critique, the interagency study of *Global 2000* was able to move forward. Its outcome and reception at the White House could not be foreseen as of early 1984. Meanwhile, however, the actions of the Reagan administration presented a confusing but generally negative picture.

Down to Cases: Environmental Policy Specifics

Six policy issues will be reviewed here in which the Reagan administration appeared to reverse or reinterpret prior positions or commitments of the United States on international environmental issues.

Transboundary Air Pollution: Acid Rain. On August 5, 1980, the governments of Canada and the United States signed a memorandum of intent that committed each country to take measures to reduce atmospheric contamination coming largely from coal-fired furnaces and resulting in the deposition of acidic fallout in the northeastern states and Canada. The causes and effects of acid deposition have been thoroughly treated elsewhere and need not be recounted here; biotic impoverishment of lakes and streams and damage to crops and forests have been major consequences. The apparent backing off by the Reagan administration from the United States's earlier commitment to take measures to abate the sulfur dioxide and nitrogen oxide emissions from coal-fired furnaces was an alleged reversal of international policy on acid rain.

Consistent with the administration's promise to ease governmental burdens on the private sector of the economy and an apparent lack of interest in environmental issues, Reagan spokesmen declared that more research was needed before major efforts would be required of industry to abate sulfate emissions. The administration opposed strengthening of the Clean Air Act to mandate control measures and sought to weaken controls in the existing law limiting sulfur emissions from new plants *(see Chapter 11)*. The administration favored changes in the Clean Air Act to extend deadlines for meeting sulfur dioxide abatement standards, while research on the causes and effects of acid rain continued. The administration allowed an increase in sulfur dioxide emissions of 1.5 million tons per year. It also reversed a requirement proposed under the Carter administration that power plants with tall smokestacks must reduce sulfur dioxide emissions by 412,000 tons per year.[17] Under the Reagan administration the EPA required a reduction of only 166,800 tons per year. Although the administration did increase funding for acid rain research, some scientists expressed fears that the research would be concentrated into periods of time too short to reveal the full effects of acid rain, which may require as much as a decade to become manifest. The problem was obviously complex and adequate research very belated. But the problem was nonetheless urgent, being a major international issue in Western Europe as well as in North America.[18]

Although sulfur dioxide emissions originate on both sides of the U.S.-Canadian border, by far the greater (although unspecified) amount is generated in the United States. Canadians interpreted signals from Washington to mean that the administration would delay any real implementation of the memorandum of intent. When Reagan made his first presidential visit to Canada in March 1981, he was greeted in Ottawa by an angry crowd brandishing signs protesting acid rain. Professor John Carroll of the University of New Hampshire declared in his study of U.S.-Canadian environmental diplomacy that environmental conflict, of which acid rain is probably the most critical issue, could become a greater source of transboundary friction than traditional political and economic relations.[19]

It cannot fairly be said that the Reagan administration actually reversed the commitment to abate acid rain, but it seems clear that the commitment of the U.S. government to do so significantly declined in priority as contrasted with "reindustrialization," the promotion of economic growth, and the reduction of government regulations affecting the private sector. But circumstances sometimes change presidential priorities. The scandals that followed one after another in the EPA during the first quarter of 1983 appear to have shaken the administration. Reagan called the first administrator of the EPA, William D. Ruckelshaus, back to the agency as administrator and at the ceremony in which the new EPA chief was sworn into office, the president singled out acid rain as the first priority of a reformed and revitalized agency. How far this apparent change in policy will be carried remains to be seen. The current release of a number of science-based reports on the issue, however, underscored its reality and importance.[20] Evasion of the issue or downplaying of its significance no longer appeared to be feasible options for the Reagan administration.

Of less immediate urgency, but of major ultimate significance, is the effect of the buildup of carbon dioxide in the earth's atmosphere. Upon coming into office the Reagan people dismissed the nonpolitical head of the research program on the effects of carbon dioxide in the earth's atmosphere, which had been established during the previous administration in the Department of Energy. In contrast to the opinions of a large number of atmospheric scientists and climatologists in the United States and in other countries, the Reagan administration, if it has a position on carbon dioxide in the atmosphere, does not appear to regard the issue as a presently serious agenda item.

Convention on the Law of the Sea. Since the year 1958, when the first United Nations Law of the Sea Conference (UNCLOS) convened in Geneva, the nations of the world have sought to bring some general legal order to that 72 percent of the earth's surface covered by the oceans. The effort has been slow, halting, and at times acrimonious. The issues have been complex and the interests that the various nations have in the oceans differ widely, as do their capabilities for utilizing the oceans for economic purposes.

Treaties for the conservation of living resources of the sea (for example, fisheries) and prevention of pollution (for example, ocean dumping) were adopted during the 1970s, usually with strong support from the United States. Boundary issues and economic rights of coastal and landlocked states remained troublesome, however, and were prominent in UNCLOS negotiations. In 1967 the Maltese delegate to the U.N. General Assembly proposed that the bed of the deep sea and mineral deposits therein be treated as the "heritage of mankind" and that their exploitation be supervised by a United Nations agency, with revenues allocated in part to the economic development of the poorer countries.[21] The United States, in principle, supported the proposal.

In 1981, after 10 years of labor, the third United Nations Law of the Sea Conference reached general agreement upon a draft treaty. This event, however, coincided with the coming into office of the Reagan administration. The American delegation to the Law of the Sea Conference, headed by a prominent Republican, Elliot Richardson, was summarily dismissed and a new delegation appointed for the purpose of reassessing America's position on the treaty and vigorously opposing the provision that would have internationalized control over deep-sea mining. Some months passed during 1981 and 1982 before the administration could decide on the official position it would take. Although the United States signed the resolution authorizing the Law of the Sea Treaty, the American representative declined to sign the actual document at official ceremonies held at Montego Bay, Jamaica, on December 10, 1982.[22]

Not only did the United States decline to sign the treaty, but it also persuaded some of its close allies, notably the United Kingdom, West Germany, France, and Japan, to abstain, although subsequently France and Japan did sign. By early May 1983, 125 countries had signed the treaty. Some of the signatories lacked the economic or technical or military power to play an effective role in treaty implementation. But the United States, a major power in oceanic affairs and a major mover for such a treaty, declined to participate in its implementation although most of its provisions were uncontested.

The Reagan administration had no real objection to the greater part of the treaty, but it opposed control of deep-sea mining by a multinational authority called "The Enterprise," an agency that would license seabed mining and distribute profits (if any) and in which the United States would not necessarily have a voice. The Reagan people saw the future of private enterprise in the sea rendered uncertain and probably onerous by an international bureaucracy controlled by socialist governments of the Third World. Although some concessions were made at the conference to make the treaty acceptable to the U.S. delegation, the basic premise of international ownership and control was clearly contrary to the Reagan principle of "individual ownership of property" and "free and well-developed markets in products and capital."

Control of Trade in Hazardous Substances. As a result of growing concern in the United States and abroad over the export of pesticides, herbicides, and other potentially toxic or hazardous materials from industrialized countries to the Third World, President Carter on January 15, 1981, issued Executive Order 12264 "on federal policy regarding the export of banned or significantly restricted substances." This action was taken because it was not considered good policy for the United States to export to other countries materials that were severely restricted or banned at home. Resentment was growing in Third World countries over this practice. Governments in many Third World countries are not subject to popular control or to influence by scientists, environmentalists, or public health experts. Ineffective public administration and the susceptibility of some public officials to "considerations" have made many countries vulnerable to the "dumping" of banned or restricted materials from the industrialized world, and this despite protest by concerned citizens in both developed and less developed countries.[23]

On February 17, 1981, shortly after taking office, Reagan rescinded Carter's Executive Order 12264. The administration's position was that the United States should not tell other nations how to order their public affairs. If a country does not wish to have pesticides, herbicides, pharmaceuticals, and other products of dubious safety imported, the administration argued, that country should restrict or prohibit them itself and not rely upon the United States to be its policeman. When the issue of international trade in hazardous substances came before the General Assembly of the United Nations in January 1983, the United States cast the one dissenting vote; all the other nations represented in the General Assembly voted for the measure (146 to 1).[24]

Meanwhile the Reagan administration, represented by EPA's Funkhouser, was alleged to have delayed and obstructed negotiation sponsored by the Organization for Economic Cooperation and Development (OECD) among western industrialized nations regarding regulation of toxic substances in international commerce.[25] The issue was of great concern to European states, whose need to control the transborder flow of toxic chemicals was becoming urgent. Scandals, such as the mystery of the missing barrels of dioxin from the cleanup of a chemical plant explosion in Italy, dramatized the problem, which of course had many other dimensions. A subcommittee of the House Committee on Science and Technology, which was investigating charges of collusion between Funkhouser and officials of the Dow Chemical Co. in relation to adoption of an international chemical testing agreement, heard allegations of improprieties in the role of EPA in these negotiations. What may have been an overzealous effort to carry out what he believed to be the president's policies put Funkhouser in bad standing with the Department of State and with the Congress and led to his subsequent resignation during the 1983 reorganization of EPA.

International Sale of Nuclear Materials. The Reagan administration, reversing a previous U.S. policy of restricting trade in fissionable material, such as uranium, suitable for use in nuclear weapons, adopted a policy of promoting nuclear exports.[26] The reason for this switch appeared to be the need to maintain a viable nuclear industry in the United States. Public opposition to nuclear energy and to the construction and operation of nuclear reactors has been growing in the United States, and it therefore seems doubtful that any significant extension of a domestic nuclear energy industry can be anticipated in the foreseeable future. Consequently, to maintain a nuclear industry for military purposes, the administration apparently thought it desirable to cultivate foreign markets to replace or offset diminished opportunities at home.

Financial Support for International Programs. Under general policy commitments and treaty provisions, and in accordance with NEPA, the United States has made significant financial contributions to various international environmental protection efforts. The Reagan administration has sought to reverse or scale down these commitments. It proposed eliminating U.S. contributions to the World Heritage Convention for the protection of natural areas of unique importance, although the concept of the World Heritage fund and program originated in the United States and was advocated by prominent conservative Republicans. The administration also proposed to reduce U.S. funding for the United Nations Environment Programme by 80 percent in fiscal 1982. (Indeed, it was rumored that the administration would have preferred to eliminate the contribution entirely.) Although Congress refused to accept the administration's budget recommendations for so radical a reduction of the UNEP contribution, the funds were cut severely nevertheless. The administration also cut off funding for the UNESCO-sponsored Man and the Biosphere program.[27] As with the UNEP appropriation, efforts were made in Congress to restore the budget cuts. Clearly, however, the administration placed very low priority on this form of international scientific cooperation. In late 1983 the administration gave notice of intent to withdraw the United States from UNESCO. How, or if, the United States would subsequently assist nonpolitical scientific programs sponsored by UNESCO was not evident in early 1984.

Although concerned about the spread of social unrest and communism in the Caribbean, the United States under the Reagan administration refused to provide funds for a major regional cooperation program to reduce pollution in the Caribbean.[28] European countries, including France and the United Kingdom (perhaps with less at stake in the long run in the Caribbean), have been contributing to the program. Finally, the administration threatened to drastically reduce U.S. support for international population programs, but was prevented from doing so by public outcry and the unwillingness of Congress to consent.[29]

United Nations World Charter for Nature. The U.N. General Assembly adopted the World Charter for Nature on October 28, 1982, by a vote of 111 with 18 abstentions and the United States casting the single negative vote.[30] Once again, as in the cases of the Law of the Sea Treaty and the export of hazardous materials, the Reagan administration took the position of the United States versus the rest of the world. The charter idea originated with an address by President Mobutu of Zaire to the 12th General Assembly of the International Union for Conservation of Nature and Natural Resources (IUCN), which met in Kinshasa in September 1975. A draft charter by which "all human conduct affecting nature must be guided and judged" was adopted by the IUCN and endorsed by the Organization of African Unity (OAU). The OAU sponsorship attracted further support from the nonaligned nations, the so-called Group of 77, representing the less-developed or Third World countries. The Soviet bloc joined in support, possibly to demonstrate solidarity with the Third World. The European Community, although regretting some of the imperative wording in the English language draft of the charter, nevertheless voted for it in principle. Abstaining nations included members of the Treaty of Amazonian Coopera-tion, led by Brazil, whose objections related to the principle of absolute national sovereignty over natural resources.[31]

The administration's position appeared to be less opposed to the objectives of the treaty than to the language of the text, which the U.S. delegation regarded as incapable of implementation. It is plausible, however, to believe that ideological considerations underlay the Reagan position on this as on many other international environmental issues. The president and his closest advisers appear to see the world much as it was probably seen by Dwight D. Eisenhower, perhaps even by Calvin Coolidge. A half-century of scientific findings and of changing perceptions of relationships between mankind and its natural environment seems beyond their self-limited range of vision.

Conclusions

The Reagan administration's international environmental policies are intelligible largely in the context of its effort to return the government of the United States, in principle, to something resembling its pre-World War II condition—the magnitude of the military establishment excepted. The admin-istration's ideology is more properly described as Reaganism than Republi-canism, in view of its strong preference for things private over things public.

Ronald Reagan and his advisers appear to have a profound distrust for *res publica* and have tried wherever possible to privatize activities undertaken by government that might be performed in the private sector.

Whether Reagan's policies will seriously affect the international environmental movement is not yet clear. Withdrawal of the United States from a position of leadership on international environmental issues actually might strengthen environmental commitments elsewhere. For many reasons, there is worldwide resentment today against the U.S. government's global environmental policies. In 1972 many Third World leaders distrusted international environmental protection efforts as a subterfuge to discourage economic development in their countries. The United States was suspected of ulterior motives in its vigorous support of international environmental initiatives. A decade later the circumstances were nearly reversed.

During the 1960s and 1970s American presidents (or highly placed officials) spoke forcibly for international environmental cooperation. Whatever their reasons, Johnson, Nixon, and Carter wished to be perceived as supportive of international cooperative efforts, and during their presidencies, the U.S. government generally supported and often initiated international environmental cooperative proposals. During the early 1980s, in contrast, international initiatives came from Asian and African leaders (for example, Tolba of Egypt, Mobutu of Zaire, Bunbei Hara of Japan, and Koh of Singapore), and it was U.S. representatives who suspected that global environmental proposals were surreptitious attempts to thwart the growth of the American economy.[32]

The impact of Ronald Reagan's administration on global environmental cooperation has been largely negative. Reagan's personal views on environmental issues at home and abroad have never been clear—perhaps because he has never had very clear views on environmental matters and does not believe that environmental issues are as important as his critics think. His apparent lack of knowledge and interest in environmental and scientific affairs is evident. It is a dangerous deficiency all too common in twentieth-century political leaders and will become more dangerous as technology overreaches human self-discipline, foresight, and restraint. Nevertheless, Reagan has demonstrated a capacity to learn from experience and to change the direction of policy without appearing to do so. Thus, this assessment of the international environmental policies of the Reagan administration should be read as an interim report. A conclusive evaluation must await future events.

Notes

1. Erwan Fouere, "Clashing Over the Environment," *Europe* 237 (May-June 1983): 12-15.
2. See Lester W. Milbrath, "Environmental Values and Beliefs of the General Public and Leaders in the United States, England and Germany," in *Environmental Policy Formation: The Impact of Values, Ideology and Standards,* ed. Dean E. Mann (Lexington, Mass.: Lexington Books, 1981), 43-61; also Peter Ester, "Environmental Concern in the Netherlands," in *Progress in Resources Management and Environ-*

mental Planning, vol. 3, ed. T. O'Riordan and R. Kerry Turner (New York: Wiley, 1981), 81-108.

3. Philip Shabecoff, "U.S. Tells Ecology Parley to Trust Free Enterprise," *New York Times,* May 12, 1982. Gorsuch declared that "the United States shall continue to support sound international environmental practices," but her credibility was diminished by action taken (or not taken) in Washington.

4. For example, see Vincent Ostrom and Elinor Ostrom, "Public Choice: A Different Approach to the Study of Public Administration," *Public Administration Review* 31 (March-April 1971): 203-216; Fred R. Glahe and Dwight R. Lee, "The Economic Analysis of Political Decision Making," in *Microeconomics: Theory and Applications* (New York: Harcourt Brace Jovanovich, 1981); and Norman Furniss, "The Political Implications of the Public Choice Property Rights School," *American Political Science Review* 72 (June 1978): 399-410.

5. Anne Gorsuch, statement for the press, May 11, 1982, 7-8.

6. Lynton K. Caldwell, *In Defense of Earth: International Protection of the Biosphere* (Bloomington: Indiana University Press, 1972), 133.

7. Ibid.

8. See Richard D. Lyons, "Oceanic Experts Favor New Laws: Meeting Here Backs Global Curbs to Guard Resources," *New York Times,* December 28, 1967.

9. See Francis M. Allegra, "Executive Order 12114—Environmental Effects Abroad; Does It Really Further the Purpose of NEPA?" *Cleveland State Law Review* 29, no. 1 (1980): 109-139; U.S. Department of Justice, "Assessment of Extraterritorial Environmental Impacts under NEPA and Executive Order 12114," *Land and Natural Resources Division Journal* 17 (September-October 1980): 2-12; Dick Kirschten, "Exporting the Environment," *National Journal,* February 25, 1980, 318. See also Nicholas Yost, "American Governmental Responsibility for the Environmental Effects of Actions Abroad," *Albany Law Review* 43 (Spring 1979): 528-537; and Charles N. Brower, "Is NEPA Exportable?" 43 (Spring 1979): 513-519.

10. Council on Environmental Quality and the Department of State, *The Global 2000 Report to the President: Entering the Twenty-First Century,* 3 vols. (Washington, D.C.: U.S. Government Printing Office, 1980). The complete report has been reprinted in a single volume by Penguin Books, 1982.

11. Russell Peterson, "The Audubon View: No Common Ground," *Audubon Magazine* 48, no. 2 (March 1982): 107.

12. *Ronald Reagan and the American Environment: An Indictment,* prepared by Friends of the Earth, Natural Resources Defense Council, The Wilderness Society, Sierra Club, National Audubon Society, Environmental Defense Fund, Environmental Policy Center, Environmental Action, Defenders of Wildlife, and Solar Lobby (Andover, Mass.: Brick House Publishing, 1982), 6. References to this report are cited not as evidence of the acts in question, but merely as a source of the charge.

13. *Proceedings of the U.S. Strategy Conference on Biological Diversity—November 16-18, 1981* (Washington, D.C.: U.S. Department of State Publication 9262, April 1982).

14. See testimony of Richard Funkhouser in *Review of the Global Environment 10 Years after Stockholm,* Hearings before the Subcommittee on Human Rights and International Organizations of the Committee on Foreign Affairs, House of Representatives, 97th Cong., 2d sess., March 30, April 1 and 20, 1982 (Washington, D.C.: U.S. Government Printing Office, 1982), 290-317.

15. See *Global 2000 Revised* (Washington, D.C.: Heritage Foundation, 1983), introduction by Julian L. Simon and Herman Kahn. An interagency assessment of *Global 2000* and its implications was submitted to President Carter in January 1981, based on reports from 19 federal agencies: *Global Future; Time to Act. Report to the President on Global Resources, Environment and Population* (Washington, D.C.:

Government Printing Office, January 1981). For analysis of these reports and the issues they raise, see Constance Holden, "Simon and Kahn versus Global 2000," *Science* 221 (July 22, 1983): 341-343.

16. "Global Sustainability and United States Policy: The Administration View," a press release by the Honorable A. Alan Hill, chairman, Council on Environmental Quality, to the Global Tomorrow Conference, Washington, D.C., June 2, 1983, 1-2.

17. *Ronald Reagan and the American Environment,* 9.

18. A timely and comprehensive source of information on the acid rain issue in Europe is *Acid News: A Newsletter from the Swedish and Norwegian NGO Secretariats on Acid Rain.* See also *Acidification,* published in English, German, and Swedish by the Swedish Ministry of Agriculture.

19. John E. Carroll, *Environmental Diplomacy: An Examination of Canadian-U.S. Transboundary Environmental Relations* (Ann Arbor: University of Michigan Press, 1983), 263-266; "Fists Across the Undefended Border," *Maclean's,* May 2, 1983, 49.

20. For an analysis of these reports, see "News and Comment," *Science* 221 (July 15, 1983): 241-242, 254.

21. Caldwell, *In Defense of Earth,* 137-138.

22. See Bernard D. Nossiter, "Sea Law Signed by 117 Nations; U.S. Opposes It; 46 Countries Also Refuse to Back Treaty," *New York Times,* late edition, December 11, 1982.

23. *Export of Hazardous Products,* Hearings before the House Subcommittee on International Economic Policy and Trade of the Committee on Foreign Affairs, 96th Cong., 2d sess., June 5, September 9 and 12, 1980. See also Barry I. Castleman, "The Export of Hazardous Factories to Developing Countries," *International Journal of Health Services* 9, no. 4 (1979): 569-606; Robert Richter, "Pills and Pesticides: For Export Only," parts I and II, Transcript of Television Broadcast on Public Broadcasting Service, October 7, 1981; Ruth Norris, ed., *Pills, Pesticides, and Profits: The International Trade in Toxic Substances* (Aurora, Ill.: Caroline House, 1982); and R. Jeffrey Smith, "Hazardous Products May Be Exported," *Science* 216 (June 18, 1982): 1301.

24. Libby Bassett, "U.N. Votes to Protect People from Harmful Imports," *World Environment Report* 9 (January 15, 1983): 1-2. See also U.N. General Assembly, "Report of the Economic and Social Council: Protection Against Products Harmful to Health and Environment," A/C./37/L.65/ Rev. 1, December 7, 1982.

25. See Fouere, "Clashing Over the Environment," 13-14; and Cass Peterson, "Facing House Investigation EPA Official Offers to Quit," *Washington Post,* May 1, 1983, A5.

26. *Ronald Reagan and the American Environment,* 30.

27. The U.S. Man and the Biosphere Program was the inadvertent victim of administration budget cutting aimed at UNESCO. See *World Environment Report* 9 (March 15, 1983): 1-2.

28. Ibid, 35; Lawrence Mosher, "Maybe Later, U.S. Says in Response to Bid for Caribbean Cleanup Funds," *National Journal* May 2, 1981, 783-784.

29. *Ronald Reagan and the American Environment,* 35.

30. Libby Bassett, "U.N. Votes to Adopt World Nature Charter," *World Environment Report* 8 (November 30, 1982): 2-3.

31. For an illustration of the awkwardness of the United States in the General Assembly debate on the charter, see U.N. General Assembly, "Consideration and Adoption of the Revised World Charter for Nature," Agenda Item 21, Provisional Verbatim Record of the Forty-Eighth Meeting, New York, October 28, 1982, A/37/PV.48, 87-90.

32. The contrast in leadership roles was noted by Maurice F. Strong, who had been secretary general of the 1972 U.N. conference in Stockholm. In a news conference in

Nairobi at the 10th anniversary commemoration of Stockholm, Strong remarked: "It is quite clear that the United States' role at this meeting is in stark contrast to its leadership role in Stockholm." He added: "It is quite significant that the Japanese have chosen to take the lead." From Shabecoff, "U.S. Tells Ecology Parley to Trust Free Enterprise."

Part IV

EVALUATION AND SUMMARY

16. REAGANOMICS AND THE ENVIRONMENT: AN EVALUATION

Edwin H. Clark II

President Ronald Reagan's economic policies have been at least as radical as his environmental policies. Entitled "supply side" economics by its proponents, "voodoo" economics by some of its detractors, and "Reaganomics" by the press, the plan was supposed to stimulate a large increase in private investment, which, so the theory went, would generate increased economic growth while simultaneously reducing inflation. The major components of the program were substantial tax cuts (particularly for businesses and high-income taxpayers), massive reductions in the federal budget (except for defense expenditures, which were increased significantly), and an attempt to free businesses from government regulation. The public responsibility for the last of these was assigned to Vice President George Bush, whom the president appointed as head of a regulatory reform task force.

Environmental regulations were a major target of this regulatory relief effort. Under the new administration, environmental policies seemed to be evaluated more in terms of their contribution to the economic program than their contribution to environmental quality.[1] Thus, one question that arises in reviewing the administration's record is how much its environmental regulatory relief efforts have contributed and will continue to contribute to the economy's apparent resurgence, and at what environmental cost. But this is not the only link between the economy and the environment. Other aspects of the economic program also have potentially significant impacts upon environmental quality. The interplay between economic and environmental policies is the subject of this chapter.[2]

In assessing this interplay, it is important to distinguish between the theoretical reasons for undertaking a policy and the policy's actual effects. They may differ substantially. First of all, it is necessary to understand what the policies have been and why they were adopted. The Reagan administration has not particularly aided this understanding, having provided remarkably few coherent statements of what its policies are in either the economic or the environmental realms.[3] Apparently, the theory of the economic program was most eloquently summarized in some sketches on a restaurant napkin (although the proponents of the new supply side economics vigorously deny that this is the program that was actually implemented). But the environmental policies do not even have the support of a dirty napkin. The few efforts by the administration to articulate these policies have been neither elucidating (they usually involve little more than a vague statement that the president and his appointees are in favor of protecting the environment) nor particularly consistent with the actions that the administration has taken.

The problem of identifying and rationalizing the policies is, however, relatively easy compared with the problem of evaluating what their effects have been. The fact that there have been two radical policies introduced together makes it extremely difficult to gain a coherent perspective on how the one has interacted with the other. And the short time that has elapsed since their adoption, combined with the economic and environmental confusion that the country has experienced over this period, makes a systematic empirical assessment virtually impossible.

Nevertheless, recognizing all the difficulties, this chapter attempts to present both the theoretical and the empirical assessments. The following section focuses on the administration's environmental policies, identifying those that appear to have the potential for creating economic impacts, describing what one might expect these impacts to be, and then attempting to determine what effect they actually have had or will have. The next section provides a similar analysis for Reagan's major economic policies.

The Environmental Program's Economic Effects

Do environmental policies significantly affect economic conditions? Since the major increase in federal environmental programs in the early 1970s, this question has been debated intensely.[4] With Reagan's election, however, the debate ended—or at least became irrelevant. The new administration did not ask the question because it was sure it knew the answer: yes, they do. Thus, it was not a matter of discussing and analyzing what the effects were or where they came from, but rather of implementing programs that would substantially reduce or eliminate them.

Environmental Policies

Although there is no clear set of environmental policies adopted for economic reasons, we have identified six as potentially most important. We will consider the kinds of effects that theoretically might be expected from each policy and then analyze what their actual influence has been.

Reduced Stringency of Standards. Theoretically, relaxing environmental standards should reduce the cost of all business activities affected by these standards. Such cost reductions could produce a number of economic benefits. Goods could be produced more cheaply leading to increased sales and higher profits. The increased profits would attract more investment, leading to greater economic growth.

The cheaper products also would help lower the rate of inflation. In turn, reduced inflation could stimulate additional investment and economic growth. A successful program to relax standards could eliminate much of the uncertainty about how stringent the standards would be, thus again promoting more investment. Finally, such a policy could make American products more competitive in foreign trade, providing yet another economic stimulus.

All of these arguments made the relaxation of environmental regulations seem the most important item on the environmental-economic agenda.

Increased Regulatory Analysis. One way of ensuring that proposed regulations are not so stringent that they might interfere with the economic agenda is to subject them to rigorous analysis before they are issued. Thus the regulatory review process, instituted under previous presidents, was substantially expanded—both in terms of the extent of the economic analyses that were required and in terms of the amount of power the Office of Management and Budget (OMB) exercised over how stringent the final regulations would be *(see Chapter 8)*.

The regulatory analysis requirements also had the advantage of substantially delaying new regulatory efforts. The analyses could take years to complete (the delay being exacerbated by reductions in agency personnel) and consume a significant amount of the agency's financial and staff resources. And if these delays did not suffice, and the new managers could not ensure that only relatively lax regulations would be proposed (for instance, because of unassailable statutory requirements), OMB seemed to have an almost unlimited authority to delay a regulation by sending it back to the issuing agency for further analysis.

Reduced Enforcement. The policies of relaxed standards and increased regulatory analysis might adequately avoid future problems, but they did little to reduce the effects of existing regulations. What could be done about them? One obvious answer was not to enforce them. If businesses could be confident that pollution control regulations, for instance, would not be enforced, they could save money by not operating their pollution control equipment. These cost savings should have the same economic impacts as a reduction in the stringency of the regulations. True, many of these businesses already had made the expensive investments required to conform to the regulatory requirements and had to pay for these investments regardless of enforcement policy. But the savings in operation and maintenance costs would not be inconsequential.[5] And the reductions in inspections and other enforcement activities also could lessen potential disruptions and allow the managers to focus on other aspects of the firm's operations.

"Privatization" and Accelerated Leasing of Natural Resources. Accelerating the sale and leasing of government-owned natural resources also could provide some economic stimulus, even though the push for "privatization" was probably based more on conservative ideology than on an assessment of likely economic benefits.

The accelerated leasing and sale of natural resources would be expected to lower their price. The price of products made from these resources would then drop, thereby reducing inflation and increasing the profits of those firms able to purchase the cheaper resources. For instance, the accelerated leasing of coal would drive down the lease price, making the coal less expensive, thereby reducing the cost of generating electricity from coal-fired power plants. The lower cost of electricity, then, could ease production costs for businesses in general.

These benefits probably would not occur immediately, however, and they might not occur in the form of lower prices. For instance, if one company already had a monopoly on the resource and also acquired the new sales or leases, then the beneficial effects would be substantially delayed and would quite possibly only occur in the form of higher future profits for that company.

Environmental Research and Information. One of the president's major goals was to reduce federal budgets for domestic programs *(see Chapter 6)*. The environmental agencies were particularly hard hit, and within the environmental agencies research efforts seemed to be a prime target. For instance, the research budget in the Environmental Protection Agency (EPA) was cut by almost half—twice as much as the rest of the agency. (After adjusting for inflation, the real reduction was by two-thirds.)[6] At Interior, the Office of Water Resources Research was abolished and research funds reduced by substantial amounts.[7]

Along with the budget cuts, the Reagan administration substantially reduced the amount of information gathered on environmental problems and rapidly eliminated many public information services.[8] Again, it is difficult to know to what extent these actions simply reflected the administration's ideology, to what extent they represented the personal approaches of particular appointees, and to what extent they were a part of the administration's economic program. To the extent they were the last of these, their economic rationale would appear to be primarily that additional knowledge and public information would make it more difficult to implement the other policies, though we should not expect to see such a rationale clearly articulated. In other words, an economic rationale might be that additional knowledge and public information would make implementation of the other policies more difficult.

Emphasis on the Free Market. A major tenet of the administration's ideology is that the free market can make the best decisions about how resources should be used. This view (not entirely limited to this administration) justifies many of the policies previously discussed, such as "privatization" and reduced data collection. For instance, in its proposed amendments to regulations on "dredge and fill" permits, the Corps of Engineers added a section eliminating any independent government assessment of the economic benefits of proposed private activities on wetlands, for "When private enterprise makes application for a permit, it will generally be assumed that appropriate economic evaluations have been completed and, therefore, the

Figure 16-1 Pollution Abatement and Control Expenditures, 1972-1979 (in 1972 constant dollars)

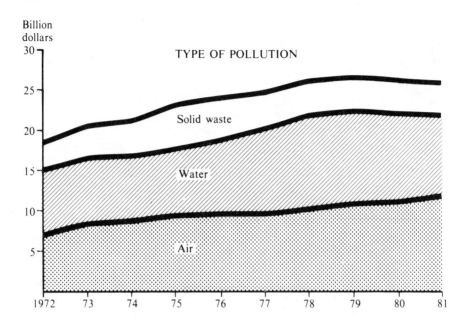

Billion
dollars

TYPE OF POLLUTION

Solid waste

Water

Air

1972 73 74 75 76 77 78 79 80 81

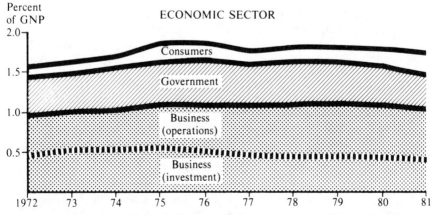

Percent
of GNP

ECONOMIC SECTOR

Consumers

Government

Business
(operations)

Business
(investment)

1972 73 74 75 76 77 78 79 80 81

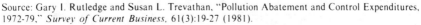

Source: Gary I. Rutledge and Susan L. Trevathan, "Pollution Abatement and Control Expenditures, 1972-79," *Survey of Current Business,* 61(3):19-27 (1981).

proposal is economically viable and there is a need for it in the market-place." [9]

Such a policy implicitly equates private profitability with social good. Presumably this is based on the assumption that anything increasing private profits furthers the nation's economic growth and thus benefits the administration's economic program.

An Evaluation

These were the various effects that the administration's environmental policies might theoretically be expected to have on the economy. Have these expectations been realized? The simple answer is, of course, no. During the first three years, little turned out as promised. The administration's economic policies were supposed to bring accelerated economic growth and increased employment along with reduced inflation rates. Inflation has been reduced, but for the rest, the major economic characteristic of the initial years of the Reagan administration was a severe recession. But how about the longer run? By the middle of 1983, the economy was pulling out of the recession. Will the environmental policies contribute to this period of growth?

To help answer this question, we will review some of the earlier efforts to evaluate the economic impact of environmental programs. Some of these evaluations by previous administrations even attempted to estimate how much the economy would benefit if environmental regulations were substantially relaxed in a manner such as the Reagan administration proposed. There is no question that the nation's environmental expenditures are large. The Bureau of Economic Analysis estimates that the nation spent $60.3 billion, or about 2 percent of its Gross National Product (GNP), on pollution control in 1981 (equivalent to about $26.4 billion in 1972 dollars).[10] Figure 16-1 shows the trends in these expenditures from 1972 through 1981. But the magnitude of the expenditures does not necessarily indicate that their impact is significant.

The most recent analysis of these impacts (completed in 1981), like most of those undertaken earlier, indicates that they have not been and would not be significant.[11] The programs have some economic impact, but it is much smaller and less serious than is often claimed *(see Figure 16-2)*. This analysis was based on a comparison between projected economic performance without pollution control programs and the actual and projected performance with the programs in effect.[12]

The study concluded that in 1981 the real GNP was 0.2 percent lower, the Consumer Price Index was increasing 0.5 percentage points faster, business fixed investment in constant dollars was 0.8 percent higher, and the unemployment rate was 0.3 percentage points lower with the programs than would have been the case without them. During the past 10 years, the real GNP has been slightly higher than it otherwise would have been because of the programs, but since 1976 it has been growing at a slower rate, and after 1981 would probably fall slightly below the level it would have attained without the programs. Various measures of inflation are slightly higher because of pollution control programs throughout the entire analysis. Unem-

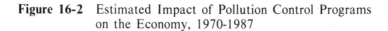

Figure 16-2 Estimated Impact of Pollution Control Programs
on the Economy, 1970-1987

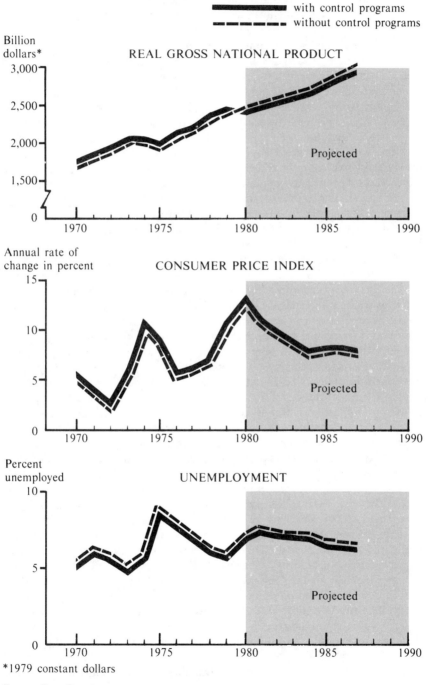

*1979 constant dollars

Source: Data Resources

ployment is lower by an average of 0.2 percentage points.

An earlier analysis of the same type attempted to predict the economic impacts of a rapid fall off in pollution control investment.[13] In this analysis expected expenditures were reduced to zero over a five-year period.[14] The results of this scenario are summarized in Table 16-1.

The economy is actually in worse shape during the first five years after the reduction in expenditures begins. At the end of five years (when new expenditures have fallen off to zero), the GNP (in constant dollars) is 0.6 percent lower, fixed investment in producer's durable equipment (in constant dollars) is 7.3 percent lower, and unemployment is 0.2 percent higher, respectively, then they are projected to be with pollution control expenditures continuing at the expected level. Eight years after the reduction begins, the economy is projected to be recovering from the policy change, with GNP only 0.2 percent lower, and the unemployment rate no higher than with the expenditures. The only measure that does better with the reduction in expenditures is inflation; the Consumer Price Index is 0.4 percent lower at the end of five years and 1.6 percent lower at the end of eight years. But this hardly represents a significant improvement.

The economic conditions and assumptions on which this scenario is based differ from those that existed during the early 1980s. Thus, the results are not directly transferable. However, it is not clear whether they would be better or worse if the analysis had been based on the actual conditions. In any case, this analysis is consistent with all the other macroeconomic analyses in indicating that pollution control programs were not the serious drag on the economy that the Reagan administration apparently believed them to be.[15]

Although such analyses represent the best that can be done with available information and analytical tools, they do not take into account some potentially important considerations. For instance, they do not completely reflect the impact of pollution control programs on industries that may be particularly affected by these programs. But here, too, evidence indicates that the impacts are less serious than many have claimed. For instance, in 1978 the Council on Environmental Quality (CEQ) reported that the iron and steel industry would have to invest $6.8 billion in 1975 dollars, equivalent to $9.9 billion in 1980 dollars, for air and water pollution control between 1975 and 1983.[16] A more recent EPA study based on a survey of firms estimated that the actual expenditures from 1974 to 1983 would be $8.5 billion in 1980 dollars, 14 percent less than the earlier estimate, which covered a shorter period.[17] CEQ reported that pollution control expenditures would consume 20 percent of total industry investment; EPA estimates that this proportion will be about 10 percent. Similarly, in 1978 CEQ reported that between 1975 and 1983 the pulp and paper industry would have to invest the equivalent of $9.4 billion (in 1980 dollars) for air and water pollution control.[18] A more recent EPA analysis indicates that from 1970 through 1983 these expenditures will amount to only $6.2 billion, a 34 percent decrease from the earlier estimate.[19]

Such direct comparisons are not available for other industries, but there

Table 16-1 Economic Impacts of Reduced Pollution Control Expenditures

Economic Measure	Effect 5 years later	Effect 8 years later
Gross National Product (constant dollars)	−0.6%	−0.2%
Fixed Investment in Producer's Durable Equipment (constant dollars)	−7.3	−2.5
Unemployment Rate	+0.2	0
Consumer Price Index	−0.4	−1.6

Source: Data Resources Inc., 1978

is substantial evidence that the same conclusion applies: the costs and impacts of pollution control regulation are often less than earlier estimates indicated. For instance, metal finishing was thought to be one of the most severely affected industrial categories, requiring investment of $460 million (in 1977 dollars) for water pollution control, with annual compliance costs of $129 million and forced closure of as many as 20 percent of the firms.[20] EPA now expects most firms to be able to adopt lower-cost control technologies, which in many cases provide the added benefit of allowing valuable metals to be captured and recycled.[21]

Thus, the analyses that have been completed suggest that the basic premise of the administration's environmental-economic programs was incorrect. At least insofar as can be measured by standard economic analytical tools, the programs have a very limited negative effect, and their relaxation would create an even smaller positive effect. But are the administration's programs likely to be able to capture even these small benefits? For a number of reasons it appears that their success will be very limited. In spite of some substantial efforts, the administration has not succeeded in actually relaxing many existing regulations, although it has prevented or at least delayed new regulations. But the cost of the regulations avoided was relatively small compared to the cost of all the regulations already in place, making the "benefits" the administration can claim very modest.

Even if the administration had succeeded in relaxing most regulations, the recession would have prevented firms from taking advantage of these changes. Gross private domestic investment fell off substantially—almost 13 percent from 1981 to 1982.[22] It is these new investments that would be most likely to benefit from regulatory relief.

Of course, investments for pollution control also have fallen off—even more rapidly than total investment. A survey in early 1983 indicated that real investment for pollution abatement plants and equipment would fall by about 25 percent between 1980 and 1983.[23] However, it is impossible to determine from the existing data whether the fall off during these years, even though it is the sharpest since such records began to be kept, has been any sharper than it would have been had the Reagan administration not been in office.

Similarly, the cutback in enforcement efforts may have created some economic benefits *(see Chapters 7-9)*. Although there are no good data on the extent to which reduced enforcement efforts have been reflected in increased noncompliance, it is probably safe to assume that there are more firms not complying with the regulations than there would have been under another administration. But the cost savings still may be limited (particularly in comparison with total production costs), although, as suggested in the following section, they may be sufficient to stimulate steadily increasing levels of noncompliance in the future. Such a trend clearly would have adverse environmental effects even if the economic benefits remained modest.

The only other element of environmental policy that might have significant economic benefit is the selling and leasing of publicly owned natural resources at very low cost. Again, this program is very unlikely to have had any short-term benefits. Because of the recession and an overall reduction in demand for energy and other natural resources, on top of the fact that firms already had substantial reserves on hand, the firms obtaining these low-cost leases had little opportunity to profit from them. To do so, they will have to wait, hoping that prices go up in the future. They then may have the opportunity to make significant profits. But in the meantime, the low-cost leases are unlikely to generate significant economic benefits.

Thus, the overall economic effect of the environmental policies is modest at best. It could even be negative. Many businessmen argue that what is most useful to stimulate investments is economic stability and reasonable certainty about what regulations they will have to satisfy. One thing that the Reagan administration has not created in its environmental policies is certainty. It has been unclear which regulations it intends to change; even when the particular regulation is clear, it is unclear what changes will be made. For instance, the administration attempted to relax the requirement for reducing the lead content in gasoline and instead ended up making it more stringent *(see Chapter 11)*. That is uncertainty.

Even when the administration finally issues a regulation, businesses cannot be confident that it will be upheld by the courts, or that state or local agencies will not take a more aggressive position in reaction to the federal re- laxation. Thus, uncertainty is both substantial and lasting. Finally, looking at the longer term, the radical relaxation of environmental regulations proposed by this administration—regardless of whether it did in fact occur—is highly likely to create a significant reaction. This reaction could be substantial enough to result in more stringent environmental regulations than if the administration had followed a more moderate course. In this case, of course, the results of the administration's efforts would be just the opposite of what they intended them to be.

Environmental Implications of Economic Programs

Although aggressively concerned with the economic implications of environmental policies, the Reagan administration seemed unconcerned, and perhaps even unaware, of the environmental implications of its economic program. The administration undertook vigorous efforts to reduce federal nondefense budget expenditures, presumably in the hope that the domestic budget could be cut sufficiently to compensate for the reduction in tax revenues and increases in defense expenditures, and to make room in the economy for the expected surge in private investment. This did not happen. The responsibility for reducing inflation and otherwise controlling the economy thus fell to the Federal Reserve Board. Independent of the executive branch and Congress, the "Fed" influences economic conditions by controlling the amount of money in the economy. It reduces inflationary pressures by reducing the money supply. The reduction in the money supply drives up interest rates, discouraging investment and thus reducing aggregate demand.

This somewhat simplistic summary of the economic program should suffice for analyzing the expected effects of these policies on the environment. But, as with environmental policies, it is necessary to assess whether the expected results did, in fact, occur and what the environmental implications of these policies are likely to be.

Expected Effects

The main rationale for the administration's economic program was that it would stimulate a substantial increase in private investment, which, because of technological advances, would result in a large increase in the availability of less expensive goods. This would help both to reduce inflation, since the surplus of cheaper goods would prevent prices from going up, and to create substantial employment opportunities.

In many respects a surge in private investment could be good for the environment. The largest areas of economic growth have been those industries, such as communication, finance, services, and wholesale and retail trade, that are not in themselves particularly damaging to the environment.[24] More environmentally damaging industries, such as manufacturing, transportation, agriculture, and mining, have been growing more slowly. Of course, not all growth in the manufacturing sector has been slow, and some of the faster growing industries—petroleum refining, chemicals, and even motor vehicles—can create serious environmental problems.

The environmental implications of these shifts, however, are generally positive. Even the growth in motor vehicles implies, at least in part, a substitution of less polluting newer vehicles for those that are already on the road. Similarly, investments in the dirtier industries tend to replace old, marginal facilities with newer, less polluting facilities. In general, one would expect higher efficiency and less pollution from a new steel mill than from one built 90 to 100 years ago.[25] New industries also tend to locate away from the center of older industrialized areas, which have experienced the most severe environmental degradation. Thus, even if there were no change in air pollution emissions, the substitution of a new plant in the suburbs for an old plant in the central city would result in an improvement in ambient air quality.

But this very fact demonstrates a potential environmental cost of accelerated investment. Because new plants will be located in new areas, they can accelerate the destruction of prime farmland, wetlands, and other natural areas and increase urban sprawl. About 3 million acres of forest, crop, pasture, or other types of land are transferred into urban uses every year.[26] And the shift will create increased difficulties for older urban areas in maintaining their economic and social viability.

On the whole, however, a program to stimulate new investment could have environmental benefits. But the magnitude of those benefits would depend upon the particular tools used to stimulate the investment. And here the policies adopted by the new administration appear less favorable than the program itself.

Tax reductions have been the major policy tool. The Economic Recovery Tax Act of 1981 was projected to leave an estimated $100 billion to $300 billion a year in the private sector (money that otherwise would have been collected in taxes) from 1983 to 1987.[27] This amount is many times larger than the savings in investment that could possibly be achieved by any reduction in environmental regulations. The direct environmental implications of this tax reduction are limited, but the social implications are significant. Although the evidence for savings and consumption patterns is unclear, assuming higher income individuals have a higher propensity to save additional income than those with lower incomes, the tax reduction has probably resulted in a smaller increase in consumption than would have occurred had the changes been more evenly distributed. This could be interpreted as having beneficial environmental implications.[28]

The second tool has been the aggressive effort to reduce federal government expenditures. The environmental implications of these budget cuts would depend, of course, on which programs and activities were cut. The federal government supports significant amounts of many environmentally destructive activities such as some water resource projects. Reducing expenditures on these would create environmental benefits. Its largest expenditures, however, are for social programs that have no direct effects on the environment. Reducing expenditures on these would create only indirect environmental impacts by affecting aggregate consumption levels. Finally, the federal government has been spending increasing amounts on environmentally beneficial activities such as pollution control programs.[29] Budget reductions here would have serious environmental implications.

The problem facing any administration attempting to make significant budget cuts is that there is only a small portion of the budget over which it has any real control, as Robert Bartlett points out in Chapter 6. Given the fact that most of the environmental protection programs were in this small part of the budget that is "discretionary," they were prime targets for large cuts, quite apart from any ideological considerations.

Another effort to offset the budgetary effects of the tax cut has involved the accelerated sale of federal resources and property. The administration projected more than $10 billion of increased revenues from accelerated leasing and sales of public property.[30] The environmental implications of such accelerated leasing and sales were likely to be negative. These negative effects, however, would be offset to the extent that the development and use of public resources substituted for development and use of private resources, depending on where the development was more environmentally damaging.

The implications of the third leg of the program—regulatory relief— were discussed in the previous section. They would be expected to be predominately negative.

An Evaluation

During its initial months, the administration's success in getting the new program adopted was phenomenal. Congress passed the largest tax cut in U.S. history and initially supported many of the proposed budget cuts. But the program soon bogged down. The administration was unable to identify the substantial amounts of waste that it claimed existed in the government and which it had proposed eliminating to help fund the program. It apparently had not realized how little discretion it had over the budget without amending existing statutes—and its efforts to enact such amendments met with little success. Thus, the budget cuts could not offset the tax cut and increased defense expenditures. This meant that the desired increase in private investment would have come on top of a seriously unbalanced federal budget. If the Federal Reserve Board had not stepped in and put the brake on the money supply, the result would have been a continuation and acceleration of the already high inflation rates.

The Fed's action succeeded in controlling inflation, but it served to nullify, at least in the short run, the administration's whole economic program. High interest rates—exceeding 20 percent for a period—substantially discouraged new investment, and the policy ended up creating the worst recession since the Depression of the 1930s. The economic record of 1980-1982 is certainly impressive—two recessions in two years (a new record), more people unemployed than at any time since the 1930s, record high interest rates, inflation rates higher than at any time since the end of World War II, and low rates of economic growth and productivity increase.[31] The anticipated spurt in investment never occurred.

Ironically, some environmental benefits did result. With the substantial fall off in industrial production, fewer pollution-creating facilities were in operation. EPA found in preparing its "National Air Quality Emissions Trends Report, 1975-1981" that an observed decrease in air pollution emissions could be explained predominantly by reduced industrial production.[32] For all major pollutants—sulfur dioxide, nitrogen dioxide, ozone, carbon monoxide, and particulates—the recession-induced decline in industrial production, energy consumption, and automobile driving was probably a major cause of reduced emissions.

Some of these reductions are likely to be permanent. The recession undoubtedly forced some older, highly polluting facilities permanently out of business. But smaller, growing businesses usually suffer the greatest mortality during such economic slowdowns, and there were record levels of business failures in 1981 and 1982.[33] There is no way of knowing what the long-term implications of these business failures will be. They could result in an absence of small, growing companies, or they could provide more opportunity for new entrepreneurs to substitute for those who have gone under. They could discourage innovation, or they could stimulate it. The actual effects will begin to appear only as the economy assumes a fairly vigorous growth rate.

On the other hand, there is relatively little question about the long-term environmental impacts of that part of President Reagan's program focused on regulatory relief and on reducing the federal budget. They are likely to have both a short-term and a long-term negative impact.

No matter what happens to the regulatory programs, there has been a hiatus. Problems that might have been dealt with were not. The net effect will most likely be a general delay in further environmental initiatives, with the magnitude of the environmental costs related to the length of delay and the seriousness of the environmental problems that remain unaddressed.

The administration's relaxation of enforcement could have an even more telling effect. In the past, EPA has relied on a very high degree of "voluntary" compliance—sometimes estimated as high as 95 percent.[34] This means that the agency could concentrate its limited enforcement activities on a relatively small proportion of firms. It probably will be more difficult to focus these activities so sharply and effectively in the future. Even if the reduction in enforcement effort had a relatively small impact on the extent of voluntary compliance—for instance, reducing it from 95 percent to 90 percent—that still would represent a doubling of EPA's enforcement load. The agency does not have the resources to handle such an increase. As a result, firms may recognize that their noncompliance will not stimulate rigorous enforcement efforts. If this is the case, it will increase the incentive for other firms not to comply with their permits, again increasing EPA's enforcement load and reducing the likelihood that any one firm will face enforcement action. This feedback mechanism—the more firms there are out of compliance, the less likely it will be that any firm will face enforcement action—obviously could generate significant environmental costs.

This problem is reinforced by the substantial budget cuts that the environmental agencies experienced during the first two years of the Reagan administration. Both because it was forced to and for ideological reasons, the Reagan administration focused many of its budget cuts on consumer and environmental protection activities. Those programs that were primarily concerned with helping the private sector were cut very little or even increased.

A particularly good example of this bias is provided by the administration's energy program *(see Chapter 10)*. EPA's efforts to evaluate the health and environmental effects of energy production and use were cut in half, the solar energy research efforts in the Department of Energy were to be cut 85 percent and the department's conservation efforts 97 percent.[35] At the same time, the administration proposed increasing expenditures on the construction of the Clinch River breeder reactor by 47 percent and on the development of fusion-based energy sources by 18 percent. It also agreed to more than $3 billion in loan guarantees for private synfuels projects.

These budget policies, combined with the hostility many of the new political appointees displayed toward government workers, forced many qualified, experienced people to leave the government. Even in the best of times, it would be hard to replace many of these experts, but it will be extremely difficult to replace them under the economic and budget conditions that the federal government faces in the foreseeable future. EPA's budget did not keep pace with its responsibilities during the 1970s, and the constraints are likely to be even tighter over the next decade. This, then, may be the most costly effect of the administration's economic policies in the long run.

Conclusions

By early 1984, neither President Reagan's environmental program nor his economic program had produced the results he promised. Although inflation seemed to be at least temporarily under control, the president had little else to boast about.

At the same time, there was little observable effect on the environment during the president's first three years. The air was, if anything, somewhat cleaner because of recession-induced decreases in driving and industrial production. Due to the delay that occurs between the time the government makes a decision and the physical actions that occur in response to that action, most of the adverse environmental effects of the administration's other policies will not be apparent for at least several years.

What about the future? The answer appears to be the same: the change in environmental programs is unlikely to benefit the economy much. Indeed, there seems to be relatively little reason to have ever expected it to do so. And there seems to be limited interest and perhaps even less opportunity to carry these efforts on into the future. One could conclude that the net effect of the whole program will be negligible.

But this is not entirely true. There have been some actions that may have serious long-term effects, both environmental and economic. One of these is the reduction in the ability of regulatory agencies such as EPA to carry out their statutory responsibilities. The administration has assured the nation of a continued budget problem that probably will prevent these agencies from acquiring the resources they need to do their job properly. And even if they were to acquire the financial resources, it could take many years for them to recreate the experienced staff they had been building over the previous decade.

But the environment will not be the only area to suffer. These reductions and other activities from 1981 to 1983 also may adversely affect private enterprise and could even slow economic growth. In the past, pollution control regulations often have been attacked as being too inflexible, but we may not have seen anything yet. Many members of the public and Congress believe that the Reagan administration has seriously abused what discretion it had under these laws. The natural reaction is to give the agencies even less flexibility in the future.[36]

In fact, one of the major casualties of this administration may well be the sincere efforts at "regulatory reform" that were initiated in previous administrations and are considered necessary by many observers on both sides of the issue. The administration failed to carry through with some of these reforms. Moreover, because regulatory reform was turned into "regulatory relief," any attempts to reintroduce reasonable reforms in the future are likely to be greeted with great suspicion.[37]

This failure may well be the most lasting legacy of the Reagan administration. The environment may suffer because constructive and workable reforms have been delayed. But private business and the economy could suffer more. In the end, it may be that instead of promoting increased economic growth at the cost of environmental degradation, the administration's policies have made the nation worse off in both respects.

Notes

1. Anne Gorsuch (later Burford) made this clear in her speech to the EPA staff, shortly after being sworn in as administrator, by emphasizing the fact that she was there to contribute to the president's economic program. She only referred to an obligation to protect the environment once or twice in passing.
2. For a fuller discussion of the environmental implications of various macroeconomic conditions, see The Conservation Foundation, *State of the Environment: 1982* (Washington, D.C.: The Conservation Foundation, 1982), 21-36.
3. For an official statement of the administration's economic policy, see Council of Economic Advisers, *Economic Report of the President: 1982* (Washington, D.C.: Government Printing Office, 1982). For a statement on the administration's environmental policy, see Council on Environmental Quality, *Environmental Quality 1981* (Washington, D.C.: Government Printing Office, 1983), chapter 1.
4. For a recent summary of these issues, see Henry M. Peskin et al., *Environmental Regulations and the U.S. Economy* (Baltimore: Johns Hopkins, 1981). The economics chapters in the Council on Environmental Quality's annual reports, *Environmental Quality,* also summarize the most recent analyses on economic impacts. Probably the best known analysis attacking the cost of regulatory efforts is that prepared by Murray

L. Weidenbaum for the Subcommittee on Economic Growth and Stabilization of the Joint Economic Committee, *The Cost of Environmental Regulation of Business,* Joint Committee Print, 95th Cong., 2d sess., 1978.

5. For nonfarm residential business, "current costs" began to exceed capital costs for the first time in 1981. Gary L. Rutledge and Susan Lease-Trevathan, "Pollution Abatement and Control Expenditures 1972-81," *Survey of Current Business* 63, no. 2 (1983): 15-23.

6. American Environmental Safety Council, Washington, D.C., June 1983.

7. Laurence Mosher, "Water, Water Everywhere," *National Journal* 14, no. 5 (1982): 207.

8. Probably the extreme manifestation of this approach was the proposal to sell the weather bureau.

9. 48 *Federal Register* 93 (May 12, 1983): 21,470.

10. Gary L. Rutledge and Susan Lease-Trevathan, "Pollution Abatement and Control Expenditures 1972-81," 17.

11. Data Resources, *The Macro-Economic Impact of Federal Pollution Control Programs: 1981 Assessment,* prepared for the U.S. Environmental Protection Agency (Washington, D.C.: EPA, 1981).

12. This analysis was conducted using a large-scale computer model of the U.S. economy by Data Resources, an independent consulting firm that does substantial amounts of work for both private industry and government.

13. Data Resources, *Macro-Economic Impacts of Federal Pollution Control Programs: 1978 Assessment,* prepared for the Council on Environmental Quality and the U.S. Environmental Protection Agency (Washington, D.C.: Council on Environmental Quality, 1978).

14. These were "incremental expenditures"—that is, expenditures that firms were making for pollution control because of federal pollution control regulations, that they would not have made in the absence of these regulations.

15. The fact that this was the only analysis of its kind completed before the new administration took office makes it appear that their environmental-economic policies were based more on ideology than on evaluation.

16. Council on Environmental Quality, *Environmental Quality—1979* (Washington, D.C.: Government Printing Office, 1979), 437.

17. Temple, Barker, and Sloan, "An Economic Analysis of Proposed Effluent Limitations Guidelines, New Source Performance Standards, and Pretreatment Standards for the Iron and Steel Point Source Category," prepared for the U.S. Environmental Protection Agency, Office of Planning and Evaluation (Washington, D.C.: U.S. Environmental Protection Agency, 1980), III-5, IV-2; and *Survey of Current Business* 61, no. 6 (1981): 19-30. The EPA estimates of pollution control expenditures in past years are significantly higher than those reported in surveys undertaken by the Bureau of Economic Analysis (BEA). If the EPA historical estimates are replaced by the results of the BEA surveys, the total for 1975-1983 investments becomes $5.58 billion in 1980 dollars, 44 percent less than the 1978 CEQ-reported estimate.

18. Council of Environmental Quality, *Environmental Quality—1978,* 437.

19. Environmental Protection Agency, Office of Policy Analysis, *Cost of Clean Air and Water Report,* draft (Washington, D.C.: U.S. Environmental Protection Agency, 1982), 813; and Council on Environmental Quality, *Environmental Quality—1978,* 437. Again, the EPA estimates for investments made from 1970 through 1980 are much higher than those reported by the Bureau of Economic Analysis. If the BEA figures for 1975 through 1978 are combined with EPA's estimates for 1979-1983, the total becomes $3.7 billion in 1980 dollars, 61 percent less than the 1978 CEQ-reported estimates.

20. Council on Environmental Quality, *Environmental Quality—1978,* 438.

21. Information provided by Environmental Protection Agency, Office of Planning and Evaluation, May 13, 1982.
22. Council of Economic Advisers, *Economic Report of President: 1983,* 164.
23. William J. Russo, Jr., and Gary L. Rutledge, "Plant and Equipment Expenditures for Pollution Abatement, 1982 and Planned 1983," *Survey of Current Business* 63, no. 6 (1983): 24-26.
24. Department of Commerce, Bureau of Industrial Economics, *1982 U.S. Industrial Outlook for 200 Industries with Projections for 1985* (Washington, D.C.: Government Printing Office, January 1981), xxii.
25. Robert G. Healy, *America's Industrial Future: An Environmental Perspective* (Washington, D.C.: The Conservation Foundation, 1982).
26. The Conservation Foundation, *State of the Environment: 1982,* 295.
27. U.S. Congress, Congressional Budget Office, *Reducing the Federal Deficit: Strategies and Options: A Report to the Senate and House Committees on the Budget—Part III* (Washington, D.C.: Government Printing Office, 1982), 187.
28. For a discussion of the implications of the tax act, see John L. Palmer and Isabel V. Sawhill, eds., *The Reagan Experiment* (Washington, D.C.: Urban Institute Press, 1982), chapter 4.
29. For a summary of these changes, see annual budget issues (usually issued in February) of The Conservation Foundation, *The Conservation Foundation Letter* (Washington, D.C.); and Executive Office of the President, Office of Management and Budget, *Special Analyses, Budget of the United States Government* (Washington, D.C.: Government Printing Office, annual).
30. Executive Office of the President, Office of Management and Budget, *Budget of the United States Government: Fiscal Year 1983* (Washington, D.C.: Government Printing Office, 1982), 3-11, 3-12.
31. The Conservation Foundation, *State of the Environment: 1982,* 21.
32. *Air/Water Pollution Report,* 21, no. 13 (April 4, 1983), 123.
33. *Business Week,* December 27, 1982, to January 3, 1983, 16.
34. In this sense, "voluntary" only means that the source is in compliance with the regulation without enforcement actions having been taken against it.
35. The Conservation Foundation, *State of the Environment: 1982,* 392-396.
36. This tendency may well be reinforced by the 1983 Supreme Court decision declaring the congressional veto unconstitutional *(see Chapter 9).*
37. Robert W. Crandall, "Has Reagan Dropped the Ball?" *Regulation* 5, no. 5 (September/October 1981): 15-18.

17. EPILOGUE

Michael E. Kraft and Norman J. Vig

The inauguration of Ronald Reagan in January 1981 began a year of radical changes in U.S. environmental policy. The president quickly put into effect a conservative policy agenda that departed markedly from the well-established, bipartisan consensus on environmental policy goals that had existed for the previous decade. The chapters in this book provide abundant details on the Reagan agenda and on the way in which the goals, values, and ideas it represented were translated into specific and often dramatic changes in environmental institutions and public policies. Those chapters for the most part were written during the summer of 1983. This epilogue summarizes the major consequences of environmental policy change in the Reagan presidency and reviews some of the more significant policy activities of fall and early winter 1983.

In many respects 1983 was as eventful a year for students of environmental policy as was 1981. In March Anne Burford (formerly Gorsuch), administrator of the Environmental Protection Agency (EPA), was forced to resign and was replaced by William D. Ruckelshaus, the first EPA administrator. In October Interior Secretary James G. Watt resigned under pressure and was replaced by William P. Clark, the president's national security adviser. Both Ruckelshaus and Clark adopted administrative styles that indicated a shift from the confrontational posture characteristic of their predecessors to one of conciliation and compromise. They made early and well-publicized overtures to environmental groups and promised a more receptive hearing for their views in the future. Ruckelshaus brought to the upper reaches of EPA a new team of policy officials whom even environmentalists credited as competent, experienced, and professional.

These personnel changes and activities led to speculation that the Reagan administration had changed course and was moderating its environmental policy, largely over concern for the political price it would have to pay for the Gorsuch and Watt policies as the 1984 election grew near. Despite his strongly ideological approach to policy issues, President Reagan had shown a capacity for pragmatism and moderation when politically necessary. Was the administration about to mount such a strategic retreat in its environmental policy? The evidence to date does not support such a conclusion; decisions made late in 1983 suggest that the Reagan White House has not altered appreciably its environmental policy priorities.

Looking ahead to 1984, we also see more continuity than change. And depending on the outcome of the 1984 presidential election, environmental policy in the rest of the decade may continue to be influenced by the new agenda Reagan brought to office. Thus the nature of the institutional and policy changes made in the early 1980s, the political strategies used to create and sustain them, and the impact they are likely to have on environmental quality in the future all bear close examination and appraisal.

Politicized Administration Under Watt and Gorsuch

As we suggested in Chapter 1, the most relevant criteria for evaluating actions early in the Reagan administration are policy legitimation and what might be termed institutional capacity for effective policy implementation. We argued that under the direction of Watt and Gorsuch the Reagan administration moved sharply away from the consensus of the 1970s, and that this abrupt shift could be criticized in terms of both criteria. Radical policy change was imposed largely through an aggressive administrative strategy that Richard Nathan has aptly described as "founded on the appointment of loyal and determined policy officials." Appointees ideologically compatible with the president "penetrated administrative operations by grabbing hold of spending, regulatory and personnel decisions." [1] Reorganization of administrative offices and transfer or removal of officials believed to be unsupportive of the president's policy objectives were additional components of the strategy. There were many advantages to this approach. Policy changes could be directed by the White House and the Office of Management and Budget (OMB), put into effect more quickly, defended credibly, if not always accurately, as vital to economic recovery, and made to appear consistent with public demands for regulatory reform. Such policy changes also would be more subtle and less visible to potential opponents than would a direct assault on the statutes themselves.

There were, of course, major weaknesses to such a strategy. Public support for ongoing programs was ignored; environmental groups were excluded from decision making; and Congress was either not consulted prior to major policy initiatives or was given insufficient opportunity to challenge administrative actions. Many administrative decisions were based more on ideology than on sound economic or scientific analysis, and many were taken with little apparent regard for their effects on environmental quality and public health. Weakening of toxic substances policy implementation provides perhaps the clearest example. Institutional capacity was undermined through severe personnel and budgetary cuts, leaving the EPA, for example, ill-prepared to implement major environmental statutes. In short, however appropriate the Reagan agenda itself may have been, we have argued that the strategy used to institute it bypassed the normal process of legitimation or consensus building, invited technical breakdowns or policy failure, was likely to impose long-term costs that exceeded the apparent short-term economic gains, and was likely to produce sustained and adverse consequences for environmental quality.

In part because the Reagan White House opposed a broad public consensus on existing environmental policy goals, was perceived as strongly probusiness, and was often inflexible in pursuit of its conservative policy objectives, it was not as successful as it might have been. Its legislative accomplishments were the least impressive. Although half a dozen major environmental statutes were due to expire between 1981 and 1984 (including the Clean Air and Clean Water acts and key statutes dealing with toxic substances and pesticides), the administration made little effort to change those statutes and had little success where it did try. While most of these statutory revisions are still to be made in 1984, the administration seems to have lost the opportunity to fashion policies more in tune with its new agenda. Regulatory reform suffered a similar fate. At the beginning of the decade a promising climate for reform existed (such as for improving program efficiency through the use of cost-benefit analysis and consideration of alternatives to regulation); but the administration's politicization of the OMB review process and its probusiness bias weakened support for such measures. Thus the much-touted regulatory reform bill, strongly pushed by the Reagan administration, died in late 1982 when the White House failed to convince House Democratic leaders to back the proposal. Finally, as Robert Bartlett shows in Chapter 6, Congress generally appropriated more funds than Reagan requested for environmental programs in 1982 and 1983.

The administration was more successful in achieving its policy objectives in the bureaucracy. Here policy change normally is made by altering formal and informal administrative rules and regulations and the structures, personnel, resources and capabilities of agencies responsible for policy implementation. The Reagan administration most frequently used tactics involving informal regulations and practices; formal regulations were not changed extensively, and few new regulations were proposed. But as Richard Andrews, Paul Culhane, and other contributors show, the EPA under Gorsuch and the Interior Department under Watt raised to unprecedented levels the practices of reinterpretation of existing rules and regulations, delay, and selective enforcement.

Six chapters in the book address the particular changes attempted and achieved in air and water quality, toxic and hazardous materials, public lands, energy, and international environmental policies. As might be expected, the type and extent of policy change is not uniform. The most extensive changes were made in the areas of toxic substances, public lands, and energy, and the least in air and water quality. Some statutes provide for more administrative discretion, thus creating opportunities for this kind of policy change. Other reasons for the variation may be that newer policies and agencies have less well-established routines and smaller or weaker supportive constituencies, making them more vulnerable.

Although the full effects of such administrative change are not yet apparent, public reaction clearly slowed down the process. The very aggressiveness used by the White House to achieve its policy objectives created something of a backlash by 1983. As Henry and Margaret Kenski show, Congress was disturbed by the appearance of informal rule making, secret negotiations with regulated parties, and "sweetheart deals" that the nation's press brought to its attention, particularly in early 1983. At the year's end, congressional oversight committees were still busy investigating actions taken during Gorsuch's tenure at the EPA.[2] In addition, environmental groups did not hesitate to seek redress in the judiciary, as Lettie Wenner demonstrates in Chapter 9. By late 1983 many of Watt's prodevelopment initiatives at the Interior Department still were being contested in the federal courts.

The Reagan administration also sought to change public policy indirectly by reshaping the policy agenda and influencing public opinion. In comparison with the Carter, Ford, and Nixon administrations, it achieved remarkable changes in rhetoric, values, and policy commitments. Policy officials from the president on down made good use of the many opportunities available to an administration to articulate its political philosophy and to try to win public support for its policy positions. The administration's conservative ideology found expression in its redefinition of environmental and resource issues, the solutions considered to be acceptable, and the priority of those concerns in comparison to economic development. Although the effects of these efforts are difficult to determine, the Reagan administration also made less headway here than it doubtless hoped to in its first three years. As Robert Mitchell's review of public opinion data indicates, the American public maintained its strong support for environmental protection. The extreme rhetoric and abrasive style used by Watt and Gorsuch seemed mainly to polarize environmental policy debate, turn public opinion against the president's policies, and even alarm the business community.

Despite a negative public reaction to the administration's attempt at policy change and the limited success noted, the consequences will be both significant and long lasting. The most important of these affect the capacity of environmental agencies, especially EPA, to implement policies effectively. The loss of experienced and capable staff and the setbacks in research and development caused by greatly diminished financial resources cannot be reversed easily. Even with a return of budgets to pre-Reagan levels, the EPA would take years to recover from the damage inflicted.

The arrival of a new environmental policy team in 1983 prompts the question of whether some of those consequences may be averted or minimized. It also raises a broader question of whether the appointment of Ruckelshaus and Clark reflected a new direction in Reagan's environmental policy or whether it represented a change more in style than in substance.

Policy Moderation Under Ruckelshaus and Clark?

to EPA reflected the degree to which personnel practices and thus agency credibility had changed.

basic policy direction occurred in 1983 or can be expected in 1984 or in a second Reagan term. Clearly the White House concluded, albeit belatedly, that Watt and Gorsuch were political liabilities for the president. The selection of Ruckelshaus to replace Gorsuch was carefully calculated to rebuild public confidence in an EPA that was widely considered mismanaged and ineffectual. The replacement of Watt with Clark reflected Watt's propensity for insensitive public statements more than his leadership of the Interior Department, but it was also a well-considered move to limit political damage from Watt's policies at Interior.

The Reagan White House might have used the opportunity created by the resignations to announce a change in policy direction, but it chose not to do so. Instead the president strongly defended his policies. Although there were definite signs of new leadership and vigor at EPA, the outlook for a reversal of Reagan's policies was not encouraging. By late 1983 Ruckelshaus had learned that his determination to rebuild a strong EPA would founder on the rocks of persistent economic and budgetary difficulties. William Clark provided little evidence that he would seek significant policy changes at Interior; instead, he would be a loyal servant of the White House and largely follow the path charted by Watt. By year's end it seemed likely that the administration's dedication to conservative ideology, economic revitalization, regulatory relief, and reduction in government spending would prevent restoration of vigorous environmental protection policies. Space allows only a brief survey of the major developments, but that should suffice to support these conclusions.

Ruckelshaus at EPA

Among the significant developments at EPA in late 1983, special attention should be given to personnel and budgetary changes, proposal of a national risk policy, a new emphasis on toxic substances control, a reversal of Gorsuch's policy on water quality, and efforts to formulate an acid rain policy. By November 1983, six months after his return as administrator, EPA had replaced all the top officials swept out of office with Gorsuch, and Ruckelshaus had made much progress in improving staff morale and restoring the credibility of the agency.[3] His recruitment of top-notch scientists to EPA signaled the degree to which personnel practices and thus agency credibility had changed.

Improving the budget was more difficult. In June 1983 Reagan approved Ruckelshaus's request to increase EPA's operating budget for fiscal 1984 by $165.5 million; it was a modest sign that EPA's resources might fare better in the future than they had in the previous two years. By late 1983, however, that prognosis was in doubt. Ruckelshaus asked for a fiscal 1985 operating budget of $1.35 billion, about the same amount Congress approved for fiscal 1981, the last Carter budget. David A. Stockman, director of OMB, approved only $1.14 billion, roughly the same amount as for fiscal 1984.[4] Although Ruckelshaus might persuade OMB or the White House to increase the amount, and Congress might provide more funds, OMB opposition was an important indicator of constraints on budgetary growth and of Ruckelshaus's limited ability to do much about the problem.

Ruckelshaus decided to give special attention to a policy issue that had been incubating on the nation's regulatory agenda for several years. The issue was development of a uniform federal policy on assessment and regulation of risks to public health, safety, and the environment. He announced his intention to the National Academy of Sciences in his first major address after assuming office and found broad support within the administration for such a policy. Here he was more in tune philosophically with the Reagan White House; indeed, the *Washington Post* in December 1983 described Ruckelshaus's second tour of duty at EPA as having "taken on the character of a crusade to persuade the public of the need to balance costs of environmental controls against their benefits." [5] Such a stance leaves environmentalists skeptical.

Yet White House Science Adviser George A. Keyworth in November 1983 characterized the EPA as "alarmist," in reacting to its strong report on the so-called greenhouse effect—carbon dioxide buildup that might lead to warming of the Earth. At about the same time, Christopher DeMuth of OMB criticized an EPA ruling on "significant new use" of toxic chemicals; DeMuth wrote to Ruckelshaus that EPA's "excessively conservative decisions" could "discourage chemical innovation." Some risks, DeMuth argued, "should be regarded as reasonable." [6]

Hazardous wastes and toxic chemicals were high on EPA's priority list for its fiscal 1985 programs, which was symbolically important because much of the controversy over Gorsuch's management of EPA focused on toxic-waste-cleanup programs. Consistent with the effort to establish uniform national risk assessment, Ruckelshaus and Alvin L. Alm, deputy administrator of the agency, proposed a more integrated and concerted program to speed action on toxic and hazardous materials. The results to date are mixed. The first decision under this new policy, announced in mid-December 1983, concerned industrial emissions of benzene, a strong carcinogen; it represented a weakening of standards proposed by the Carter administration. Environmentalists criticized that decision as well as three related actions in late 1983 and early 1984. EPA proposed higher risk levels for radiation from active uranium mills and arsenic emitted into the air, and the agency delayed for two years stricter pollution controls for diesel-powered autos and light trucks. By early 1984 Ruckelshaus found that pleasing both the White House and environmentalists would be a difficult task.

Environmentalists were elated, however, with a decision Ruckelshaus made on water quality. On October 31, 1983, he agreed to reverse a decision made by Gorsuch that would have allowed states to weaken water-quality regulations in order to promote industrial growth. Ruckelshaus promised that he would soon publish new regulations that would strengthen protection for streams, rivers, and lakes. In this case he also had to battle others in the Reagan administration who wanted to weaken regulations implementing these provisions in the Clean Water Act. [7]

Perhaps the most important decision Ruckelshaus faced in 1983 concerned acid rain. As Richard Tobin notes in Chapter 11, acid rain had become a significant component of both clean air and energy policy discussions. International issues also were prominent as Canada displayed increasing impatience with the U.S. government's failure to act. Several major scientific studies released in mid-1983 provided additional evidence on the severity of the problem and outlined possible actions. Ruckelshaus had promised a new policy on this complex and thorny issue, and he actively sought further scientific advice from an EPA study group established for that purpose.

Yet his much publicized search for a moderate position around which he might build consensus proved disappointing. On September 21, 1983, he submitted a draft plan to the Cabinet Council on Natural Resources and Environment. The plan called for a very limited and experimental program that would reduce sulfur dioxide emissions by about 3 million tons per year, a much lower reduction than that favored by many scientists and environmentalists, who wanted a decrease of at least 10 million tons per year. However, even the limited draft plan—with its $1.5 billion to $2.5 billion price tag— was unacceptable to the administration. The Department of Energy, OMB, and others criticized it as too costly, premature, and politically unacceptable. In mid-October Ruckelshaus discussed his plan with White House aides, including Chief of Staff James Baker, Counselor Edwin Meese III, and OMB's Stockman; the outcome was a decision to consider other options. By late October a discouraged Ruckelshaus announced that formulation of an acid rain policy was being postponed indefinitely. In mid-January 1984 he proposed a substantially weaker plan to the president at another meeting of the cabinet council, and the president indicated he would announce a decision on acid rain policy early in 1984.[8]

The acid rain decision underscored both the complexity of the issues and the resoluteness of White House priorities for federal spending reductions and regulatory relief for industry. Many viewed Ruckelshaus's failure to produce a plan acceptable to the White House as an indication of his limited influence in the administration and of the future challenges he would face. Meanwhile, environmentalists looked to Congress to devise a solution to the problem. At the end of 1983 several bills were under active consideration. Acid rain also became a prominent issue in the well-publicized New Hampshire primary election campaign when most of the Democratic presidential candidates attended a conference on the problem sponsored by environmental and citizen groups. At the conference Sen. John Glenn, a presidential candidate from Ohio, sought environmentalist support by proposing detailed legislation to control acid rain.

How well does the EPA under Ruckelshaus stand up to our two evaluative criteria of policy legitimation and institutional capabilities? There was more success on the first than the second. The most striking change occurred in EPA's relations with Congress and with environmental groups. A writer for the *Washington Post* captured the change in political style:

"Articulate, possessed of a leavening wit and ever-conscious of the protocol of power in Washington, Ruckelshaus is a smash hit with Congress." Sen. Robert T. Stafford, Republican chairman of the Environment and Public Works Committee, was impressed: "At the end of six months things are so much better than before that I can't begin to describe it." [9] Similarly, even before his confirmation by the Senate, Ruckelshaus arranged a meeting with 26 representatives of the leading environmental organizations to discuss his goals for the agency, thus indicating a willingness to listen to their views. By October 1983 he even issued guidelines to "set a tone for the agency" after its "period of turmoil." Agency employees were advised to treat people decently, enforce the law as it is written, and avoid "excessive rigidity or the absence of common sense." [10]

The more limited success in dealing with agency capabilities and White House priorities has already been described. To his credit, Ruckelshaus brought to an end active hostility to environmental regulation, helped restore staff morale, increased the agency's credibility, and increased the budget modestly. Most importantly, he tried to bring back to the agency a commitment to professional environmental management and to reduce the politicization that led to Gorsuch's downfall. His approach and priorities were consistent with the pre-Reagan consensus on environmental policy, and they promised to show dividends across a wide range of decisions. He was unable, however, to find much support in the White House for new policy directions. This should not have surprised him. When his nomination was still being considered by the White House, Ruckelshaus met with Watt to discuss how independent the new EPA administrator might be. Watt described the meeting: "We talked about the commitment Bill Ruckelshaus and I have to the Reagan philosophy, the concept of teamwork, that we work together in carrying out the Reagan agenda, and his [Ruckelshaus's] full commitment to team membership." [11] By late 1983 Rep. James J. Florio, a Democrat from New Jersey and chairman of a House Energy and Commerce subcommittee that was a leading source of criticism of Gorsuch, expressed the reservations that environmentalists still held:

> He's just in neutral. He's never going to do anything that's wrong, but this administration's environmental philosophy is not going to be an aggressive philosophy until Ruckelshaus decides he doesn't want to be a good soldier. [12]

From Watt to Clark at Interior

William Clark assumed office in November 1983 and consequently had fewer opportunities than Ruckelshaus for major decisions by the end of the year. Yet there is less reason in Clark's case to expect significant change in policy. The president's decision to appoint Clark to the Interior post, statements made at his confirmation hearings, and his early actions at the department suggest that the administration's natural resource policies will continue largely unchanged in 1984.

Watt announced his resignation on October 9, 1983, as support was growing for a Senate resolution calling for his removal from office. In his letter of resignation, he cited his record of achievements and praised the president for his support but concluded that "my usefulness to you in this Administration has come to an end. A different type of leadership at the Department of Interior will best serve you and the nation." [13] Watt announced later that he would accept a short-term appointment as "visiting distinguished fellow in energy and natural resources policy" at the conservative Heritage Foundation and would begin work on several books. In great demand as a public speaker, he reportedly earned $15,000 a speech. Other accounts indicated he planned to serve as a liaison between conservative groups and the Republican party in 1984; during 1982 Watt was the top fund raiser for the party, bringing in some $1 million.

Clark was nominated for the Interior job on October 13, following much speculation on whom the president would select. Watt's successor at Interior would not be colorful, but his policy positions would be similar. Appearing on public television's MacNeil-Lehrer News Hour, White House Counselor Edwin Meese talked openly about the unlikelihood of policy change: "Generally the policies of this administration, inaugurated by Jim Watt and approved by Ronald Reagan, will be the policies that will continue under the stewardship of Bill Clark." [14] Despite some criticism of Clark's apparent lack of qualifications for the job, the president was satisfied that he would serve the administration well: "He is a God-fearing Westerner, fourth-generation rancher, a person I trust." The nomination surprised nearly everyone, and it was a shrewd political move by Reagan. Clark would help to build support for the president in the West, would be respected as fair and honest, and would be a loyal and trusted friend of the White House at the sensitive Interior position. As a noncontroversial and rather bland administrator in comparison to Watt, Clark would help to bury environmental issues before the 1984 election. Moreover, unlike the situation at EPA, there was little demand outside the predictable environmentalist circles to remove other policy officials at the department. Most of Watt's ideological lieutenants would remain at Interior to carry on the administration's battles.

Although five major environmental groups, including the Sierra Club and the Wilderness Society, opposed Clark's confirmation, there was never much doubt about the Senate's approval. Clark said little during the hearings on policy or personnel changes; he declined every opportunity offered by members of the Senate Energy and Natural Resources Committee to repudiate Watt's controversial policies on oil and natural gas leasing and on national parks and other public lands. His responses to questions were generally noncommittal, leading Sen. Paul E. Tsongas of Massachusetts to wonder "whether Judge Clark is just a James Watt who took a Dale Carnegie course in civil behavior." [15] Clark did emphasize, however, his respect for Interior's career staff, many of whom Watt had fired, transferred, downgraded, or subordinated to political appointees. Clark was confirmed on November 18 by a vote of 71 to 18. The confirmation followed a 48 to 42 vote late the night before rejecting a "sense of the Senate" resolution that criticized

Watt's policies and called for Reagan and Clark to ensure that Interior Department programs "conform with the expressed will of Congress." [16]

After his first month in office Clark, like Ruckelshaus, adopted a more moderate style than his predecessor. He met on several occasions with leaders of environmental groups and promised to increase their access to policy officials at Interior. At one of those meetings he announced that he would not be tied to Watt's policies and that Reagan had given him a free hand for a full policy review. Clark also expressed a desire to settle out of court as many as possible of the 4,000 lawsuits pending against the department. Thus, efforts to improve policy legitimation by lowering the decibel level in debates over environmental protection and energy development and by broadening the constituencies consulted were under way by the end of the year.

Less evidence of substantive changes in policy, personnel, and budgets emerged, although environmentalists and congressional critics continued to press for change. Using an appropriations bill for fiscal 1984, Congress had imposed some controls over Watt's coal and offshore oil leasing policies. Hoping for additional changes, the Wilderness Society late in the year issued a well-documented report accusing Watt of "unprecedented abuse of administrative power" in these and other policy areas.[17] Environmentalists continued to express concern that the policy officials Watt brought to Interior remained well entrenched and that Watt's legacy of newly reinterpreted rules and regulations would be used to carry on his policies.

In late December, Clark announced that he was realigning land, water, and energy offices at Interior and replacing three of Watt's top aides. Ann D. McLaughlin, selected to fill the number two position in the department, under secretary, said her job would involve improving Interior's communications with Congress, environmental groups, the news media, and other groups. McLaughlin had served as director of public affairs at EPA in the mid-1970s. Environmentalists responded to these announcements by asserting that the three aides replaced were just "the tip of the iceberg." Speaking to the National Association of Manufacturers a short time later, Clark said the replacement of some of Watt's aides at Interior did not signal a change in administration policy. He announced also that his department's fiscal 1985 budget would be reduced by $200 million from the 1984 appropriation of $6.7 billion.[18]

The Executive Office and Environmental Policy

As Norman Vig argues in Chapter 4, the Reagan presidency has made full use of the powers and resources of the Executive Office to implement its new environmental agenda. The appointment of Watt and Gorsuch and their activities in office reflected Ronald Reagan's political philosophy and his intention to bring about major changes in environmental and natural resources policies. An examination of the Task Force on Regulatory Relief, OMB decisions, and the posture of the White House itself in late 1983 suggests no significant policy redirection is in sight.

In August 1983, in what seemed like political posturing on regulation in anticipation of the 1984 elections, the task force issued a final report and announced it was going out of business, its work essentially completed. It asserted that the "executive branch has now done what it can" to reduce the scope and cost of federal regulation and implied that any further reductions would have to come from Capitol Hill. Its 124-page report on the administration's deregulation program cited some $150 billion that business and consumers would save over the next decade thanks to White House initiatives. Consumer advocates promptly challenged this figure, criticizing especially the contention that elimination of regulations had been accomplished "without compromising important environmental, health or safety objectives." [19] Among the list of goals that went unmet by the task force were revisions of the clean air and water acts and passage of the regulatory reform bill. The demise of the task force hardly implied that deregulation would cease; it was instead a testimony to the extent to which more institutionalized solutions (such as within OMB) were discovered for dealing with the alleged burden of overregulation that has so preoccupied the Reagan presidency.

As Richard Andrews notes in Chapter 8, most of the daily work of regulatory review was performed by the Office of Information and Regulatory Affairs in OMB under the president's executive order on cost-benefit analysis. The White House also issued a report card on its success there. As of mid-1983 OMB had reviewed nearly seven thousand rules under the executive order and caused changes to be made in about one out of every nine. The figures tell only a part of the story. OMB's role in environmental regulation was particularly strong, as Ruckelshaus discovered on the acid rain issue. And OMB had the full support of the president for its actions inasmuch as it was the lead office for meeting the administration's economic and budgetary reduction goals. Not surprisingly, allegations emerged that OMB had overstepped its legal authority on some environmental issues. For example, during testimony before one congressional investigative committee in fall 1983, John E. Daniel, EPA chief of staff under Gorsuch, charged that OMB had acted improperly in promoting industry interests. He asserted that OMB had tried to dictate regulations to EPA, had urged that cost factors be considered in setting health rules when the Clean Air Act prohibited them, had threatened reprisals against the agency, and had shown proposed rule changes to industry officials before they were made public.[20] At the end of 1983 the OMB review process was still in place, and all signs pointed toward its vigorous use during the rest of the administration's tenure.

One of the more remarkable aspects of the tangled course of Reagan's environmental policy over the last three years is the degree to which the president himself has escaped criticism for the political and policy disasters at EPA and Interior. Although polls during 1983 showed a majority of the public did not trust Reagan administration *officials* on environmental policy, a CBS-*New York Times* poll in April found that by a margin of 48 percent to 38 percent the public still trusted Reagan himself to make the right decisions on the environment.[21] At about the same time several ABC News/*Washington Post* polls found 50 percent or more of the public believed the

president "cares more about protecting the firms that are violating antipollution laws" than about enforcing those laws. His administration would still
pay a political price, but it seemed that the damage limitation strategy
adopted by the White House was at least partly successful. Rita Lavelle,
assistant administrator for hazardous waste under Gorsuch, ultimately paid a
greater price than Ronald Reagan for her efforts on his behalf. In early
December 1983 she was convicted of perjury and of obstructing a congressional investigation. She was sentenced to six months in prison and fined
$10,000. A Justice Department investigation of the EPA scandal that led to
Lavelle's conviction found no "competent evidence" to support a charge of
White House involvement in political manipulation of toxic-waste-cleanup
funds. It also found insufficient evidence to warrant criminal prosecution of
Gorsuch and five other former EPA officials it had investigated. Congressional critics charged that the investigation was too limited and the report
unconvincing.[22]

Environmental Policy Choices for the 1980s

By the end of the 1970s environmental policy issues had secured a stable
place on the nation's political agenda. In the early 1980s the Reagan
presidency helped propel them to even greater prominence as it launched a
broad attack on what it viewed as burdensome environmental regulation.
Public reaction to Reagan's policies confirmed a strong base of support
nationwide for vigorous environmental protection as well as the political
influence of the environmental lobby in Washington, D.C. Thus, controversies over environmental protection are likely to be more significant in the 1984
elections than they have been in recent years. Environmentalists will be out in
force during 1984 trying to influence elections at all levels in the United
States, and they are likely to give special emphasis to the presidential election.
But the degree to which Reagan's record on environmental policy becomes a
major campaign issue will depend also on the priority given to it by
Democratic contenders for the presidency.

In January 1984 White House officials openly acknowledged that a
reelection-year shift in the tone and substance of the administration's
environmental policy would be necessary to convince voters that President
Reagan had not neglected enforcement of environmental protection laws.
However, they said the president planned to accomplish this mainly by
avoiding the kind of controversies that characterized the first two and one half
years of his administration, not by a major change in its policies or budgetary
priorities. The "next phase" of environmental policy, as they called it, was to
be put into effect by Ruckelshaus and Clark. A senior White House official
decribed the plan:

> The change is almost automatic when you change from Burford to
> Ruckelshaus. . . . You get more respect for environmental protection, more
> respect for scientific evidence and due process, and more respect for the
> political process. Ruckelshaus enjoys the benefit of the doubt. It was less a
> matter of conscious strategy, and more you just pick the man. . . . Now we

have an opportunity, even if there is no major change in policy. . . .Tone is an important element here. You are balancing a lot of competing interests.[23]

This book has dealt with two sets of concerns related to the role of environmental issues in 1984 and beyond. We have focused on the scope and nature of environmental policy issues in the 1980s, and on how policy implementation in the Reagan administration has departed from the pre-1981 consensus on policy goals. As we argued in Chapter 1, the issues of the 1980s differ from those of the 1970s. Whatever conclusions one reaches about the legitimacy or impact of environmental policy change during the Reagan administration, the challenges posed by the range and complexity of environmental problems will continue throughout the 1980s. Dealing seriously with them will require not only respect for scientific evidence and competent administration but also informed and responsible leadership from the White House. Formulation of effective policies also requires that difficult choices be made in balancing competing public values and in setting policy priorities during a period of scarce budgetary resources.

At one level, environmental controversies in the Reagan administration have involved precisely such conflicts over policy priorities. Had the administration approached those conflicts with greater consideration of the prevailing consensus on environmental policy goals, it might have accomplished more and avoided the political price it may pay in the 1984 elections. Improving programs, however, is not an easy task under the best of circumstances. Certainly one would not predict success when those objectives are pursued with more interest in providing relief for the business community than in genuine reform of environmental policy. For example, the idea of using analytical techniques such as risk analysis and cost-benft analysis to help set policy priorities is now widely accepted. But the Reagan administration demonstrated the difficulty and pitfalls of putting that proposal into practice. Thus, Ruckelshaus has encouraged greater use of risk analysis in environmental regulation, but OMB under Stockman has been concerned mainly with using cost-benefit analysis as a tool for deregulation.[24] The two approaches may not be compatible.

These kinds of internal conflicts raise the broader question of the extent to which economic rationality, embodied in these analytical techniques, can guide reform of environmental programs in the Reagan administration. In cases such as dioxin contamination in Times Beach, Missouri, and the intense pressure early in 1984 to set safety guidelines for the highly carcinogenic pesticide ethylene dibromide (EDB), the administration found itself reacting to crises and developing emergency procedures to address the problems. Economic losses and the costs to public health that resulted from failing to act more promptly may greatly exceed what might have been spent on better environmental regulation in the first place.[25] Thus actions intended to economize often cost more in the long run than they save in the short run.

For these reasons and because of the existence of severe budgetary constraints, environmental policy making in the 1980s will remain a tough challenge. Effective solutions will emerge only from a combination of sound analysis and accountable decision making. But decisions aimed at balancing public values must be made without full knowledge of environmental risks and costs, and environmental agencies must cope for some time with the budget and staff reductions imposed in the early 1980s. Unfortunately, the prospects for continued large federal deficits will make it difficult to improve the situation. Using an optimistic economic forecast and assuming no major tax increases or further spending reductions, the Reagan administration estimates deficits will remain in the range of $190 billion to $200 billion for the rest of the 1980s.[26] Although spending on environmental protection and natural resources programs had increased to 2.4 percent of the federal budget by 1980, it fell back to an estimated 1.5 percent by 1983; it was projected to decrease to 1.2 percent for fiscal 1984. Under Reagan budget projections, by 1986 it would fall to 0.88 percent. These sharp reductions in the priority of federal spending on the environment symbolize the policy reversal described in this book. A government that is not willing to pay for the environment is not likely to succeed in protecting it.[27]

There are no easy ways to choose policy priorities under these conditions. But making those decisions through political processes that encourage reasoned consideration of policy alternatives and accountability to the public offers the greatest promise for success. We hope the analyses offered in this book suggest some of the more productive ways to go about making such choices for the future.

Notes

1. Richard P. Nathan, *The Administrative Presidency* (New York: John Wiley, 1983), 69, and "The Reagan Presidency in Domestic Affairs," in *The Reagan Presidency: An Early Assessment,* ed. Fred I. Greenstein (Baltimore: Johns Hopkins, 1983), 71.
2. Joseph A. Davis, "Few Legislative Changes Made As Result of EPA Investigations," *Congressional Quarterly Weekly Report,* December 10, 1983, 2619-2621.
3. Cass Peterson, "Ruckelshaus Rocks No Boats at EPA," *Washington Post National Weekly Edition,* December 12, 1983; Joseph A. Davis, "Ruckelshaus Team Moving Into Place at EPA," *Congressional Quarterly Weekly Report,* November 12, 1983, 2391.
4. Lawrence Mosher, "Ruckelshaus's First Mark on EPA—Another $165.5 Million for Its Budget," *National Journal,* June 25, 1983, 1344; Philip Shabecoff, "New E.P.A. Chief Seeks More Funds," *New York Times,* December 6, 1983, 8. *(See note 27.)*
5. Peterson, "Ruckelshaus Rocks No Boats."
6. Philip Shabecoff, "Monitoring the Cleanup at the E.P.A.," *New York Times,* November 20, 1983, 4E, and *National Journal,* December 3, 1983, 2511.
7. Philip Shabecoff, "E.P.A. to Reverse Easing of Water Rules," *New York Times,* November 1, 1983, 10.
8. Philip Shabecoff, "Monitoring the Cleanup at the E.P.A."; "Ruckelshaus Postpones Plans to Curb Acid Rain," *New York Times,* October 23, 1983, 16; and *New York Times,* January 18, 1984, 11. *(See note 27.)*
9. Peterson, "Ruckelshaus Rocks No Boats"; Shabecoff, "Monitoring the Cleanup."

10. *New York Times,* October 21, 1983, 8.
11. Joseph A. Davis, "Quick Confirmation Likely for Ruckelshaus as EPA Head," *Congressional Quarterly Weekly Report,* March 26, 1983, 623.
12. Peterson, "Ruckelshaus Rocks No Boats."
13. *The New York Times,* October 10, 1983, 14.
14. Joseph A. Davis, "Senate Energy to Vote on Clark Nomination," *Congressional Quarterly Weekly Report,* November 5, 1983, 2332.
15. Associated Press release, November 2, 1983.
16. Joseph A. Davis, "Senate Confirms Clark as Interior Secretary," *Congressional Quarterly Weekly Report,* November 19, 1983, 2412.
17. Lawrence Mosher, "Watt's Departure from Interior May Not Mean A Sharp Break with His Policies," *National Journal,* November 5, 1983, 2306.
18. Philip Shabecoff, "Clark Names New Under Secretary and Realigns Resource Agencies," *New York Times,* December 23, 1983, 9; Associated Press release, December 23, 1983; *New York Times,* January 11, 1984, 11; and Dale Russakoff and Cass Peterson, "Will Shuffles at Interior Matter?" *Washington Post National Weekly Edition,* January 9, 1984, 11.
19. Kenneth B. Noble, "U.S. Expects Deregulation to Save Up to $150 Billion," *New York Times,* August 12, 1983, 6; Michael Wines, "Mission Accomplished, Bush Says of His Rules Task Force," *National Journal,* August 20, 1983, 1749.
20. "Ex-E.P.A. Aide Says Budget Office Put Case for Industry," *New York Times,* September 28, 1983, 1, 11. See also Susan J. Tolchin and Martin Tolchin, *Dismantling America: The Rush to Deregulate* (Boston: Houghton Mifflin, 1983).
21. Cited in newsletter from League of Conservation Voters, October 1983. See also Barry Sussman, "Poll Says Most Think Reagan Prefers to Protect Polluters," *Washington Post,* March 5, 1983.
22. Stuart Taylor, Jr., "U.S. Won't Charge Ex-E.P.A. Officials," *New York Times,* August 12, 1983, 1, 7.
23. David Hoffman, "Reagan Is Trying to Clean Up His Environmental Image," *Washington Post National Weekly Edition,* January 9, 1984, 10.
24. Tolchin and Tolchin, *Dismantling America.* See also, V. K. Smith, ed., *Environmental Policy Under Reagan's Executive Order: The Role of Benefit-Cost Analysis* (Chapel Hill: University of North Carolina Press, forthcoming, 1984).
25. Cass Peterson, "Weighing a Ban on EDB, the Super Carcinogen," *Washington Post National Weekly Edition,* January 9, 1984, 8; and Philip Shabecoff, "Intense Pressure on E.P.A. to Take Action on Pesticide," *New York Times,* January 12, 1984, 15. EDB is the most powerful chemical carcinogen ever tested by EPA, and it has now pervaded the nation's food supply.
26. Jonathan Fuerbringer, "Reagan Said to Oppose Panel on Paring Deficits," *New York Times,* January 17, 1984, 12.
27. As this volume went to press, President Reagan announced some minor environmental initiatives in his annual State of the Union address on January 25, 1984. He proposed a $50 million supplemental appropriation for EPA hazardous waste programs in 1984; extension of the Superfund beyond 1985; doubling of the acid rain research budget; $157 million for park and other conservation land acquisition (which Congress normally appropriates anyway); additional efforts to clean up the Chesapeake Bay; and greater state and public participation in offshore oil leasing (already announced by William Clark). According to the OMB, EPA's operating budget will increase by 8.5 percent from $1,114 million

in fiscal 1984 to $1,290 million in 1985, the largest budget increase for any nondefense agency. However, this increase was less than half of the $236 million increase that William Ruckelshaus had requested, and it would leave EPA's budget more than 10 percent less than it was in the last year of the Carter administration and about equal to its level of 10 years ago after accounting for inflation. Ruckelshaus also lost his battle for an acid rain control program, having been unable to convince the president that enough is known to begin a new regulatory effort. For the text of Reagan's address, see *New York Times,* January 26, 1984; see also Philip Shabecoff, "Head of E.P.A. Defends Reagan Plan for Further Acid Rain Study," *New York Times,* January 27, 1984; and Cass Peterson, "EPA's Ruckelshaus To Get Half the Budget Increase He Sought," *Washington Post,* January 27, 1984.

CONTRIBUTORS

Richard N. L. Andrews is professor of environmental sciences and engineering and director of the Institute for Environmental Studies at the University of North Carolina, Chapel Hill. Formerly chairman of the Natural Resource Policy and Management Program at the University of Michigan and a budget examiner at the U.S. Office of Management and Budget, he is the author of *Environmental Policy and Administrative Change* (1976) and of numerous journal articles on environmental policy, impact assessments, and budget-cost analysis.

Regina S. Axelrod is chairperson of the Department of Political Studies and on the faculty of the Institute for Urban Studies at Adelphi University. Current research interests are energy and environmental policy. She is the editor and a contributing author of *Environment, Energy, Public Policy: Toward a Rational Future* (1981) and the author of *Energy and Urban Environment: Consolidated Edison versus the City of New York* (1982).

Robert V. Bartlett teaches public policy and public administration at Texas Tech University. He is the author of *The Reserve Mining Controversy: Science, Technology and Public Policy* (1980) and of several articles and papers. He is currently involved in a research project on the use of science in implementation of the National Environmental Policy Act.

Lynton K. Caldwell is the Bentley Professor of Political Science at Indiana University. He was consultant to the U.S. Senate in drafting the National Environmental Policy Act, and he has written, among other books, *Science and the National Environmental Policy Act: Redirecting Policy Through Procedural Reform* (1982) and *International Environmental Policy: Emergence and Dimensions* (1984).

Edwin H. Clark II is a senior associate at The Conservation Foundation in Washington, D.C., where, among other responsibilities, he directs the preparation of its reports entitled *The State of the Environment*. He was formerly senior economist at the Council on Environmental Quality and economics adviser to the administrator of the Environmental Protection Agency.

Steven Cohen teaches public policy and administration at Columbia University. A former staff member in the Superfund Office of the Environmental Protection Agency, he was responsible for developing

Superfund's community relations policy. He has written a number of articles and reports on environmental and energy issues, and he is a consultant on nuclear waste and hazardous waste for the Department of Energy.

Paul J. Culhane is a research political scientist at Northwestern University. He is the author of *Public Lands Politics* (1981) and various articles and book chapters on natural resources policy. He is currently writing books on the outcomes of federal environmental assessments, theories of American bureaucratic politics, and the politics of MX missile basing.

J. Clarence Davies is executive vice president of The Conservation Foundation. He has held positions with Resources for the Future and the President's Council on Environmental Quality and has taught at Princeton University and Bowdoin College. He is the author of *The Politics of Pollution*, 2d ed. (1975) and numerous magazine articles on environmental policy.

Helen M. Ingram is a professor of political science at the University of Arizona, where she also teaches a course in environmental policy. She has specialized in natural resources, particularly water policy, and is a coauthor of *A Policy Approach to Political Representation: Lessons From the Four Corners States* (1980).

Henry C. Kenski teaches political science at the University of Arizona. A former American Political Science Association congressional fellow, he is the author of various articles and book chapters on public opinion, elections, Congress, the presidency, and public policy. In 1981 he served as legislative staff director for Rep. Morris K. Udall, a Democrat from Arizona.

Margaret Corgan Kenski teaches political science at Pima Community College. She is the author of various articles and book chapters on Congress, environmental policy, and teaching political science. In 1980 and 1982 she served as a political consultant in several Arizona congressional campaigns.

Michael E. Kraft is a professor of political science and public administration at the University of Wisconsin, Green Bay. His research and teaching interests include public policy making, policy analysis, and environmental politics. His work has appeared in a number of edited collections on public policy and in journals such as *Policy Studies Review, Policy Studies Journal,* and *Political Science Quarterly.*

Dean E. Mann is professor of political science, University of California, Santa Barbara. He has written extensively on the management of natural resources, particularly in the West, and is editor of *Environmental Policy Formulation* (1981) and *Environmental Policy Implementation* (1982). He currently serves as editor of *Western Political Quarterly* and associate editor for environmental policy for the *Policy Studies Journal.*

Robert Cameron Mitchell, a sociologist, is a senior fellow at Resources for the Future, a nonprofit research organization in Washington, D.C. His articles on the environmental movement and environmental public opinion have appeared in *Natural Resources Journal, Society, Public Opinion, Western Political Quarterly,* and as chapters in several volumes. Among the national surveys he has conducted is a comprehensive survey of environmental attitudes commissioned by the President's Council on Environmental Quality for the 1980 CEQ report.

Richard J. Tobin is an associate professor of political science at the State University of New York at Buffalo. His interests focus on regulatory and environmental policy. He is the author of *The Social Gamble: Determining Acceptable Levels of Air Quality* (1979) and has published in *Energy Policy, Environmental Conservation, Environmental Affairs,* and *The Environmental Professional.*

Norman J. Vig is professor of political science and director of the Science, Technology, and Public Policy Program at Carleton College. He is the author of *Science and Technology in British Politics* (1968) and coeditor and a contributing author of *Politics in Advanced Nations* (1974) and *Political Economy in Advanced Industrial Societies* (forthcoming).

Lettie McSpadden Wenner is associate professor of political science at the University of Illinois at Chicago. She is the author of *The Environmental Decade in Court* (1982), *One Environment Under Law* (1976), and numerous journal articles on environmental policy issues ranging from effluent charges for pollution to referendums on nuclear moratoriums.